Translated Documents of Greece and Rome

Robert K. Sherk, Editor

VOLUME 1

Archaic Times to the End of the Peloponnesian War

Archaic Times to the end of the Peloponnesian War

EDITED AND TRANSLATED BY
CHARLES W. FORNARA
*Professor of Classics and History, Brown University,
Providence, Rhode Island*

CAMBRIDGE
UNIVERSITY PRESS

PUBLISHED BY THE PRESS SYNDICATE OF THE UNIVERSITY OF CAMBRIDGE
The Pitt Building, Trumpington Street, Cambridge CB2 1RP, United Kingdom

CAMBRIDGE UNIVERSITY PRESS
The Edinburgh Building, Cambridge CB2 2RU, UK http://www.cup.cam.ac.uk
40 West 20th Street, New York, NY 10011–4211, USA http://www.cup.org
10 Stamford Road, Oakleigh, Melbourne 3166, Australia

First edition first published by the Johns Hopkins University Press 1977
Second edition first published by Cambridge University Press 1983
Reprinted 1986, 1988, 1989, 1994, 1995, 1998 (twice)

Printed in the United Kingdom at the University Press, Cambridge

Library of Congress catalogue card number: 79-54018

British Library Cataloguing in Publication data
Archaic times to the end of the Peloponnesian
War. – 2nd ed. – (translated documents of Greece and Rome; v. 1).
1. Greece – History – to 404/3 B.C. –
Sources
I. Fornara, Charles W. II. Series
938'.008 DF222

ISBN 0 521 25019 6 hardback
ISBN 0 521 29946 2 paperback

B.B.

SERIES EDITORS' INTRODUCTION

Greek and Roman history has always been in an ambivalent position in American higher education, having to find a home either in a Department of History or in a Department of Classics, and in both it is usually regarded as marginal. Moreover, in a History Department the subject tends to be taught without regard to the fact that the nature of the evidence is, on the whole, very different from that for American, English, or French history, while in a Classics Department it tends to be viewed as a 'philological' subject and taught by methods appropriate to Greek and Latin authors. Even on the undergraduate level the difference may be important, but on the graduate level, where future teachers and scholars, who are to engage in original research, are trained, it becomes quite clear that neither of these solutions is adequate.

One problem is the standard of proficiency that should be required in Greek and Latin – both difficult languages, necessitating years of study; and few students start the study, even of Latin, let alone Greek, before they come to college. The editors recognize that for the student aiming at a Ph.D. in the subject and at advancing present knowledge of it there can be no substitute for a thorough training in the two languages. Nevertheless, they believe that it is possible to extend serious instruction at a high level to graduate students aiming at reaching the M.A. level and to make them into competent teachers. It is also possible to bring about a great improvement in the standard of undergraduate courses not requiring the ancient languages – courses that instructors themselves usually find unsatisfactory, since much of the source material cannot be used.

In order to use this material, at both graduate and serious undergraduate levels, the instructor must, in fact, be able to range far beyond the standard authors who have been translated many times. Harpocration, Valerius Maximus, and the *Suda* are often necessary tools, but they are usually unknown to anyone except the advanced scholar. Inscriptions, papyri, and scholia can be baffling even to the student who does have a grounding in the ancient languages.

It is the aim of the series of which this is the first volume to supply that need – which colleagues have often discussed with the editors – for translations of materials not readily available in English. The principal historical authors (authors like Herodotus, Thucydides, Livy, and Tacitus) are not included; they are easy enough to find in adequate translations, and the student will have to read far more of them than could be provided in a general source book. References to important passages in the works of those authors have been given at suitable points, but it is assumed that the instructor will direct the student's reading in them. While doing that reading, the student will now be able to have at his side a comprehensive reference book. Occasionally a passage from an otherwise accessible author (not a main historical source) has been included, so that the student may be spared the temptation of failing to search for it. But most of the material collected in this series would be hard for him to find anywhere in English, and much of it has never been translated at all.

Such translations of documentary sources as exist (and there are some major projects in translation among them, e.g. in the field of legal texts, which are intended to be far more than source books for students) tend to be seriously misleading in that they offer continuous texts where the original is (so often) fragmentary. The student cannot be aware of how much actually survives on the document and how much is modern conjecture – whether quite certain or mere guesswork. This series aims at presenting the translation of fragmentary sources in something like the way in which original documents are presented to the scholar: a variety of type fonts and brackets (which will be fully explained) have been used for this, and even though the page may at first sight appear forbidding to one unaccustomed to this, he will learn to differentiate between text and restoration and (with the instructor's help and the use of the notes provided) between the dubious, the probable, and the certain restoration. Naturally, the English can never correspond perfectly to the Greek or Latin, but the translation aims at as close a correspondence as can be achieved, so that the run of the original and (where necessary) the amount surviving can be clearly shown. Finer points of English idiom have deliberately been sacrificed in order to produce this increased accuracy, though it is hoped that there will be nothing in the translation so unnatural as to baffle the student. In the case of inscriptions (except for those with excessively short lines) line-by-line correspondence has been the aim, so that the student who sees a precise line reference in a modern work will be able to find it in the translation.

Translation is an art as well as a science; there are bound to be differing opinions on the precise interpretation and on the best rendering of any given passage. The general editors have tried to collaborate with volume editors in achieving the aims outlined above. But there is always room for improvement, and a need for it. Suggestions and corrections from users of the series will always be welcome.

The general editors sincerely hope that the present series will make a major contribution to raising the standard of ancient history teaching in the U.S.A. and, indeed, wherever English is the medium of instruction, and that it will help to convey to students not fully proficient in

Greek or Latin, or even entirely ignorant of those languages, some of the immediacy and excitement of real (as distinct from textbook) history. Perhaps some will be encouraged to develop their skill in the two languages so as to go on to a fuller understanding of the ancient world, or even to professional study of it.

    We wish to express our gratitude to the Andrew V. V. Raymond Chair in the Department of Classics at the State University of New York at Buffalo for financial aid in the publication of the first volume in this series.

Harvard University   E.B.
State University of New York at Buffalo   R.K.S.

FOR MY SON CHARLIE

CONTENTS

Contents

Contents

Contents

Contents

PREFACE TO THE SECOND EDITION

The decision to publish a second edition of *Archaic Times to the End of the Peloponnesian War* has enabled me and the Editors of the Series of which this volume is a part to subject the book to intensive scrutiny. Many errors in the text and indices have been removed, and there has been some augmentation of the material contained in the volume, limited though it was by the need to retain the numeration of the first edition. The typography and format have also been modified in order to produce a better-looking page that will make it easier going for the reader.

I have a number of obligations to others which it is a pleasure to record. I am grateful to the Syndics of the Cambridge University Press for their willingness to publish this volume in the second edition. As before, I gratefully acknowledge my enormous debt to Professors E. Badian and Robert K. Sherk for their tireless assistance and salutary criticism. I am also indebted to a considerable number of other scholars for their corrections and kindly criticisms. Of these D. M. Lewis was especially generous and helpful, even to the point of providing me with the appropriate references to *IG* I^3. Those errors that still remain are entirely my own, though their number was diminished by a useful list of errata and suggestions presented by Professor D. J. Geagan. Finally, I record here my deep thanks to Katrina Avery for working closely with me in my revision of the book. Many improvements and corrections are directly the result of her energy and dedication.

Acknowledgment is made to the University of Chicago Press and to the American Oriental Society for permission to quote material under their copyright.

April 1980   C.W.F.

VOLUME EDITOR'S INTRODUCTION

The primary purpose of this volume is to supplement the standard and easily accessible sources of the history of the Greek world from the Archaic period to the end of the Peloponnesian War.

The predominance of fifth-century Athenian inscriptions in the documents translated here is due almost as much to the unflagging willingness of the Athenians to carve their decrees and accounts on marble and to the long and successful excavations in the Athenian Agora as to their intrinsic importance. An attempt, nevertheless, has been made to provide a selection of the more important, or interesting, non-Athenian documents. Here I follow closely and owe a debt to Marcus Niebuhr Tod for volume I of his *Greek historical inscriptions* and to Russell Meiggs and David Lewis for their expanded and updated successor volume.

Much of the material in this volume derives from secondary authors, particularly scholiasts, ancient scholars who themselves wrote commentaries on the 'classical' authors. Mainly, these were men living in Hellenistic times, having access to sources not extant today, and their work, in turn, was quoted (and abbreviated) by scholars who came after them. The scholia (material written by ancient scholars in the margins of texts) to Aristophanes and Pindar provide examples of such mines of information, and the lexicographers of Roman and Byzantine times – e.g. Harpocration in his *Lexicon* and the compilation called the *Suda* – provide another. The fragments of the writings of forgotten Greek historians, some of which are translated here, frequently derive from sources such as these, though also from other writers whose works managed to survive. The standard source for this information is Felix Jacoby's *Die Fragmente der griechischen Historiker*, uncompleted at his death but under continuation. It is a series of companion volumes, one with the ancient texts, the other with commentary written in German, except in the case of IIIb (Suppl.), which is written in English and provides an invaluable commentary on those historians of Athens known as the 'Atthidographers.'

In the presentation of these documents, epigraphical and literary, I have attempted to be as objective as possible. Many are notoriously in dispute as to date, interpretation, and even historical authenticity, but polemical or tendentious reporting would be out of place in a book of this kind. Items are therefore arranged without prejudice in strict chronological order according to the earliest date ascribed to each by serious scholars – even if later dates would appear to me to be preferable. However, other dates that have been proposed are indicated as alternatives, and a brief bibliography of works published in English is added, to permit the student to explore conflicting views when they exist.

A few words are required here about the general format used. In the case of inscriptions, the heading identifies the material of the item (e.g. marble or bronze), form (e.g. plaque, stele, or statue base), the dialect used (when not obvious), peculiarities of the script (if there are such), and the locality in which it was found. A section below the heading provides a list, not all-inclusive, of various texts of the inscription that have been consulted, the text principally followed being specially marked. In addition, literary sources bearing on the inscription are cited. Another section follows in most instances, with bibliography relevant to the inscription.

In the translation of the inscriptions I have followed the format set down by the General Editors and have tried to adhere as closely as possible to the actual word order, even at the cost of some clumsiness. Line endings have been marked. Missing letters of proper names are enclosed in square brackets [ ] when restored; otherwise, when there are missing letters, the entire word or words of which they are a part are italicized, except in some instances where the lacuna is so trivial that italicization would convey the wrong impression of the stone. But it should be borne in mind that restorations are rarely *certain*; and whenever, in my opinion, a proposed restoration is *hazardous* or merely *possible*, I have bracketed or italicized the word or words even though the restoration is quite compatible with the letters or the traces of letters that survive. Furthermore, if a proposed restoration is purely theoretical or deduced from extrinsic considerations, I have placed it in a note below the text and not in the text itself. There are also cases of restorations so inventive that they are not included even in the notes. However, exceptions arise. Some historical arguments of considerable importance have been constructed on the basis of conjectural restorations. Since the student must be able to grasp purported evidence, many of these are reported in the notes or in alternative versions of texts (Nos. 71, 94). The notes themselves are as succinct as possible and are limited to explanations of obscurities in the text or of terms not covered in the Glossary that probably would be unfamiliar to the reader. Here, too, I have tried to avoid making comments supporting any particular view or minimizing difficulties inherent in one or another of them.

Those items that are literary extracts are treated in the same way, though the presentation is, of course, less complex.

The indices of this volume are correlated with the item numbers and not the pages. This system will not only obviate confusion when the same indexed rubrics appear in two items placed on the same page, but it will also permit the reader quickly and instructively to use the indices in combination with the table of contents so that the general context of each indexed rubric will be immediately apparent.

The great number of personal and place names occurring in this volume suggests that the most reasonable course to be followed in rendering them is that of direct transliteration, and most names are therefore so treated, even though Alkibiades or Thoukydides or Kroisos may require getting used to by the student. On the other hand, the names of authors are given in their familiar English or Latinized form. Polydeukes is Pollux; the historian Thoukydides is Thucydides; and Ploutarchos is Plutarch. Place names follow a less ironclad rule. I have transliterated the less familiar and used the English or the Latinized forms of the more familiar.

Symbols used and miscellaneous information[1]

*	indicates the text on which the translation of an inscription here given is based
( )	indicate an explanatory addition to the text
[ ]	enclose letters or words that no longer stand in the text as it survives, but have been restored by modern scholars
[. . .]	indicates by the number of dots the exact number of missing letters where no restoration is attempted
[- - -]	indicates an indeterminate number of missing letters
{ }	indicate apparently superfluous letters or words
⟨ ⟩	enclose letters or words thought to be accidentally omitted on the original document
[[ ]]	enclose letters or words that were deliberately erased in ancient times
|	indicates the end of a line in an inscription
||	indicate the beginning of every fifth line in an inscription
/	indicates the end of a line of verse
//	indicate the beginning of every fifth line of verse
v	indicates a vacant letter space in the original document
vv	indicate that there is more than one letter space vacant in the original document
vacat	indicates that an entire line or a space between entire lines was left vacant

1 Some of these items are further explained in the Series Editors' Introduction, above.

lacuna indicates that a portion of the document is missing

Italics indicate that only a part of the original word is extant on the document.

A dot underneath a letter indicates that the preserved traces on the stone are compatible with the letter printed, but not with that letter only.

The term 'stoichedon' indicates a style of engraving in which letters are aligned vertically and horizontally in checkerboard fashion, so that (in a perfect example) all lines of an inscription have the same number of letters.

In the transliteration of numerals, the practice followed has been to use arabic numerals when Greek numerals were used and to use words when the Greek numbers were written out. As to deme names (demotics), they customarily appear in the Greek in the adjectival form (e.g. Perikles Cholargeus), though I give instead the place name with 'of' (of Cholargos).

Athenian time reckoning

The twelve Athenian months are

Hekatombaion	(June/July)	Gamelion	(December/January)
Metageitnion	(July/August)	Anthesterion	(January/February)
Boedromion	(August/September)	Elaphebolion	(February/March)
Pyanopsion	(September/October)	Mounichion	(March/April)
Maimakterion	(October/November)	Thargelion	(April/May)
Posideion	(November/December)	Skirophorion	(May/June)

The Athenians counted time in two ways. The 'archon' or 'festival' year followed the order of the months and was the 'official' year for the preponderance of the magistrates, e.g. archons, generals; others, such as the Treasurers of Athena, seem to have held their tenure from Panathenaic festival to Panathenaic festival (Hekatombaion 28). Since the 'ordinary' year of twelve lunar months of twenty-nine or thirty days falls short of the solar year by a little more than eleven days, the practice was to intercalate a thirteenth month from time to time. In addition, the archon eponymous was free to intercalate days into the year (in order, for example, to postpone a festival on a day of ill-omen).

Time was also reckoned by the Conciliar calendar. Each of the ten Athenian tribes served in the Boule as prytany (see the Glossary) for approximately one tenth of the year. In the fourth century, at least, the first four prytanies served thirty-six days each, and the last six served thirty-five days each. Whether this also applied in the fifth century is the subject of considerable dispute. For calendric equations linking the two calendars, no. 158 deserves close study.

The ten Athenian Tribes in their official order

I. Erechtheis   VI. Oineis
II. Aigeis   VII. Kekropis
III. Pandionis   VIII. Hippothontis
IV. Leontis   IX. Aiantis
V. Akamantis   X. Antiochis

Numbers and coinage

The Attic system of numerals worked, like the Roman, by the combination of different units, each a multiple of the next. A different symbol existed for each of the numerals 10,000; 5,000; 1,000; 500; 100; 10; 5; 1; and when a number was written in numerals, the largest symbol always appeared first, with the others juxtaposed in descending order. No smaller numeral was repeated when a larger would serve instead (e.g. never two fives instead of a ten).

The Attic system of coinage and weights was based on the drachma.

6 obols (ob.) = 1 drachma (dr.)
100 dr. = 1 mna
6,000 dr. (60 mnai) = 1 talent (T.)

Sums of money were normally expressed by Attic numerals, standing for drachmai, with a special symbol for 1 drachma. There were also special symbols for talents, obols and fractions of obols. Talents preceded and obols and their fractions followed the numerals indicating drachmai. (The mna was not used as an accounting unit.) Consequently, in the restoration of inscriptions involving sums of money, this system of numeration permits assured calculation of the maximum and minimum figures allowable, when the beginning of a series of numerals is preserved but not the end. For example, if a series started with the symbol for 1,000 (drachmai) and six letter spaces were known to be missing after it, in no case could the sum be less than 1,019 or more than 4,700. In the first case, the figures would be 10, 5, and 1 (this last written four times); in the second, 1,000 written three times, 500, and 100 written twice.

Similarly, one can work backwards when only the last portion of a figure is preserved and calculate at least the minimum possible sum. To take a real example: no. 120, the Parthenon accounts, gives in the left-hand column as the cost for 'expenditures on purchases' (lines 22f.) a sum of five digits, of which the first three are missing, while the last two are symbols for 100 dr. The three missing symbols must be equal to or greater than the symbols following them, which are preserved. But if they were merely equal (i.e. if there were five symbols for 100 dr.), the sum (500 dr.) must have been expressed by its own proper symbol. Therefore the first symbol must be at least 500, and the lowest possible sum consists of $500 + 4 \times 100$ dr. $= 900$ dr. By the same process, the next alternative after 900 dr. is 1,400 dr. $(1,000 + 4 \times 100)$, and, after that, 1,800 dr. $(1,000 + 500 + 3 \times 100)$. It therefore follows also that a sum in which a space in its middle has been effaced can sometimes be restored with complete certainty.

It would be idle to attempt to calculate the value of the drachma in terms of the American dollar (especially in these times). However, in absolute terms, the usual assumption is that average wages in Athens in the second half of the fifth century amounted to about a drachma per day. Thus an inscription (*IG* I^2 372 (I^3 474)) of 409 B.C. recording sums paid out by Athens for the completion of the Erechtheum indicates that amount as the pay to sawyers. Sailors also were paid a drachma a day in 415 (Thucydides 6.31.3), though the pay dropped in 413 to 3 obols a day (Thucydides 8.45.2; cf. Xenophon, *Hellenica* 1.5.3–7). During the first part of the Peloponnesian War (Aristophanes, *Wasps* 684) jury pay was three obols a day.

ABBREVIATIONS

AC	*L'Antiquité classique*
AHR	*American Historical Review*
AJA	*American Journal of Archaeology*
AJAH	*American Journal of Ancient History*
AJP	*American Journal of Philology*
Arch. Eph.	*Archaiologike Ephemeris*
ATL	B. D. Meritt, H. T. Wade-Gery, and M. F. McGregor, *The Athenian tribute lists*, 4 vols.: I, Cambridge (Mass.) 1939; II–IV, Princeton 1949–53
BCH	*Bulletin de Correspondance hellénique*
BSA	*Annual of the British School at Athens*
Bradeen–McGregor, *Studies*	Donald W. Bradeen and Malcolm F. McGregor, *Studies in fifth-century Attic epigraphy*, University of Cincinnati Classical Studies 4, Norman, Okla. 1973
Buck	Carl D. Buck, *The Greek dialects*, Chicago 1955
Bury–Meiggs	J. B. Bury, *A history of Greece*, 4th ed. by Russell Meiggs, London 1975
CAH	*The Cambridge ancient history*, 1st ed., Cambridge 1923–39
CP	*Classical Philology*
CQ	*Classical Quarterly*
CR	*Classical Review*
CRAI	*Comptes rendus de l'Académie des Inscriptions et Belles-Lettres*
CSCA	*California Studies in Classical Antiquity*
DAA	A. E. Raubitschek, *Dedications from the Athenian Akropolis*, Cambridge (Mass.) 1949
de Ste Croix, *Origins*	G. E. M. de Ste Croix, *The origins of the Peloponnesian War*, London 1972
Ehrenberg studies	*Ancient society and institutions: studies presented to Victor Ehrenberg on his seventy-fifth birthday*, Oxford 1966
FGrHist	F. Jacoby, *Die Fragmente der griechischen Historiker*, Berlin and Leiden 1923–
FHG	Karl Müller, *Fragmenta historicorum graecorum*, 5 vols., Paris 1841–70
Fornara, *Generals*	*The Athenian board of Generals from 501 to 404*, Historia Einzelschriften 16, Wiesbaden 1971
GHI	R. Meiggs and D. M. Lewis, *A selection of Greek historical inscriptions to the end of the fifth century BC*, Oxford 1969
GRBS	*Greek Roman and Byzantine Studies*
Gomme, etc., *HCT*	A. W. Gomme, A. Andrewes, and K. J. Dover, *A historical commentary on Thucydides*, 4 vols. (Books I–VII), Oxford 1945–70

Abbreviations

Graham, *Colony*	A. J. Graham, *Colony and mother city in ancient Greece*, Manchester 1964
HSCP	*Harvard Studies in Classical Philology*
HTR	*Harvard Theological Review*
Hammond, *History*	N. G. L. Hammond, *History of Greece*, 2nd ed., Oxford 1967
Hammond, *Studies*	N. G. L. Hammond, *Studies in Greek history*, Oxford 1973
Harrison 1	A. R. W. Harrison, *The law of Athens. The family and property*, Oxford 1968
Harrison 2	A. R. W. Harrison, *The law of Athens. Procedure*, Oxford 1971
Hignett, *Constitution*	C. Hignett, *A history of the Athenian constitution*, Oxford 1952
Hignett, *Invasion*	C. Hignett, *Xerxes' invasion of Greece*, Oxford 1963
Hill, *Sources*[2]	G. F. Hill, *Sources for Greek history between the Persian and Peloponnesian Wars*, 2nd ed. by R. Meiggs and A. Andrewes, Oxford 1951
Historia	*Historia, Zeitschrift für Alte Geschichte*
Huxley, *Sparta*	G. L. Huxley, *Early Sparta*, Cambridge (Mass.) 1962
IC	*Inscriptiones Creticae*, ed. M. Guarducci, 4 vols., Rome 1935–50
IG	*Inscriptiones Graecae*, Berlin 1873–
JHS	*Journal of Hellenic Studies*
Jeffery, *Greece*	L. H. Jeffery, *Archaic Greece. The city-states c. 700–500 BC*, London and Tonbridge 1976
Jeffery, *LSAG*	L. H. Jeffery, *The local scripts of Archaic Greece*, Oxford 1961
Jones, *Democracy*	A. H. M. Jones, *Athenian democracy*, Oxford 1957
Kagan, *Outbreak*	D. Kagan, *The outbreak of the Peloponnesian War*, Ithaca 1969
Meiggs, *Empire*	R. Meiggs, *The Athenian Empire*, Oxford 1972
Michell, *Sparta*	H. Michell, *Sparta*, Cambridge 1952
Mosshammer, *Eusebius*	A. A. Mosshammer, *The Chronicles of Eusebius and Greek chronological tradition*, Lewisburg, Pa. 1977
PACA	*Proceedings of the African Classical Associations*
Phoros	*Phoros. Tribute to Benjamin Dean Meritt*, New York 1974
REG	*Revue des Etudes grecques*
RFIC	*Rivista di Filologia e di Istruzione Classica*
Rhodes, *Boule*	P. J. Rhodes, *The Athenian Boule*, Oxford 1972
SEG	*Supplementum Epigraphicum Graecum*
SIG	W. Dittenberger, *Sylloge inscriptionum Graecarum*, 3rd ed., Leipzig 1915–24
Sealey, *History*	R. Sealey, *A history of the Greek city-states, ca. 700–338 BC*, Berkeley 1976
TAPA	*Transactions of the American Philological Association*
Tod	M. N. Tod, *A selection of Greek historical inscriptions to the end of the fifth century BC*, 2nd ed., 2 vols.: I Oxford 1946; II Oxford 1948
Wade-Gery, *Essays*	H. T. Wade-Gery, *Essays in Greek history*, Oxford 1958
YCS	*Yale Classical Studies*
ZPE	*Zeitschrift für Papyrologie und Epigraphik*

1 Ancient Chronology

A: The Parian Marble (*FGrHist* 239). 264/3 B.C. Two fragments of a marble stele. Paros. B: Eusebius, *Chronica* (ed. Helm), early fourth century A.D.

E. Bickerman, *Chronology of the ancient world* (Ithaca 1968) 87–9; D. S. Wallace-Hadrill, *Eusebius of Caesarea* (Westminster, Md. 1961) 155–67; Mosshammer, *Eusebius.*

A. Extracts from the Parian Marble

THE HEADING [---] | [From] *all sorts* [of records and general histories] I have recorded the [ti|mes] from the beginning, starting with Kekrops, the first King of Athens, down to the archonship, in Paros, | of [....] yanax, and, at Athens, of Diognetos (264/3).

45 895/3 From the time when Ph[ei]don of Argos published [his] *measures* [and] | established *weights* and struck silver coins in Aegina, he being the eleventh (in line of descent) from Herakles, (it has been) 631 years, and the King of Athens was | [Pherekl]es.[1]

48 683/2 From the time when the (Athenian) Archon held office year by year, 420 years.[2]

50 605/3 From the time when A[lyatte]s became *King* of the Lydia[ns, | 3]41 years, and Aristokles was Archon at Athens.[3]

52 591/0 [From the time when] the Am[phikt]yo[nians[4] held sacrificial celebration] after they had *subju|gated* Kyrrha[5] and the gymnastic contest was established for a money prize from the spoils, [3]27 years, and Simon was Archon at Athens.

56 561/0 From the time when Peisistratos became tyrant of Athens, 297 years, and K[o]m[e]as was Archon [at Athens].[6]

56 556/5 From the time when Kroisos from Asia [sent envoys to] Delphi, | [29]2 years, and Euthydemos was Archon at Athens.[7]

59 511/10 From the time when Harmodios and [Aristoge]iton killed || [Hippa]rchos, the [successor] of Peisistratos, and the Athenians [drove out] the Peisistratidai from [the P]elasgian Wall, 248 years, and the Archon at Athens was Ha[r]p[ak|tides.[8]

69 478/7 From the time when G[e]lon son of Deinomenes became tyrant [of the] S[yrac]u[sans,] 215 years, and Timosthen[es] was Archon at Athens.

1

76 420/19 From the time when Archelaos became King of the Macedo-
nians, Perdikkas having died, 1[57] years, | and Astyphilos was
Archon at Athens.[9]

B. Eusebius, *Chronica*

798/7 Fidon (=Pheidon) of Argos was the first man to devise measures
and weights.[10]

789/8 The first trireme made sail at Corinth.[11]

758/7 The first Ephor, which is the name of a magistrate, was appointed in Lacedaemonia. Lacedaemonia had been under the rule
of the Kings for 350 years.[12]

746/5 The Lacedaemonians waged their twenty-year struggle with
the neighboring Messenians.[13]

720/19 The war which was waged in Thyrea between the Lacedaemonians and Argives.[14]

661/0 Kypselus held the tyranny in Corinth for 28 years.[15]

624/3 As some believe, Draco the legislator became celebrated.[16]

607/6 Pittacus of Mytilene,[17] who was one of the Seven Wise Men,[18]
slew Frynon (=Phrynon) the Athenian in combat at the Olympic Games.

597/6 Epimenides purified Athens.[19]

594/3 Solon established his own laws, the laws of Dracon having become antiquated except for those relating to homicide.[20]

562/1 Peisistratus, tyrant of the Athenians, crossed over into Italy.[21]

520/19 Harmodius and Aristogeiton slew Hipparchus the tyrant.
Leaena, a courtesan and their mistress, bit off her tongue when
put to the torture to betray her comrades.[22]

488/7 Egypt fell away from Darius.[23]

472/1 Themistocles fled to the Persians.[24]

461/0 Kimon defeated the Persians at the Eurymedon in a battle by
land and sea.[25] The Persian War came to an end.

445/4 Herodotus was honored when he read out his books in the
Council[26] at Athens.[27]

439/8 Fidias (=Pheidias) made the ivory Minerva (Athena).[28]

This selection from material in the Parian Marble and Eusebius provides some
examples of the Greeks' investigation of their own chronology. The dates are not all
reliable, nor were the ancients unanimous about them, as may be seen from comparison of the Parian Marble at the year 895 with Eusebius at 798. Indeed, it is fair
to say that the earlier the date, the more debatable its validity. In addition, error
and confusion on the part of the chronographers need to be taken into account.
Thus, there are numerous signs of chronological confusion in the Parian Marble,
where the dates given are frequently in conflict with orthodox chronology. The fact
that its author used different systems of reckoning, counted years inclusively and

exclusively, and that the mason may occasionally have inverted the order of some items (see note 1) is insufficient to explain many simple errors, however ingeniously some scholars have attempted to account for them. It should also be noted that although we may be confident that the actual dates ascribed to events in the Parian Marble are for the most part at least the dates the author intended to give, considerable uncertainty exists on this score with regard to Eusebius. His work on chronology survives only in an Armenian version, a Latin translation by Saint Jerome (from which the citations translated here derive), and in some other chronicles as well. Furthermore, the complicated arrangement adopted by Eusebius made for error and imprecision in the copying. Hence the discrepancies that are to be found not only in the various versions vis-à-vis each other, but even within the manuscript tradition of Saint Jerome's version. The result is to obscure precisely what dates Eusebius intended, the margin of error being about one to three years.

1 The very next item in the Parian Marble names Archias the Bacchiad of Corinth and founder of Syracuse as tenth in line of descent from Temenos – precisely what Ephorus (see no. 4A) alleged of Pheidon of Argos. The author of the Parian Marble or the mason may have wrongly interchanged these details (Jacoby); if so, Ephorus' date for Pheidon harmonizes with that in the (corrected) Parian Marble, Archias having actually been designated as the eleventh in descent from Herakles (and seventh from Temenos).
2 Cf. Pausanias 4.5.10, 15.1.
3 Cf. Herodotus 1.18–22.
4 I.e. members of the Amphictyonic League. See no. 16.
5 See no. 16.
6 Cf. Hdt. 1.59–64, Aristotle, *Athenaion Politeia* 14.
7 Cf. Hdt. 1.47.
8 Cf. Hdt. 5.55, Thucydides 1.20.2, 6.54.1, Arist. *Ath. Pol.* 18. This item telescopes the assassination of Hipparchos in 514 and the expulsion of his brother Hippias in 511/10, when the tyranny ended. Cf. Eusebius at the year 520/19.
9 Cf. Thuc. 2.100.2.
10 Cf. the Parian Marble (A) at the year 895.
11 Cf. Thuc. 1.13.2, Diodorus 14.42.3.
12 Cf. Arist. *Politics* 5.11.1313a26, Plutarch, *Lykourgos* 7, Diogenes Laertius 1.68.
13 See no. 12 below, Tyrtaeus F 4.
14 Cf. Hdt. 1.82.
15 Cf. Hdt. 5.92, Diod. 7.9.6.
16 I.e. he effected his judicial reform in that year. Cf. Arist. *Ath. Pol.* 4, Diod. 9.17, *Suda* s.v. 'Drakon,' and no. 15 below.
17 Cf. Hdt. 1.27, Arist. *Pol.* 3.14.1285a.
18 See Plato, *Protagoras* 343a for the canon of the 'Seven Sages.'
19 Cf. Arist. *Ath. Pol.* 1, Plut. *Solon* 12.
20 Cf. Arist. *Ath. Pol.* 7. The Armenian version here says that Solon abrogated the laws of Drakon.
21 The error was Eusebius' own, as we may tell by its repetition in Syncellus (another source for the *Chronica*) 239c (454, 7). It is a mistake for Eretria: cf. Hdt. 1.61.
22 Cf. the Parian Marble at the year 511/10 and note 8 above.
23 Cf. Hdt. 7.1.3.
24 Cf. Thuc. 1.135–8, Diod. 11.56.4.
25 The account is confused. See Thuc. 1.100.1, Diod. 11.61.
26 I.e. Boule.

27 Cf. Plut. *On the Malignity of Herodotus* 26.
28 See no. 114 below.

2 The Date of Lykourgos of Sparta. Ninth *or* eighth *or* seventh century B.C.

A: Scholiast to Pindar, *Pythian Odes* 1.120b (Ephorus, *FGrHist* 70 F 173); B: Aristotle, *Politics* 2.7.1271b24–6; C: Athenaeus 14.37, p. 635ef (Hellanicus, *FGrHist* 4 F 85a; Sosibius, *FGrHist* 595 F 3; Hieronymus F 33 Wehrli). D: Strabo 8.5.5, p. 366 (Hellanicus, *FGrHist* 4 F 116; Ephorus, *FGrHist* 70 F 118); E: Plutarch, *Lykourgos* 1 (Aristotle F 533 Rose). Cf. Herodotus 1.65f.; Thucydides 1.18.

Michell, *Sparta* 21f.; Huxley, *Sparta* 42f.; W. G. Forrest, *A history of Sparta* (London 1968) 55–60; Bury–Meiggs 98f.; Sealey, *History* 69, 74; Mosshammer, *Eusebius* 173–92.

A. Scholiast to Pindar, *Pythian Odes* 1.120b

Pindar, *Pythian Odes* 1.119–21: (Let us celebrate Deinomenes, son of Hieron and king of Aetna,) for whom Hieron founded that city with god-built freedom by the laws of the rule of Hyllos.[1]

Scholion: The legislation of Lykourgos. For he was eleventh (in descent) from Herakles (about 870), as Ephorus relates.

B. Aristotle, *Politics* 2.7.1271b24–6

They say that Lykourgos, when he gave up the guardianship of Charillos[2] the king and withdrew from the country, then spent most of his time around Crete because of Crete's kinship (with Sparta).

C. Athenaeus 14.37, p. 635ef

It is clear from this that Terpander is older than Anacreon: Terpander was the first man of all to win the Karneia, as Hellanicus narrates in his metrical *Victors at the Karneia* and in his prose *Catalogue* (of their names). The establishment of the Karneia came about in the twenty-sixth Olympiad (676/5–673/2), as Sosibius says in his *On Chronology*. Hieronymus, in *On Harp Singers*, which is the fifth book of his *On Poets*, says that Terpander lived in the time of Lykourgos the lawgiver, who is said by all in common agreement to have arranged the first numbered celebration of the Olympic Games together with Iphitos of Elis.

D. Strabo 8.5.5, p. 366

Hellanicus says that Eurysthenes and Prokles arranged the constitution. Ephorus censures him, saying that he makes no mention anywhere of

Lykourgos, and attributes his deeds to those who are unconnected with them.[3]

E. Plutarch, *Lykourgos 1*

See no. 3B.

1 Hyllos the son of Herakles was believed to have given his name to one of the three Dorian tribes, Hylleis, Dymanes, Pamphyloi (see no. 12C (1)).
2 His name is spelled elsewhere 'Charilaos.'
3 It is to be noted that Hellanicus had nothing to say about Lykourgos and therefore is not responsible for associating him with the Karneia.

3 The Establishment of the Olympic Games. (?) 776 B.C.

A: Plutarch, *Numa* 1 (Hippias of Elis, *FGrHist* 6 F 2); B: Plutarch, *Lykourgos* 1 (Aristotle F 533 Rose); C: Strabo 8.3.33, p. 358 (Ephorus, *FGrHist* 70 F 115.11–17); D: Pausanias 5.20.1; E: Athenaeus 14.37, p. 635ef (Hellanicus, *FGrHist* 4 F 85a; Sosibius, *FGrHist* 595 F 3; Hieronymus F 33 Wehrli); F: Eusebius, *Chronica* (ed. Helm) at 776.

H. T. Wade-Gery, *CAH* 3.544–8; Jeffery, *LSAG* 217f., *Greece* 168; Huxley, *Sparta* 109f.; Bury-Meiggs 101–3; Sealey, *History* 40–3; M. I. Finley and H. W. Pleket, *The Olympic Games* (London 1976); Mosshammer, *Eusebius* 86–8.

A. Plutarch, *Numa 1*

It is difficult for chronology to be known accurately, especially that calculated from the Olympic victors. They say that Hippias of Elis published lists of them, at a later date, based on nothing that would compel credence.

B. Plutarch, *Lykourgos 1*

Some say that Lykourgos flourished at the same time as Iphitos and that he joined in the establishment of the Olympic Truce, and even Aristotle the philosopher is among their number. He put forward in evidence the discus at Olympia, on which the name of Lykourgos is written down and preserved.

C. Strabo 8.3.33, p. 358

(The Aetolians won Elis from the Epeians. Because of the friendship which had existed between the Aetolian Oxylos and the Herakleidai, it was agreed to make) Elis sacred to Zeus and to make any man marching against this country accursed and equally so the man who failed to use all his force to repel him. As a result, those who founded the city of the Eleians left it unfortified thereafter; those who marched on campaign through the country surrendered their arms and received them back after leaving the boundaries; and Iphitos established the Olympic festival, the Eleians being under divine protection.

D. Pausanias 5.20.1

The discus of Iphitos does not have the truce which the Eleians proclaim at the Olympic Games written in a straight line. The letters go around the discus in a circle.

E. Athenaeus 14.37, p. 635ef

See no. 2C.

F. Eusebius, *Chronica* at the year 776 B.C.

Africanus writes that the first Olympiad occurred in the time of Ioatham, King of the Hebrews. Our computation also sets it in the same time.

4 Pheidon of Argos. Early eighth century *or* 748 B.C. *or* 669 B.C.

A: Strabo 8.3.33, p. 358 (Ephorus, *FGrHist* 70 F 115.20–35); B: Pausanias 6.22.2; C: Parian Marble, *FGrHist* 239 F 30 (895–893 B.C.); D: Strabo 8.6.16, p. 376 (Ephorus, *FGrHist* 70 F 176); E: *Etymologicum Magnum* 3.613.13 (Orion s.v. 'obol'); F: *Excerpta de Insidiis* 10.27 (Nicolaus of Damascus, *FGrHist* 90 F 35). Cf. Herodotus 6.127.3; Aristotle, *Politics* 5.10.1310b, *Athenaion Politeia* 10.

H. T. Wade-Gery, *CAH* 3.539–43; A. Andrewes, *CQ* 43 (1949) 70–8; Huxley, *Sparta* 28–30; Bury-Meiggs 524; Sealey, *History* 40–5; Jeffery, *Greece* 134–6.

A. Strabo 8.3.33, p. 358

(Elis enjoyed peace because sacred to Zeus as the site of the Olympic Games.)[1] But Pheidon of Argos, who was tenth in the line of Temenos[2] (803–770) and who held more power than any man of his time – through which he regained the 'Portion of Temenos,' which had broken up into many parts – and who invented the so-called Pheidonian measures and weights, and struck coins, especially of silver, in addition also attacked the cities taken by Herakles and deemed it fitting for himself to preside at those contests which Herakles had established and of which the Olympic Games were one. Coming by force he presided at them, nor did the Eleians have arms with which to prevent him because of the peace which had prevailed, while the rest were subject to his rule. However, the Eleians did not register in their record that celebration of the Games, but acquired arms because of it and began to defend themselves.

The Lacedaemonians joined with them either because they envied the good fortune that came to them from the peace or because they believed that they would also have them as allies in destroying Pheidon, who had deprived them of the hegemony over the Peloponnesians which earlier they had possessed. And they indeed helped to bring down Pheidon and joined the Eleians in organizing the territory of Pisa and Triphylia.

B. Pausanias 6.22.2

The Pisaians brought disaster upon themselves of their own volition by incurring the hatred of the Eleians and by their eagerness to administer the Olympic Games in the place of the Eleians. In the eighth[3] Olympiad (748) they brought in Pheidon of Argos, who of all Greek tyrants acted most outrageously, and they administered the Games together with Pheidon.

C. Parian Marble at 895–893 B.C.

See No. 1A.

D. Strabo 8.6.16, p. 376

Ephorus says that silver was first minted in Aegina by Pheidon. She became a merchant-state because her men plied the sea as merchants because of the poverty of their land. Thus petty wares are called 'Aeginetan profit.'

E. *Etymologicum Magnum* 3.613.13

Pheidon of Argos was the first man of all to mint coin (and he did so) in Aegina. Distributing the coin and taking back the spits[4] he dedicated them to Argive Hera.[5]

F. *Excerpta de Insidiis* 10.27

(Nicolaus relates) that Pheidon went out of friendship to render assistance to the Corinthians, who were undergoing party strife, and that he died when an attack was launched by his associates.[6]

1 See no. 3C.
2 One of the great-grandsons of Herakles. On the 'Return of the Herakleidai,' he received Argos as his portion; the two sons of his brother Aristodemos, Prokles and Eurysthenes, received Lacedaemonia; and Kresphontes obtained Messenia.
3 '⟨twenty-⟩eighth': Falconer (= 669 B.C.).
4 The 'obolos' (an Attic weight or coin) is a dialectical form of *obelos*, 'spit'; see Plutarch, *Lysander* 17.5 for the early use of nails or spits as money. Iron spits have in fact been excavated at the temple of Hera at Argos. See Jeffery, *Greece* 135.

5 Cf. Aelian, *VH* 12.10: '(the Aeginetans) were the first to mint money and from them coin was called "Aeginetan." '
6 Arist. *Pol.* 2.3.7.1265b speaks of 'Pheidon of Corinth, a most ancient lawgiver.' This formulation is inappropriate to the Argive.

5 The Foundation of Naxos and Megara in Sicily. Late eighth century B.C.

A: Strabo 6.2.2, p. 267 (Ephorus, *FGrHist* 70 F 137); B: Stephanus of Byzantium s.v. 'Chalkis' (Hellanicus, *FGrHist* 4 F 82). Cf. Thucydides 6.3ff.[1]

E. A. Freeman, *The history of Sicily* (Oxford 1891) 1.314–16; Gomme, etc., *HCT* 4.207–10; Bury-Meiggs 76f.; Sealey, *History* 32: C. Starr, *The economic and social growth of early Greece* (New York 1977) 43f., 62–4; Mosshammer, *Eusebius* 114f.

A Strabo 6.2.2, p. 267

Ephorus says that these cities (Naxos and Megara) were the first Hellenic cities to be established in Sicily, in the tenth generation after the Trojan War. For people before that time were afraid of Etruscan piracy and of the cruelty of the barbarians there, with the result that they did not even sail there for purposes of trade. Theokles of Athens (continues Ephorus) was driven by a storm to Sicily and observed its uninhabited state and the excellence of its soil. Returning home, he failed to persuade the Athenians (to venture upon a colony). But taking a considerable number of the Chalcidians of Euboea and some Ionians, and in addition some Dorians, of whom the greater number were Megarians, he sailed (off to Sicily). The Chalcidians thus settled Naxos while the Dorians (colonized) Megara, previously called Hybla.

B. Stephanus of Byzantium s.v. 'Chalkis'

... Hellanicus in the *Priestesses of Hera*, Book 2: 'Theokles of Chalcis established the city (of Naxos) in Sicily with Chalcidians and Naxians.'

1 Thucydides gives the following sequence: Naxos, Syracuse, Leontini, Katane, Thapsus, Megara.

6 The Foundation of Croton. Late eighth century B.C.

A: Strabo 6.1.12, p. 262 (Antiochus of Syracuse, *FGrHist* 555 F 10; Ephorus, *FGrHist* 70 F 140); B: Zenobius, *Proverbs* 3.42 (Hippys of Rhegium, *FGrHist* 554 F 1). Cf. Diodorus 8.17; Pausanias 3.3.1.

Gomme, etc., *HCT* 4.201, 206f.; Bury-Meiggs 78f.

A. Strabo 6.1.12, p. 262

(Croton was founded when Trojan women burned the ships of the Achaean heroes when they wandered to the site.) But Antiochus says that when the god (Apollo at Delphi) directed the Achaeans by oracle to found Croton, Myskellos departed to examine the site. Because Sybaris was already established,[1] having the same name as the nearby river, he judged that site (i.e. Sybaris) to be better. He thus returned and asked the god again whether that place would be given to him to colonize in place of the other. The god replied – for Myskellos happened to be hump-backed – 'Myskellos of the short back, *pass by*! In searching for something else / you hunt for *morsels* (?).[2] Praise the gift you are given.' He returned and founded Croton. Archias[3] the founder of Syracuse also shared in the task, having sailed up by chance, when he was setting out upon the establishment of Syracuse. As Ephorus says, Iapygians previously dwelled in Croton.

B. Zenobius, *Proverbs* 3.42

'Praise the gift you are given': this is a clause of the oracle which was given to Myskellos of Rhypes (in Achaea) at that time when he did not wish to found Croton but rather Sybaris, as Hippys says in his *On Chronology*. He says the oracle was as follows: 'Myskellos of the short back, by searching for some things contrary to the god / *you will not find other things*. Praise the gift you are given.'[4]

1 Cf. Eusebius in Hieronymus (Jerome), Ol. 18, 3 (709 B.C.): 'Croton, Parium and Sybaris were founded.'
2 The italicized words of these dactylic hexameters are corrupt.
3 See no. 1, note 1.
4 See note 2.

7 The Lelantine War. Late eighth century B.C.

A: Strabo 10.1.12, p. 448; B: Plutarch, *Banquet of the Seven Sages* 10 (*Moralia* 153f); C: Proclus on Hesiod, *Works and Days* 650–62 (Plutarch F 84 Sandbach); D: Plutarch, *Erotica* 17 (=*Moralia* 760e–761a (Aristotle F 98 Rose)). Cf. Herodotus 5.99; Thucydides 1.15.3.

J. Boardman, *BSA* 52 (1957) 27–9; W. G. Forrest, *Historia* 6 (1957) 160–75; A. R. Burn, *The lyric age of Greece* (London 1960) 90–3; Bury–Meiggs, 107; Sealey, *History* 35; Jeffery, *Greece* 64–7.

A. Strabo 10.1.12, p. 448

Generally these cities (Chalcis and Eretria) were in amity with each other; in their dispute about the Lelantine plain they did not so completely cease (from amity) as to act remorselessly in the war, but agreed on the conditions under which they would engage in the struggle. This too[1] is made evident by a stele in the (temple of Artemis) Amarysia which states that long-range missiles are not to be used.[2]

B. Plutarch, *Moralia* 153ef

For we hear that of those who were wise men in that time the most distinguished poets congregated at Chalcis for the burial rites of Amphidamas. Amphidamas was a warlike man and he fell after making much trouble for the Eretrians in the battles around Lelantos.

C. Proclus on Hesiod, *Works and Days* 650–62

Hesiod, *Works and Days* 654–6: Then I crossed over into Chalcis to the contests of warlike Amphidamas. The sons of great-hearted (Amphidamas) had proclaimed and established many contests.

Scholion: All this about Chalcis, Amphidamas, the contest and the tripod Plutarch says was interpolated and is not genuine. Amphidamas died fighting by sea[3] for the Lelantine plain against the Eretrians. Prizes and contests were established in his honor by his children after he died.

D. Plutarch, *Moralia* 760e–761a

Do you know the reason why Kleomachos of Pharsalus died in battle? .... He came as an ally of the Chalcidians ⟨with⟩[4] the Thessalian force when the war with Eretria was at its height. It appeared to the Chalcidians that their infantry was strong, but it was difficult to repulse the enemy horse. The allies urged Kleomachos, who possessed a vigorous spirit, to be the first to charge against the cavalry .... Donning his helmet, Kleomachos, in exultation, gathered around himself the bravest of the Thessalians, rode out boldly, and fell upon the enemy, so as to disarrange and rout the cavalry. Because of this the hoplites also fled and the Chalcidians won mightily. However, it chanced that Kleomachos met his death, and the Chalcidians point out his grave in the agora, and the great column stands upon it even now .... Aristotle says that Kleomachos died in a different manner when he had conquered the Eretrians in battle.

1 Strabo had just pointed out (10.1.10, p. 448) that a stele in the temple of Artemis in Eretria put Eretrian forces at 3,000 hoplites, 600 knights, 60 chariots.
2 See Archilochus F 3 West, who writes that the sword, not bows or slings will be used in combat by the 'spear-famed masters of Euboea' when they fight 'on a plain.' Polybius 13.3.4 (cf. Livy 42.47.5) discusses the question of the rules of war in such a way as to indicate that this compact between Chalcis and Eretria was a well-known historical example. See F. W. Walbank, *A historical commentary on Polybius* 2 (Oxford 1967) 416.

3 Emended by K. F. Hermann to 'fighting in single combat.'
4 An addition by Hermann; the text in Plutarch is unacceptable as it stands: 'he came as an ally of the Chalcidians when the Thessalian war against the Eretrians was at its height.'

8 The Use of the Word 'Tyrant.' About 700 B.C.

A: Summary, Sophocles, *Oedipus Rex* (Hippias of Elis, *FGrHist* 6 F 6); B: Clement of Alexandria, *Miscellanies* 1.21.117.8-9, p. 74.14 Stählin (Theopompus, *FGrHist* 115 F 205; Euphorion, Müller, *FHG* 3, p. 71).

E. A. Freeman, *The history of Sicily* (Oxford 1891) 2.49-55; A. Andrewes, *The Greek tyrants* (London 1956) 20-30; Bury-Meiggs, 105; Sealey, *History* 38f.; C. Starr, *The economic and social growth of early Greece* (New York 1977) 178-81.

A. Summary, Sophocles, *Oedipus Rex*

The poets after Homer have done a curious thing in denoting the kings before the period of the Trojan war as 'tyrants.' This word became current among the Hellenes at a later date, in the time of Archilochus, as Hippias the sophist says. For Homer (*Odyssey* 18.85) calls Echetos, the most lawless of rulers, 'king' and not 'tyrant': 'to King Echetos, destroyer of mortals.' They say that the tyrant derived his name from the Tyrrhenians. For they became troublesome as pirates.[1]

B. Clement of Alexandria, *Miscellanies* 1.21.117.8-9

Theopompus in fact states in the forty-third book of the *Philippika* that Homer flourished five hundred years after the expedition at Ilium.[2] Euphorion in his *On the Aleuadai* says that he flourished in the time of Gyges, who began his kingship in the eighteenth Olympiad (708/4), and he also states that he (Gyges) was the first person to be called 'tyrant.'

1. It is notable that Herodotus conversely can speak of Aristagoras' fear of losing the 'kingship' of Miletus (5.35.1).
2. I.e. about 700. This is the latest date given for Homer in the ancient literature. Herodotus, for example, placed him (with Hesiod) in the ninth century (2.53); the Parian Marble, line 45 (*FGrHist* 239 A 29; see no. 1A above) assigns him to the years 907/5, a generation after Hesiod (A 28), probably following Ephorus, *FGrHist* 70 F 1, F 101, F 102. Ephorus also claimed Homer for his own city, Kyme, and asserted that Hesiod and Homer were related.

9 The Foundation of Tarentum by the Partheniai of Sparta. About 700 B.C.[1]

A: Strabo 6.3.2-3, pp. 278f. (Antiochus, *FGrHist* 555 F 13; Ephorus, *FGrHist* 70 F 216); B: Athenaeus 6.101, p. 271cd (Theopompus, *FGrHist* 115 F 171). Cf. Aristotle, *Politics* 5.7.1306b; Pausanias 10.10.6-8; Diodorus 8.21; Justin 3.4.

9 The foundation of Tarentum by the Partheniai of Sparta

J. L. Myres, *CAH* 3.674; T. J. Dunbabin, *The Western Greeks* (Oxford 1948) 28-31; Huxley, *Sparta* 37f.; Bury–Meiggs 79.

A. Strabo 6.3.2-3, pp. 278f.

In speaking of the foundation (of Tarentum) Antiochus states that when the Messenian War occurred, those Lacedaemonians who did not take part in the campaign were considered slaves and named 'helots,' while those children who were born during the campaign they named Partheniai (sons of concubines) and judged as being without citizen rights. These did not suffer it, and they were many; and they plotted against the government . . . . (When the plot was betrayed, instead of punishing them the Spartans sent to Delphi to enquire about using them as colonists.) The oracle responded: 'I give you Satyrion and the rich land of Tarentum / to dwell in and to become a woe to the Iapygians.' Thus the Partheniai went with (their leader) Phalanthos . . . . They named the city Taras after a certain hero. [3] Ephorus speaks as follows about its foundation. The Lacedaemonians made war against the Messenians since they had slain King Teleklos when he went to Messenia to make a sacrifice. They swore that they would not return home before they destroyed Messenia or were themselves all slain. . . . (In the tenth year, in response to the complaints of those Lacedaemonian women who had been left as if widows and who feared for the manpower of their country, the strongest and youngest men – who therefore had no part in the oath because they had joined the ranks after it was pledged – were sent back to Sparta.) They commanded all of them to have intercourse with all the virgins, believing that they would be the more fruitful. Because of this the children were named Partheniai (= 'the sons of the virgins'). . . . But when (the men of the army) returned home (after conquering Messenia), they did not give the Partheniai equal honor with the rest because they were illegitimate. The Partheniai joined with the helots . . . (but their plot was discovered and) they were persuaded by their fathers to found a colony. If they secured a satisfactory site they were to stay there; if not, they were to return and receive the fifth part of Messenia. They were sent out and came upon the Achaeans, who were fighting with the barbarians. Sharing in the danger they founded Tarentum.

B. Athenaeus 6.101, p. 271cd

As to the so-called Epeunaktoi[2] among the Lacedaemonians (for these too are slaves), Theopompus clearly expounds the matter in Book 32 of his *Histories*, speaking as follows: 'After many Lacedaemonians had died in the Messenian War, those who remained were fearful

that their lack of numbers would become evident to their enemies.
They put some of the helots on each mattress of those who had died.
Later they made them citizens but called them Epeunaktoi because
they had been set on the mattresses of the dead.'³

1 Eusebius dates the colony's foundation to 706 B.C.
2 Hesychius s.v. 'Epeunaktoi': 'bedfellows.'
3 Diod. 8.21 identifies Epeunaktai and Partheniai.

10 Orthagoras, Tyrant of Sicyon. About 650 B.C.

Oxyrhynchus Papyri 11.1365 (*FGrHist* 105 F 2). Cf. Aristotle, *Politics* 5.12.1315b;
Diodorus 8.24; Plutarch, *Moralia* 553ab. This extract is a papyrus fragment;
Ephorus has been suggested as its author. It is a good example of the ancient pro-
clivity to invent circumstantial detail.

A. Andrewes, *The Greek tyrants* (London 1956) 57; M. White, *Phoenix* 12 (1958)
2-14; D . M. Leahy, *Historia* 17 (1968) 3 n. 5; Bury–Meiggs 109; Sealey, *History*
60-5.

    [being] a man of the people *and* | *of low birth*, | he disregarded | the
5   oracle. The || other sacrifices which | were enjoined upon him by |
10 Delphi he rendered | to the gods, but the ty|ranny which was fal|ted
    to come about he *dis*|*regarded.* To An|[d]r̞[e]̤as was born | a son,
15 whom he rai|sed and gave the name || Orthagoras. Until | *adulthood he*
20 *was all* | *the time* brought up | and educated | just as was suit||able for
    the son of a *co*|*ok* and a *common* | citizen. Whe|n his chi|ldhood was
25 ended, || he became | one of the patrols | *guarding* the | *land*, and when
30 war brok|e out between the Sicyo||nians and the Pelle|neans, he was at
35 a|ll times a|*ctive* and accomplished. | When a foray was made || by the
    Pelleneans | and they *attacked un*|*expectedly, he went to meet them* |
40 and killed | *some of the* enemy [and] || was by far *the most dist*|*lin-*
    guished | of the *patrol.* | In return for this the S[icyoni]|ans appointed
45 him patrol [commander] || by election. [Immediately] | on having
    won [this] | honor [he conquered] | the *enemy* [even] | more impres-
50 sively, [so that || many] of the citizens | were won over *and became*
    att|*ached* to him. As [time] | passed [they elect|ed] him Polemarch, ||
55 primarily *becau*|*se* of his bravery [and] | good fortune | in war, and
60 [al|so] (because) the majority [of the] || citizens were well disposed
    [to] h|im. *When he had wag*|*ed war* [during his tenure] | of that office
65 [with valor] | and kept the territory || which was theirs *se*|*cure* and
    caused [much] *da*|*mage* to the *enemy* | to be done, [the] | People of
70 the [Sicyo]||nians once again [- - -]

11   Law of the City of Dreros (Crete). 650–600 B.C.
Block of schist, lines 1, 3, 4, right to left; line 2, left to right; Dreros.
Probably the earliest surviving Greek law.

Jeffery, *LSAG*, no. 1a, p. 311 and Plate 59; *GHI*, no. 2, pp. 2f.

V. Ehrenberg, *CQ* 37 (1943) 14–18; R. F. Willetts, *Aristocratic society in ancient Crete* (London 1955) 106, 167–9; idem, *Ancient Crete* (London 1965) 68f.

May God be kind (?).[1] This has been decided by the city: When a man has been Kosmos,[2] for ten years that s l ame man shall not be Kosmos. If he should become Kosmos, whatever judgments he gives, he himself shall owe double, and he | shall be useless[3] as long as he lives, and what he does as Kosmos shall be as nothing. *vv* | The swearers (to this shall be) the Kosmos, the Demioi and the Twenty of the city.[4] *vv*

1   The meaning of the first ten letters is quite uncertain.
2   Apparently the chief magistrate, as elsewhere in Crete; here a single office.
3   This means either 'deprived of the right to some or all offices' or 'deprived of citizen-rights.'
4   The function of the Demioi and the nature of the Twenty are unknown. The word *city* (*polis*) appears here for the first time in a political sense.

**12   Tyrtaeus of Sparta, the Messenian Wars, and the Great Rhetra.
Middle seventh century B.C.**

A: Strabo 8.4.10, p. 362 (Tyrtaeus F 2 West; Philochorus, Callisthenes, *ap. FGrHist* 580 F 2); B: Scholiast to Plato, *Laws* 1.629a (*FGrHist* 580 F 5); C: Tyrtaeus Fragments 19, 2, 4–7 West. Cf. Pausanias 4.4–24; Diodorus 15.66.3–4; Plutarch, *Lykourgos* 6.

Michell, *Sparta* 16–19; Huxley, *Sparta* 127, n. 349; Jacoby, *FGrHist* IIIb Suppl. 1. 583f. On the Messenian Wars and the 'Great Rhetra', see Wade-Gery, *Essays* 37–85; Michell 8f.; Huxley 26ff., 53–6; Hammond, *Studies* 47ff., esp. 62–7; Bury-Meiggs 94; Sealey, *History* 74–8; Mosshammer, *Eusebius* 204–9.

A. Strabo 8.4.10, p. 362

They went to war several times because of the Messenian revolts. Tyrtaeus says in his poems that the first acquisition of Messenia came in the time of his (generation's) fathers' fathers. The second occurred when they revolted and chose as their allies the Argives, Eleians, ⟨Arcadians⟩[1] and Pisatans. The Arcadians provided Aristokrates, king of Orchomenos, as general, and the Pisatans, Panteleon son of Omphaleon, at the time when (Tyrtaeus) says that he himself was general for the Lacedaemonians in the war. And he says that he was from Lacedaemonia in the elegy which they named the *Eunomia* (F 2.12–15 West): 'For the son of Kronos himself, husband of lovely-chapleted Hera, / Zeus, gave this city to the Herakleidai. / Together with them, having left windy Erineon, / we came to the wide island of Pelops' (i.e. the Peloponnesus). Thus either the elegy is not authentic or Philochorus must be disbelieved when he says that he (Tyrtaeus) was an Athenian and from (the deme) Aphidna, as well as Callisthenes and many others when they say that he came from Athens when the Lacedaemonians requested it in accordance with an oracle which commanded them to take their leader from the Athenians.[2] It was in Tyrtaeus' time, then, that the second war began.

B. Scholiast to Plato, *Laws* 1.629a

Pl. *Laws* 1.629a: Let us then cite Tyrtaeus (on the matter of external war and internal revolution – he who was Athenian in origin and became a citizen of theirs (the Spartans).

Scholion: This Tyrtaeus was born an Athenian . . . . When he came to Sparta and became inspired, he advised them to renew the war against the Messenians. He urged them on in every way, and among his remarks is the well-known verse 'Messenia, excellent for plowing and excellent for planting' (F 5.3 West, given in C(4) below).

C. Fragments of the Poetry of Tyrtaeus

(1) TYRTAEUS F 19 WEST

2 *slingers* of stones *and* [bowmen] / [- -] *like* hosts [of wasps[3]] / [- -]
5 Ares the plague of men, *insatiable* [of war-cry] // [- -] *headlong* (?)
while they *beyond* (?) [- - -] / [- -] like [- -] / *fenced in* with hollow
shields, / (each group) separately, Pamphyloi, Hylleis *and* [Dymanes,[4] /
10 holding] *up* in their hands their murderous ashen spears. // [. . . .
placing] *everything* in (the hands of the) immortal gods / [- -] we shall
obey [- -] *leader(s)* / but all together [we] shall immediately smite, /
standing close to the spear-bearing *men*. / Dreadful will be the din of
15 both [- -] // [of men] *striking* their well-rounded *shields* with spears, /
[- -] will hurl as they [fall] against each other, / [corslets of mail]
round men's [- -] chests / they shall fall back shattered [before the
20 destruction / while,] struck by [great] boulders, // [(their) bronze
helmets] will ring.

(2) TYRTAEUS F 2.12–15 WEST
See A.

15

(3) TYRTAEUS F 4 WEST

(a)

Plut. *Lyk.* 6.7: The Kings Polydoros and Theopompos made this addition to the rhetra: 'If the People formulate[5] crookedly, the Elders and the Leaders (Kings) shall be the decliners (of the proposal),' that is to say, they shall not validate (the motion) but simply dismiss the People as ruining the motion and changing it for the worse. But they were able to persuade the city that the god had commanded this, as Tyrtaeus apparently recalled in the following (F 4.1-6 West): 'Having heard Phoibos they brought back to their home from Delphi / the oracles of the god and words that were sure. / "The god-honored Kings shall rule the
5   Boule, / they who care for the lovely city of Sparta, // and the reverend Elders, and next the men of the People, / obedient to straightforward agreements." '[6]

(b)

Diod. 7.12.5-6: That the same Lykourgos brought from Delphi as an oracle on (Spartan) cupidity that which is remembered as a proverb: 'Greed for money[7] and nothing else will destroy Sparta.' The Pythia gave her oracular response on constitutional affairs to Lykourgos as follows.[8] 'For thus did the lord Apollo, of the silver bow, the one who works from afar, / golden-haired, make response from the rich inner sanctuary / (F 4.3-10 West): "The god-honoured Kings shall rule the
5   Boule, / they who care for the lovely city of Sparta // and the reverend Elders, and next the men of the People, / obedient to straightforward agreements.[9] / They shall speak what is good and do everything justly / and counsel nothing for the city (that is crooked[10]). / Victory and
10 authority shall accompany the majority of the People. // For Phoibos has so revealed this to the city." '

(4) TYRTAEUS F 5 WEST

Paus. 4.6.5: This Theopompos was the man who put an end to the war. My evidence is the elegiac lines of Tyrtaeus (lines 1-2 follow). Scholiast to Pl. *Laws* 1.629a, p. 375: see (B) above (line 3 follows). Strabo 6.3.3, p. 279: Messenia was taken after nineteen years of war, just as Tyrtaeus also says (lines 4-8 follow).

Tyrtaeus F 5: With our King, Theopompos dear to the gods, / through whom we took wide Messenia, / Messenia, excellent for plowing and
5   excellent for planting. / They fought it for nineteen years, // without ever a pause, possessing an enduring spirit, / the spearmen, fathers of our fathers. / In the twentieth year they (the Messenians) abandoned their rich fields / and fled out from the great mountains of Ithome.

(5) TYRTAEUS F 6–F 7 WEST

Paus. 4.4.15: As for the punishments with which they maltreated the Messenians, they have been described in Tyrtaeus' poem (lines 1–3 (= 6 West) follow). That they were compelled even to join in (Spartan) mourning is shown in the following lines (lines 4f. (= 7 West) follow).

Tyrtaeus F 6–F 7: Like asses worn down by great burdens, / bringing to their masters out of grievous necessity / the half of all the crop the tilled land bears / [- - -] wailing for their masters, the wives and the men alike, / // whenever the destructive doom of death comes upon any.[11]

5

1   Strabo's editors (e.g. Meineke, Jones) add 'Arcadians' on the strength of Pausanias 4.15.4, 4.17.2.
2   According to the *Suda* s.v. 'Tyrtaios,' he was 'either Laconian or Milesian.'
3   Sitzler (cited in M. L. West, *Iambi et Elegi Graeci* (Oxford 1972) 160).
4   The original three tribes of the Dorians. Tyrtaeus in lines 7–9 is either speaking of his own time or contrasting an earlier period with the present occasion (lines 11ff.); what is preserved in the papyrus permits no certain conclusion. In the former case the three Dorian tribes would have been the basis of the Spartan military organization in Tyrtaeus' own lifetime; in the latter case we may assume that the Dorian tribes had ceased to be the basic military unit.
5   Some emend the verb to 'vote.'
6   Cf. no. 167.
7   Or 'laws' (of Lykourgos); the word used is *rhetra*.
8   This sentence is written in the margin of the codex.
9   See note 7.
10 I.e. 'distorted.'
11 At least one verse is missing between lines 3 and 4; hence the incomplete sentence in 4–5.

13   Spartan Treatment of Helots. After about 650 B.C.

A: Athenaeus 14.74, p. 657cd (Myron of Priene, *FGrHist* 106 F 2); B: Pausanias 4.14.5 (Tyrtaeus F 6–F 7 West); C: Athenaeus 6.101, p. 271cd. Cf. Plutarch, *Lykourgos* 28; Pausanias 3.20.6.

Michell, *Sparta* 79–84; Bury–Meiggs 96.

A. Athenaeus 14.74, p. 657cd

That the Lacedaemonians used the helots very cruelly is also related by Myron of Priene in the second book of his *Messenian History*, where he writes as follows: 'They assign the helots every shameful task leading to every disgrace. For they ordained that each one of them be required to wear a dogskin cap and to wrap himself in leather and to receive a stipulated number of blows every year apart from any wrongdoing so that they would never forget that they were slaves. In addition, if any exceeded the vigor proper to a slave's condition, they made death the penalty;[1] and they assigned a punishment to their owners if they did not rebuke those who were growing fat. And on handing the land (over to them), they set them a portion (of produce) which they were constantly to hand over to them.'[2]

B. Pausanias 4.14.5

See no. 12C. Tyrtaeus F 6–F 7 West.

C. Athenaeus 6.101, p. 271cd

See no. 9B.

1 Cf. Thuc. 4.80.
2 See Paus. 4.6.4, for a characterization of Myron's unreliability.

14 Memorial to a Locrian Proxenos at Corcyra. About 625–600 B.C.
A cylindrical limestone cenotaph, inscribed in one continuous line round the monument, from right to left. Hexameter verse, Doric Greek, Corcyra.

IG IX 1.867; Jeffery, *LSAG*, no. 9, p. 232; *GHI*, no. 4, pp. 4f.

Of Tlasias' son Menekrates is this the memorial, /[1] an Oianthian[2] by race, and this the People made for him. / For he was the cherished Proxenos[3] of the People. But in the sea / he was lost, and a public grief
5   [--][4] // Praximenes came on his behalf from his father*land* / and built, together with the People, this monument to his brother.

1 The beginning is marked by a lozenge (◊). The division here indicated is that into verses.
2 In Ozolian Locris. See no. 87.
3 This is the earliest mention of this title: see the Glossary under 'metics.'
4 '[came to all]': Peek. Other restorations do not greatly differ in meaning.

15 Drakon's Law on Homicide. 621/0 B.C.

A: Eusebius, *Chronica,* in Hieronymus (Jerome) 97b6 Helm (at the year 624/3);
B: *IG* I[2] 115+ (I[3] 104); *GHI*, no. 86, pp. 264–7; *R.S. Stroud, *Drakon's law on homicide* (Berkeley and Los Angeles 1968) 1–18, with photo in back insert. Marble stele, stoichedon, Athens. Cf. Andocides 1.83; Aristotle, *Athenaion Politeia* 4.1, 7.1; Plutarch, *Solon* 17.1. The authenticity of the law has been disputed. As the heading indicates, this stele was inscribed in 409/8 B.C.

D. M. MacDowell, *Athenian homicide law in the age of the orators* (Manchester 1963) 117–25; Stroud, passim; W. T. Loomis, *JHS* 92 (1972) 86–95; Bury–Meiggs 121; Sealey, *History* 99–105.

A. Eusebius, *Chronica* 97b6 Helm

See no. 1B at the year 624/3.

B. *IG* I² 115+ (I³ 104)

Diognetos of Phrearrhos[1] was Secretary, | Diokles was Archon.[2] |
Resolved by the Boule and the People, Akamantis held the prytany,
[D]io[g]lnetos was Secretary, Euthydikos presided, [..]e[...]anes
5 made the motion. The II law of Drakon about *homicide* shall be inscribed
by the Recorderls of the laws (Anagrapheis), after they have received it
from the *King Archon, jointly with the Secretarly* of the Boule, on a
marble stele, and they shall set it up *in front* of the Stola Basileia. The
Poletai shall let the contract *according to the* lalw. The Hellenotamiai
10 shall supply the *money.* II First Axon.[3] *vv* | Even if without *premedi-*
tation [someone kills someone, he shall be exiled.] Juldgment shall be
passed (on him) by the Kings[4] as guilty of homicide[5] *either* (?) [-17-]
or (?) the man who ploltted (the death). The Ephetai *shall give the ver-*
dict. [Pardon may be granted, if the father] is alivle, or brothers, or
sons, by all of them (in agreement), or the one [opposing it shall pre-
15 vail: if none] of thllese men exists, (then by the male relatives) as far as
the degree of cousin's son and [cousin, if all] | are willing [to pardon].
The opposer *shall prevail.* [If none of these exists, and the] *killling* was
involuntary, and judgment is passed by the [Fifty-One, the Ephetai,
that it was involuntary] | homicide, he may be admitted (into the
country) by [members of his phratry, ten in number, if they wish.
These] thle Fifty-One [shall elect] *according to their rank.* [And those
20 also who] *priollr* (to this time) *committed homicide* [shall be bound
by this ordinance. Proclamation shall be made] against the hlomicide
[in the] *agora*[6] [(by relatives) as far as the degree of cousin's son and
cousin. Prosecution shall be made jointly] | by *cousins,* [sons of cous-
ins, sons-in-law, fathers-in-law] alnd *members of the phratry* [-36-]
25 reponslible for *homicide* [-26- The Fifty-]llOne [-42-] of homicide |
are convicted [-35-If] *anyone* | [kills the homicide or is responsible
for his murder when he has kept away from the market] on the froln-
tier *and* [from the games and from the Amphictyonic rites,[7] (then) just
as one by whom an] *Athenian is* klilled, [just so shall he be treated.
30 The verdict shall be brought in by the] *Ephetai.* II [---] | [---] | [---] |
35 [--initiating] aclts [of injustice --] *acts* of injustice, *should* kllill
[--Verdict shall be brought in] by the *Elphetai* [--] he is a frele man.

And [if a man unjustly carrying away one's property by force is imme-
diately] repelle|d and killed, [there shall be no recompense for his
death --] | [---]⁸

1 From the time of Kleisthenes, citizens of Athens were officially identified by
   the name of the deme in which they were registered.
2 I.e. of 409/8 B.C., when this law was published on stone. The first two lines are
   set out as a heading.
3 This heading is written in slightly larger letters, more widely spaced.
4 This is either a reference (in the plural) to the king archon of different years or
   to the phylobasileis.
5 Stroud; 'decide on the cases of the homicide' and 'hold trials for accusations of
   homicide' are alternative explanations.
6 The word can mean either 'in the marketplace' or 'in the Assembly.'
7 I.e. those common to all Greeks as members of the League.
8 The inscription continues for more than twenty lines, with only a few letters
   preserved on the right-hand edge. But '*Second* Axon' can be restored on line 56
   from traces of letters set out as in the heading in line 10.

16   The First Sacred War. Late seventh century B.C.

A: Athenaeus 13.10, p. 560bc (Callisthenes, *FGrHist* 124 F 1); B: Aeschines 3.107-
9; C: Harpocration s.v. 'Krauallidai' (Didymus; Xenagoras, *FGrHist* 240 F 22);
D: Scholiast to Pindar, *Summary* (of the origins) *of the Pythian Festival* b (p. 3
Drachmann); E: *Parian Marble, FGrHist* 239 F 37. Cf. Aeschines 2.15; Plutarch,
Solon 11.

M. Cary, *CAH* 3.604-6; T. J. Cadoux, *JHS* 68 (1948) 99f.; W. G. Forrest, *BCH* 80
(1956) 33-52; V. Ehrenberg, *The Greek state* (Oxford 1960) 254; Bury–Meiggs
110f.; Sealey, *History* 47.

A. Athenaeus 13.10, p. 560bc

And the war called Krisaian, as Callisthenes says in his *On the Sacred
War*, when the Kirraians fought against Phocis, was also (i.e. like the
Trojan War) ten years long. The Kirraians had abducted Megisto, the
daughter of Pelagon, son of Phokeus, and the daughters of Argives, as
they were returning from the Pythian shrine. Kirra too was taken in the
tenth year.

B. Aeschines 3.107-9

Once that territory (of the Kirraian plain) was occupied by the Kirraians
and Kragalidai, both very lawless peoples, and they dealt impiously
with the Delphian shrine and dedications and also offended against the
Amphictyonians . . . [108]. (The oracle, consulted by the Athenians,
incited the League to sacred war.) On receiving the oracular response,
the Amphictyony voted on Solon's motion . . . to go to war against the

accursed ones as the oracle of the god declared. [109] Collecting together a great force of the Amphictyonians they enslaved the people and utterly destroyed their harbor and their city and dedicated their territory (to the god) in accordance with the god's oracle.

C. Harpocration s.v. 'Krauallidai'

... Didymus says that it should be written 'Kraugallidai.' For the territory in Phocis near Kirra is thus called Kraugallion, as Xenagoras also narrates in (Book) 4 of his *Chronology*.

D. Scholiast to Pindar, *Summary of the Pythian Festival* b

Eurylochos of Thessaly renewed the festival of the god after defeating the Kirraians. The Kirraians had been acting as brigands and were murdering those who approached the precincts of the god. He overcame them in the archonship of Simon[1] at Athens (591/0) and of Gylidas at Delphi. All those Kirraians who chanced to survive fled to Kirphis, which is adjacent to Mt Parnassus. Leaving behind some of the Thessalians under the general Hippias to defeat the survivors, he proceeded to renew the festival. He established only the contest for money. Hippias' men having, after six years, subdued the Kirraians who were left, in the archonship of Damasias at Athens (582/1) and of Diodoros at Delphi, they later also established the contest awarding a wreath because of (this) success.

E. *The Parian Marble, FGrHist* 239 F 37

See no. 1A at the year 591/0.

1 The text reads Simonides, though the scholiast of Summary d, like the author of the Parian Marble, has the correct name Simon.

17 Battos, the Founder of Cyrene. Late seventh century B.C.

Scholiast to Pindar, *Pythian Odes* 4.10a (Menecles of Barca, *FGrHist* 270 F 6). Cf. Herodotus 4.145–60 and no. 18 following.

F. Chamoux, *Cyrène sous la monarchie des Battiades* (Paris 1953) 69–73, 93–9, 104–20; A. R. Burn, *The lyric age of Greece* (London 1960) 136f.; Bury–Meiggs 85f.

Pind. *Pyth.* 4.5f.: ... the priestess named Battos in an oracle as the founder of harvest-bearing Libya.
    Scholion: About the (cause of the) arrival of Battos at the seat of the oracle writers are not in agreement. For some (Hdt. 4.155.3) say

that he (came) on account of his (stuttering) voice and they never stop
repeating the oracle: 'Battos, you came because of your voice, but the
King, Phoibos Apollo, / is sending you to sheep-feeding Libya as founder.' But some (say that he went to the oracle) because of civil disruption (in Thera). At any rate Menecles says that the motive of disruption
seems persuasive while that about his voice[1] seems somewhat mythical.
He says that the citizens of Thera fell into civil strife and became es-
tranged from each other, and that Battos was the leader of one of the
factions. When the struggle of the factions ended, the result was that
Battos' party was driven from the city and fled the country. Renounc-
ing the thought of returning to his country, they considered founding
a colony. Battos went to Delphi and asked whether they should carry
on the internal struggle (?)[2] or should establish a colony at some different place. The god responded: 'Your first enquiry is bad, but the
second is good. / Go, leave the sea-girt land, the mainland is better / in
the east. Cast away the prior ruse, yielding to persuasion. / -?- land
piously, which is great, and he hates impiety.[3] / As a man acts, such will
be his fruits.'

1 The word Battos was taken by Hesychius s.v. to mean 'stutterer.'
2 The meaning is uncertain.
3 The line is corrupt.

18   The Foundation of Cyrene. Late seventh century B.C.

Marble stele, nonstoichedon, Doric Greek, Cyrene. This inscription
actually dates from the fourth century, but embodies in lines 23–40
what is allegedly the original decree passed by the Therans, though its
authenticity is in question.

GHI, no. 5, pp. 5–9; L. H. Jeffery, *Historia* 10 (1961) 139–47; J. H. Oliver, *GRBS*
7 (1966) 25–9.

Graham, *Colony* 27, 40, 224–6; Bury–Meiggs 85f.; Jeffery, *Greece* 186f. (See no.
17.)

God. Good Fortune. | Damis son of Bathykles made the motion. As to
what is said by the Therans, | Kleudamas son of Euthykles,[1] in order
that the city may prosper and the Pe|ople of Cyrene enjoy good for-
5   tune, the Therans shall be given t|l|he citizenship according to that ances-
tral custom which our forefathers establish|ed, both those who *founded*
Cyrene from Thera and those at Thera who *re|mained* – just as Apollo
granted Battos and the Thera|ns who founded Cyrene good fortune if
they abided by *the* | sworn agreement[2] which our ancestors concluded
10   with them when || they sent out the colony according to the command

of Apol|lo *Archagetes.*[3] With good fortune. It has been resolved by the People | that the Therans shall continue to enjoy equal citizenship in Cyrene in the sa|me way (as of old). There shall be sworn by all Therans
15   who are domicil|ed in Cyrene the same oath which the others onc|le swore, and they shall be assigned to a tribe and a phratry and n|ine Hetaireiai.[4] This decree shall be written on a stele | of marble and placed in the ancestral shrine of | Apollo Pythios; and that sworn agreement[5] also shall be written down on the stele | which was made by the col-
20   onists when they sailed to Libya *wit*||*h* Battos from Thera to Cyrene. As to the expenditure necessary for *the s|tone* or for the engraving, let the Superintendents of the Accounts *pr|ovide* it from Apollos's revenues. *vv* | The sworn agreement of the settlers.[6] | Resolved by the Assembly.
25   Since Apollo spontaneously told B[at]||tos and the Therans *to colonize* Cyrene, it has been decided by the Ther|ans to send Battos off to *Libya,* as Archagetes | *and* as King, with the Therans to sail *as his Companions.* On equal a|nd fair terms shall they sail *according to family* (?), with
30   one son to be consc|ripted [-*c.* 21-][7] adults and from the [ot||her] Therans those who are free-born [-6-][8] shall sail. If they (the colonists) establi|sh the settlement, *kinsmen* who sail | later to *Libya* shall be entitled to *citizenship* and offices | and *shall be allotted* portions of the land *which has no owner.* But if they do not successfully estab|lish the
35   settlement and *the Therans* are incapable of giving it assistan||ce, and they are pressed by hardship for five years, from that land *shall* they depart, | without fear, to Thera, to their own property, and they shall be citiz|ens. Any man who, if the city sends him, refuses to sail, will be liable to the death-|penalty and his property shall be confiscated. The man ha|rboring him or concealing him, whether he be a father (aiding his)
40   son or a brother his brot||her, is to suffer the same penalty as the man who refuses to sail. On these conditions a sworn agreement was ma|de by those who stayed there and by those who sailed to foun|d the col- ony, and they invoked curses against those transgressors who would not ab|ide by it – whether they were those settling in Libya or those who rem|ained. They made waxen images and burnt them, calling down (the
45   following) c||urse, everyone having assembled together, men, wom|en, boys, girls: 'The person who does not abide by this | sworn agreement but transgresses it shall melt away and di|ssolve like the images – him- self, his descendants and his prope|rty; but those who abide by the
50   sworn agreement – those || sailing to Libya *and* [those] *staying* in Thera – shall have an abundance of good things, both *themselves* [and] *their descendants.*'

1 I suspect a lacuna, though an apparent parallel for the asyndeton has been pro-
    vided by F. Chamoux, *Cyrène sous la monarchie des Battiades* (Paris 1953) 109
    n. 1 (from an unpublished Cyrenaic inscription).

2 *Or* 'original agreement': *GHI*, p. 7.
3 This reading, like many others which are here italicized, derives from Oliverio, *RFIC* 56 (1928) 224f., who read letters not seen by others, which 'should probably rank higher than mere restorations' (*GHI*, p. 7). - Archagetes: 'Founder'; a title of Apollo, it was also the name for the founder of a new cult.
4 A smaller political grouping than the phratry. Compare 'Companions' (Hetairoi) in line 27, and see Graham, *JHS* 80 (1960) 108f.
5 See note 2.
6 This is set out as a heading.
7 '[from each household, and those shall sail] who are adults': Wilhelm (cited *GHI*, p. 5); '[from the perioeci (or townsmen?), one hundred are to sail] who are adults': Jeffery; '[from each household, one hundred in number,] adults': Oliver. New readings by Fraser (in *GHI*) support none of these.
8 '[whoever wished]': Graham and others; '[one hundred in number]': Jeffery.

19 Law from Chios. 600–550 B.C.

Reddish trachyte stele inscribed vertically on three sides, horizontally on the back. The writing runs from left to right and right to left in alternate lines (boustrophedon). Ionic alphabet, Chios.

L. H. Jeffery, *BSA* 51 (1956) 157–67; Wade-Gery, *Essays* 198f.; Hignett, *Constitution* 95; J. H. Oliver, *AJP* 80 (1959) 296–301; **GHI*, no. 8, pp. 14–17; M. Ostwald, *Nomos and the beginnings of the Athenian democracy* (Oxford 1969) 161–3; Bury–Meiggs 124; Jeffery, *Greece* 231f.; Sealey, *History* 121.

The Back of the Stele[1] (C)

Let him appeal to | the Boule of the Pe|ople.[2] On the third day | after
5　the Hebdomaia[3] || that Boule shall assembl|e which is the People's,
　　(which) c|an inflict fines,[4] and (which) consis|ts of fifty men fro|m a
10　tribe. The othe||r business shall be transacted which concerns the
　　Peo|ple and especially the issue *of e|very* (case) of appe|al which *arise|s*
15　in every month || in [...] | [---] | [---]

1 The other faces of the stele are poorly preserved and present extremely obscure texts. The front face (A) mentions as two officials the demarch and king (basileus). Allusion to the appeal of a judgment occurs on the right side (B), while on the left (D) there is a reference to someone's obligation to take an oath in the month of Artemesion.
2 This is the earliest secure reference to a Boule (=Council) of the People. Its power to levy fines and, apparently, to judge appeals attests the growth of the popular element within the state at a relatively early period. The Council presumably coexisted with an aristocratic council, and some have argued that it provides reason to accept the authenticity of the much-debated Solonian Council of 400 (Aristotle, *Ath. Pol.* 8.4; Plutarch, *Solon* 19.1).
3 A festival to Apollo on the seventh day of every month.
4 The adjective so translated here ('(which) can inflict fines') is difficult and may perhaps mean '(which must assemble) under penalty of a fine.'

20   Gravestone of Phanodikos of Prokonnesos. 575-550 B.C.
Marble stele, writing from left to right and right to left in alternate
lines, Sigeion. The first inscription on the stone (A) is in the Ionic dialect of Prokonnesos (an island in the Propontis); the second (B) is written in Attic.[1]

SIG, no. 2, pp. 2f.; *SEG* IV, no. 667.

M. Guarducci, *Annuario della Scuola Archeologica di Atene e delle Missioni italiane
in Oriente* 3-5 (1941-43) 135ff.; Graham, *Colony* 192f.; Jeffery, *LSAG* 72, 366f.,
with facsimile on Plate 71, 43-4.

(A)

Of Phanodikos | am I (the likeness),[2] son of Hermok|rates, of | Pro-
5 konne||sos. A mixing bow|l and a sta|nd (for it) a|nd a strainer for the
10 P|rytaneion || did he give to the Syke|eans.[3]

(B)

Of Phanodikos am I (the likeness), the son of H|ermokrates, of Proko-|
nesos, as well (as the above).[4] A mixing bowl | and a stand and a
5 strain||er for the Prytaneion I g|ave as a memorial to the Sigei|ans. If
10 harm befall|s (me), take care of me, O | Sigeians. I was ma||de by Hai-
sopos and | his brothers.

1 The doublet has been explained as an attempt to conciliate the Athenians after
   they gained Sigeion, as reflecting a second stage in the career of Phanodikos
   (when he became an exile in Sigeion), and as a re-engraving, after the first inscription had become illegible (!).
2 An image of the man was engraved on the stone.
3 I.e. Sigeians. Spelling is inconsistent; note 'Prokonesos,' B 2f.
4 The words 'as well' can also be taken with what follows, i.e. 'I too (gave) a mix-
   ing bowl. . . .'

**21   Epitaph of the Corinthians who Died at Salamis. About 600 *or*
480 B.C.**
Marble block, archaic Corinthian, Salamis.

IG I² 927 (I³ 1143); R. Carpenter, *AJA* 67 (1963) 209 (*c.* 600); Hignett, *Invasion*
411-14; A. L. Boegehold, *GRBS* 6 (1965) 179-86 (480); *GHI*, no. 24, pp. 52f.
(480). Cf. Herodotus 8.94; Plutarch, *Moralia* 870e.

[O friend! In the well watered] city of Corinth we once lived. /[1] [But
now we lie in Aia]s' [island of Salamis. / Here we captured Phoenician
ships and Persian, / and we saved holy Greece from the Medes.][2]

1 Each verse occupies one line of the inscription.
2 The epigram is restored from Plut. *Mor.* 870e.

22 The Athenian Naukrariai. 594/3–508/7 B.C.

A: Photius, *Lexicon* s.v. 'Naukraria' (Cleidemus, *FGrHist* 323 F 8); B: Pollux, *Onomasticon* 8.108; C: Bekker, *Anecdota* 1.283.20f. s.v. 'Naukraroi.' Cf. Herodotus 5.71 (with Thucydides 1.126.5); Aristotle, *Athenaion Politeia* 8.3, 21.5.

Hignett, *Constitution* 67–74; B. Jordan, *CSCA* 3 (1970) 153–75, especially 158–60; A. Andrewes, *CQ* 27 (1977) 241–8.

A. Photius, *Lexicon* s.v. 'Naukraria'

In earlier times when they used the words naukraria and naukraros, the naukraria was like a symmory[1] and a deme, and the naukraros was like the demarch. Solon so designated them, as Aristotle also says.[2] In the laws (of Solon the following phrases appear): 'if anyone has a dispute about his naukraria' and 'the naukraroi each according to his naukraria.' Later, from (the reform of) Kleisthenes, they became demes, and the demarchs were (so) named. From Aristotle's (*Athenian*) *Constitution* (8.3) (we record) the manner in which Solon regulated the city: 'There were four tribes, just as earlier, and four Phylobasileis (= 'Tribe-Kings'). Distributed into each tribe were three trittyes, with twelve naukrariai in each.' Cleidemus says in his third book that after Kleisthenes established ten tribes in place of four, they were in fact divided into fifty parts which they called naukrariai, in the same way as they now call (the units in) the division into a hundred parts 'symmories.'

B. Pollux, *Onomasticon* 8.108

Demarchs: those who are in charge of each deme. For a time they were called naukraroi, when the demes too (were called) naukrariai. A naukraria was, for a time, the twelfth part of a tribe, and there were twelve naukraroi, four to each trittys. These men handled the revenues of the demes and their expenditures. Each naukraria supplied two[3] horsemen and one ship, from which it perhaps acquired its name.[4]

C. Bekker, *Anecdota* 1.283.20f.

Naukraroi. Those who provided the ships and acted as trierarchs and were subordinate to the Polemarch.

1 Trierarchic symmories of the fourth century were groups of the richest men in each tribe, obligated to provide triremes.
2 *Ath. Pol.* 8.3, where all that Aristotle claims is that Solon used the term.

3 'Ten': Wilamowitz (*Aristoteles und Athen* (Berlin 1893) 2.163, n. 48).
4 The Greek word for ship is *naus*.

23 The Athenian Archon List. Published in the late fifth century B.C. Marble fragments (A-D), stoichedon, Athens.

B. D. Merritt, *Hesperia* 8 (1939) 59-65; D. W. Bradeen, *Hesperia* 32 (1963) 187-208; *GHI*, no. 6, pp. 9-12.

T. J. Cadoux, *JHS* 68 (1948) 77-9, 109-12; F. Jacoby, *Atthis* (Oxford 1949) 171-6; E. Badian, *Antichthon* 5 (1971) 9-11; M. F. McGregor, *Phoenix* 28 (1974) 18-21; Sealey, *History* 135-7. See also Appendix I.

(A)

[....^{1}-- | Ky]pselo[s^2 | Te]lekle[-- | Phil]omb[rotos? .... (595/4^3]

(B)

COLUMN II^4
K[---] | Pha[---] | Te[--] | Erch[sikleides (548/7)]^5 || Thes[---] |
Ph[.]r[---]|[---]

(C)

[On]eto[rides (527/6) | H]ippia[s (526/5) | K]leisthen[es (525/4) |
M]iltiades (524/3) || [Ka]lliades (523/2) | [Peisi]strat[os] (522/1)]^6

(D)

[Phain]ip[pos? (490/89) | Ar]ist[eides? (489/8)]^7

1 A, G, or N stood in the fourth space from the left.
2 Grandson of Kypselos, tyrant of Corinth, he was the father of that Miltiades who colonized the Chersonesus (Hdt. 6.34ff.). This latter is to be distinguished from Miltiades son of Kimon, Archon 524/3 (C 4), who himself went to the Chersonesus to succeed his brother Stesagoras (also the name of his grandfather); who later served as general at Marathon; and who was the father of the great Kimon, a general and early opponent of Perikles. The family tree of this clan, problematic in itself, is greatly complicated by the confused and imperfectly transmitted text of Marcellinus given in no. 26. See N. G. L. Hammond, *CQ* 6 (1956) 113-29; D. W. Bradeen, *Hesperia* 32 (1963) 193-7, 206-8.
3 Plut. *Solon* 14.3 provides the date.
4 Nothing remains of Col. 1 of (B) except, on line 5, the last letter of a name (s) coming after about twelve spaces.
5 I.e. Erxikleides. Pausanias 10.5.13 provides the name, and Eusebius, *Chronica* 103b10 Helm (which dates its context, the fire at Delphi) permits the identification.
6 The dates are secured by the name of Miltiades, who according to Dionysius of Halicarnassus was Archon in the 64th Olympiad (7.3.1). See Cadoux for the

interlocking reasons dictating the first year of this Olympiad (p. 110, note 216). Of the men listed, Hippias is the son of Peisistratos, Kleisthenes is the famous reformer and the son of Megakles, Miltiades is the general at Marathon (see note 2), and Peisistratos is the son of Hippias (see Thucydides 6.54.6f. and no. 37 below).

7 Phainippos is dated by the *Parian Marble, FGrHist* 239 F 48 (where the name wrongly appears as [Ph]a̱[i]n[i]p[pid]es); that author indicates that there was also another Archon with this name. See E. Badian, *Antichthon* 5 (1971) 11–13, for doubts as to whether the Aristeides named here was Aristeides 'the Just'; cf. Plutarch, *Aristeides* 1.8.

24 Greek Mercenaries in Egyptian Service. 591 B.C.
Scratched on the leg of a colossal statue of Rameses II before the great temple of Abu Simbel in Nubia, on the left bank of the Nile. (G) was written on a second colossus.

H. R. Hall, *CAH* 3.300-2; H. W. Parke, *Greek mercenary soldiers* (Oxford 1933) 5; Jeffery, *LSAG* 354f., *Greece* 196; *GHI*, no. 7, pp. 12f.; facsimiles in A. Bernard and C. Masson, *REG* 70 (1957) 1-20. Cf. Herodotus 2.159-61; Bury-Meiggs 85.

(A)
Doric Greek, mostly Ionic letters

When King Psammetichos[1] went to Elephantine, | this was written by those who, with Psammetichos son of Theokles, | sailed and came above Kerkis, as far as the river | allowed. Potasimto led the foreign-
5 speaking and Amasis the Egyptians. || Archon son of Amoibichos and Peleqos son of Eudamos[2] wrote us (i.e. these lines).

(B)
Helesibios of Teos

(C)
Telephos of Ialysos wrote me.

(D)
Python son of Amoibichos

(E)
[- - -] and | Krithis wrote[3] me.

(F)
Pabis of Colophon | with Psammetes

(G)

Anaxanor of Ialysos [--][4] when Ki|ng Psammetichos marched his army the first time [--][5]

1 King Psamtik II, Herodotus' Psammis.
2 Or 'Axe son of Nobody,' as these names can be translated. I.e. 'Archon cut them with his axe' (Hall, p. 301).
3 A letter is omitted in this word.
4 '[made the march]': Bernard–Masson.
5 '[with Amasis]': Bernard–Masson; '[with Potasimto]': Fraser (cited *GHI*, p. 13).

25   Alliance between Elis and Heraia in Western Arcadia. Early sixth century *or* mid-sixth century *or* about 500 B.C. Bronze tablet, Elean dialect, Olympia.

Buck, no. 62, p. 261; Tod I, no. 5, pp. 8f.; Jeffery, *LSAG*, no. 6, p. 219, with Plate 42 (*c*. 500 B.C.); *GHI*, no. 17, pp. 31–3. Cf. Strabo 8.3.2, pp. 336–7.

H. T. Wade-Gery, *CAH* 3.530, 544ff.; F. Adcock and D. J. Mosley, *Diplomacy in ancient Greece* (London 1975) 178.

This is the covenant[1] of the Eleians and the Her|aians. There shall be an alliance for one hundred years. | It shall begin from this (year). If there is any need, either of word or of d|eed, they shall stand by each other
5   in all things, especially i|n war. If they do not stand by each other, a talent | of silver shall be paid to Zeus Olympios by the wr|ong-doers for dedication to him. If anyone | does harm to this writing, whether private citizen or o|fficial or community, to the sacred penalty shall he
10   be li|l able which here is written down.

1 *Rhetra.* For the use of this word see Wade-Gery, *Essays* 62–4.

26   The Establishment of the Panathenaic Festival. 566/5 B.C.

A: Marcellinus, *Life of Thucydides* 2–5 (Pherecydes, *FGrHist* 3 F 2; Hellanicus, *FGrHist* 4 F 22); B: Harpocration, *Lexicon*, s.v. 'Panathenaia' (Hellanicus, *FGrHist* 323a F 2; Androtion, *FGrHist* 324 F 2). Cf. Plutarch, *Theseus* 24.3.

F. E. Adcock, *CAH*, 4.67; T. J. Cadoux, *JHS* 68 (1948) 104; Jacoby, *FGrHist* IIIb Suppl. 2.508f. (n. 2); J. A. Davison, *JHS* 78 (1958) 26–9; E. Vanderpool, *Phoros* 159; Bury-Meiggs 130f; H. W. Parke, *Festivals of the Athenians* (London 1977) 33f.

A. Marcellinus, *Life of Thucydides* **2-5**

For (Thucydides the historian) was related through his ancestors to Miltiades the general, and Miltiades to Aiakos son of Zeus. . . . [3] Didymus bears witness to this, declaring that Pherecydes in Book 1 of his *Histories* writes as follows: 'Philaios son of Aias settled in Athens. His son was Daikles; and his son Epilykos; and his son Akestor; and his son Agenor; and his son O⟨u⟩lios; and his son Lykes; and his son Iophon;[1] and his son Laios; and his son Agamestor; and his son Tisandros [[in whose archonship in Athens and his son Miltiades]][2] and his son Hippokleides,[3] in whose archonship ⟨in Athens⟩ the Panathenaia was established; ⟨and his son Kypselos;⟩[4] and his son Miltiades, who colonized Chersonesus.'[5] [4] Hellanicus also confirms this in the work entitled *Asopis.*[6]

B. Harpocration, *Lexicon* **s.v. 'Panathenaia'**

. . . The first person to conduct the festival was Erichthonios son of Hephaistos, according to what Hellanicus and Androtion say, each in Book 1 of his *Attic History.*[7]

1 A correction by Hertlein (cited in Jacoby's text) of 'Tophon.'
2 An interpolation or error by the copyist.
3 This is probably Megakles' unfortunate rival for the hand of Agariste, cf. Hdt. 6.126ff.
4 Added by Rutgers (cited in Jacoby's text).
5 See no. 23A with note 2. Marcellinus' text is hopelessly confused, and Rutgers' addition (note 4) hardly helps matters because it puts Kypselos and his son Miltiades far too late in the sixth century, even if it provides Miltiades with his proper father. The date 566/5 comes from Eusebius, *Chronica* 102b Helm, where the information is provided at that year that 'the athletic contest which they call the Panathenaia was held'; no mention of Hippokleides appears.
6 Marcellinus' point becomes clear later in the text (10ff.), where the younger Miltiades' marriage to Hegesipyle, daughter of King Oloros, provides the required bridge between the great clan and the historian, since Thucydides' father's name was Oloros.
7 Aristotle (F 637 Rose) assigned the organization of the Great Panathenaia to Peisistratos and, apparently, the organization of the yearly festival to the time of Erichthonios.

27 Spartan Treaty with Tegea. About 560 B.C.

Plutarch, *Greek Questions* 5 (*Moralia* 292b) (Aristotle F 592 Rose). Cf. Herodotus 1.67.

F. Jacoby, *CQ* 38 (1944) 15f.; Huxley, *Sparta* 136f.; Bury-Meiggs 133; Jeffery *Greece* 121; Sealey, *History* 83.

Who are the 'good' (*chrestoi*) among the Arcadians and Lacedaemonians? When the Lacedaemonians were reconciled with the Tegeans they made a treaty and set up a common stele on (the river) Alpheios. There was written on it among other things that (the Tegeans were) to expel the Messenians from the country and were not permitted to make them 'good.'[1] In explanation of this Aristotle says it means 'not to kill them', in order to assist those Tegeans who laconized.

1 The special meaning of the word, according to Jacoby, is 'to make them citizens,' just as the negative of it means 'to deprive them of citizen-rights': see no. 11, line 3. Aristotle evidently misunderstood the word because the dead were euphemistically called 'the good people,' a meaning which he employed here.

28 Kroisos' Gifts to the Temple of Artemis at Ephesus. About 550 B.C.

Fragments of dedicatory inscriptions carved on three column bases and written in the Ionic alphabet.

*Tod I, no. 6, pp. 9f.; A. R. Burn, *The lyric age of Greece* (London 1960) 212–14; Jeffery, *LSAG* 339; Bury–Meiggs 143–5. See Herodotus 1.92 for Kroisos' connection with the temple. It was begun in his reign and took some 120 years to complete.

(A)
[King] Kr[oisos] *made the dedication.*

(B)
King [Kroisos] *made the dedication.*

(C)
[King Kroisos] made the dedication.

29 Treaty between Sybaris and the Serdaioi. (?) 550–525 B.C.

Bronze plate, Achaean colonial script, Olympia.

Jeffery, *LSAG* 251f.; *GHI*, no. 10, pp. 18f. Cf. Strabo 6.1.13, p. 263.

T. J. Dunbabin, *The Western Greeks* (Oxford 1948) 24–7; Jeffery, *Greece* 169.

Agreement was made by the Sybari|tes and their allies and the | Ser-
5 daioi for friendshi|p faithful and guileless fo|rever. Protectors:[1] Ze|us and Apollo and the other g|ods and the city Poseido|nia.

This is perhaps the earliest preserved Greek treaty as well as the single known epigraphical document of Sybaris. The Serdaioi are an unidentified people supposed on the basis of a series of coins to have been an Achaean colony in South Italy.

1 The word *proxenos* is here used in a special sense. For its normal meaning see nos. 14, 67C and the Glossary.

30 The Wives of Hippias and Hipparchos, the Sons of Peisistratos of Athens. About 546 B.C.

A: Athenaeus 13.89, p. 609cd (Cleidemus, *FGrHist* 323 F 15); B: Scholiast to Aristophanes, *Knights* 449 (425/4). Cf. Herodotus 1.60; Thucydides 6.55.1; Aristotle, *Athenaion Politeia* 14.4

F. Jacoby, *FGrHist* IIIb Suppl. 1.70ff.

A. Athenaeus 13.89, p. 609cd

The woman who led Peisistratos back to the tyranny, as having the appearance of Athena,[1] is said to have been beautiful, and indeed to have resembled the goddess in her beauty. She was a wreath-seller, and Peisistratos gave her in marriage to his son Hipparchos, as Cleidemus narrates in the eighth book of the *Homeward Journeys*.[2] 'He gave to his son Hipparchos the woman who stood by his side in the chariot, Phya the daughter of Sokrates. The daughter of Charmos[3] the ex-Polemarch, ⟨Myrrhina⟩, who was most beautiful, he took for Hippias, the man who became tyrant after himself. It happened,' says Cleidemus, 'that Charmos had been the lover of Hippias, and was the first (?) to set up the Eros by the Academy, on which there is inscribed: "Eros, full of all manner of tricks, / this altar was set up for you / by Charmos on the shady bounds of the Gymnasium." '[4]

B. Scholiast to Aristophanes, *Knights* 449 (425/4)

Aristophanes, *Knights* 447-9: (Sausage-seller) I say that your grandfather / was one of the bodyguard – (Kleon) Which? Speak! / (Sausage-seller) That of Byrsina, the wife of Hippias.

Scholion: . . . Myrrhina became the wife of Peisistratos [*sic*]. She was the mother of Hippias and Hipparchos. (Aristophanes) has said Byrsina instead of Myrrhina[5] because he is again satirizing Kleon as a leather-seller.[6] When Peisistratos led her into Athens on a chariot he said that she was Athena because he wished to be tyrant.

1 The text is partly corrupt here.

2   The title of cyclic epics describing the return of Homer's heroes from Troy. The reference is almost certainly wrong.
3   The manuscripts of Thucydides give the name as Kallias.
4   So also Pausanias 1.30.1. Peisistratos is said to have been the dedicator in Plutarch, *Solon* 1.7.
5   The earlier form of this name was Myrsina.
6   *Byrsa* is the Greek word for 'hide.'

31   The Nature of Peisistratos' Rule. 546/5–528/7 B.C.

A: Athenaeus 12.44, p. 532f–533a (Theopompus, *FGrHist* 115 F 135); B: Plato, *Hipparchos* 229b. Cf. Herodotus 1.59.6; Thucydides 6.54.5f.; Aristotle, *Athenaion Politeia* 16. For a negative view of the tyranny see Isocrates, *Panathenaicus* 148, *On the Team of Horses* 25–6.

F. E. Adcock, *CAH* 4, 65–8; Hignett, *Constitution* 110–23; W. G. Forrest, *The Emergence of Greek democracy* (London 1966) 175–89; Bury-Meiggs 127–32; Sealey, *History* 134ff.

A. Athenaeus 12.44, p. 532f–533a

And yet their father, Peisistratos, was moderate in his pleasures. He did not even station guards over his lands or orchards, according to Theopompus in Book 21, but he allowed anyone who wished to come in and enjoy and take whatever he needed – the very thing that Kimon also did later in imitation of him.

B. Plato, *Hipparchos* 229b

Since you are my friend I would not dare to deceive you and to disregard[1] such a man (as Hipparchos). It was in fact on his death that the Athenians became subject to the tyranny of his brother Hippias, and you have heard from every ancient witness that only in those years was there a (true) 'tyranny' in Athens. For the rest of the period (preceding 514) the Athenians lived virtually as in the time of the rule of Kronos.[2]

1   A pentameter inscription of a herm of Hipparchos has just been quoted saying 'This is the monument of Hipparchos: do not deceive a friend.'
2   Traditionally, the 'Golden Age.'

32   Polykrates. Tyrant of Samos. About 540–522 B.C.

Athenaeus 12.57, p. 540d–f (Alexis, *FGrHist* 539 F 2; Clearchus F 44 Wehrli). Cf. Herodotus 3.39–46.

A. Andrewes, *The Greek tyrants* (London 1956) 118–23; G. L. Huxley, *The early Ionians* (London 1966) 125–30; Bury-Meiggs 148f.; Jeffery, *Greece* 214–19; Mosshammer, *Eusebius* 290–7.

Alexis in the third book of his *Samian Annals* says that Samos was adorned by Polykrates from (the resources of) many cities. He introduced Molossian and Lacedaemonian hounds, goats from Scyrus and Naxos, cattle from Miletus and Attica. Alexis also says that he summoned craftsmen at very high rates of pay. Having had fashioned for himself, before his tyranny, expensive couches and drinking-cups, he gave them over for the use of those becoming married or engaging in very large festivities. Because of all this there is good reason to marvel at the fact that the tyrant is not mentioned as having sent for women or boys from anywhere, despite his passion for liaisons with males; for he was even a jealous rival for the love of Anacreon the poet, when he cut off in anger the hair of his lover. Polykrates was the first man to build ships and name them 'Samian' after his country. But Clearchus says that Polykrates, the tyrant of luxurious Samos, was destroyed because of the intemperance of his ways by cultivating the Lydian effeminacies.[1] It was for this reason that he set up the Samian bazaar in the city to vie with the one known in Sardis as Sweet Embrace;[2] and as against the 'flowers of the Lydians' he constructed the notorious 'flowers of the Samians.'[3] Of these (neighborhoods), the Samian bazaar was an alley (of) courtesans. The alley truly filled Hellas with every food tending towards enjoyment and incontinence.

1 The corruptive influence of the Lydians was spoken of from at least the time of Xenophanes (about 570–503), who alluded to its effect upon Colophon (H. Diels, *Die Fragmente der Vorsokratiker*[5] 21 B F 3).
2 A euphemistic expression for a quarter of the town containing brothels.
3 Properly, 'products of luxury,' but here streets of brothels.

33 Law from a Locrian Community Settling New Territory. 525–500 B.C.

Bronze plaque found either near Naupactus or at Psoriani (in Aetolia). The writing, in Locrian or Aetolian Greek, runs from left to right and right to left in alternate lines.

*Buck, no. 59, pp. 255–7; Jeffery, *LSAG* 104f., and Plate 14; *GHI*, no. 13, pp. 22–5.

Graham, *Colony* 56f., 65; J. A. O. Larsen, *Greek federal states* (Oxford 1968) 54.

(Obverse)

(A)

This covenant about the land shall be valid in accordance with the | division of the plain of Hyla[1] and Liskara, both for the d|ivided (?) lots and for the public ones. Pasturage-rights[2] shall belong to pa|rents and son; if no son exists, to an unmarried daughter; if no unmarried daughter

5   exists, ‖ to a brother; if no brother exists, by degree of family connec-
tion let a man pasture according to what is | just. If (there is) not (any
such relative), to the man who pastures –,[3] and whatever he shall plant, |
he shall be immune from its seizure. Unless under compulsion of war it
is resolved by | a majority of the one hundred and one men, chosen
according to birth, that two | hundred fighting men, at the least, are to
10 be brought in as additional settlers, whoe‖ver proposes a division (of
land) or puts it to the vote in the Council of Elders or in the city or i|n
the Select Council or who creates civil discord relating to the distribu-
tion of land, that man | shall be accursed and all his posterity, and his
property shall be confiscated | and his house leveled to the ground in
accordance with the homicide l|aw.[4] This covenant shall be sacred to
15 Pythian Apollo *and the gods sharing his s*‖*anctuary.* [May there be for
the man] who transgresses *these conditions* destruction for himself and
his posterity and his *po*|*ssessions*, but may (the god) be propitious to
the man who piously observes them. Of the *land*, [the half of it] [5]

(Reverse)

(B)

they should receive, he shall be capable of bestowing his property on
whomever he wishes.

(An uninscribed space follows)

(C)

shall belong to the earlier, and half shall belong to the additional settlers.

(An uninscribed space follows)

(D)

They shall distribute the valley portions. Let exchanges be valid, but
exchanging shall be done before the magistrate.[6]

(An uninscribed space follows)

(E)

(The tablet was turned upside down for this text)

[If the] Demiourgoi[7] gain profit in anything other | than what is pre-
scribed, as sacred to Apollo | it shall be held as an offering for (a period
of) nine ye|ars,[8] and it shall not be counted as profit.

1 'wooded Plax': Wilamowitz (cited *GHI*, p. 221), taking the word 'plain' as the
proper noun and making *hyla* its adjective. An alternative meaning for 'd|ivided
lots' is 's|acred precincts.'

2 Some scholars understand the word to mean not pasturage but 'inheritance-rights.'

3 A baffling word – or the erasure of one – follows here. Jeffery understands text (B) as a line which had been left out at this point (where an error was committed and then erased): 'If the heirs do not take it, etc.'

4 This cumbrous sentence can (and perhaps should) be divided differently. Its beginning (lines 7ff.) can be taken instead with the preceding sentence, a full stop coming at 'additional settlers' (line 9). A new sentence would then begin with 'Whoever. . . .'

5 The sentence continues on the reverse, text (C).

6 This fragment is written in larger lettering. It seems to be a later addition.

7 See the Glossary.

8 Cf. Aristotle, *Ath. Pol.* 55.5.; *GHI*, taking *echeto* ('it shall be held') as an epithet of Apollo, translate: 'let them dedicate a statue to Apollo Echetos at the end of nine years.'

34 A List of Dareios' Subjects. 516–509 B.C.
Old Persian, on the south retaining wall of the Palace at Persepolis.

R. G. Kent, *Old Persian*[2] (New Haven 1953), no. DPe, p. 136. Cf. Herodotus 3.89ff. (satrapy list).

W. W. How and J. Wells, *A commentary on Herodotus* (Oxford 1928) 1.405f.;
G. B. Gray and M. Cary, *CAH* 4.183, 194–201; Hignett, *Invasion* 81f.; G. G. Cameron, *Journal of Near Eastern Studies* 32 (1973) 47–56; Bury–Meiggs 149f.

[1.1–5] I am Dareios the Great King, King of Kings, King of many countries, son of Hystaspes, an Achaemenian. [2.5–18] Saith Dareios the King: By the favor of Ahuramazda these are the countries which I got into my possession along with this Persian people, which felt fear of me (and) bore me tribute: Elam, Media, Babylonia, Arabia, Assyria, Egypt, Armenia, Cappadocia, Sardis, Ionians who are of the mainland and (those) who are by the sea, and countries which are across the sea;[1] Sagartia, Parthia, Drangiana, Aria, Bactria, Sogdiana, Chorasmia, Sattagydia, Arachosia, Sind, Gandara, Scythians, Maka. [3.18–24] Saith Dareios the King: If thus thou shalt think, 'May I not feel fear of (any) other,' protect this Persian people; if the Persian people shall be protected, thereafter for the longest while happiness unbroken – this will through Ahura come down upon this royal house.[2]

Herodotus' satrapy list corresponds neither with this list nor with another engraved at Behistun. It is therefore possible that Dareios' lists were catalogues of the peoples of his empire rather than of the satrapal organization. It is also possible that Herodotus is mistaken.

1 I.e. Mediterranean islands such as Cyprus, Lesbos, Samos.

2 Kent's translation is given here, in a slightly modified version, with the permission of the American Oriental Society.

35   Letter of Dareios. 521–486 B.C.

Marble block, near Magnesia on the Maeander, letter forms of the second century A.D.[1]

SIG, no. 22, pp. 20f.; *GHI, no. 12, pp. 20-2. Cf. Xenophon, *Oeconomicus* 4.8; Athenaeus 1.51, p. 28d. For some literary parallels, see no. 34 and Thucydides 1.129.3.

M. van den Hout, *Mnemosyne*, n.s. 2 (1949) 144-52.

The King of Kin|gs Dareios son of Hys|taspes to Gadatas, | his slave,
5   thus speaks: || I find that as to | my injunctions | you are not com-
10   pletely obe|dient. Because | you are cultivating my || land, transplant-
     ing[2] from (the province) beyond the Eu|phrates[3] fruit trees to | the
15   western Asian re|gions, I prai|se your purpose and || in consequence
     there will be laid up in store for you | great favor in the Roy|al House.
     But because | my religious disposi|tions are being nullified by you, I
20   shall give || you, unless you make a change, | a proof of a wronged
     (King's) an|ger. For the gardeners | sacred to Apollo | have been made
25   to pay tribute to you; and land || which is profane they have dug up at
     your com|mand. You are ignorant of my | ancestors' attitude to the
30   god, | who told the Persians | *all* of the truth and [. . .] || [- - -]

1 As Dittenberger inferred (*SIG*, p. 20), the letter probably was inscribed at this
   late date in order to document the sacredness of the land.
2 The verb is in line 13.
3 The official Persian name for Syria.

36   An Argive Rule about the Use of Sacred Treasures. Sixth century B.C.

Limestone block, writing from left to right and right to left in succeeding lines, Argos.

W. Vollgraff, *Mnemosyne* 7 (1929) 206-34, with photo on Plate 2; Buck, no. 83, pp. 283f.; *F. Sokolowski, *Lois sacrées des cités grecques*, Suppl. (Paris 1962), no. 27, pp. 64f.; D. Levi, *AJA* 49 (1945) 301f.

When these men were Demiourgoi,[1] these things | were made *in* (the temple) of Athena. The obj|ects and the heirlooms and the [·5·] |
5   [. . . . were dedicated] to Athena Polias. || The heirlooms for the u|se

of the Goddess shall not be us|ed by a private person[2] outside of | the
10   sacred precinct of A[then|a] Polias. But the Sta||te shall use them *for*
[the | sacred rites]. If anyone damages them, he shall repa|ir them. The
Demiourgos shall *impose* the amount. | The temple warden shall see to
these matters.

1   A list of the names of six men appears vertically in lines 5–10, the text of the
    inscription being indented at that point.
2   The meaning of this word is uncertain. Another interpretation (Vollgraff) is that
    it denotes a member of the subject population.

37   Dedication of Peisistratos Son of Hippias. About 521 B.C. *or* early fifth century
Sculptured marble cornice, Athens.

IG I² 761; Jeffery, *LSAG*, Plate 4, 37, with p. 75 (no later than 511/10); **GHI*, no.
11, pp. 19f. Cf. Thucydides 6.54.6. *DAA* 449f. (early fifth century). The same
mason carved the lettering on the base of a dedication by Hipparchos, probably
Hippias' brother, at the Ptoion in Boeotia. See *LSAG*, no. 38, p. 75.

Gomme, etc., *HCT* 4.331.

This memorial of his magistracy[1] Peisist[ratos Hippias'] son | dedicated
in Apollo Pyth[i]os' sacred precinct.[2]

1   For his archonship see no. 23C.
2   The lines are in verse, coinciding with the lines of the inscription.

38   A Spartan Dedication. Sixth century *or* 490–480 *or* about 460 B.C.
Stone base, Olympia. The nature of the base suggests that the statue
was a bronze pillar-statue of the archaic style.

Buck, no. 68, p. 266 (sixth century); Jeffery, *LSAG*, no. 49, p. 196 (490–80);
*GHI, no. 22, p. 47. Cf., for Spartan activity in Messenia *c.* 490, Plato, *Laws* 3.692d,
698d–e; Strabo 8.4.10, p. 362; Pausanias 4.23.5–10. See no. 67 for hostilities *c.*
460. The epigram is quoted by Pausanias 5.24.3.

Huxley, *Sparta* 88; W. E. den Boer, *Historia* 5 (1956) 168–74.

[Accept,] Lord son of Kronos, Zeus Olympian, this fine statue | with
gracious *spirit* from the Lacedaemonians.[1]

1   The lines of the inscription coincide with the verses.

39 The Liberation of Athens. 514–511/10 B.C.

A: Athenian drinking songs celebrating Harmodios and Aristogeiton. (1) Athenaeus 15.50, p. 695ab; (2) Scholiast to Aristophanes, *Acharnians* 980 (426/5). Cf. Pausanias 1.8.5; Plutarch, *Aristeides* 27.6. See also no. 1A at 511/10, 1B at 520/19. B: The Rylands Papyrus 18. *D. M. Leahy, *Bulletin of the John Rylands Library* 38 (1956) 406–35; *FGrHist* 105 F 1. Cf. Herodotus 5.55–65, 5.92a, 6.123.1–2; Thucydides 6.54–9.

A: M. Bowra, *Greek lyric poetry*[2] (Oxford 1961) 392–6; M. Ostwald, *Nomos and the beginnings of the Athenian democracy* (Oxford 1969) 121–7; C. W. Fornara, *Philologus* 114 (1970) 155–80; H. W. Pleket, *Talanta* 4 (1972) 68–81; Bury–Meiggs 134; Sealey, *History* 145f.
B: G. Dickens, *JHS* 32 (1912) 25f.; N. G. L. Hammond, *CQ* 6 (1956) 48–50; Huxley, *Sparta* 69–71; Jacoby, *FGrHist* IIC.236f.

A. Athenian drinking songs celebrating Harmodios and Aristogeiton

(1) ATHENAEUS 15.50, p. 695ab
I shall bear my sword in a branch of myrtle / like Harmodios and Aristogeiton / when they killed the tyrant / and made Athens a place of isonomia.[1]

Dearest Harmodios, you are surely not dead / but are in the Islands of the Blest, they say, / where fleet-footed Achilleus is / and, they say, good Diomedes the son of Tydeus.

I shall bear my sword in a branch of myrtle / like Harmodios and Aristogeiton / when at the festival of Athena / they killed the tyrant Hipparchos.

Your fame shall be throughout the world forever, / dearest Harmodios and Aristogeiton, / because you killed the tyrant / and made Athens a place of isonomia.

(2) SCHOLIAST TO ARISTOPHANES, *ACHARNIANS* 980 (426/5)
Aristoph. *Acharnians* 980: Nor shall he (War) sing the Harmodios (song) in my company.
    Scholion: In their drinking gatherings (the Athenians) sang a certain song called that of Harmodios, the beginning of which was 'Dearest Harmodios, you are surely not dead.' They sang it for Harmodios and Aristogeiton because they destroyed the tyranny of the Peisistratidai....

B. Rylands Papyrus 18, Column 2 (lines 12–24)[2]

15   [-11-] *having crossed* | *over to* the mainland,[3] | *much* of the *seacoa‖st skirting the mountains* was established (with cities) by [him]. | But[4] Chilon, the Lakedaimonian, | having been Ephor and *gener‖al*, [and]

20 Anaxandrida[s],⁵ | amongst the Hell[en]es, || brought the *tyrannies*
do|wn: in Sikyon | Ai[sch]ines, Hippias | [at Athens], Peisist[ra|tos'
successor.⁶]⁷

1 'Equality of law.'
2 Column 1 consists of lines 1-11, and is very fragmentary; possibly the word
   'Spar[ta' appeared. Column 2 ends with line 23, line 24 being my supplement.
   The nature of this work is highly uncertain. Hammond considers it the epitome
   of a Greek history, Leahy and Jacoby suggest that it may be a tract on the Seven
   Wise Men, Huxley suggests that it is a history of Sparta.
3 Identification of the 'mainland' (*epeiros*) depends on the identity of the subject
   of the sentence. *Epeiros* was a term meaning 'land' originally applied to northwest Greece (whence the later name of the region, 'Epirus'). The term subsequently developed the meaning of 'continent' and as such was especially applied
   to Asia. Thus, if the subject of the sentence is Polykrates, 'Epeiros' is Asia; if
   Periander (Leahy), Epirus; if Ariston, king of Sparta (Huxley), it is Kythera and
   the Argive possessions on the Peloponnesus.
4 Or 'And.'
5 Chilon's ephorate was traditionally set in Olympiad 55 (560-557, Diogenes
   Laertius 1.68; see, however, Hammond, *Studies* 84 n. 4). Anaxandridas ruled
   about 550-520.
6 Bilabel (cited in Jacoby, *FGrHist* IIC (Komm.) 336).
7 Compare Plutarch, *On the Malignity of Herodotus* 21, *Moralia* 859d: '(Did not
   the Spartans) expel the Kypselids from Corinth and Ambrakia, Lygdamis from
   Naxos, the sons of Peisistratos from Athens, Aischines from Sikyon, Sym-
   machos from Thasos, Aulis from Phokis, Aristogenes from Miletus, and end the
   close oligarchy (*dynasteia*) in Thessaly by bringing down Aristomedes and
   Angelos through the agency of Leotychidas the king?'

40 The Rebuilding of the Temple at Delphi by the Alkmeonidai. 513-510 B.C. (?)

A: Scholiast to Pindar, *Pythian Odes* 7.9b (486) (Philochorus, *FGrHist* 328 F 115);
B: Scholiast to Demosthenes 21.144 (9.623 Dindorf). Cf. Herodotus 6.123; Aristotle, *Athenaion Politeia* 19.4.

Jacoby, *FGrHist* IIIb Suppl. 1.449ff.; C. W. Fornara, *Philologus* 114 (1970) 163-5;
K. H. Kinzl, *Hermes* 102 (1974) 179-90; Bury-Meiggs 134f.; Sealey, *History* 146.

A. Scholiast to Pindar, *Pythian Odes* 7.9b (486)

Pindar, *Pyth.* 7.1-9: Athens the greatest of cities is the finest / preamble
to the powerful family of the Alkmeonidai / to lay as the foundation of
my song to their horses. / For what native city, what family, if you live
5 there, will you name // more illustrious / for Hellas to hear of? / For
report has gone to all the cities, / Apollo, of the townsmen of Erech-
theus who made your home / in shining Delphi wondrous.
    Scholion: . . . It is said that when the temple at Delphi was burned

down – as some declare, by the sons of Peisistratos – the Alkmeonidai, who had been banished by the sons of Peisistratos, promised to rebuild it. After they attacked the Peisistratidai and when they had conquered, they rebuilt the precinct of the god with greater beneficence, as Philochorus relates, since they earlier made that vow to the god.

B. Scholiast to Demosthenes 21.144

Demosthenes 21.144: For he (Alkibiades), O men of Athens, is said to have been an Alkmeonid on his father's side – and they say that these (the members of this family) were banished by the tyrants when they engaged in political strife on behalf of the people. Borrowing money from Delphi they liberated the city and expelled the sons of Peisistratos . . . .

Scholion: Megakles married the daughter of Peisistratos (*sic*). When (Peisistratos) had unnatural relations with her,[1] Megakles cast off the daughter and himself went to Delphi. At that time the temple of Apollo had been burned down[2] and the Delphians announced that they would contract for the construction of the temple. Megakles accepted the contract. Taking ten talents he spent three for construction and by means of the (other) seven he collected together a force and he persuaded the Lacedaemonians to provide assistance against Athens. He did not capture Peisistratos, who was no longer alive, but he expelled Hippias, his son, the tyrant.

1 Hdt. 1.61.1.
2 See no. 23, note 5.

41   Ostracism at Athens. Just prior to 508, 508/7, *or* Just prior to 488/7 B.C.

A: The date of the introduction of ostracism. (1) Harpocration s.v. 'Hipparchos' (Androtion, *FGrHist* 324 F 6); (2) Vaticanus Graecus 1144, fol. 222rv (*AJP* 93 (1972) 87f.); (3) Aelian, *Varia Historia* 13.24. Cf. Aristotle, *Athenaion Politeia* 22, *Politics* 3.13.1284a; Diodorus 11.55.1. B: Procedure. (1) *Lexicon Rhetoricum Cantabrigiense*, p. 354, 1 N (Philochorus, *FGrHist* 328 F 30); (2) Scholiast to Aristophanes, *Knights* 855 (425/4). Cf. Diodorus 11.55.2; Plutarch, *Aristeides* 7.2–6; Pollux 8.19–20. C: The period of banishment required by ostracism. (1) Scholiast to Aristeides 46.158.13, p. 538, 4 Dindorf (Theopompus, *FGrHist* 115 F 88); (2) Scholiast to Aristophanes, *Wasps* 947 [423/2]. D: Ostraka. *GHI*, no. 21, p. 42 (1–5); E. Vanderpool, *Ostracism at Athens*, Semple Lectures (Cincinnati 1970), Figures 19, 21, 46, 48, respectively, for nos. 6–9. See also Rudi Thomsen, *The origin of ostracism* (Copenhagen 1972).

A: Hignett, *Constitution* 159–64; G. R. Stanton, *JHS* 90 (1970) 180–3; J. J. Keaney and A. E. Raubitschek, *AJP* 93 (1972) 87–91; M. Chambers, *JHS* 99 (1979)

151-2. **B:** Jacoby, *FGrHist* IIIb Suppl. 1.315ff.; Hignett, *Constitution* 164f. **C:** Jacoby, *op. cit.* 317; Kagan, *Outbreak* 91, 103. **D:** E. Vanderpool, *Hesperia*, Suppl. 8, pp. 408-11, *Hesperia* 17 (1948) 194, Vanderpool, *Ostracism*; F. Willemsen, *Deltion* 23 (1968) 28f.; *GHI*, no. 21, pp. 40-7; Bury-Meiggs 164f.; Sealey, *History* 164-6.

A. The date of the introduction of ostracism

(1) HARPOCRATION *s.v.* 'HIPPARCHOS'

. . . There is another Hipparchos about whom Lykourgos in the *Against Lykophron* says 'Hipparchos son of Peisistratos.' Hipparchos son of Charmos is a different man, as Lykourgos says in the *Against Leokrates* (117). Of him Androtion says in Book 2 that he was a relative of Peisistratos the tyrant and was the first man to be ostracized, the law about ostracism having been first passed at that time[1] on account of the suspicion against those connected with Peisistratos, since he became tyrant as demagogue and general.

(2) VATICANUS GRAECUS 1144, FOL. 222rv[2]

Kleisthenes introduced the ostracism law into Athens. It was of this nature. It was the custom of the Boule, after having considered (the question) for a few days, to write down on potsherds (ostraka) (the name of) whatever citizen had to be exiled. They cast these (sherds) within the fence[3] of the Bouleuterion. Whoever received more than two hundred ostraka (was required) to be an exile for ten years, though he could reap the benefits of his property (at Athens). Later it was resolved by the People to ordain a law (to the effect) that the ostraka were to be in excess of six thousand for the man who was to be ostracized.

(3) AELIAN, *VARIA HISTORIA* 13.24

Kleisthenes the Athenian, who was the first to introduce (the law) that an ostracism should be held, was himself the first man to suffer the sentence.

B. Procedure

(1) *LEXICON RHETORICUM CANTABRIGIENSE* P. 354, 1 N

The manner of ostracism. Philochorus explains ostracism in his third book by writing as follows: 'Ostracism [is as follows]. The people took a preliminary vote before the eighth prytany as to whether it seemed best to hold an ostracism. When it was resolved to do so, the agora was fenced off with planks. Ten entrances were left through which (the Athenians) entered according to tribe and deposited their sherds, keeping what they had written turned downwards. The nine Archons and the Boule presided. After (the sherds) had been counted up, whoever received the greatest number and not less than 6,000,[4] was required to settle his private legal commitments in ten days and to depart from the city for ten years – though later it became five – receiving the income from his property but not going within Geraistos, the promontory of Euboea.[5] Hyperbolos was the only man without reputation to be ostracized because of his evil habits[6] and not because he was suspected of aiming at a tyranny. After him the custom was ended, it having been begun when Kleisthenes passed his laws, when he put an end to the tyrants, in order also to expel their friends.[7]

(2) SCHOLIAST TO ARISTOPHANES, *KNIGHTS* 855 (425/4)
Knights 855: And so if you get angry and are about to play the ostrakon game . . .
   Scholion: This was the nature of the ostracism . . . . If 6,000 (sherds) were not cast (against a person), he was not banished. The Athenians were not alone in having the ostracism, but the Argives, Milesians, and Megarians also did. Virtually all of the most accomplished men were ostracized: Aristeides, Kimon, Themistokles, Thoukydides, Alkibiades.

C. The period of banishment

(1) SCHOLIAST TO ARISTEIDES 46.158.13, p. 528, 4 Dindorf
See no. 76

(2) SCHOLIAST TO ARISTOPHANES, *WASPS* 947
Wasps 946f.: No, but he seems to me to have experienced / what Thoukydides too once suffered when he went into exile.
   Scholion: He is speaking of Thoukydides son of Melesias of Alopeke. The Athenians ostracized him for the (statutory) ten years according to the law. It is not strange that elsewhere (Aristophanes) says that he has been 'ostracized' and now says that he is in 'exile.' Ostracism is a species of exile and the genus (exile) comprehends the species. One can reasonably term ostracism exile although exile is not ostracism. Exile (i.e. in the strict use of the term) differs from ostracism in that the property of exiles is confiscated while that of those who change their residence because of ostracism is not . . . .

D. Ostraka

1. Arist[eides,] Da[tis'] | *brother*
2. [(?) Aristeides | son of Lysim]achos, | [who had] *the* suppliants |
[pushed away]

3. [Kall]ixenos | [the] *traitor*
4. [---]s, (may he) lose his *rights*!
5. Of all the cursed *leaders* [this] ostrakon says that Xanth[ippos] |
the son of [Arri]phron does the most evil.[8]
6. Themistokles son of Neokles, out with him!
7. Ma! Vengeance on Hippochrates[9]
8. Kallixen[os][10]
9. [Of the Alk]meon[idai Kal]lixen[os son of Ar]isto[nymos]

1   Keaney, *Historia* 19 (1970) 3, emends to read 'the law having been enacted
    before this time.'
2   This parchment manuscript volume was written by a Byzantine in the fifteenth
    century, and it is an open question whether he is transmitting an ancient source.
3   The Bouleuterion had no fence.
4   According to Plut. *Aristeides* 7.6, it is a matter of a quorum: 'if those bearing
    ostraka number less than 6,000, the ostracism is void.'
5   Jacoby believes that another limit has dropped out of the text; cf. Arist. *Ath.
    Pol.* 22.8.
6   See no. 145.
7   Cf. Diod. 11.55.
8   Wilhelm (cited *GHI*, p. 42). The word order of this couplet cannot be repro-
    duced in English. Other interpretations: 'This ostrakon says that the cursed
    Xanthippos most wrongs the *sacred hearth*': Raubitschek (cited *GHI*, p. 42);
    ' . . . most wrongs the Prytaneion': Broneer (cited *GHI*, p. 42).
9   'Ma' is an exclamation; note the misspelling of Hippokrates.
10 This ostrakon contains a sketch of Kallixenos and is further embellished with
    the drawing of a fish and a branch.

42   Epigrams Celebrating an Athenian Victory over Boeotia and Chalcis. About 506 B.C.[1]

A: Block of dark Eleusinian limestone, nonstoichedon, near the Propylaia; B: Four fragments from a marble base, stoichedon, on the Acropolis.

IG I² 394 (I³ 501). *DAA*, no. 173, pp. 201-5; *GHI*, no. 15, pp. 28f. Cf. Herodotus
5.75-7.

Hammond, *History* 192; Bury-Meiggs 138f.; C. W. Fornara, *CSCA* 10 (1978) 45-7.

(A)

[In dismal chains of iron they quelled their] pride, |[2] the sons [of the
Athenians, by deed in battle, | when they crushed the people of Boeotia
and of Chalcis,] | from whom (these) horses, as a [tithe, they dedicated
to Pallas (Athena).]

(B)

[When they] *crushed* [the people of Boeotia and of Chalcis,] | *the sons*
of the Athenians, *by deeds* [in battle, | in dismal chains of iron] *quel-*

led [their pride,] | *from whom* (these) horses, as a *tithe*, [they dedicated to Pallas.]

1   The Athenian victory in 506 over the Boeotians and Chalcidians led to the erection of a monument carrying epigram A. Epigram B (with transposition of two of A's hexameters) appears on the base of another monument set up in the middle of the fifth century. The letters are less archaic, though three-bar sigma is used. The occasion for the apparent renewal of A by B is unknown, though it has been associated with the battle of Oenophyta *c.* 457 (*DAA*, p. 203), and with the repression of the revolt of Euboea in 446 (Tod I, p. 87 [see no. 103] ; Jacoby, *JHS* 64 (1944) 45). Restoration of these inscriptions is assured from the quotation of the epigram in Herodotus 5.77.

2   On both inscriptions, verse endings and line endings coincide.

43   Dedication of the Athenian Portico at Delphi. 506 *or* 500–480 *or* 479 B.C.

On the top step of the stylobate of the portico, Delphi.

Tod I, no. 18, pp. 21f.; *GHI*, no. 25, pp. 53f.

The Athenians dedicated the Portico, having seized both the arms[1] and the ship ornaments from the enemy.

1   The word is understood by P. Amandry (see *GHI*, p. 54, and now Amandry, *BCH* 102 (1978) 582-6), perhaps correctly, to mean the cable from the Persian bridge of boats spanning the Hellespont. Others assume the dedication followed Salamis (480), the Aeginetan-Athenian War (about 500–480) or the battle against Chalcis in 506 B.C. Pausanias 10.11.6 associates it with the victories of Phormion in the Corinthian Gulf (429), but the archaic writing excludes so late a date.

44   Athenian Klerouchy at Salamis. Late sixth century B.C.

A: Scholiast to Pindar, *Nemean Odes* 2.19; B: *IG* I^2 1 (I^3 1); B. D. Meritt, *Hesperia* 10 (1941) 301-7; H. T. Wade-Gery, *CQ* 40 (1946) 101-4; N. G. L. Hammond, *JHS* 76 (1956) 48 [=*Studies* 261] ; *GHI*, no. 14, pp. 25-7; Bury–Meiggs 526. Marble stele, stoichedon (with variations), Athens.

A. Scholiast to Pindar, *Nemean Odes* 2.19

Pindar, *Nem.* 2.13–15 (Bowra): Truly is Salamis able to rear a fighting-man. / In Troy Hektor learned of Aias. O Timodamos, your staunch

15   courage // in the pankration will exalt you.

Scholion: The question is why he has brought the business about Salamis into the subject of Timodemos.[1] For he says outright (v. 16) that his deme is Acharnai (and Timodemos is therefore an Athenian and not a Salaminian) . . . . Asclepiades says that he probably is one of the Athenians who became klerouchs at Salamis. Thus it is probable that though he was born at Athens he was 'reared' in Salamis.

B. *IG* I^2 1

Resolved by the People. [Those in S]alam[is who are -8-]^2 | shall be allowed to dwell in Salamis [-20-] | [.]^3 pay taxes and *perform military service.* [But their property in Salamis] *shall n|ot be leased* (by
5 them) unless [-23-]^4 *I||f a man leases it, there shall be a penalty paid* [by the lessee and by the] *l|essor*, each of them, [-19-]^5 | into the public treasury. [It shall be exacted by the] *a|rchon.*^{6} If [not, he will be called to account at his euthyna.]^7 *The|ir* arms [they shall furnish
10 themselves at the cost of] *th||irty drachmas.* [When they are arme|d,] the archon [shall pass their arms under rev|iew.] *In* (the year of?) the *Boule* [-11-]

1 The spelling of the name given by the scholiast is normal Attic; Pindar wrote Doric Greek.
2 'Athenians]': Meritt; 'klerouchs]': Luria (cited *GHI*, p. 26); 'inhabitants]': Wilhelm (cited *GHI*, p. 26).
3 '[forever, except that they must at Athen|s]': Meritt; '[and pay taxes just as the city-dweller|s]': Wade-Gery.
4 '*a kinsman* [is the lessor] ': Wade-Gery; '*dwellers* [there also lease it]': Meritt.
5 '[of one-tenth the rent] ': Wade-Gery; '[of three times the rent]': Tod.
6 A term used for a governor or ruling magistrate as well as for the eponymous Archon; see the Glossary.
7 "[They shall be mobilized by the] *a|rchon* if [any need arises': Wade-Gery.

45 Rations for Ionian Mothers Working at Persepolis. About 500 B.C.

One of a series of tablets discovered in the fortification wall of the Persepolis terrace, Elamite, Persepolis. R. T. Hallock, *Persepolis fortification tablets*, The University of Chicago Oriental Institute Publications 92 (Chicago 1969) 349, PF 1224. Copyright ©1969 by the University of Chicago. Hallock, p. 2; C. Nylander, *AJA* 59 (1965) 55. Cf. no. 46.

[1–13] 32 BAR^1 (of) grain, supplied by Ašbašuptiš. Šedda the hatarmabattiš^2 (at) Persepolis, for whom Abbateya sets the apportionments, received, and gave (it as) kamakaš^3 to Ionian women who have just given birth (at) Persepolis, irrigation (?) (workers), whose apportionments are set by Abbateya and Miššabadda. [13–16] 9 women (who) bore male children received (each) 2 BAR, and 14 women (who) bore girls received each 1 BAR.
[16–17] Twelfth month, 22nd year.^{4}

Note that double payments of grain are made to the mothers of boys, either as a reward (Hallock) or for hierarchic reasons (suggested by Badian).

1 A BAR is a dry measure equivalent to ten quarts.
2 An official serving as agent for payment of special rations.
3 A word of uncertain meaning.
4 The twenty-second year of the reign of Dareios (521–486 B.C.). The translation given here follows that of Hallock (reprinted with permission).

46 An Ionian Contractor at Persepolis. About 500 B.C.
Carved on a cliff amidst limestone quarries, Ionic lettering, near Persepolis.

G. Pugliese Carratelli, *East and West*, n.s. 16 (1966) 31–3.

E. Schmidt, *Persepolis* 1 (Chicago 1963) 160f.; C. Nylander, *AJA* 69 (1965) 55; R. T. Hallock, *Persepolis fortification tablets*, The University of Chicago Oriental Institute Publications 92 (Chicago 1969) 2; A. Momigliano, *Alien wisdom* (Cambridge 1975) 125. Cf. no. 45.

I am (the property) of Pytharchos[1] | *To the gods.*[2]

1 The 'speaker' of the inscription is the cliff itself. Cf., for example, no. 20.
2 This expression is written below the Pytharchos inscription in much smaller script, and it may or may not have been written by Pytharchos himself.

47 Law of the Eastern (Hypocnemidian) Locrians about their Colony at Naupactus. 500–470 B.C.
Bronze plaque. Locrian dialect, Chaleion (modern Galaxidi).

Buck, no. 57, pp. 248–53; Jeffery, *LSAG* 104–6; **GHI*, no. 20, pp. 35–40. The lower limit for the date of the law is given by Thucydides 1.103.3 (the seizure of Naupactus by Athens).

Graham, *Colony* 40–60, 226–8; J. A. O. Larsen, *Greek federal states* (Oxford 1968) 45–58; Jeffery, *Greece* 75f.

The settlement at Naupactus (is to be established) on these conditions. A Hypocnemidian Locrian, wh|en he becomes a Naupactian, shall as a Naupactian be allowed to have a share as a guest-friend[1] in religious privileges | and to make sacrifice, when he is present, if he wishes. If he wishes, he shall (instead) make sacrifices and s|hare in them as a member of (his former) community and association,[2] both he himself and his posterity forever. As to taxes, t|l|he colonists of the Hypocnemidian
5 Locrians shall not pay (them) to the | Hypocnemidian Locrians (unless and) until a man again becomes a Hypocnemidian Locrian. Should | he

wish to return, if he leaves at his hearth an adult son or brother, he shall
be pe|rmitted to do so without entry-fees. If compulsion drives out
from Naupactus the | Hypocnemidian Locrians, they shall be allowed
10 to return, each to his place of origin, without e||ntry-fees. They shall
pay no tax except in common with the Locrians of the Wes|t.[3] I.[4] The
colonists (sent) to Naupactus are bound by oath not to rebel against the
Opuntians[5] | by any pretext or device of their own free will. It shall be
lawful for the oath, if they wi|sh, thirty years from the time of the
(first) oath-taking, to be administered by one hundred men | of the
Naupactians to the Opuntians and (similarly) to the Naupactians by the
15 Opuntians. II. If any man defaults in his taxe||s in Naupactus who is a
colonist, he shall be excluded from the Locrians until he pays back
what is due | by law to the Naupactians. III. If there is no natural suc-
cessor left at the hearth (of a deceased man) and no heir among the
col|onists in Naupactus, that Hypocnemidian Locrian who is next of
k|in shall take (his property), from whatever part of Locris he may be,
if he goes there, be he man or boy, within three m|onths. Otherwise,
20 Naupactian law shall apply. IV. If from Naupactus a man re||turns to
Hypocnemidian Locris, he shall proclaim it at Naupactus in the A|ssem-
bly,[6] and in the city of his origin among the Hypocnemidian Locrians
he shall proclaim it in the | Assembly.[7] V. When one of the Perkothariai
and Mysacheis[8] becomes a Naupactian | himself,[9] his property in Nau-
pactus shall also be subject to Naupactian (law), | while as to his pro-
25 perty in Hypocnemidian Locris, Hypocnemidi||an |

(Reverse side of the plaque)

law shall apply, whatever the law may be in the various cities of the |
Hypocnemidian Locrians. If anyone returns under the laws governing
the colonists and is of the Perkothariа|i and Mysacheis, they shall each
of them be subject to their own laws, each according to his city. | VI.
If there are any brothers of a man living in Naupactus, in accordance
30 with the || law governing each (community) of the Hypocnemidian
Locrians, if (a brother) dies, his p|roperty shall come into the posses-
sion of the colonist – that which it is proper for him to possess.[10] VII. |
The colonists at Naupactus shall bring suit with right of precedence
before the j|udges, and they shall bring suit and submit to it in Opus –[11]
on the very day. Fr|om the Hypocnemidian Locrians appointment shall
35 be made of a prostates[12] – one of the Locrians for the col||onist(s) and
one of the colonists for the Locrian(s) – by whoever are in office for
the year.[13] VIII. If any|one leaves behind (in Locris) his father and a
portion of his property (which he has consigned) to his father, when |
(his father) dies, the colonist to Naupactus shall be permitted to recover
his portion. | IX. Whoever violates these resolutions by any pretext or

device in eve|n one point, unless it is with the agreement of both parties
40 – the Opuntian Thousand by majority || vote and the Naupactian colonists by majority vote – shall lose his citizen-rights and his pro|perty shall be confiscated. To the man bringing suit, the magistrate shall grant trial | within thirty days – (that is,) he shall grant it if thirty days are lef|t to his term of office. If he does not grant trial to the one bringing suit, his (own) citizen-righ|ts shall be forfeit and his property confisca-
45 ted, (both) his real property and his sl|laves. The customary oath is to be sworn (by the jury and) into an urn are their vot|es to be cast. Furthermore, the ordinance for the Hypocnemidian Locrians shall equally be valid for the Chaleians[14] led by Antiphates.

1 'in the places where a stranger is permitted by sacred law': Graham.
2 A grouping smaller than the political unit and probably not presupposed by it. Whether it was based on kinship or the observation of common religious rites is unknown.
3 I.e. they are to be subject to no special taxes since they are colonists. The Locrians of central Greece were Greeks of a common identity, split (possibly as the result of an invasion) by Phocis and flanking it from the east and west. The Western Locrians, in whose territory Naupactus lay, were also called Ozolian.
4 Separate sections of the inscription were marked off by number.
5 Opus was the political center of the Eastern Locrians; thus the Thousand of the Opuntians (line 39) is the assembly of *all* the Hypocnemidian Locrians; see Larsen, p. 53.
6 Or, 'in the marketplace.'
7 Or as in n. 6.
8 Apparently religious castes subject to special regulations as regards their property.
9 A punctuation mark inscribed just before this word may indicate that we should translate 'he and his property' (thus *GHI*), though then there will be a grammatical error. But a punctuation mark is misplaced also on line 7 and the marks are often arbitrarily placed.
10 This sentence is oddly constructed because the first thought (that a colonist would be entitled to inherit his brother's property) led to a second (that the right needed to be limited), which was then accommodated to the same sentence.
11 Eight letters (probably two words) in this space are a puzzle. Buck suggested 'against themselves'; Tod I, no. 24, p. 35: 'so far as (they are) concerned.'
12 That person who sponsors a foreigner in civil actions. (See Glossary, 'Metics.') Another interpretation is 'surety.'
13 This sentence is difficult and perhaps erroneously inscribed.
14 Chaleion was a community of the Western Locrians; see no. 86.

48 The Persian Cavalry at Marathon. 490 B.C.

Suda s.v. *choris hippeis* ('the cavalry are apart'). Cf. Herodotus 6.107ff.; Nepos, *Miltiades* 5.5; no. 90 below.

N. G. L. Hammond, *JHS* 88 (1968) 39f. [=*Studies* 214ff.] ; A. R. Burn, *JHS* 89 (1969) 118; Bury-Meiggs 529; Sealey, *History* 190f.; G. Shrimpton, *Phoenix* 34 (1980) 20-37.

When Datis had invaded Attica, they say that the Ionians, when he had withdrawn, went up to the trees,[1] and signaled to the Athenians that the cavalry were apart. Miltiades, learning of their departure, thus attacked and conquered. Hence the proverb is applied to those who break ranks.

1 Or, 'into the trees.'

49   Dedication of Kallimachos. 490 B.C.
Fragments of an Ionic column, nonstoichedon, five hexameters, set out in two lines, Athens.

IG I² 609 (I³ 784); *DAA*, no. 13, pp. 18-20; B. B. Shefton, *BSA* 45 (1950) 140-64, *BSA* 47 (1952) 278; **GHI*, no. 18, pp. 33f. Cf. Herodotus 6.109-11, 114.

F. Jacoby, *Hesperia* 14 (1945) 158 n. 8; E. B. Harrison, *GRBS* 12 (1971) 5-24 (with drawing of inscription); Bury-Meiggs 158-61.

[Kallimachos] of Aphidna *dedicated* [me] to Athena, / (the) *messenger of the immortals*[1] who dwell in [Olympian homes,] /l [-8-]² *Polemarch* of the Athenians the battle / of Ma[rathon - - -]³ // to the sons of the Athenians [-23-].

1 If the figure of a winged woman found on the Acropolis belongs to this monument (*DAA*), the 'messenger' dedicated would be Iris or Nike (Victory).
2 '[he who, causing as]': Shefton.
3 '[on the behalf] *of the Hellenes* [brought renown] // to the sons of the Athenians [and passed on the] *remembrance* [of his virtue]': Shefton; '*he did win* [whom baneful Ares slew, // leaving behind] *remembrance* [and grief] to the sons of the Athenians': Fraenkel (*Eranos* 49 (1951) 64). Harrison, taking the beginning of 'Ma[rathon' as the start of a different word and reading the fifth verse as an elegiac pentameter (and not a hexameter), restores, from verse 4: 'of the *very* [brave] *won a name* [that was fairest] // [and] *remembrance* [of his virtue] for the sons of the Athenians.'

50   Athenian Thank-Offering for Marathon. 490 B.C.
On a limestone base against the front of the south wall of the Athenian treasury, Delphi. Re-inscribed (probably) in the third century.

*SIG, no. 23, pp. 22f. (A and B); *GHI*, no. 19, p. 35 (B).

(A)

The [A]theni[ans dedicated (this as)] *first-fruits* [of the battle of Marathon; from the Medes][1]

(B)

The Athenians to Apollo [from the Med]es as *first-fruits* of the *battle* of Marathon.

1 Pausanias 10.11.5 associated this dedication with the building of the treasury. Some scholars instead assume (see *GHI*, p. 35) that the treasury (as opposed to the base) was built between 506 and 490.

51 Athenian Epigrams on the Persian Wars. 490 *or* 490 (B) and 480 (A) *or* 480 (B) and 490 (A) *or* 480 B.C.[1]
Two fragments of a marble base; (A) stoichedon; (B) nonstoichedon; Athens.

IG I^2 763+ (I^3 503); F. Jacoby, *Hesperia* 14 (1945) 161–85 (490); Gomme, etc., *HCT* 3.98f. (480); B. D. Meritt, *AJP* 83 (1962) 294–8 (490, 480); W. K. Pritchett, *AJP* 85 (1964) 50–5 (480, 490); **GHI*, no. 26, pp. 54–7 (480, 490); Hammond, *Studies* 191–3 (480–79, 490).

(A)

These men's courage [-9-[2] imperishable[3]] forever, /| [-- gods grant][4] /|
For they checked, as footsoldiers [and on swift-faring ships], /| all of Hellas from [witnessing the day] of slavery.

(B)

They truly possessed an *adamantine* [---][5] when the spear /| was poised in front of the gates *in the face of* [---][6] /| [who wished] to burn the sea-girt [---][7] /| city, turning back by force the Persian [power.]

1 The normal assumption would be that both epigrams relate to the same battle. But if it is Marathon, the phrase 'on swift-faring ships' of (A) must refer to fighting on the ships of the enemy, which would be a singular usage; and if it is Salamis, the fact that Athens indeed was burned by the Persians, counter to the clear indication of (B), is equally troublesome. Hence the inclination of some to ascribe the first to Salamis and the second (which was inscribed some time later than the first) to Marathon. But even then, we have prominent reference to 'footsoldiers' in (A) and the implication (though hardly inevitable) in (B) of a battle fought in view of the city. Hence the lively dispute among scholars.
2 '*Of* these men's courage [the fame shall be': Peek (cited *GHI*, p. 55); '[shall be a shining light,': Meritt.

3 This word, like the supplements in the following three verses, derives from a fourth-century copy, identified by Meritt, which gives the last part of each verse: [---] *imperishable* [--] /| [---] gods grant /| [---] on swift-faring ships /| [---] see the day.
4 '[no matter to whom in deeds of war the gods may grant success]': Meritt. The number of letters in line 2 is in dispute.
5 '[spirit in their breast]': Wilhelm (cited *GHI*, p. 54); others offer minor variations.
6 '[bowmen]': Wilhelm; '[myriads]': Meritt; '[enemies]': Peek.
7 '[splendid]': Meritt; '[(city), but who saved (the)]': Wilhelm, Peek.

52 The Greek Embassy to Gelon. 480 B.C.

Scholiast to Pindar, *Pythian Odes* 1.146b Drachmann (Ephorus, *FGrHist* 70 F 186). Cf. Herodotus 7.157-67; Diodorus 11.1.4.

R. W. Macan, *Herodotus: The seventh, eighth and ninth books* (London 1908) 2.226-9; Hignett, *Invasion* 17; C. W. Fornara, *Herodotus* (Oxford 1971) 82-4.

Pind. *Pyth*. 1.71-5 (Bowra): Grant, I pray, son of Kronos, / that the Phoenician[1] and Etruscan battle-cry may become peaceful and remain at home since it has seen its insolence bring lamentation on their ships off Cumae.[2] / Such losses did they suffer when they were crushed by the lord of the Syracusans / – (a fate) which hurled their youth from
75 the swift-faring ships into the sea, // delivering Hellas from grievous slavery.

Scholion: Some take this Hellas as Sicily, others as Attica. It is likely that Pindar, coming upon the history of Ephorus,[3] followed his authority. For Ephorus narrates that when Xerxes was preparing his expedition against Hellas, envoys appeared before the tyrant Gelon imploring him to come to the common assembly of the Greeks. Ambassadors from the Persians and Phoenicians (also went) to the Carthaginians with the injunction that an expedition of the greatest size should invade Sicily 〈and〉, after subduing the Hellenic faction (there), sail to the Peloponesus. Both sides accepted. When Hieron[4] was ready to aid the Hellenes and the Carthaginians were ready to cooperate with Xerxes, Gelon, after he had equipped 200 ships, 2,000 horse and 10,000 foot,[5] learned of the Carthaginian expedition sailing against Sicily. He fought with them and brought liberty not only to Sicily but to all of Hellas. It is therefore likely that Pindar happened to read this history.

1 I.e. Carthaginian.
2 In 474 B.C.; see no. 64.
3 Pindar wrote in the first half of the fifth century, Ephorus in the middle of the fourth.
4 A mistake for 'Gelon.'
5 Cf. Hdt. 7.158.4. Diod. 11.21.1 gives 50,000 men and 5,000 horse.

53   A Supplication by Corinthian Women during Xerxes' War. 480–479 B.C.

Scholiast to Pindar, *Olympian Odes* 13.32b Drachmann (Theopompus, *FGrHist* 115 F 285b). Cf. Plutarch, *On the Malignity of Herodotus* 39 (*Moralia* 871ab); Athenaeus 13.32, p. 573c–e.

Pind. *Olympian Odes* 13.22–3b (Bowra): The sweet-breathing Muse / (flourishes in Corinth) and Ares flourishes with the deadly spears of young men.

Scholion: He says that Ares is glorious in Corinth because he is alluding to the Persian affair in which the Corinthians distinguished themselves on behalf of the preservation of the Hellenes. Theopompus says that even their women prayed to Aphrodite to instill into their husbands the love of fighting the Medes on behalf of Hellas. (To do this,) they went into the temple of Aphrodite, which they say was founded by Medea at the command of Hera. The elegy inscribed exists even now (he says), positioned on the left as one enters the temple: 'On behalf of the Hellenes and their (own) citizen-warriors these women / stood in prayer to Lady Kypris. / For shining Aphrodite did not wish[1] / to give
5   over to the bow-carrying Medes[2] // the Akropolis of the Hellenes.'

1   A variant: 'was not minded.'
2   'Persians' is a variant.

54   Gelon's Thank-Offering for the Victory at Himera. 480 B.C.
Limestone tripod-base, Delphi. Lines 4 and 5 are in a different hand.

C. D. Buck, *CP* 8 (1913) 137; Jeffery, *LSAG* 266 and Plate 51.6; **GHI*, no. 28, pp. 60f. Cf. Diodorus 11.26.7; Athenaeus 6.20, p. 231f.

E. A. Freeman, *The history of Sicily* (Oxford 1891) 2.212; Bury–Meiggs 189f.

Gelon son [of] Deinomenes | dedicated (this tripod) to Apollo, | (Gelon) the Syracusan. | The tripod and the Victory were made by ||
5   Bion son of Diodoros of Miletus.[1]

1   He is mentioned by Diogenes Laertius at 4.58.

55   The Decree of Themistokles. 480 B.C.
Marble stele, third-century lettering, stoichedon (with slight irregularities), Troezen. The authenticity of this decree is contested.

*GHI, no. 23, pp. 48–52; H. Berve, Bayerische Akademie der Wissenschaften, Phil.-Hist. Klasse, Sitzungsberichte (no. 3, 1961) 1–50 (favorable to authenticity); C. Habicht, Hermes 89 (1961) 1–35 (hostile); M. Jameson, Hesperia 31 (1962) 310–15 (favorable); B. D. Meritt, Semple Lectures (Cincinnati 1962) 21–34 (favorable); Hignett, Invasion 458–68 (hostile); M. Chambers, Philologus 111 (1967) 166–9 (hostile); C. W. Fornara, AHR 73 (1967) 425–33 (favorable); Sealey, History 214–16 (hostile). Cf. Herodotus 7.140–4; 8.40.2; Demosthenes 19.303; Plutarch, Themistocles 10.4; Bury–Meiggs 172; critical bibliography by Dow (cited GHI, p. 48):

[Gods.] | Resolved by the Boule and the People, | Themis[tokl]es son of Neokles of Phrearrhioi made the motion.[1] | The city shall be entrus-
5 ted to Athena, Athen||s' [Protectress, and to the] other gods, all of them, for protectio|n and [defense against the] Barbarian on behalf of the country. The Athenian|s [in their entirety and the aliens] who live in Athens | shall place [their children and their women] in Troezen |
10 [-21-][2] the Founder of the land. [T||he elderly and (movable)] pro-perty shall (for safety) be deposited at Salamis. | [The Treasurers and] the Priestesses are [to remain] on the Akropoli|s [and guard the posses-sions of the] gods.[3] The rest of the Athe|[nians in their entirety and those] aliens who have reached young manhood shall em|bark [on the
15 readied] two hundred ships and they shall repu||lse the [Barbarian for the sake of] liberty, both their | own [and that of the other Hellenes,] in common with the Lacedaemonians, Co|rin[thians, Aeginetans] and the others who wis|h to have a share [in the danger.][4] Appointment will also be made of trie|rarchs [two hundred in number, one for] each
20 ship, by the g||enerals, [beginning] tomorrow, from among those who are own|ers [of both land and home] in Athens and who have children | who are legitimate. [They shall not be more] than fifty years old and t|he lot shall determine each man's ship. (The generals) shall also en-
25 list mar|ines, ten [for each] ship,[5] from men over twenty years o||f age [up to] thirty, and archers, fou|r (in number). [They shall also by lot appoint] the specialist officers[6] for each ship wh|en they appoint [the] trierarchs by lot. A list shall be mad|e also [of the rest,[7] ship by] ship, by the generals, on n|otice boards, [with the] Athenians (to be selec-
30 ted) from the lexiarchic re||gisters,[8] [the] aliens from the list of names (registered) wi|th the Polemarch. They shall write them up, assigning them by div|isions, up to two hundred (divisions, each) [of up to] one hundred (men),[9] and they shall appen|d to each division the name of the trireme and the tri|erarch and the specialist officers,[10] so that they
35 may know on w||hat trireme each division shall embark. When assign-|ment of all the divisions has been made and they have been allotted to the tri|remes, all the two hundred shall be manned by (order of) the Boule | and the generals, after they have sacrificed to appease Zeus the
40 | All-powerful and Athena and Nike[11] and Posei||don the Securer.[12] vv

When they have completed the manning of | the ships, with one hundred of them they shall bring assistance to the Artemis|ium in Euboea,[13] while with the other hundred they shall, all round Salam|is and the rest of Attica, lie at anchor and guard | the country. To ensure that in a
45 spirit of concord all Athenians || will ward off the Barbarian, those banished for the [t|en-]year span[14] shall leave for Salamis and they are to remain [ther|e until the People] decide about them. Those [-6-] | [---][15]

1 This kind of prescript, which gives the mover's patronymic and deme, is not customary in Athenian inscriptions until about 350 B.C.

2 '[their Protector being Pittheus]': Jameson; '[to be entrusted to Theseus *or* to Pittheus]': Habicht. Neither seems to fit in with the traces of letters legible.

3 Cf. Hdt. 8.51.2, where those who remained at Athens are 'Treasurers of the shrine and poor men.'

4 Cf. for the language, Hdt. 7.144.3, 178.2.

5 Cf. Hdt. 6.15.1 (70 Chiot marines per ship at Lade), 7.184.2. But see also Thucydides 1.14.3, Plutarch, *Kimon* 12.2.

6 *Or* 'the servicemen': Jameson. See B. Jordan, *CSCA* 2 (1969) 183-207.

7 *Or* '[of the sailors].'

8 Registers in which all Athenian citizens, with the possible exception of the thetes, were enrolled. According to Pollux 8.104 s.v. 'lexiarchoi,' 'the person listed in the lexiarchic register had already inherited his family property. Family property is also called *lexis*.' According to the *Suda* s.v. (Adler, no. 462), 'the names of Athenian citizens of the age to hold office were written up with their demes added. From those records they allotted the offices.'

9 The normal number was 200 (Hdt. 8.17).

10 See note 6.

11 'to Zeus (and) to the | All-powerful and to Athena Nike': Amandry (cited *GHI*, p. 48), assuming the word 'and' was misplaced. Pankrates ('All-powerful') was a hero usually distinct from Zeus, while Nike ('Victory') is generally Athena Nike and not a separate deity.

12 These gods are invoked by titles appropriate to the special situation: Zeus 'Allvictorious,' 'Athena (bringing) Victory,' Poseidon 'the Securer' or 'who never slips,' the aspect of Poseidon most crucial to sailors.

13 The Artemisium = the temple of Artemis. There were 147 Athenian ships at the Artemisium, 20 manned by Chalcis (Hdt. 8.1.2); 53 more came later as reinforcements (8.14.1).

14 I.e. ostracized. In Aristotle's *Athenaion Politeia* 22.8, the ostracized had already been recalled in the archonship of Hypsichides (481/80). What seems envisaged here (for which there is otherwise no support) is that the men were recalled but confined to Salamis without yet receiving their full citizen-rights.

15 '[who have been deprived of citizen-right|s are to have their rights restored ---]': Jameson.

56   Contribution of the Naxians to the War Effort against the Persians. 480 B.C.

Plutarch, *On the Malignity of Herodotus* 36 (=*Moralia* 869a–c) (Hellanicus, *FGrHist* 323a F 28; Ephorus, *FGrHist* 70 F 187; Simonides F 65 Diehl). Cf. Diodorus 5.52.3.

F. Jacoby, *FGrHist* IIIb Suppl. 1.55f.; Hignett, *Invasion* 14.

'For the Naxians sent three triremes as allies of the barbarians, but one of the trierarchs, Demokritos, persuaded the others to choose the cause of the Hellenes.'[1] Thus he (Herodotus) did not even know how to confer praise without blame, but in order that one man might be praised, an entire city and people must be defamed.[2] Yet he is ⟨contra⟩dicted both by Hellanicus, of the more ancient historians, and by Ephorus, of the more recent. For in their accounts the one says that the Naxians came to bear aid to the Hellenes with six ships, while the other says with five . . . . (Herodotus passed over in silence Naxian bravery against Datis in 490 B.C.)[3] That he did not want to praise Demokritos but fabricated the lie to shame the Naxians is plain from his totally ignoring and omitting his achievement and his bravery, which Simonides set forth in an epigram: 'Demokritos was the third to begin the fight when at Salamis / the Hellenes joined battle with the Medes at sea. / He captured five ships of the enemy, and a sixth, † from the hand / of the barbarian he secured †,[4] a Dorian ship being captured.'

1   Plutarch is quoting from Herodotus 8.46.3.
2   Plutarch has just excoriated Herodotus (8.30) for accusing the Phocians of taking the Hellenic side merely out of hatred for the Thessalians.
3   It is worth noting that Plutarch's evidence for this comes from the local historians of Naxos, hardly disinterested parties.
4   The Greek between daggers is corrupt.

57   Oath of the Athenians Taken before the Battle of Plataea. 479 B.C.
Marble stele, fourth-century lettering,[1] stoichedon, Acharnai. Its authenticity is contested.

Tod II, no. 204, pp. 303–7; P. Siewert, **Der Eid von Plataiai*, Vestigia 16 (Munich 1972) pp. 6f. Cf. Herodotus 7.132.2; Lycurgus, *Against Leokrates* 81; Diodorus 11.29.3; Theopompus, *FGrHist* 115 F 153 (no. 95D below).

Hignett, *Invasion* 460f.; A. E. Raubitschek, *TAPA* 91 (1960) 178–83; F. W. Walbank, *A historical commentary on Polybius* 2 (Oxford 1967) 180–2; P. Siewert, *Der Eid von Plataiai* (cited above).

21   The oath which the Athenians took when they were about | to fight
against the barbarians: vv^2 | 'I shall fight as long as I live, and I shall not
25   consider it more important | to be alive than to be free, a||nd I shall
not fail the Taxiarch[3] or th|e Enomotarch, be he alive or de|ad, and I
shall not retreat unless the Hegemones[4] | lead (the army) away, and I
30   shall do whatever the gener|als command. Those who di||e, of the allied
fighting-men, I shall bury on the sp|ot and I shall leave no one unburied.
After b|eating the barbarians in battle I shall ti|the[5] the city of the
35   Thebans; and I shall not des|troy Athens or Sparta or Platae||a or any
other city of those which shared in the fi|ghting. Nor shall I allo|w
(them) to be coerced by famine, nor shall flowing stream|s be kept
from them by me, be they friends or enem|ies.[6] If I remain faithful to
40   the o||ath's terms, may my city be free from sickness; | if not, may it
become sick. And may my city go unsack|ed; if not, may it be sacked.
And may my (land) bear (its fruits); i|f not, may it be barren. And may
women bea|r children like to their parents; if not, (may they bear)
45   monsters. || And may cattle bear issue like to cattl|e; if not, monsters.'
After swearing this, cove|ring over the sacrifices with their shields, at
th|e trumpet-blast, they called a curse down upon themselves if any of
the | terms of the oath should be violated by them and if they should
50   not main||tain the stipulations of the oath: | (namely) that pollution of
guilt be upon them who swore it.[7]

1   This oath follows another on the same stele (lines 1–20), described as the 'ancestral Ephebic oath.'
2   Not indicated in Siewert's text.
3   Daux (*Revue Archéologique* 17 (1941) 177); Robert (cited Tod I, 303f.), followed by Tod, read 'Taxilochos,' a Spartan division commander equivalent to
the Taxiarch.
4   'Leaders'; it is the normal Spartan term.
5   I.e. sell it, with its inhabitants, and give a tithe of the proceeds to the gods. Cf.
Hdt. 7.132.2.
6   This sentence may derive from the oath of the Amphictyonic states; see
Aeschines 2.115.
7   The last sentence is clearly not part of any original document.

58   The Number of the Athenian Dead at Plataea. 479 B.C.

Plutarch, *Aristeides* 19.5-6 (Cleidemus, *FGrHist* 323 F 22). Cf. Herodotus 9.70;
Plutarch, *Aristeides* 11.3-4.

F. Jacoby, *FGrHist* IIIb Suppl. 1.82f.; Bury–Meiggs 181-4.

Of those who struggled on behalf of Hellas there fell in all one thousand
three hundred sixty men. [6] Fifty-two of these were Athenians, all of

them from the tribe Aiantis, as Cleidemus says, it having fought most valiantly. That is why the men of Aiantis used to celebrate in honor of the Nymphs of Sphragidion[1] the sacrifice declared by the Pythian oracle for the victory. They take the money required from the public treasury.

1 See Pausanias 9.3.9 for the location, near Mt Cithaeron.

59   Greek Thank-Offering for Victory in the Persian War. 479 B.C.

Engraved on the bronze coils of the 'Serpent-Column.' Phocian writing, Delphi (though discovered in Istanbul).[1]

Tod I, no. 19, pp. 22-4; *GHI, no. 27, pp. 57-60; Jeffery, *LSAG* 102 and Plate 13.15. Cf. Herodotus 9.81; Thucydides 1.132.2-3; Pausanias 5.23.1-3 (for the names on the offering at Olympia); Plutarch, *Themistocles* 20.3.

ATL 3.95-100; P. A. Brunt, *Historia* 2 (1953) 146-8; Hignett, *Invasion* 435-8.

(Coil 1) *By these* [the] | war wals fought. | (2) Laced[aemonians,] | Athenians, | Corinthians, | (3) Tegeans, | Sicyonians, | Aeginetans, | (4) Megarians, | Epidaurians, | Erchomenians, | (5) Phleiasians, | Troezenians, | Hermionians, | (6) Tirynthians, | Plataeans, | Thespians, | (7) Mycenians, | Ceians, | Melians, | Tenians,[2] | (8) Naxians, | Eretrians, | Chalcidians, | (9) Styrians, | Haleians, | Potidaeans, | (10) Leucadians, | Anactorians, | Cythnians, | Siphnians,[2] | (11) Ambraciots, | Lepreans.

1 A golden tripod rested on this column until melted down by the Phocians about 354 B.C. during the Third Sacred War. The column remained at Delphi until brought to Constantinople by the Emperor Constantine.
2 This people was inscribed later.

60   Megarian Memorial of the Persian War. 479 B.C.

Limestone slab, writing of the fourth or fifth century A.D., near Megara.

Tod I, no. 20, pp. 24f. Cf. Herodotus 9.69 (Megarian action at Plataea); Pausanias 1.43.3.

H. T. Wade-Gery, *JHS* 53 (1933) 95-7; Tod I, no. 20; Hignett, *Invasion* 150, 338 n. 10.

The epitaph of those who died in the Persian War and who lie | here[1] as heroes, since it has been lost in the passage of time, Helladios the High-Priest had inscrlibed in honor of the fallen and of the city. Simonides | composed it.[2] || 'To foster the day of freedom for Hellas and for the Megarians / did we strive, and we received death as our fate, / some below Euboea and Pelion, where is / the precinct of holy Artemis the

5

10 Archeress; / some at Mount Mycale; some before Salamis, // [---]³ /
some on the Boeotian plain, who dared / to lay their hand on men who
fought from horses. / Our townsmen, [Megarians,]⁴ provided us this
15 honor around the altar / in the hospitable agora of the Nisaeans.'⁵ || Up
to our own day the city sacrifices a bull to the heroes.⁶

1 The memorial was actually a cenotaph.
2 The rest of the inscription (except for line 15) is an epigram in elegiac couplets;
   the lines coincide with the verses. It was virtually automatic to attribute Simoni-
   dean authorship to poetry of this date and type.
3 The pentameter which normally would follow the hexameter of line 10 was apparently omitted by the mason or by Helladios.
4 Added by Kaibel, since a word, as we know from the meter, has dropped out of
   the verse. Wade-Gery's addition yields: 'Our townsmen provided us this [col-
   lective] honor.'
5 Wade-Gery, emending the text, which reads: 'in the agora of the hospitable
   Nisaeans.'
6 The last line is in prose.

61 Pausanias, Regent of Sparta, and his Actions after the Victory at Plataea.

A: Pausanias' return to Byzantium. (1) Nepos, *Pausanias* 3.1-3; (2) Athenaeus
12.50, p. 536ab (Nymphis, *FGrHist* 432 F 9). Cf. Thucydides 1.128.3; 1.131.1.
B: Pausanias' expulsion from Byzantium. (1) Justin, *Epitoma* 9.1.3; (2) *Oxyrhynchus Papyri* 13.1610 F 6. Cf. Thucydides 1.131.1; Plutarch, *Kimon* 6.6; Diodorus
11.60.2. C: Collusion with helots. Aristotle, *Politics* 5.7.1307a. Cf. Thucydides
1.132.4; Nepos, *Pausanias* 3.6. D: His death: Pausanias 3.17.7-9. Cf. Thucydides
1.132-4; Diodorus 11.45; Plutarch, *Themistocles* 23.4, *Kimon* 6.7; and see no.
65B2. For Pausanias' actions in 478, see Thucydides 1.94, 1.128.5; Diodorus
11.44.1-3.

M. E. White, *JHS* (1964) 140-52; C. W. Fornara, *Historia* 15 (1966) 267-70; J. D.
Smart, *JHS* 87 (1967) 136-8; P. J. Rhodes, *Historia* 19 (1970) 387-400; Meiggs,
Empire 465-8; de Ste Croix, *Origins* 171-4; Bury-Meiggs 531.

A. Pausanias' return to Byzantium

(1) NEPOS, *PAUSANIAS* 3.1-3
But not long afterwards he returned of his own will¹ to the army and
there he revealed his plans in a fashion that was not clever but insane.
For he abandoned not only the customs of his country but altered even
his external appearance and dress. He made use of royal splendor and of
the clothing of the Medes. A Median and Egyptian bodyguard followed
him about. He dined in the Persian fashion more sumptuously than those
who were with him could endure. He gave no access for meeting him to

those who sought it; he made prideful answers and gave orders cruelly.
He was unwilling to return to Sparta but betook himself to Colonae, a
place in the region of the Troad. There he began to foment plans as
dangerous for his country as for himself.

(2) ATHENAEUS 12.50, p. 536ab
Nymphis of Heracleia in the sixth book of his *On My Native City* says:
'Pausanias, the victor over Mardonios at Plataea, the man who disregar-
ded Spartan customs and became arrogant, when staying at Byzantium,[2]
dared to write on the brazen bowl, dedicated to the gods whose statues
were set up at the mouth (of the passage leading to the Euxine Sea), and
which is even now in existence, that he himself had dedicated it. He added
this epigram, having lost all control of himself out of luxury and over-
weening pride: "As a remembrance of his excellence was this dedication
made to Poseidon the Lord / by Pausanias, ruler of broad Hellas, / at
the Euxine Sea, a Lacedaemonian by race, the son / of Kleombrotos, of
the ancient stem of Herakles." '

B. Pausanias' expulsion from Byzantium

(1) JUSTIN, *EPITOMA* 9.1.3
For this city (Byzantium) was first founded by Pausanias, the King of
the Spartans, and it was held (by him?) for seven years. Thereafter it
was under the power of the Lacedaemonians or the Athenians according as either was victorious.

(2) *OXYRHYNCHUS PAPYRI* 13.1610 F 6[3]
[-- from the point at which] | *we made our digression.* The A[the]|nians,
40 with K[i]mon | son of Miltiades as gen||eral, saile|d forth from Byzan-
ti|um with the all|ies (and) [Ei]on, the (city) on the | Str[ymo]n
45 (river), (which) the Persians h||eld, was captured[4] and | [Scyru]s, an
island which

(The fragment breaks off)

C. Collusion with helots. Aristotle, *Politics* 5.7.1307a

(The causes of discord in aristocracies arise) when someone is powerful
and is capable of becoming even more so, (and he will promote discord)
in order to become sovereign, just as Pausanias appears (to have done)
in Lacedaemonia – he who held the command in the war against the
Medes.

D. Pausanias' death. Pausanias 3.17.7–9

Next to the altar of the (goddess of) the Brazen House two statues of
Pausanias are standing – the man who held the command at (the battle

of) Plataea. I shall not speak to people who are aware of it of the special fate that befell him. For that which has been narrated by men of earlier times is sufficiently accurate. It is enough for me to follow up (their accounts). I have heard from a Byzantine that Pausanias was caught in his plotting and was the only man who supplicated (Athena of) the Brazen House in vain simply because he was unable to wash away a curse. [8] For when he was occupying himself at the Hellespont along with the fleet of the Lacedaemonians and the other Hellenes, he developed a lust for a Byzantine virgin. As soon as night came, those who were so commanded brought in Kleonike – for that was the girl's name. Then a noise awakened Pausanias when he was sleeping. For as she went to his side she inadvertently knocked down the lighted lamp. Inasmuch as Pausanias was self-conscious about his betrayal of Hellas and because of it was constantly upset and fearful, he then jumped up and struck the girl with his Persian sword. [9] It was impossible for Pausanias to avert (the) curse (arising from) this, though he attempted every kind of purification, supplication to Zeus Phyxios (God of Flight), and even went to the necromancers in Arcadian Phigalia. But he paid a proper penalty to Kleonike and the god. The Lacedaemonians, in fulfillment of a command from Delphi, made those bronze statues and pay honor to the spirit Epidotes ('the bountiful one'), because they say that it is this Epidotes who averts the wrath of the God of Suppliants arising from Pausanias.

1 Or, 'on his own authority': cf. Thuc. 1.128.3.
2 Cf. Herodotus 4.81.3; Thuc. 1.95, 1.130. It is unclear whether Nymphis' description applies to Pausanias' first or second tenure of Byzantium.
3 The fragment, which is probably an epitome of Ephorus (compare line 36 with Diod. 11.59.4–60), consists of all the lines translated.
4 What is in question is the date of Pausanias' expulsion. Some assume that Kimon's departure from Byzantium presupposes that Pausanias had been removed forcibly from the city at a date prior to the capture of Eion and Scyros, i.e. before 476/5 (rather than in 472/1); see no. 62.

62 Attempts at Colonizing Ennea Hodoi in Thrace. 476/5–437/6 B.C.

Scholiast to Aeschines 2.31 (Blass=34 Dindorf). Cf. Thucydides 1.100.2-3; 4.102.2.

ATL 3.106–10; Gomme, etc., *HCT* 1.296f., 3.573; Meiggs, *Empire* 416; W. E. Thompson, *Phoros* 149; Bury–Meiggs 210.

Aeschin. 2.31: As to the original possession of the territory and of the so-called Ennea Hodoi (Nine Ways). . . .
    Scholion: Ennea Hodoi. The Athenians met with misfortune nine times at the so-called Nine Ways, which is a place in Thrace now named

Chersonesus. They suffered misfortune because of the curses of Phyllis, who loved Demophon[1] and expected him to return in order to fulfill his promises to her. After going to the place nine times, since he did not come, she prayed for the Athenians to suffer misfortune that number of times at the place. The disasters occurred as follows: first, when Lysistratos, Lykourgos, and Kratinos campaigned against Eion[2] on the (river) Strymon, (the Athenians) were destroyed by the Thracians after they seized Eion, in the archonship of Phaidon (476/5) at Athens. Second, the klerouchs with Leagros,[3] in the archonship of Lysikrates.[4] . . . When Hagnon,[5] the Athenian, colonized Ennea Hodoi, he named it Amphipolis, in the archonship of Euthymenes (437/6) at Athens.

1 Son of Theseus.
2 See no. 61B2.
3 A correction of 'Leagoras.'
4 An apparent error for Lysistratos (467/6) or Lysanias (466/5) or Lysitheos (465/4). Seven Athenian defeats, between 425 and 360 B.C., are then listed here.
5 Cf. Thuc. 4.102.3.

63   Regulations of the Teians. 475–470 B.C.
Marble stelai near Teos (known from copies).

Buck, no. 3, pp. 186f.; *GHI, no. 30, pp. 62-6.

(A)

Whoever makes drugs that are poison|ous (for use) against the Teian|s as a community or against a private citizen, t|hat man shall die, both
5 h|l|imself and his family. | If into the land of Teos anyone p|revents grain from being imported | by any pretext or device, either b|y sea
10 or by the mainlan|l|d, or, after it is imported, re-export it, th|at man shall die, both himself and his family.

(B)

[---] | [--] in it [--][1] | Whichever Teian (by whom) the *Public Examiner*
5 (Euthynos) | or Aisymnetes[2] [-6-][3] or || who rises up against [-6-] | [-5-][4] he shall die, both himself and his famil|y. Whoever in future is
10 Aisym|netes in Teos or in the territory of Te|l|os [-6-] | [--- know-| ingly] *betrays* [...] the *ci|ty* [and territory] of the Tei|ans, or the men
15 [on the] is|l|land[5] or on the *sea* in the | *future* [or the] | Aroian *fort* (?); [or (whoever) in the] | future *commits treason* [or] *brig|andage,*
20 or takes brigands under his || protection or commits piracy, or t|akes pirates under his protection, with ful|l| knowledge, (men) who from the

territory of Teos or from the s|ea bear off plunder, or [(whoever)
25 hatches some] e|vil plot against the T[ei]|lan community, with full know-
ledge, (in collusion) either *with* | Hellenes or with barbari|ans,[6] that
man shall die, both him|self and his family. | If those serving as Timou-
30 choi[7] || do not have the curse invoke|d when by the statue of Dynamis
there is seate|d (the crowd for) the festival in (the months of) Anthes-
35 terio|n and Herakleon | and Dios, the curs||e shall apply to them. Who-
ever (takes) the stel|ai on which the curse is wri|tten and breaks them or
40 cuts the let|ters[8] out or makes them illeg|ible, he shall di||e, both him-
self and | [his] family.

1 Traces of words are preserved on these lines.
2 Normally, an elected and temporary 'tyrant' (Aristotle, *Politics* 3.14.1285a31).
  The implication of line 8, if not line 4, is that the official is here regularly elected.
3 '[is given] *aid*': Bannier (cited *GHI*, p. 63).
4 The two copies which are all that remains of this inscription provide different
  and contradictory readings. In one copy, '*the Ai|symnetes*' can be restored here;
  the other suggests '*or oppos|es.*' Reading the latter, another restoration than that
  given for line 4 (note 3) is needed – the title of the official not to be opposed.
5 Perhaps the island Aspis, otherwise called Arkonesos, lying between Teos and
  Lebedos (Strabo 14.643).
6 'Presumably Persians are intended': *GHI*, p. 65.
7 Little is known of these officials (whom Hiller, *SIG* no. 38, p. 42, n. 17, supposed to be officeholders in general); see G. Gottlieb, *Timuchen* (Heidelberg
  1967).
8 Literally, 'Phoenician things'; cf. Herodotus 5.58.

64 Hieron's Thank-Offering for the Victory at Cumae. 474 B.C.
Two Etruscan helmets of bronze. (A) Olympia; (B) from the Alpheios
River. Doric Greek, (A) probably metrical.

A: Jeffery, *LSAG*, no. 7, p. 275 and Plate 51; *GHI, no. 29, p. 62. B: G. Daux,
BCH 84 (1960) 721, with photo. Cf. Pindar, *Pythian Odes* 1.71ff. (no. 52 above);
Diodorus 11.51; E. A. Freeman, *The history of Sicily* (Oxford 1891) 2.250f.;
Bury–Meiggs 191.

(A)

Hieron, son of Deinomenes, | and the Syracusans | to Zeus: Etruscan
spoils from Cumae.

(B)

Hieron, son of Deinomenes, | and the Syracusans | to Zeus, from the
Etruscans, from Cu[mae].

65   Themistokles' Ostracism and Flight to Persia. 473 B.C. or after

A: Themistokles' ostracism. (1) Aristodemus, *FGrHist* 104 F 6.1; (2) Cicero, *De Amicitia* 12.42. Cf. Thucydides 1.135.3; Diodorus 11.55.1-3; Plutarch, *Themistocles* 22-3. B: Trial for medism and exile. (1) *Lexicon Rhetoricum Cantabrigiense*, p. 337, 15 N (Caecilius, Theophrastus; Craterus, *FGrHist* 342 F 11); (2) Scholiast to Aristophanes, *Knights* 84 (425/4). Cf. Thucydides 1.135-8; Diodorus 11.55-6; Plutarch, *Themistocles* 21, 24-9.

R. J. Lenardon, *Historia* 8 (1959) 23-48; W. G. Forrest, *CQ* 54 (1960) 221-41; Kagan, *Outbreak* 58-61; D. W. Knight, *Some studies in Athenian politics*, Historia Einzelschrift 13 (1970) 41-4; P. J. Rhodes, *Historia* 18 (1970) 387-400; de Ste Croix, *Origins* 169-79; Bury-Meiggs 206-8; Sealey, *History* 255.

A. Themistokles' ostracism

(1) ARISTODEMUS, *FGRHIST* 104 F 6.1
Themistokles, envied because of his transcendent intelligence and excellence, was banished by the Athenians and came to stay at Argos.

(2) CICERO, *DE AMICITIA* 12.42
Who was more famous in Greece, or who more powerful, than Themistocles? After he had, as general, freed Greece from slavery in the Persian war, and because he had been sent into exile because of envy, he did not tolerate the injustice of an ungrateful country as he should have, but he did the same thing which twenty years before (491 B.C.) Coriolanus had done.[1]

B. Themistokles' banishment and flight

(1) *LEXICON RHETORICUM CANTABRIGIENSE*, P. 337, 15 N
Eisangelia (is a process directed) against new and unwritten offenses. This is the opinion of Caecilius. Theophrastus in the fourth book of his *On Laws* says that (the legal process) comes about if an orator tries to dissolve the democracy, or does not advocate the best policy because he is receiving money, or if someone betrays a place or ships or an army on land; or if someone goes over to the enemy or † is conquered amongst them †[2]; or if someone engages in a campaign with them or takes bribes. Consistent with the remarks of Theophrastus is the eisangelia against Themistokles which was introduced, according to Craterus, by Leobotes, the son of Alkmeon of the deme Agryle.[3]

(2) SCHOLIAST TO ARISTOPHANES, *KNIGHTS* 84
Aristoph. *Knights* 83f.: (Nikias) The best thing for us is to drink bull's blood. / For the death Themistokles died is preferable.

Scholion: Themistokles (is the man who) destroyed the barbarians in the sea-battle off Salamis and then, banished by the Athenians for treason on a false charge, fled to Artaxerxes, the son of Xerxes, and received the greatest honors from him, such that he obtained three cities for his sauce, bread and drink: Magnesia, Myous, and Lampsacus. He had announced to the King that he would enslave Hellas if he received an armed force. But when he arrived at Magnesia with the army, he judged that it would be an act of guilt on his part if the Hellenes who had been preserved because of him should become enslaved to the barbarians because of him. Using the excuse that he wished to perform sacrifice and sacred rites to the Artemis called Leukophryis, he put the vial under the bull and, drawing off the blood, he gulped it down and immediately died.[4] But some say that Themistokles was conscious of being incapable of accomplishing for the King what he had announced (he would do), and thus came to the choice of death.

1   Whether Cicero's date applies to the ostracism of Themistokles or his banishment is disputed, and we cannot be sure how precise Cicero's date is.
2   The phrase between daggers is corrupt.
3   Leobotes' father's name makes it virtually certain that the Alkmeonidai were involved in this attack.
4   The same superstition is reflected in Herodotus' tale (3.15.3) of the suicide of Psammenitis of Egypt. How the belief originated is unknown, but Aristotle, who accepted it (*History of Animals* 3.19), supposed that the blood coagulated so swiftly that the drinker was choked.

66   Political Expulsions from Miletus. 470–440 B.C.
Marble base, stoichedon,[1] Miletus.

Tod I, no. 35, pp. 67f.; *GHI*, no. 43, pp. 105–7. Cf. [Xenophon], *Athenaion Politeia* 3.11 (no. 105); Nicolaus of Damascus, *FGrHist* 90 F 53.

G. Glotz, *CRAI* 1906, 511–29, who associated this inscription with no. 92 (450 or thereafter); J. P. Barron, *JHS* 82 (1962) 1–6 (443 or 442); Meiggs, *Empire* 562–5 (452 or earlier).

[-21- the sons[2] of N]ympharetos, and Alki[mos | and K]resphontes,[3] [the] sons of Stratonax, shall suffer *blood-guilt* | [banishment,] both they themselves *and* their descendants, and by whomsoever any one of them *might be* | *killed*, one hundred staters shall be given to him from
5   the || [property] of the family of Nym[phare]tos. The Epimenioi[4] in office when a claim is made | *by the* slayers shall pay the money. If (they do) not, they themselves | *shall be liable to pay* (the fine[5]). If the city *should get* (the condemned men) *into its power*, they shall be put to death | by the Epimenioi in whose term of office they are seized. If

they do not put them to | death, they shall *each* be liable to pay fifty
10   staters. ‖ The (presiding) Epimenios, if he does not put (the matter) up
for decision, shall owe a fine of one hundred staters. | Successive boards
of Epimenioi shall always proceed according to this decree. | Otherwise,
they shall be liable to the same penalty.

1   The ends of some lines have blank spaces while others continue on to the right-
hand side of the base in order that the lines may end without arbitrary division
of words or natural parts of words.
2   Or 'son.'
3   The names suggest that the family was Neleid (which had held the kingship in
Miletus), for, according to the scholiast (B) to *Iliad* 11.692, the son of Neleus
was named Alkimos; see especially Nicolaus of Damascus, op. cit.
4   'Monthly officers.' Apparently the presiding officers of the state, monthly officials like the Athenian prytaneis, though it is also possible that they were religious officials.
5   I.e. the Epimenioi would themselves be penalized by a fine identical in amount
to that which they were obligated to pay qualified claimants. Cf. no. 169, lines
4ff. I thank Katrina Avery for the suggestion.

67   The Messenian Revolt. 469-60 *or* 465/4-460/59 *or* 465/4-455/4 B.C.

A: Scholiast to Aristophanes, *Lysistrata* 1138 (412/11) (Philochorus, *FGrHist* 328
F 117), 1144; B: Pausanias 3.11.8; C: Pausanias 4.24.5-6. Cf. Thucydides 1.101.3,
1.128.1; Pausanias 1.29.8; Diodorus 11.63-5 (under the year 469/8), 84.7-8;
Plutarch, *Kimon* 16-17.

Gomme, etc., *HCT* 1.401-11 (465/4-460/59); *ATL* 3.158-80 (464-61); N. G. L.
Hammond, *Historia* 4 (1955) 371f. (469-60); Jacoby, *FGrHist* IIIb Suppl. 1.455-
61; D. W. Reece, *JHS* 82 (1962) 111-20 (ended 455); P. Deane, *Thucydides'
dates* (Ontario 1972) 18-30 (464-455/4); J. R. Cole, *GRBS* 15 (1974) 369-85;
Bury-Meiggs 213; Sealey, *History* 255-7.

A. Scholiast to Aristophanes, *Lysistrata* 1138, 1144

Lys. 1137-44: And then, O Laconians - for I turn to you - / do you
not know that Perikleidas once came here / and as a suppliant of Athe-
140   nians sat, a Laconian, // at the altars, pale in his dark red cloak, / begging
for an army. At that time Messenia / pressed on you and the god was
shaking (the earth) as well. / But coming with four thousand hoplites /
Kimon saved all Lacedaemonia.

Scholion at 1138: Those who have compiled the local histories of
Athens relate this about the Lacedaemonians. Philochorus says that the
Athenians also acquired the hegemony because of the disasters which
overwhelmed Lacedaemonia.

Scholion at 1144: Kimon, in the twelfth[1] year after the battle at

Plataea (468/7). This was in the archonship of Theagenides. A part of (Mount) Taygetos broke away and (with it) the music-hall, other buildings, and most of the houses. The Messenians rebelled and began to make war, and the helots rose up – until Kimon came because of the (Spartan) supplication and saved them.

B. Pausanias 3.11.8

The fourth time (Tisamenos) fought against the helots from the Isthmus[2] who went in rebellion to Ithome. Not all the helots rebelled, but rather the Messenian body, which had separated itself off from the ancient helots . . . . At that time the Lacedaemonians allowed the insurgents to depart under truce in obedience to Tisamenos and the Delphic oracle.

C. Pausanias 4.24.5-7

It happened that the Messenians who had been caught in the land and who were forcibly made to belong to the helots later rebelled in the seventy-ninth Olympiad (464), when Xenophon of Corinth was (Olympic) victor, and when Archimedes[3] was Archon at Athens. They found this chance to rebel: some Lacedaemonians who were condemned to death on a certain charge fled to Tainaros as suppliants. The college of Ephors thereupon dragged them away from the altar and put them to death. [24.6] Since the Spartans took no account of the suppliants the anger of Poseidon came upon them, and the god hurled their entire city down to the ground. At this catastrophe, all of the helots who originally had been Messenians went in rebellion to Mount Ithome. The Lacedaemonians called their allies in against them, especially Kimon son of Miltiades, their proxenos, and Athenian forces. But when the Athenians had arrived, (the Spartans) seem to have suspected them of possibly intending to foment revolution, and because of this suspicion to have not long afterwards sent them back from Ithome. [24.7] The Athenians, because they were aware of the suspicion of the Lacedaemonians against themselves both became allies of the Argives because of it and gave Naupactus to the Messenians besieged in Ithome after they had retired from it under truce. (The Athenians) had taken it from the Locrians, called Ozolian, who abutted Aetolia. The strength of the place (i.e. Ithome) secured the Messenians' departure – as well as the response of the Pythia to the Lacedaemonians that truly a judgment would come upon them if they sinned against the suppliant of Zeus of Ithome.

---

1   The date is apparently corrupt. Jacoby substitutes 'the eighteenth year after the battle of Plataea' (i.e. 462/1). See *FGrHist* IIIb Suppl. 1.455ff.

2 Cf. Herodotus 9.35.2, which states that the fourth contest of Tisamenos was 'against the Messenians at the Isthmus.' The word *Isthmus* has been emended, in the text of Herodotus, to *Ithome.*
3 The name is attested elsewhere as Archedemides (archon 464/3).

68 Athenian Relations with Phaselis. 469–450 *or* after 428/7 B.C.
Marble stele, Ionic writing, stoichedon, Athens.

IG I² 16+ (I³ 10); Wade-Gery, *Essays* 180–200 (469–462); *GHI*, no. 31, pp. 66–9; *Bradeen and McGregor, *Studies* 116.

G. E. M. de Ste Croix, *CQ* 55 (1961) 100–8; H. B. Mattingly, *PACA* 7 (1964) 37–9; R. Sealey, *CP* 59 (1964) 16f.; R. Seager, *Historia* 15 (1966) 509f.; Meiggs, *Empire* 231f.; C. W. Fornara, *CQ* 29 (1979) 49–52.

Resolved by the Boule and the *Pe⎸ople*, Akamanti[s] held the prytany,
5 ⎸ [...]sippos[1] was Secretary, Ne⎸[...]edes[2] presided, Leo[n] *ma⎸⎸de the motion. For the* Phaselites this dec⎸ree shall be *inscribed.* Whatever *legal dispute* arises at Ath[ens] ⎸ [against][3] a Phaselite, [at] Athe[n⎸s
10 the] *suit* shall be tried *i⎸⎸n* (the court of) [the] *Polemarch,* just as ⎸ [with the] Ch⎸[ians, and] in no place else whatever. [As to th⎸e other cases] arising from legal disputes, ⎸ [the present] mutual legal arrange-
15 ments with Phal[selis] will *be* applicable in litigation. The ⎸⎸ [--10--][4] shall be abolished. If [a⎸ny other] magistrate accepts a [l⎸lawsuit against] any Phaselite ⎸ [-8-][5], *if he* finds again⎸st (him), [the judgment] shall be
20 *void.* [I⎸⎸f anyone violates] this de⎸cree, let him [be liable to pay] ten thousand dr⎸achmas (to be) *consecrated* to Athena. *T⎸his decree* shall
25 be inscrib⎸ed *by the Secretary* of the Boule ⎸⎸ [on a stele of] *marble* and [he shall] *set it* ⎸ up [on the Akropolis] at the *expense* of th⎸e [Phaselites.] *vv* ⎸ *vacat*

1 [Ona]sippos and [Mna]sippos are possible names.
2 The first letter of this name (N) could instead be the last letter of the preceding word (so Bradeen–McGregor). Hence E⎸[...]edes is possible. The name Epimedes has been suggested.
3 The preposition that must be restored here (*pros*) implies that the measure is directed at Phaselite defendants (Fornara), though the phrase has traditionally been translated neutrally: '*legal dispute* . . . [involving] a Phaselite.'
4 '[provisions for appeal]': Dittenberger (cited *GHI*, p. 67).
5 '[contrary to this (decree)]': Photiades (cited *GHI*, p. 66); '[in Athens]': Wilhelm (cited *GHI*, p. 67).

69 The Ban against Arthmios of Zeleia. 469–461 *or* about 450 B.C.

Scholiast to Aristeides 2.287 Dindorf (Craterus, *FGrHist* 342 F 14). Cf. Demosthenes 9.41; Aeschines 3.258; Deinarchus 2.24.

M. Cary, *CQ* 29 (1935) 177ff. (469–461); R. Meiggs, *JHS* 63 (1943) 23ff. (about 450), *Empire* 508–12.

Aristeides 2.287: The same spirit is found on the stele which they set up later than this[1] and which stated the following: Arthmios son of Pythonax of Zeleia shall be without rights and be the enemy of the People of the Athenians, both himself and his family, because he brought the gold of the Medes into the Peloponnesus.

Scholion: There was a certain Craterus who compiled all the votes of the People passed in Hellas. This decree inscribed on the stele was proposed by Kimon; though Aristeides says it is by Themistokles.

1 The Persian embassy to the Athenians in 479 B.C.

70 A Halicarnassian Law concerning Disputed Property. 465–450 B.C.
Marble stele, Ionic Greek, nonstoichedon, Halicarnassus.

SIG, no. 45, pp. 52–4; Buck, no. 2, pp. 184–6; *GHI*, no. 32, pp. 69–72.

This was determined by the joint meeting | of the Halicarnassians and the Salmaki|tians[1] and Lygdamis[2] in the sacred | Agora in the month
5 of Hermaion, on the fif||th day from its beginning, when Leon was Pry|tanis, the son of Oassassis, an|d Sa[ryss]ollos son of Thekyilos[3] was in *char|ge of the temple. For* the Recorders:[4] There shall be no
10 *trans|ferral* of land or house||s to the Recorders when Apollo|nides son of Lygdamis is Reco|rder and Panamyes son of Kasbo|llis (is Recorder),
15 and when the Salmakitian Rec|orders are Megabates son of A||phyasis and Phormion son of P[a]|nyassis.[5] If anyone wishes to bring su|it about land or houses, let him *bring* his acti|on within eighteen months
20 from *when* | this decision was made. According to law, just *a||s* at present, shall the jurors (dikasts) *take* the oath. *What* | the Recorders know[6] | shall be binding. If anyone thereafter | brings action, after the
25 period of the | eighteen months, an oath shall be taken by t||he possessor of the land or the hous|es, and the oath shall be administered by the jurors after ei|ght obols have been paid to them. The oath shall | be (administered) in the presence of the adversary. | Possession of land and
30 houses shall be secure for those || who held possession at the time when Apollonides and Pana|myes were Recorders, unless they late|r sold it. As to this law, | if anyone wishes to invalidate it or to make a proposa||l
35 by vote so as to repeal this la||w, let his property be sold | and (the proceeds) be consecrated to Apollo and the man h|imself be in exile forever. If he should not poss|ess (property) worth ten staters, he shall
40 himself be s|old for exportation (as a slave) and have no man||ner of

return to Halicarn⎮assus. Any of the Halicarnassians in their e⎮ntirety shall be allowed, if he does not violate these terms a⎮s sanctioned by
45 oath and as record⎮led in the temple of Apollo, to bring suit (according to this decree).

1 Salmakis apparently was a Carian settlement which retained its own government though it also associated itself with Halicarnassus.
2 Apparently the tyrant. Cf. the *Suda*, s.v. 'Herodotus': '(Herodotus) was the son of Lyxes and Dryo of Halicarnassus, a noble, whose brother was Theodoros. He went to Samos because of Lygdamis who became the third tyrant of Halicarnassus from (the line of) Artemisia. For Pisindelis was the son of Artemisia and Lygdamis (was) the son of Pisindelis. . . . Returning to Halicarnassus and expelling the tyrant, . . . (Herodotus went to Thurii [see no. 108] because he was envied).' However, the name of Lygdamis was not rare in Halicarnassus, and the relationship of the tyrant Lygdamis to Artemisia is uncertain (see *GHI*, p. 72).
3 These names testify to the admixture of the Greeks with the inhabitants of Asia Minor. (Cf. the names of Herodotus' parents as given by the *Suda* [note 2].)
4 Mnemones or 'rememberers.' According to Aristotle, *Politics* 6.8.1321b, these officials were empowered 'to register private contracts and verdicts from the courts.' In this case, their purview was wider.
5 Megabates is a good Persian name (cf. Herodotus 5.32). A Panyassis, according to the *Suda* s.v., was an epic poet and the uncle of Herodotus. Duris of Samos (in a difficult passage: *FGrHist* 76 F 64) claimed him as a Samian citizen (by way of immigration), just as he claimed Herodotus was a Thurian. Some suppose that the Panyassis named in this incription was the alleged uncle of Herodotus.
6 I.e. judge to be the case on the basis of their knowledge.

71 Regulations Imposed by the Athenians on Erythrae. Middle 460s *or* 453/2 B.C.

From a copy of a now lost inscription found at Athens, probably stoichedon.

A: *IG* I^2 10 (I^3 14); B: **ATL* 2.D10, pp. 54-7 and Figure 4 on p. 38 (453/2); *GHI*, no. 40, pp. 89-94 (early 450s on).

L. Highby, *Klio* Beiheft 36 (1936) 33-5 (middle 460s); *ATL* 3.254-8; Meiggs, *Empire* 579f.; Bury-Meiggs 210; Sealey, *History* 275f. Other inscriptions, rightly or wrongly, have been associated with this decree: *IG* I^2 11, 12/13a (I^3 15), which seem to belong in the 460s.[1]

A. *IG* I^2 10

[-*c. 7*-] presided, L[-- made the motion. The sacrificial victims] ⎮ *shall be brought* [by the Erythrae]ans [in their entirety] *to* [the] *Great* Panathenaia (and they shall have the) *value* [of not ⎮ less] than three mnas, and *distribution shall be made* to *those* Erythraeans *who are pre-*

sent | [of the meat by the] Hieropoioi (who shall dispense) [a drachma
5   to each]. *If* [they bring || the victims but (they are)] *less* in value *than
three mnas according to* [what has been laid down,] *purchase shall be
made* [by the | Hieropoioi] *of victims,* [and] the *People of the* [Er]y-
[thra]eans [shall owe one thousand] *drach|mas.* [It shall be allowed] to
anyone who wishes [to take away a portion] *of the meat.* Among the
Erythraeans *lo|ts shall be drawn* for a Boule of one hundred and *twenty*
men. The man [all|otted (the office) shall undergo scrutiny] in *the*
E[ry]th[rae]an Boule. ⟨No one shall⟩[2] be allowed to *serve as member of*
10   *the Boule* || (who is) less than *thirty* years *of age.* Prosecution shall lie
[agains|t those] *found guilty,* and they shall not be members of the
Boule for the space *of* four years. *The all|otment* shall be carried out
and the establishment of *the* Boule (effected) *for the present by the*
[Episk|opoi (Inspectors)] and [the] *Phrour|arch* (Garrison Commander),
in future by the Boule and the *Phrour|arch. Each* future *member of the*
15   *Boule at* [E]ry[th]rae shall, [before] he *enters* [the Boul|le,] take an
oath [to Z]eus *and* Apollo and Deme[ter,] *calling down dest|ruction*
[upon himself if he swears falsely] *and* [destruction] *upon his children.*
The oath shall be [sw|orn] over *burning sacrifices.* The [member of]
the Boule shall act in the Boule according [to the] | *existing* [law].
Otherwise, he shall be *liable to a fine* of [one thousand drachmas] |
20   [and he shall pay] no less [to the] Erythraean People. || [The] Boule
shall swear [the following]: 'I shall deliberate *as best I can* [an|d] *as
justly* (as I can) for the Erythraean People and (the People) of the Athe-
nians and their [all|lies] *and* I shall not *rebel* from the People of the
Athenians or from [th|e] allies of the Athenians, either on my own
initiative *nor shall I be persuaded* (to do so) *by anyone else.* | [Nor
shall I desert,] *either on my own initiative* nor [shall I be persuaded] *by
25   anyone else,* [not anyone.] || [Nor] shall I *receive back* any *of the
exiles* either [on my own initiative] nor | *shall I be persuaded* [by any-
one else. Of those] *who fled* [to the] Medes, without *the* [assent of
the | Athe]nians and of the *People,* I shall *not* banish (those) who re-
main (in Erythrae) [without] *the* [ass|ent] *of the* Athenians and [the]
People. If any [Erythrae]an kills | another Erythraean [[aean]] he shall
30   be put to death if he is *judged guilty.* [If ban|lishment] *is the sentence,*
he shall be exiled from *all the* Athenian *alliance* [a|nd his] property
shall become the public property of the Erythraeans. If *someone is*
[caught be|traying [[..]][3] the [city] of the Erythraeans to the tyrants,
he shall [with | impunity] be put to death, (he) [and the] children
sprung from *him, unless* [-6-] | [-14-][4] *having* [the] children sprung
35   from *him shall reveal*[5] [to the People || of the] Erythraeans and [the
(People of the)] Athenians. The property [of the convic|ted man] *shall
be declared in its entirety* [by his] children [and they shall have] *half,*

[the rest to be] con|*fiscated.* In *the same way* [if someone is convicted
... the] *People* of the Athenians [or | the] *garrison which* [[-7-]]⁶ at
Erythrae [---] | [.....] the *Phrourarch* [and] *the* Athenian [garrison
40 (?) --] || [---]⁷

B. *ATL* 2.D10

[Resolved by the Boule and the People, -c.8- held the prytany, ...] |
[....] presided, L[ysi]k[rates⁸ was Archon (453/2). Judgment of the
Commissioners. The Er|ythraea]ns *shall bring wheat to* [the] *Great
Panathenaia* (which is) *worth* [not l|ess] than three mnas and *distribu-*
5 *tion shall be made* to *those* Erythraeans *who are present* [of the w|lheat
by the]Hieropoioi *of half a chous⁹ to each. If* [they bring le|ss] *in value
than three mnas, they* (the Hieropoioi) *shall, in accordance with this
order, purchase* [whea|t and the E]rythraean [People] *shall* owe ten
mnas. | [But it shall be lawful] for any Erythraean who wishes [to pro-
vide the wheat.] *B|y* lot *there shall be a* Boule *consisting* of one hun-
10 dred and *twenty men.* The men [all|lotted (the office) shall undergo
examination] in *the* Boule and it shall [not] be lawful for *a foreigner to
serve as member of the Boule* | [nor] (for anyone) less than *thirty* years
of age. Prosecution shall lie [against t|hose] *found guilty.* (No one)
shall be a member of the Boule [twice] *within* four years. *The al|lot-
ment* shall be carried out and the establishment of the *present Boule*
shall be effected by *the* [Episk|opoi] and [the] *Phrourarch,* in future,
15 by the Boule and the *Phrour||arch* [not] *less than thirty days before
the term of office expires* [for the Boul|e]. (Its members) shall take
oath by [Z]eus and Apollo and Deme[ter,] *calling destruction down
upon themselves* | [if they swear falsely]¹⁰ *and destruction* on their
children. [The oath shall be swo|rn] *over burning sacrifices.* [The]
Boule [shall burn in sacrifice nothing less | than a cow as victim.]
20 *Otherwise,* it shall be liable to a fine of [one thousand drachma|ls; and
whenever the] *People take their oath,* the People *shall burn* no less. |
[The following] shall be sworn *by the Boule:* 'I shall deliberate *as best
[I can a|nd as justly (as I can)]* for the Erythraean People and (the
People of the) Athenians and their | [allies] *and I shall not rebel* from
the People of the Athenians or from [t|he] allies of the Athenians,
either on my own initiative *nor shall I be persuaded* (to do so) *by any-
25 one else,* || *nor shall I desert,* either on my own initiative nor [shall I
be persuaded] *by anyone else* [nor shall I e|ver] receive back any of the
[exiles] either [on my own initiative nor] | *shall I be persuaded* [by
anyone else, (namely, of) those who fled to the] Medes, without (the
permission) *of the Boule of the* | Athenians and *the People. Nor* shall I
banish *any of those* who remain (in Erythrae) [without] (the consent

of) *the* [Bo|ule] *of the* Athenians and the People. If any [Erythraean]
30   kills || another Er[ythraean,] he shall be put to death *if he is judged
guilty*; [if exile] | *is his sentence,* he shall be exiled from *all the* Athe-
nian *alliance* [and h|is] property *shall become the public property* of
the Erythraeans. If *someone is* [caught be|traying] the [city of the]
Erythraeans to the tyrants, he | shall be put to death [with impunity,
35   (he) and the] children sprung from *him.* [If it is evil|dent that his]
children *are friendly* [to the Peopl|e of the] Erythraeans and [to the
(People of the)] Athenians, [they are to be spared] and his property *i|n
its entirety shall be declared by the children* [and they shall take] *half*
[and] the [rest shall be con|fiscated.] The [Phrourarch] of the Athe-
nians *shall establish* [the nec|essary] *garrison* [everywhere] at Erythrae
[-21-] [11]

1   The copy of this inscription, which we know of only through another copy, is
    of poor quality. Editors have been led increasingly to depart from it in the
    effort to supply a more or less continuous text. Brackets and/or underlinings
    (often) therefore indicate not gaps in the copy itself but letters which require
    radical transformation in order to yield a required or desired meaning. The two
    versions of the copy here presented indicate the comparatively wide range of
    interpretation it permits.
2   Hiller's addition (in *IG* I[2]).
3   Letters disruptive of Hiller's context, which he assumed erroneous.
4   The letters of the copy seemed unintelligible to Hiller.
5   The verb stands in line 35.
6   See note 4.
7   Though the copy continues for another five lines, supplements are without
    substantive value.
8   It should be pointed out (for what it is worth) that the dotted k is incompa-
    tible with the mark in the copy, which is not a mere vertical but a vertical with
    the beginning of a horizontal joined to it at the top, thus suggesting G or T as
    possibilities. No such archon is available. But the date of the inscription does
    not suggest that an archon's name would have been mentioned in it.
9   A *chous* contained 12 kotylai=6 pints.
10 A gap of six letter spaces (ignored by *ATL*) is indicated at this point in the
    copy.
11 See note 7.

72   Egypt Rebels from Persia. After 464 B.C.

Photius, *Bibliotheca* 40ab (Ctesias, *The Persian History, FGrHist* 688 F 14.36f.);
cf. Herodotus 7.7; Thucydides 1.104, 1.109-10; Diodorus 11.71.3-6, 74f., 77. Cf.
nos. 77, 78. Photius provides an epitome of Ctesias' history.

H. D. Westlake, *Essays on the Greek historians and Greek history* (Manchester
1969) 61-73; J. Libourel, *AJP* 92 (1971) 605-15; Meiggs, *Empire* 473-6; Bury-
Meiggs 219; Sealey, *History* 269-72.

[36] Egypt rebels. Inaros a Libyan and another person, an Egyptian, foment the revolt. Preparations are made for war. The Athenians also send forty ships at his (Inaros') request. Artaxerxes himself prepares to take the field, but since his friends advise against it he sends his brother Achaimenides with an army of four hundred thousand foot and 80 ships. Inaros joins battle with Achaimenides and the Egyptians win. Achaimenides is struck by Inaros and dies, and his corpse is sent to Artaxerxes. Inaros was also victorious by sea. Charitimides, the admiral in command of the 40[1] ships from Athens, distinguished himself. Of fifty Persian ships 20 were taken with their crew and thirty were destroyed. [37] Then Megabyzos is sent against Inaros bringing, in addition to the preceding army, a force of two hundred thousand foot and 200 ships commanded by Horiskos. Thus, apart from the ships, the rest of the force totalled five hundred thousand men. For at Achaimenides' death, one hundred thousand of the 400,000 men he led also perished. The fighting thus becomes fierce and many fall on both sides, though the Egyptians suffer more. Megabyzos wounds Inaros in the thigh and routs him. The Persians win overwhelmingly. Inaros flees to Byblos – this is a fortified city in Egypt – together with those Hellenes who did not perish along with Charitimides in the battle.

1 Diod. 11.74.3 gives the number as two hundred.

73 Spartan Aid to Thebes. After 464 B.C.

Justin, *Epitoma* 3.6.10; cf. Diodorus 11.81.2.

Kagan, *Outbreak* 89f.; Meiggs, *Empire* 475.

Then, summoned back to the Messenian War, the Lacedaemonians, so as not to leave the Athenians unengaged in the intervening period, agreed with the Thebans to restore to them the hegemony of Boeotia which they had lost in the time of the Persian War, on condition that they take up war against Athens.

74 Perikles' Oratory. About 461–429 B.C.

A: Scholiast to Aristophanes, *Acharnians* 530 (426/5) (Eupolis F 94 Kock; cf. Diodorus 12.40.6). B: Aristotle, *Rhetoric* 1.7.34.1365a; 3.4.3.1407a; 3.10.7.1411a; C: Plutarch, *Precepts of Statecraft* 5 (*Moralia* 802c). Cf. Thucydides 2.65; Plato, *Phaedrus* 269e–270a; Plutarch, *Perikles* 7, 8, 15; Bury–Meiggs 215; Sealey, *History* 301.

A. Scholiast to Aristophanes, *Acharnians* 530

Aristoph. *Acharnians* 530: Then Perikles the Olympian . . .

Scholion: . . . Eupolis (writes as follows) in his *Demes* (412 B.C.): He was the most powerful orator among men. / Whenever he came forward to speak, like great runners, / he beat the orators in speaking by ten 5 feet. / But though you call him swift, in addition to that speed, // a kind of persuasion rested on his lips. / And so he mesmerized (his audience) and was the only orator / to leave the sting inside those who heard him.

B. Aristotle, *Rhetoric*

1.7.34.1365a: And the greatest part of what is great (is rhetorically effective). Thus Perikles in the funeral oration, (when he said that) the youth had been removed from the city just as if the spring had been removed from the year.[1]

3.4.3.1407a: And Perikles (in his speech) against the Samians compared them to children who take the morsel (of food) but go on crying. And against the Boeotians (he said) that they were like oaks. For just as they are chopped down by themselves,[2] so are the Boeotians, fighting among each other.

3.10.7.1411a: And Perikles bade them remove Aegina, the eyesore of the Piraeus.

C. Plutarch, *Precepts of Statecraft* 5 (*Moralia* 802bc)

Because of this the constitution in the time of Perikles was in name a democracy, as Thucydides says (2.65.9), but in fact the rule of the first man (in the state) because of his power of oratory. For although Kimon too was good, and so were Ephialtes and Thoukydides (son of Melesias), nevertheless, when (Thoukydides) was asked by Archidamos, the Spartan King, who wrestled best, Perikles or he, he said, 'No one knows. For when I wrestle him down, he says he did not fall, and wins by persuading the audience.' This not only brought him fame but brought safety to the city. For being persuaded by him, the city preserved the prosperity it had achieved and refrained from foreign (adventures).

1 This famous phrase has been associated either with an oration Perikles delivered in 439 (cf. Plut. *Per.* 28.4 and the next extract from Aristotle) or one in 431 (Thucydides 1.34ff.). See C. W. Fornara, *Herodotus* (Oxford 1971) 83.
2 In the form of axe handles.

75 Athenian Regulation of the Eleusinian Mysteries. About 460 B.C.
Marble stele, stoichedon, Athens.

SIG, no. 42, pp. 46-9; *IG* I² 6, 9 (I³ 6); B. D. Meritt, *Hesperia* 14 (1945) 61-81;
F. Sokolowski, *HTR* 52 (1959) 1-7. (B) F. Sokolowski, *Lois sacrées des cités
grecques*, Suppl. (Paris 1962), no. 3, pp. 13-18; (C) *K. Clinton, *The Sacred Officials of the Eleusinian Mysteries*, Transactions of the American Philosophical Society,
n.s. 64 (1974) 10-13.[1]

(B)

[- - t|(45)hat] (done) inadvertently | (shall be expiated) by the regular
(penalty), that (done) *i|ntentionally, by a doubl|e* (penalty). A truce
5   *shall be in e||ffect* for the init|(50)iates, both *for the | epoptai*[2] [a|nd]
10   for their *follo|wers,* and the *p||roperty* of the *f|(55)oreigners,* and for
     the [Ath|e]nians *in their en|tirety.* There shall be a beginning | of the
15   period o||f the truce in | (60) Metageitnio|n, from | the full moon, |
20   through Boedro||mion and into P|(65)yanopsion, | until the ten|th of
25   the month. T|he truce || shall be in force in all thos|(70)e cities which |
30   pay observance to th|e shrine and for the A|thenians p||resent in those
35 | (75)same citie|s. For the Le|sser Myste|ries, the t||ruce shall extend |
40   (80)from Gamelion, | from the fu|ll moon, | through Anthester||ion
     and into El|(85)aphebolion, | until the tent|h of the month.

(C)

5 || [-12-] *obol* [-5-]|[-13-][3] sacr[i-5-]|[-10] *half-obol da|ily* [from
10   each] initiate. | The *priestess* of Deme[t]er || *shall receive* at the *Lesser
     Mysteries* | from *each initiate* | an obol, and (shall also receive) [at the
15   Greater] | *Mysteries* an [obol from] each [i|nitiate. All the] obo||ls
     [shall become the property] of the *two goddesses*[4] [except for] *si|x-
     teen hundred drachm|as. From* the *sixteen* | hundred *drachmas* [the]
20   priestes|s [shall provide for] the expenses *just as* || was done hitherto.
     The (families of the) E[umolpid]ai an|d Ker[yk]es [shall] receive
     [from] | *each* initiate [-12-] | [-9-].[5] *Female* [-7-] | [-5-][6] *initiate* not
25   [-10-] || [. no one] *except* the (child) who is a *public* [initi|ate.][7]
     The Kerykes *shall initiate* [separately] | *each* initiate [and the Eumo|
     l]p[i]dai (shall do) the same. *If* (they initiate) *b|y groups,* they [shall]
30   be fined [-6-] || [.][8] drachmas. The initiation shall be performed
     [-8-] | [...]Kerykes and Eu[molpidai.][9] | (As to) [the first-fruits][10]
     of the *sacred* money, | *it shall be permissible* [for the] Athen[ians ...]
35 | [-5-][11] *however* [they] wish, [just] || as with Athena['s money] | on
     the Akropolis. But as to the [money (itself), th|e] Hieropoioi (shall
     take) *this* (money) [of the two goddesses] | (and) administer it [on

40 the] Akropo'lis. [-6-] | [--] in the [--] || [--] *of the orphans*[12] [-5-] |
[.] *all* the orphans [and the] | initiates, each [-9-][13] | *Those* initiates in
Ele[usis who are initi|ated] (shall be initiated) in *the* hall [-5-[14] of the
45 s||anctuary], while those in the city [who are initiate|d] (shall be ini-
tiated) in the Eleusinion. [-7-] | The priest of the altar and *the* [herald][15]|
of the two goddesses and the [all-sacred] priest | shall receive, each *of*
50 *them*, [an obol from] || *each initiate* [(to be) dedicated to the two god-
desses.][16]

1 The character of the writing and the general order of the subject matter indicate that these rules were not published at one time 'but grew slowly as the
current customs and popular need dictated' (Sokolowski, *HTR* cit. 6). The
inscription consists of three parts: (A) carved on the front of the stele, poorly
preserved and not included here; (B) carved on the right side of the stone; (C)
carved on the back. Numbers in parentheses in (B) give the line numbers in
IG I[2].
2 Those initiates who had attained the third and highest stage of initiation into
the mysteries, the first two stages being mere initiation (*myēsis*) and the 'preliminary' (*teletē*).
3 '[from | each initiate': S(okolowski).
4 Demeter and Kore (Persephone).
5 '[all parts from th|e victims sacrificed.]': S.
6 '[or m|ale] not [of the prescribed age shall not become an]': S.
7 I.e. children selected for the service of the cult.
8 'One thousand', 'ten thousand' and 'one hundred' have been suggested.
9 'shall be performed [by those] | Kerykes and Eu[molpidai who are adult':
Meritt; 'who are selected by lot': S.
10 Clinton; '[protection]': Meritt; '[expenditure]': S.
11 'to u|se it]': Clinton, in his commentary.
12 'Though the restoration eludes me, the passage probably refers to the special
care taken by the state or the *genē* to assure the initiation of orphans': Clinton.
13 As restored by S from line 38: '[The Eumolp||idai] *shall have in their* [pre-
sence the g|uarantor] of the *orphans*. [There shall be performance by] | the
orphaned *children*, [and by the] | initiates, each of them, [of the preliminary
sacrifice].'
14 '[outside': Clinton; '[outside' or '[inside': E. S. Roberts and E. A. Gardner, *An
introduction to Greek epigraphy* 2 (Cambridge 1905) 6.
15 Clinton; '[Cleanser]': S.
16 Only a few letters are preserved in the remaining twelve lines.

76 Kimon's Return from Ostracism. 461/60–457/6 *or* 452/1 B.C.

Scholiast to Aristeides 46.158.13, p. 528, 4 Dindorf (Theopompus, *FGrHist* 115 F
88). Cf. Andocides 3.3; Diodorus 11.86.1; Nepos, *Cimon* 3.3; Plutarch, *Kimon*
17.8–18.1, *Perikles* 10.4.

Gomme, etc., *HCT* 1.326f. (457/6). Kagan, *Outbreak* 91f. (457/6); Meiggs, *Empire*
422f. (452); de Ste Croix, *Origins* 189 n. 79 (452/1); Bury-Meiggs 213, 220, 222;
Sealey, *History* 272f.

Aristeides 46.14f.: Thus Kimon preserved for his city that (harmonious order) which derives from the nature of things. For he made everyone orderly as far as he could. In such fashion did he govern and teach both the People in the city and those who followed him on campaign. And yet, by Zeus, they ostracized him so as not to hear his voice for ten years. But they brought him back again before the ten years expired in order to hear that voice of his, so greatly did they miss him.

Scholion: Theopompus on Kimon in the tenth book of the *Philippica*: 'Although five years (of his ostracism) had not yet passed when war broke out against the Lacedaemonians, the People recalled Kimon, believing that because of his proxenia he would conclude peace very quickly. Arriving at the city he put an end to the war.'

77 Samians Fight in Egypt. 464–454 B.C.
Marble block, developed Ionic writing, nonstoichedon, Samos.

Jeffery, *LSAG*, no. 21, p. 331 and Plate 63; *GHI*, no. 34, pp. 76f. Cf. Thuc. 1.104.2; Ctesias (above, no. 72) and no. 78, below. The association of this epigram with the Athenian expedition to Egypt is not certain.

H. D. Westlake, *Essays on the Greek historians and Greek history* (Manchester 1969) 61ff.

[To this]¹ action many [- - -]² / for the sake of³ [Mem]phis the lovely he *set* ships [to battle,] / *furious* Ares, (ships) of the Medes and Hellenes, [and the Samians / took] *fifteen ships* of the Phoenicians. //
5   [But]⁴ Hegesa[g]oras son of Zoiilotes and[- -] / [- - -]

1 Peek's restoration (cited *GHI*, p. 76). The verse endings coincide with the ends of the lines of the inscription.
2 '[testify, when on the Nile]': Peek. There are traces remaining on the stone which are compatible with this restoration.
3 Or 'roundabout.'
4 Peek. The Samian mentioned presumably died in the battle and had a statue erected in his honor (of which this block of marble was the base).

78 Casualty List of the Erechtheid Tribe of Athens. About 459 B.C.
Marble stele, stoichedon, Athens.

IG I² 929 (I³ 1147); *GHI*, no. 33, pp. 73–6. Cf. Thucydides 1.104.2; Plato, *Menexenos* 241e; Aristodemus, *FGrHist* 104 F 11.3. Cf. nos. 73, 77.

ATL 3.174f.; Fornara, *Generals* 44–6; de Ste Croix, *Origins* 182; Bury–Meiggs 219f.

Of Erechtheis | these died in the war,[1] in Cyprus, in Eg[y]|pt, in Phoenicia, at Halieis, on Aegina, at Megara, | in the same year. ||

5	Of the *generals*[2]	71 Phanyllos	130	Akryptos
	Ph[ryn]ichos[3]	Ch[..]nios		Timokrates
	P[ant]aleon	E[ug]eiton		Archelas

(The list of names continues in the three columns)

60	Amphikedes	126 Nikon	185	Araith[os]
	Xenyllos	*vacat*		*vacat*
	vacat			
	General	in Egypt		
	Hippodamos	*vacat*		
	Euthymachos	Telenikos		
65	Eumelos	Seer		
	Androsthenes	*vacat*		
	Archers Phrynos			
	Tauros			
	Theodoros			
	Aleximachos			

1 Or, 'fighting.'
2 Normally translated as a participle: 'as general.'
3 Daux (*BCH* 99 (1975) 153).

79 The Building of the Long Walls and the Middle Wall at Athens. About 459–442 B.C.

A:Scholiast to Plato, *Gorgias* 455e; B: Plutarch, *Moralia* 351a (Cratinus F 300 Kock); C: Harpocration s.v. 'The Middle Wall' (Antiphon F 37 Thalheim; Aristophanes F 556 Kock). Cf. Thucydides 1.107.1, 1.108.3; Aeschines 2.173; Plutarch, *Kimon* 13.6, *Perikles* 13.6–7. *IG* I[2] 343.90 (I[3] 440.127) gives a reference to the receipt of money from Teich[opoioi], 'wall[-builders]' by the Superintendents of the Parthenon in 443/2. Cf. nos. 118, 120.

Gomme, etc., *HCT* 1.312f.; Meiggs, *Empire* 188; Bury–Meiggs 235f.

A. Scholiast to Plato, *Gorgias* 455e

Plato, *Gorgias* 455de: (Gorgias) 'I will try, Sokrates, clearly to unveil to you the total power of rhetoric. You have yourself led the way admirably. You know, I presume, that those very shipyards (to which you alluded) and the walls of the Athenians and the construction in the harbors were built through the advice of Themistokles[1] and the other (fortifications) through (the advice of) Perikles, and not through that of the workmen.' (Sokrates) 'This is said, Gorgias, about Themistokles, and I myself have heard Perikles when he advised us about the Middle Wall.'

Scholion: He calls 'the Middle Wall' that which even until now exists in Hellas. For he built the Middle Wall as well (as the others) at Mounychia, part heading to the Piraeus and part to Phaleron, so that if the one section were thrown down, the other would largely serve.

B. Plutarch, *Moralia* 351a

He (Isocrates) sits at home shaping his phrases, taking as much time as Perikles took in erecting the Propylaia[2] and the Parthenon.[3] Yet Cratinus mocked even him as if he were proceeding slowly with the work, saying something like this about the Middle Wall: 'Perikles is building it with words, but in fact is changing nothing.'

C. Harpocration s.v. 'The Middle Wall'

The Middle Wall. (In) Antiphon's *In Reply to Nikokles*. There were three walls in Attica, as Aristophanes also says in the *Triphales*, the north wall, southern wall, and the wall to Phaleron. The southern wall was said to be 'in the middle' of the ones on each side . . . .

1 479 B.C. See Thuc. 1.89.3–93.
2 See no. 118.
3 See no. 120.

80   Thank-offering by the Lacedaemonians for the Victory at Tanagra. 458 B.C.
Marble stele, Corinthian letters, Corinthian Doric, heroic couplets, Olympia.

Jeffery, *LSAG*, no. 38, pp. 129f. and Plate 21; **GHI*, no. 36, pp. 78f. Cf. Herodotus 9.35.2; Thucydides 1.107.6–108.1; Diodorus 11.80.2–6; Plutarch, *Kimon* 17.4–8, *Perikles* 10.1–3; Bury–Meiggs 220; Sealey, *History* 270f.

[The temple] has [a golden shield;[1]] from [Tanagra /[2] the Lacedaemonians] and (their) *alliance dedicated* (it) / [as a gift (taken) from Argives, Athe]nians and [Ionians, / the tithe] (due) *because* [of victory]
5   in the *war*. // [--] Cor[inth]i[ans --] / [---]

1 Pausanias (5.10.4), who quotes the first four lines of this inscription, calls the object a golden shield on the eastern pediment of the temple of Zeus at Olym-

pia, just below the statue of Victory. It had an apotropaic Medusa's head and, because it was bow-like in form, apparently could be called (as here) a *phiale*, normally not a shield but a broad flat bowl for drinking water or pouring libations.

2   The lines of the inscription coincide with the verses.

81   Alliance of Athens and Egesta. 458/7 *or* 454/3 *or* 418/17 B.C.

Two fragments of a marble stele, developed Attic letters but 3-bar sigma, stoichedon, Akropolis.

IG I^2 19, 20 (I^3 11); Tod I, no. 31, pp. 56f. (454/3); *GHI*, no. 37, pp. 80-2 (458/7); *Bradeen and McGregor, *Studies* 71f. (458/7 or 454/3). Cf. Diodorus 11.86.2 and no. 91 (for 454 or before), Thucydides 6.6.2 (for 418/17).

A. E. Raubitschek, *TAPA* 75 (1944) 10-12; W. K. Pritchett, *AJA* 59 (1955) 58f.; H. B. Mattingly, *Historia* 12 (1963) 268f. (418/17); B. D. Meritt, *BCH* 88 (1964) 413-15 (458/7); J. D. Smart, *JHS* 92 (1972) 128-46 (418/17); *Phoenix* 31 (1977) 251 (406/5); T. Wick, *JHS* 95 (1975) 186-90 (418/17); Sealey, *History* 308.

[The Alliance and] *Oath* [of the Athenians and] Egestaeans.[1] | [Resolved by the Boule and] *the* [People, -8-] held the prytany, [....] | [-was Secretary, --] o [-presided, --]on[2] was Archon, Ar[....3] | [-made the
5   motion. --] || [---] | [---] | [--] as many *victims* [..] | [-18-swear] *the* *oath. That* it [be] swor|n [by everone shall be the] *generals' respon-*
10 *sibility* [--] || [-14-] with *the* oath-commissioners *so that* [--] | [-11-] This *decree* and the [oath shall be inscribe|d on a marble stele on the] Akropolis by the Secretary of the Boule. [The P|oletai are to let out the contract.] The Kolakretai *are to provide* [the mon|ey. Invitation
15 shall be offered for] hospitality to the embassy of the E[gestaeans || in the Prytaneion at the] accustomed time. Euphe[mos made the motion. Let | all the rest be as (resolved) by the] Boule, but in future, when [-9-] | [-19-] herald [shall] introduce [-14-] | [---]

(Lacuna)

[These are the envoys of the] Egestaeans [who swore the oath -12-] | [-7-]ikonos, Ap[-34-] | *vacat*[4]

1   The heading is in larger letters.
2   'Ha]b[r]on': Bradeen–McGregor (supporting an earlier reading by Raubitschek, rejected by Pritchett, *loc. cit.*; archon in 458/7); 'Arist]on' (454/3): Tod; 'Ant]i-phon' (418/17): Mattingly.
3   'Ar[che]de|[mos made the motion': Hiller (in *IG* I^2).
4   The beginning of another decree, concerning Halikyai, follows after the vacant space.

82 Athenian Compact Involving the Delphic Amphictyony or Phocis. About 457 B.C. *or about 448 B.C.*

Marble stele, stoichedon, Athens. Little of this text survives and inter-pretation is most uncertain.

IG I² 26 (I³ 9); Tod I, no. 39, p. 78 (renewal of alliance with Phocis, about 448); *B. D. Meritt, *AJP* 75 (1954) 369–73 (alliance with the Amphictyonic league, about 457); Meiggs, *Empire* 418–20. For the earlier dating, after Oenophyta, cf. Thucydides 1.108.2; Diodorus 11.82–3; for the later, cf. Thucydides 1.112.5; Plutarch, *Perikles* 21.

[Resolved by the] *Boule* and *the* [Peo|ple, -7-][1] *held the prytany,* Ai[...] | [....] *was Secretary,* Menyll[os p|resided, -5-]ies made the
5   motion. (The Athenians) [shall] *con||clude* [the] alliance [...] | [-12-]
Pylaia[2] [.....] | [-14-][3] the Amphi[cty|onians, those who] *share* in the
10 *shr|ine,*[4] [-9-] having taken oath in [th||e -10- by] Apollo [an|d Leto and] Artemis[5] [...] | [---] | [---]

1 Aiantis or Leontis.
2 The meeting of the Amphictyonians at Pylai.
3 '[wit|h (the) Phocians, and at the] Pylaia [ann|ounce to them and to]': Tod; '[in accor|dance with what the (messengers) from the] Pylaia [ann|ounce to all]': Meritt.
4 Tod's continuation: 'the oath] having been sworn (by them) in [th||e meeting-place'; 'and shall remain,] having sworn, in [th||e alliance,': Meritt.
5 Even less is certain after this point, though some letters can be read in lines 12–16 and line 17 can be seen. Tod restored an Athenian date in line 12: 'in Ar[ist|on's archonship' (454/3).

83 Dedication of Athenian Knights. 457–446/5 B.C.

Marble base, stoichedon, Acropolis. The style of the base does not per-mit a more precise dating.

SIG, no. 51, pp. 63f.; *DAA*, no. 135, pp. 146–52. Cf. Pausanias 1.22.4.

The *Knights* (dedicated this out of booty taken) from the *enemy*. The Hipparchs *w|ere* Lakedaimonios, Xenophon, Pronap[e]|s.[1] Lykios of Eleutherai,[2] the son of Myro[n],[3] made (it).

1 Lakedaimonios, the son of Kimon, who was general at Corcyra in 433 (Thucy-dides 1.45.2); cf. Plutarch, *Kimon* 16.1, *Perikles* 29.1–2; no. 125, 1.8. Xenophon son of Euripides of the deme Melite served as general at Samos (441/40): see no. 108. Of Pronapes son of Pronapides it is known only that he made another dedi-cation (Hill, B 36, p. 294). The *Eighth Epistle* of Themistokles (one of a collec-tion of spurious letters drawing on unverifiable historical traditions) names a

Pronapes of the deme Prasiai as an opponent of Themistokles. It is noteworthy that three hipparchs are mentioned here since the normal number attested shortly thereafter is two.
2 A town on the border of Attica and Boeotia. The name does not occur among the known Athenian demes.
3 Myron was the famed sculptor of the Diskobolos (Lucian, *Philopseudes* 18).

84 Tolmides' Circumnavigation of the Peloponnesus. 457 *or* 456/5 B.C.

Scholiast to Aeschines 2.75 (Blass=78 Dindorf). Cf. Thucydides 1.108.5; Diodorus 11.84; Pausanias 1.27.5; Plutarch, *Perikles* 19.2; Polyaenus 3.3.

ATL 3.166ff. (457 B.C.); Meiggs, *Empire* 470f.; Bury-Meiggs 221.

Aeschines 2.75: I bade you emulate . . . (the actions at Plataea, Salamis, Marathon, Artemisium) and the generalship of Tolmides, who marched without fear with one thousand picked Athenian troops through the center of the Peloponnesus though it was hostile territory.

Scholion: Tolmides. He sailed around the Peloponnesus with the Athenians and won brilliant fame and seized Boiai and Cythera when Kallias was Archon at Athens (456/5). Tolmides also set fire to the dockyards of the Lacedaemonians.

85 The First Tribute Quota List of 454/3 B.C.
Marble stele, stoichedon (with irregularity), Athens

IG I^2 191+ (I^3 259): a new fragment, Inv. no. I 7300, published by *B. D. Meritt, *Hesperia* 41 (1972) 403-17. Cf. Diodorus 12.38.2; Plutarch, *Perikles* 12.1.

ATL 3.253f.; Kagan, *Outbreak* 98-101; Meiggs, *Empire*, 115-17; Bury-Meiggs 221; Sealey, *History* 273-5.

The *lapis primus*, or first stele of the tribute quota lists, a huge block of marble measuring 3.663 m × 1.109 m × 0.385 m, contained six tribute quota lists on its obverse face (see the diagram at no. 95M). The first list now is securely dated to 454/3 because of the discovery of a new fragment giving the name of the archon, Aris[ton], in addition to a number of cities registered in Column III. The restorations of the preamble must, however, be regarded as quite tentative.

[These quotas, each separately (and) all in to]*tal* (?)[1] *from* the Hel-l[enot]amiai *for* [whom - 7-] | [-7- was Secretary] *were the first* to be *audited* [by the] *thirty* (Logistai) [for the Goddess (Athena) | from the allied tribute] *when* Aris[ton] was Archon for the A[then]ians, a mna *from* [each tal|ent.][2] *vv*

COLUMN III
5 Pedasians 200 dr.
Astyrenian[s 8 dr. 2 ob.]
Byzantine[s 1500 dr.]
[K]amirians [900 dr.]
Thermaians
10 [in] Ikaro[s 50 dr.]
[D]aunio-
teichit[ians 16 dr.] 4 ob.
Samothra[cians] 600 dr.
Astypal[aians] 200 dr.
15 Mendai[ans 80]0 dr.
Selym[b]r[ians] 900 dr.
Aigant[ians 3]3 dr. 2 ob.
Neopo[--]
Mile [--]³
20 Akr[--] 300 dr.
Co[lophon]ians 300 dr.

(The column contains an additional eight names)

1 As an alternative Meritt offers: '[These quotas, city by city in total].'
2 This offering to the goddess Athena, 1/60 of a talent of silver, was called *aparchē* (see nos. 118 note 5, 128 note 2).
3 Instead of regarding 'Mile[sians --]' and the items preceding and following it as typically independent entries, Meritt combines them to yield the following restorations: 'Mile[sians on the] ‖ pen[insul]a'; or 'Neopo[litans and] | Mile[sians on the] ‖ pen[insul]a'; or 'Neopo[litans from *vv*] | Mil[etos on White] ‖ Pen[insul]a.' 'Akr-' (line 20) is on this view the beginning of the word *akroterion* ('headland,' 'cape,' 'peninsula').

86   Limitation of Athenian Citizenship. 451/50 B.C.

Scholiast to Aristophanes, *Wasps* 718 (423/2) (Philochorus, *FGrHist* 328 F 119). Cf. Aristotle, *Athenaion Politeia* 26.4; Plutarch, *Perikles* 37.3-4.

Jacoby, *FGrHist* 3b Suppl. 1.462ff.; Hignett, *Constitution* 343-7; Sealey, *History* 299.

Aristophanes, *Wasps* 715-18: But when they are afraid, they give Euboea / to you and promise you food in batches of fifty medimnoi. / But they never gave it - except for the recent five medimnoi. / And even these you barely got - having to defend yourself from the charge of being an alien - and, at that, by single choinixes of barley.[1]
Scholion: This (is said) because who was a citizen and who was not

was investigated so strictly, when distribution of the wheat was made,
that those who were investigated appeared to be under prosecution on
a charge of being aliens (who pretended to be citizens). Now Philochorus says that on another occasion 4,760 men were found to be ille-
gally enrolled, as is set forth in the preceding quotation (of Aristophanes). The Euboean affair can also be combined with the *Catalogues
of the Dramas.*[2] For the year before, when Isarchos was Archon (424/3),
they campaigned against (Euboea), as Philochorus says. But perhaps
this is a reference to the gift from Egypt which Philochorus says Psam-
metichos sent to the People in the archonship of Lysimachides (445/4),
(which consisted) of 30,000 [[except that the numbers do not tally]][3]
medimnoi, 5 to each Athenian. Those who received it totalled 14,240.

1 A choinix was 1/48 of a medimnos and contained about one man's daily ration.
2 A compilation giving such data about plays as when they were produced.
3 An addition either by another scholiast or by a reader.

87 Treaty between Oianthia and Chaleion (in Western or Ozolian Locris) (A), and Law of Chaleion (B). About 450 B.C.

Bronze plaque, Locrian writing. Chaleion (modern Galaxidi). (A) and
(B) are written in different hands.

Buck, no. 58, pp. 253–5; *Tod I, no. 34, pp. 63–5; Jeffery, *LSAG*, no. 4, p. 106,
and Plate 15. Cf., for Locrian and Aetolian piratical practices, Thucydides 1.5.

J. A. O. Larsen, *Greek federal states* (Oxford 1968) 54f., 57.

(Front)

(A)

No one shall carry off the Oianthian stranger from the territory of
Chaleion n|or the Chaleian from the territory of Oianthia, nor his pro-
perty, if one makes a seiz|ure,[1] but one may seize the man making a
seizure with impunity. One may carry off foreign property from the sea
| with impunity from seizure – except from the harbors of the two
5 cities. If one makes unjust seizure, (the penalty is) fo|ur drachmas. If
one holds the booty for more than ten days, o|ne and a half times (the
value of) whatever he has seized shall be his penalty. If one should be
domiciled for more than a month, either | the Chaleian in Oianthia or
the Oianthian in Chaleion, the there-prevailing legal procedures s|hall
apply to him.

(B)

If the Proxenos acts falsely as Proxenos, dou|ble penalties are to be im-
posed. ||

(Back)

10   If the judges who try suits for foreigners divide in their opinion, jurors shall be chos|en by the foreigner who brings the suit, exclusive of the Proxenos | and his personal guest-friend, the best men (being selected).

   In cases of suits involving a mn|a and more, fifteen men (are to be cho-
15   sen); in cases involving | less, nine men. If citizen || takes action against citizen in accordance with the treaty, Demiourgoi | shall select the jurors from the best citizens | after having sworn the five-fold oath.[2] By the jurors shall the sam|e oath be sworn. Majority prevails.

1   I.e. private seizure of a person or property in order to compel the payment of a claim from the family or community of the person or property seized.
2   An oath naming five gods.

88   The Civil Laws of Gortyn. About 450 B.C.

Twelve columns on the inner surface of a circular wall going in sequence from right to left, archaic Cretan writing from right to left and left to right in succeeding lines, Gortyn.

Buck, no. 117, pp. 314–30; *IC* IV 72+; *R. F. Willetts, *The law code of Gortyn* (Berlin 1967) 39–50 (text and translation). Full photos and facsimiles are provided in the last two mentioned. Tod I, no. 36, pp. 68–73, and *GHI*, no. 41, pp. 94–9, give text and commentary on Columns I and IV 23–VI 1, respectively. Strabo 10.4.17, p. 481 mentions Gortyn as a preserver of its laws. Cf. Bury–Meiggs 104.

A. The property of divorced women. Col. II 45–III 49

45   *v* If a husband *and wi|fe* divorce, that which is h|er property she shall keep, whatever she had when she went t|o the husband, and (she shall
50   keep), of the produce, t|he half, if there is any (derived) from || her property, and (she shall keep) of whatever | she weaves (in the household), the [half], whatever | there may be, and five staters, if the h|usband is responsible for the *separati|on.* But *if* the husband claims [the
55   gui|l|t] *is* [not] his own, the judge | [Coll III] shall decide under oath (whether it is). If anything els|e is taken by her from the husband, five st|aters shall be her fine and whatever | she takes from him and what-
5   ever she pur||loins, she shall return it. But as to those things | she denies, (the judge) shall rule that t|he woman take oath by Ar|temis (by going) to (the) Amyklaian (temple) to the | Archeress. Whatever someone takes
10   away[1] from her when she has t||aken oath, five stat|ers shall be his fine and the th|ing itself. If a strang|er helps her carry (anything) off, ten
15   *state|rs* shall be his fine and the thi|l|ng's double value, whatever the judge | shall swear he carried off. *v* | If a man dies with children l|eft

behind, if the wife wishes, with her | property in her possession she
20   shall marr‖y and with (as well) whatever her husband gave her in accordance with the wr|itten agreements, in the presence of witnesses, th|ree in number, adult, and free. But if | she takes anything away from the children, she shall be s|ubject to trial. *v* If (the husband) is without
25   issue ‖ when he dies, her own possessions she shall kee|p and of whatever she *has woven the ha*‖*lf, and of the* produce from within (the household) she shall t|ogether with the heirs have her shar|e apportioned to
30   her and whatever the husband gave in wr‖itten agreement. If she takes anything else, she shall be su|bject to trial. *v* If the wife is without iss|ue when she dies, her | property they shall give to the heirs, | and of what-
35   ever she has woven the h‖alf, and of the produce, if there is any from | her property, the ha‖lf. If (either) wishes to give gifts (?),[2] | man or woman,
40   either clothing or twelv|e staters or a twelve-stat‖ler object, (it is permitted,) but not more. *v* If | a female serf be separated from a male serf, whether he is alive | or dead, her own propert|y she shall keep. If she takes anything else, she shall be subject to trial. *v* | If a woman gives
45   birth *when she is d*‖*ivorced*, she shall bring it to her h|usband at his house in the presence of witn|esses, three in number. If he does not acce|pt it, it shall be in the power of the mother whether the chi|ld shall be raised or exposed.

B. The inheritance line.[3] Col. V 9–28

10   LEAF[4] If a man dies or a woma‖n, if there are children or, of chil|dren, (grand)children, or of these (grandchildren, great-grand)ch|ildren, these shall possess the proper|ty. PALM If there is none of thes|e, b{b}rothers
15   of the dead per‖son and brothers' childre|n or their children, (if they exist,) the|se shall possess the property. PALM If | there is none of
20   these, (but there are) sisters | of the dead person or the‖ir children or of these children (there are) children, they shall possess the prope|rty. PALM If there is none of these, | those to whom it falls by way of the
25   origin of the pr|operty, these shall tak‖e it. PALM If there are no heir|s, those of the household | who make up the kleros[5] shall p|ossess the property. *v*

C. The marriage line for heiresses. Col. VII 15–29

15   *v* The *he*|*iress* shall marry (the) broth|er of the father, of those who are alive, who is | the oldest. If there are more hei|resses (than one) and
20   brothers of the ‖ father, to the next oldest shall she (i.e. the second heiress) be mar|ried. If there are no brother|s of the father, but sons of the brot|hers, (the heiress) shall marry the one who (is son) *of the*

25 o‖ldest. If there are more ‖ heiresses and sons of the bro‖thers, (the additional heiress) shall marry that other who is ne‖xt (in age) *to the* oldest. But (only) one ‖ heiress shall be obtained by the he‖ir, and *not* more. LEAF

1 The verb is on line 10.
2 Buck; 'Payment for maintenance': Liddell–Scott–Jones, *Greek Lexicon*; 'Payment for porterage': Willetts.
3 Cf. no. 33A.
4 Drawings of a leaf and of a palm (14, 16, etc.) set off the main article and individual sentences respectively.
5 Other free families connected by birth or neighborhood with that of the deceased. See *GHI*, p. 98.

89 Relations between Argos, Cnossus, and Tylissos. About 450 B.C.

(A) large poros fragment from Tylissos (northwest of Cnossus); (B) joining fragments of a limestone stele from Argos. Argive letters, Doric Greek, stoichedon, with some irregularity in (B).

Buck, no. 85, pp. 285-7 (B); Jeffery, *LSAG* 165; *GHI*, no. 42, pp. 99-105.

Graham, *Colony* 154-60, 235-44.

(A)

(Col. I) [. . . . sacrifice] shall be *provided* by those fr‖om [the Argives] and the skins [shall be r‖eceived by the Cn]ossians. Before the (festival
5 of the) *Tau‖rophonia* [sacrifice shall be made] in Tylissos of a [s‖heep -11-][1] and [. .]‖[-11-] *New* treaties ‖ shall not be made by eithe‖r (party) [unless] it is agreed upon by the (common?) assembl‖y.[2] The
10 Argives shall *cast* the thi‖rd [part] of the *vo‖tes*. [If] of friends ‖ (Col. II) we make enemies and o‖f our enemies (we make) friends, it will be
15 d‖one only if it is agreed upon by the as‖sembly (?). Those from Tylissos shall cast ‖ the third part of the votes. ‖ If a battle takes plac‖e with
20 the other party not present, a tr‖uce shall be made in case of nee‖‖d for five days. If an army ‖ *invades* the territory of Cno‖ssus, [the Tylissians] shall provide aid with all‖(Col. III)l their strength [-10-[3] Food] ‖
25 *shall be* provided [by the Cnossians for th‖le] Argives [(when) at Cnossus, by the] *Arg‖ives* for those [in Tylissos . . . . .]‖[---]‖[-4-][4] If [-14-]‖
30 [---]‖[.] And in Tyl[issos -11-]‖[---]‖[---]‖ [---][5]

(B)

[-13-‖-23-] the [territory of the Acha‖rnaians (?) may] be plundered [by the Tylissians] except for [th‖ose parts] *belonging* to the city [of

5   the Cnossians.] Whatever ‖ we both together win [from the enemy, in
      div|ision of that (taken) by] land, (the Tylissians) shall have a third part
      of everything. [O|f that (taken) by] sea, they shall have the half of
      everything. The *t|enth part* shall be taken by the Cnossians of whatever
      we seize in *comm|on*. The finest of the spoils shall be brought to Delphi
10   ‖ by both parties jointly, while the rest shall be dedicated to [Ares at
      Cnoss]|us by both parties jointly. [Export shall be perm|itted] from
      Cnossus to Tylissos and from Tyli[ssos to Cnossu|s.] If (a Tylissian)
      exports beyond, let him pay as much [as the Cn]|ossians; but goods
15   from Tylissos shall be exported whithersoever [desired.] *T‖o* Poseidon
      at Iutos[6] shall the Cnossian [priest sacri|fice;] to Hera in the Heraion[7]
      shall sacrifice be performed of a cow *by bo|th* (parties) jointly. They
      shall sacrifice before the Hyakinthia(n) (Festival) [-8-]|[---]

                              (Two lines lost)

21   [-34-] (the) first day o|f the month shall be kept in the same way [in
      accordance with the decision] by bo|th parties. A Cnossian may not
      possess property | in Tylissos, but a Tylissian (may do so) in Cnossus if
25   he wishe|s. Neither (party) is to cut off any of the land (of the other)
      or | take the whole. Boundaries of the land: Swine's Mountain and
      E|agles and that Artemision and the precinct of the Archos and | the
      river and towards Leukoporos and Agathoia, along the cou|rse of the
30   rainwater, and Laos. When we sacrifice to Machaneus[8] ‖ the sixty full-
      grown rams, to Hera as well | shall be given the leg of each victim. If
      se|veral cities take property from the enemy, | as the Cnossians and
      Argives jointly decide, | so shall it be. To Ares and Aphrodite shall the
35   Cnossi|an priest make sacrifice, and he shall keep the leg of each victim.
      The A|rchos shall keep the precinct at Acharna. For those who sacrifice
      | the Cnossians shall provide gifts, while the Argives (shall provide
      them) | for the chorus. If in Tylissos a Cnossian summons an em|bassy,
40   let it follow him wherever he requires; if a Tyliss|ian (in Cnossus), the
      Cnossian (shall do) the same.[9] If they do not provide hosp|itality, let
      the Boule impose a fine immediately o|n the Kosmoi,[10] and similarly in
      Tylissos with the Cnossian. | This stele was erected when Melantas was
      King.[11] | Lykotadas of the tribe Hylleis presided. Resolved by the As-
45   sembly for ‖ Sacred Matters. Architstratos of the Lykophronid phratry
      presided over the Council. | The Tylissians shall add this to the stele: |
      If a Tylissian comes to Argos, the same treatment | as the Cnossians'
      shall be his. *vv | vacat*

---

1   '[to Hermes,] and [a lamb shall be given to Daira]': Vollgraff (cited *GHI*, p.
    100).

2 Or, 'the majority.'
3 '[as far as possible]': Vollgraff, though the supplement is two letters too long.
4 Generally supplemented as 'an *army* [shall be fed (*or* paid) for thirty] d|ays.'
5 A few letters at the beginning of each line are preserved. As supplemented by Vollgraff (28–34): 'If [they send the army away, it shall] ret|urn [to its ho||me.] And in Tyl[issos the same applies. When we sacrifice a ewe to] Arth[aia, w|e shall] *render* [to Apollo a she|ep.]'
6 Possibly present Mt Juktas.
7 Probably the well-known Argive Heraion, especially in view of the provenance of this inscription.
8 Identified with Castor by Vollgraff.
9 This is either, with Vollgraff, in order to provide a means for altering the arrangements between Cnossus and Tylissos or, with *GHI* and others, in order to bind both parties to support each other's embassy.
10 See no. 11, lines 1–3.
11 Not one of the old kings of Argos but, rather, an eponymous official.

90 Nemesis and the Accounts of her Temple in the Attic Deme of Rhamnous. 450–440 B.C.

A: Pausanias 1.33.2–3; cf. Pliny, *NH* 34.29; B: Temple accounts. *GHI*, no. 53, pp. 144–6 (*IG* I³ 248).

M. I. Finley, *Studies in land and credit in ancient Athens* (New Brunswick, 1952) 284f.

A. Pausanias 1.33.2–3

Rhamnous is about sixty stades from Marathon for those taking the road along the sea (north) to Oropus. The people's dwellings are by the sea and a little inland from the sea is the temple of Nemesis (Retribution), the most implacable of the gods to men who are insolent (*hubristic*). It appears that the wrath of this goddess came upon those barbarians who disembarked at Marathon. For in their contemptuous belief that ⟨nothing⟩ would impede their taking Athens they brought a piece {which was}[1] of Parian marble for the making of a trophy for victory as if it were already brought about. [3] This stone Pheidias sculpted to be a statue of Nemesis ....[2]

B. Temple accounts, *GHI*, no. 53

5   In Autokleid|es' demarch|y.[3] Of Nemes|is' monies the t||otal in the h|ands of the | two-hundred-dr|achma borrowers:[4] | 37,000 (drachmas).
10 Of the o||ther money o|f Nemesi|s, the total: 1|2,72|9 (dr.) 3 (obols).
15 || In Mnesiptolem|os' magistracy, the tot|al of all the s|acred monies:
20 51,3|97 (dr.) 5 (ob.). || In Nausimenes' magistr|acy, the total of the sacred

monies held b|y the two hund|red-(drachma) borrowers: 37,000 (dr.).
25 || The rest: 11,723 (dr.) | 2 (ob.). | In Euainetos' magistr|acy the total
30   (outstanding) from the bor|rowers of three hundred drachmas: ||
13,500 (dr.). The grand total: | 55,712 (dr.) 1 (ob.). | In Demophanes'
35   demar|chy, the Hieropoioi's to|tal: 5,206 (dr.) 4 (ob.); || of the bor-
rowers of three hundred drachmas:| 14,400 (dr.); of the borrow|ers of
two hundred drachmas: 37,000 (dr.). | The grand total: 56,606 (dr.)
4 (ob.).

1   Deleted by Spiro (editor of the Teubner text of Pausanias), among others; pro-
    bably an erroneous repetition of the last two letters of the preceding word.
2   Pliny gives a different explanation of the statue and another sculptor (Agorakri-
    tos); see, for general reference, G. Richter, *The sculpture and sculptors of the
    Greeks* (New Haven 1950) 240-2.
3   The demarch was chief officer of the deme and is named here in a dating for-
    mula (as is the archon eponymous in documents concerning Athens as a whole).
    Note that he is indifferently referred to as 'demarch' and 'magistrate.'
4   Like the 300-drachma borrowers of line 29, these seem to represent borrowers
    of standard sums lent out by the temple - though this is doubted by Finley.

91   A Victory of Selinus. 450-413 B.C.
Reddish limestone block, local script, Doric writing, nonstoichedon,
Selinus.

Tod I, no. 37, pp. 73f. (450); W. M. Calder III, *The inscription from Temple G at
Selinus, GRBS*, Monographs 4 (413);*GHI*, no. 38, pp. 82f. Cf., for a date about
450, Diodorus 11.86.2; for the Athenian defeat in 413, cf. Thucydides 7.1.3ff.;
Calder, *GRBS* 5 (1964) 113-19.

Because of these gods the Selinuntians are victorious: | *because* of Zeus
we conquered, and because of Phobos[1] [and] | *because* of Herakles and
because of Apollo and because of P[os]|e[ido]n and because of the
5   Tyndaridai and because of Athe||na and because of Malophoros[2] and
because of Pasik|rateia[3] and because of the other gods, but because of
Zeus | most of all.[4] With peace (now) concluded, (the dedication), |
when *beaten out* in gold [and] when these names have been pu|nched
10   (into it), shall be set up [in] the Apollonion, || with Zeus' [2-3][5]
being inscribed. The gold | shall be sixty talents in worth.[6]

1   The war god of Selinus or Ares himself.
2   'Apple-bringer': epithet of Demeter.
3   Probably Persephone.
4   Calder believes lines 2-7 are in verse and comprise a Zeus-song.
5   '[(name) first]': Holm-Benndorf (cited Calder, p. 17); '[song]': Calder.
6   A solid gold shield weighing 60 talents (Calder) or costing 60 talents of silver
    (*GHI*, p. 83).

92 Regulations for Miletus. 450/49 *or* after 450/49 *or* 426/5 B.C.
Eight fragments of a marble stele, 3-bar sigma, stoichedon (with irregularity), Athens.

IG I² 22+ (I³ 21); J. H. Oliver, *TAPA* 66 (1935) 177–98 (450/49); *ATL* 2.D11, pp. 57–60; *Bradeen and McGregor, *Studies* 63–5, with Plates on pp. 26–9 and commentary (450/49). Cf. no. 66.

ATL 3.253–6 (450/49); H. B. Mattingly, *Historia* 10 (1961) 174–81, *Ehrenberg studies* 207–9, *BSA* 65 (1970) 145–7, *Phoros* 98–101 (426/5); J. B. Barron, *JHS* 82 (1962) 1–5; B. D. Meritt and H. T. Wade-Gery, *JHS* 83 (1963) 100–3 (450/49); C. W. Fornara, *AJP* 92 (1971) 473–5 (after 450/49); Meiggs, *Empire* 213–15, 562–5 (450/49); Sealey, *History* 305.

[Agreement for the Mi]lesi[ans.¹ *vv* | Resolved] by the Boule an[d the People, -8-] *held the prytany*, [-6?- was Secret|ary, -4?-]or² presided, [--³ the] *Commissioners* [-- There shall be p|erformance of the] regular ceremonies *to the* [gods, and election shall be held of] five *men* [by the
5 --] || [-5-]⁴ forthwith, [(these men to be) over fifty⁵ years] of age. [Refusal of the office shall not be allowe|d them] *nor substitution* (of another in their place). [These] shall *have the status of magistrates* and [-22-] | [--] with [--] | [--] Mil[esians --] | [-7- Mil]esians [-12-] ten
10 [--] || [--] of the troopships [--] | [--] shall supply arms [--] | [--] shall be rowers [--] | [--] *four obols⁶* [--] | [--] of each man(?) [--]
15 || [--] to the *soldiers⁷* [--] | [--] to [Athe]ns whatever [may --] | [--] as much as [they] may take [--]|

(No words are legible in lines 18–23)⁸

25 [-10-] *thirty* [--] || [-6-] envoy or [--] | [-6-] *nothing* or [--o|f the] allies what may not [seem good to the] Athe[nians. If anyone does this,] | let him [be deprived of his citizen-rights] and *his* property [be confiscated and let the tithe go to the goddess.] | Trials shall be held for
30 Milesians [--]⁹ || drachmas from the tithes [--¹⁰] | They shall deposit [the] court-fees with [--¹¹ Th|e] trials shall take place in Athens in *the* [-29 -¹² Anthes|te]rion and Elaphebolion. [--] | [..]¹³ having distributed
35 and allotted [--] || [-8-] two of the archons [-- Payment] s|hall be [made] to the jury out of [--¹⁴ --] | [he/they ...] shall provide access to the *law-court* [-- in the months | that have been] stipulated or [he/they
40 shall] *be liable* [--¹⁵ --] | [...] to the Ath[enian] archons [--] || [-5-] to Athens to the Epimeletai¹⁶ [--] | [-7-] just as formerly and [--] | [-8-] let the *five* have the responsibility [--] | [-5-] law-court convenes
45 [--] | [-7-] shall be (permitted?) for those who proceed [--] || [-7-] the Athen[ian] archons [--] | [-10-] those (cases) involving more than one hundred [drachmas --¹⁷] | [.] *on a* stele, *and* the decrees [--] | [..] not

pervert or contrive [--[18] If anyone] *trans|gresses* them, a criminal charge
50 shall be lodged against him *with* [--[19]--] || [...] shall bring him either
before one (?)[20] [--] | law-court[21] of what *should be* his punishment or
[fine--] | decrees of the Athenian[s] confisc[--] | [....] seize and re-
55 turn[22] [--] | [...] the city shall pay back the *value* [--] || and in future
[shall not] make registrations of property for the purpose of taxation
[--] | [.] concerning the money from the property-tax[23] [--] c|ondem-
nation of each other by those who [remained] at home (?) [--] | in-
habited(?) the city or by some other penalty [--] | [-10-] shall be *re-*
60 *turned* to him who has been condemned contrary [--] || [.] *return*
either property or money from [--] | [-5-] in the archonship of Euthy-
nos (450/49 *or* 426/5). Whoever does not [obey these (injunctions) shall
be compell|ed to return it by] the five archons and [--] | [--] trials
shall be held [at] Athens [--] | [--] opposed to the Athenians' [--] ||
65 [--] the Prytaneis[24] of the Miles[ians--] | [--] either group the city [--]
| [--] of the Milesians [--] | [--] the Athe[nians] on the one hand [--]
70 | [--] *administer oaths* [--] || [--] the [rest of the Mi]lesi[ans--] | [--]
the *five* [shall] administer the oaths [--] | [--] take oath [--] | [--] |
75 [--] let them have the responsibility how *best* [--] || [--] of the
[Mil]esians or *of the* garrisons they [shall] have the authority [--] |
[.. But if anyone] *deserves* a greater penalty, [to] Athens [--] | [--]
having imposed (a fine) of as much as seems *deserved* [--] | [--] *shall be*
brought before the People by the [--] | [-5-decreed] *by them* still or
80 whether some other [--] || [--] M[ile]sians. But if [they are] wise [--] |
[--] *are* necessary. As to Arnasos[25] the Boule [--] | [--] so that they can
have the authority to govern [--] | [Let the responsibility be taken by]
the Boule [for the] defense. Of *that which has been decreed* [--] | [--]
85 shall be *accomplished* the Boule [is to be] solely empowered [--] ||
[-6-let them] *send* [off the] two guard-ships and the [--] | [-15-] in
the archonship of [Euth]ynos.

(The rest of line 86 and line 87 have been erased)

1 The heading is written in larger letters.
2 'Onet]or': *ATL*.
3 'Euthynos was Archon (450/49 *or* 426/5). This (agreement) the] *Commis-*
   sioners [drafted]': B(radeen)–McG(regor) et al.
4 '[By the People from among || all citizens]': B–McG et al.
5 Mattingly, B–McG; 'thirty' was earlier restored by Oliver and others.
6 This reference to pay, and the other military allusions in the text, are explained by some (Oliver, Mattingly) as measures providing for Milesian military
   support for Athens; others (D. M. Lewis, B–McG) connect them with the present institution of the new Athenian board of five men and with a reorganiza-
   tion of the garrison.
7 Just before this, 'to [Athens]' is generally restored.
8 'To Athens' is restored by B–McG in lines 19 and 20.

9 *'just* [as for Athenians and from each talent a thousand]': B–McG.

10 '[shall be consecrated to Apollo at Didyma': B–McG.

11 '[the Athenian archons on the last day of the month': Oliver; '[with the Athenian magistrates residing in Miletus': B–McG supposing that the Athenian board of five men is meant.

12 '[months of Posideion, Gamelion': Oliver; '[Heliaia in the months Gamelion': B–McG.

13 '[The archons are to seat the jury,] | having distributed and allotted [them according to tribe in the Heliaia]': Oliver. B–McG provide a radically inventive text.

14 B–McG restore (from line 34) as follows: 'These trials shall be sc‖rutinized (?) by] two of the archons [and the Epimeletai of the suits and the payment] | shall be [given] to the jury out of *the* [court-fees.'

15 B–McG continue (after the restoration translated in the preceding note): 'Those proceeding from Miletus] | shall be granted access to the *law-court* [without fail by the archons in office in the months | that] *have already been stipulated* or [they shall be] fined one thousand drachmas.'

16 The word 'epimeletai' (see note 14 above) can designate a number of different Athenian officials, and can also mean nothing more than 'those in charge of.'

17 'shall be subject to appeal': Oliver, B–McG.

18 From the preceding line, after '*on a stele*', as restored by B–McG: '[and the Milesians shall always obey] the decrees [of the Athenians a|nd] they shall not pervert (them) or contrive [that they be dissolved.'

19 '[the Epimeletai forthwith': B–McG.

20 B–McG assume that the word 'either' is a mistake and restore (from the end of line 49): 'the Epimele‖tai] shall introduce him to one [of the archons within five days.'

21 'assessment shall be made by the] | court': B–McG.

22 According to the very hypothetical restorations of B–McG, this section deals with compensation to be granted victimized pro-Athenian loyalists by the new Milesian government set up by this decree.

23 *Eisphora*: an exceptional tax (see also Glossary). In a disputed passage (3.19), Thucydides states *either* that this tax was levied in Attica for the first time in 428 B.C. *or* that in 428 it produced a revenue of 200 talents for the first time. Whether the *eisphora* in the present passage was imposed by the Athenians or had been imposed by the prior government of Miletus is not clear. Oliver and Mattingly assume the former, B–McG the latter.

24 Originally, the supreme magistrates of the Milesian state; their powers at this time are unknown. See J. Barron, *JHS* 82 (1962) 4–5.

25 The place cannot be identified.

93 Appointment of the Priestess and Building of the Temple of Athena Nike. 450–445 *or* about 427 B.C.[1]

Marble stele, developed Attic letters, but with 3-bar sigma, stoichedon.

IG I² 24 (I³ 35); **GHI*, no. 44, pp. 107–11.

H. B. Mattingly, *Historia* 10 (1961) 169–71 (*c.* 427); B. D. Meritt and H. T. Wade-Gery, *JHS* 83 (1963) 109–11 (450–445); A. L. Boegehold, *Classical studies presented to B. E. Perry* (Illinois 1969) pp. 175–80; Meiggs, *Empire*, 495–503; Bury-Meiggs 231.

[-29-]|[-19]kos made the motion. [For | Athena Ni]ke a priestess[2]
5 who [....]|[-12-][3] from *all* Athenian women || shall be [appointed] ,
and the sanctuary shall be furnished with door|s as Kallikrates shall
prescri|be. The Poletai shall let the contract out for hire in t|he prytany
of (the tribe) Leontis. Payment to t|he priestess shall be fifty drachmas
10 (per year) and || the legs and hides from pu|blic (sacrifices). A temple
shall be constructed as | Kallikrates shall prescribe and an al|tar of
15 marble. *vv* | Hestiaios made a motion. Three men shall be elect|led from
the Boule. They, together with Kallikra|tes, after making the specifica-
tions, shall [indicate to th|e Boule] the manner in which [--4]|[---]|
[---]

1   The inscription on the reverse side of this stele is included as no. 139 below.
2   An epitaph of Myrrhine, the first priestess of Athena Nike (*SEG* 12.80), if she is
    identified with the Myrrhine of Aristophanes, *Lysistrata* (412/11), suggests a
    date after 411 for her death.
3   '[will be priestess for life]': Papademetriou (cited *GHI*, p. 107); '[elected by
    lot]': Meritt and Wade-Gery.
4   '[the contract will be] *let*': Meritt and Wade-Gery.

94   The Financing of Public Expenditures through Athena's Treasury. 450/49 *or* 431/30 B.C.

The 'Strasbourg Papyrus', a commentary on Demosthenes 22.13ff. (*Anonymus
Argentinensis*). A: U. Wilcken, *Hermes* 42 (1907) 414 (431); B: *ATL* 2.D13, p. 61
(450/49); C: H. T. Wade-Gery and B. D. Meritt, *Hesperia* 26 (1957) 164-88 (450/
49). Cf. Plutarch, *Perikles* 12.1-3.

ATL 3.281 (450/49); Gomme, etc., *HCT* 2.28-33 (431 as a possibility); R. Sealey,
Hermes 86 (1958) 442, *JHS* 85 (1965) 161f. (431); Meiggs, *Empire* 155, 515-18
(450/49); de Ste Croix, *Origins* 310f.; Bury-Meiggs 225.

Dem. 22.13f.: One could speak of many examples, both ancient and
modern (of the importance of building triremes). But that which you
are most familiar with from hearsay, this, if you will – those men who
from (the spoil of) the barbarians constructed the Propylaia and the
Parthenon and who adorned the other temples on which we all of us
pride ourselves with good reason – surely you know this from hearsay,
that it was because they had triremes that, after leaving their city and
being confined in Salamis, they won the sea-battle and saved the city
and all of their possessions, and became the source of many great benefits to the rest of Hellas, which even time cannot obscure in memory.
Very well. This is ancient history. But as to what you all have seen, you
know that recently you came to the assistance of the Euboeans in three
days' time and sent the Thebans back under a truce.

A. Strasbourg Papyrus, 3–8, ed. Wilcken

[- - - 'Constructed (?)[1] the Propylai]a and the Parthenon.' After - - *years*
5 | [- - -] they began construction (and it/they was/were) *ma*|*de* [by
Iktinos.[2] In (the archonship of) Eu]thydemos[3] Perikles moved | [and
the People decreed that] the talents stored up in the public treasury[4] |
[of silver . . .] *five thousand* [accumulated[5]] according to Aristei|[des'
assessment . . . were] to be [spent] on the city.

B. Strasbourg Papyrus, 3–8, ed. *ATL* 2.D13

[- - - 'Constructed the Propylai]a and the Parthenon.' *33 years* | [after
the Persian Wars (447/6) the temples] began to be constructed by them,
5 [and they] *ma*|*de* [the statue as well, when in (the archonship of)
Eu]thydemos Pericles moved | [that the Athenians should apply] the
talents stored up in the public treasury | [accumulated from the tribute]
(to a total of) five thousand according to Aristei|[des' assessment. - -]

C. Strasbourg Papyrus, 3–11, ed. Wade-Gery, Meritt

[- - - 'Constructed the Propylai]a and the Parthenon.' *Thi*|[rty years,[6]
approximately, after the Persian Wars] they began construction, and
5 [they had it] *do*|*ne* [from the tribute, after] Perikles [moved] a reso-
lution [in (the archonship of) Eu]thydemos | [to carry up for the Pana-
thenaia for Athena] the talents stored up in the public treasury | [which
had been accumulated from the cities] (to a total of) five thousand
according to Aristei|[des' assessment, and to carry up another three
thousand] to the Akropolis[7] after this [whi|le the works were being
effected; (and that) in order that the sea be controlled] *by them*, the
10 Boule || [should care for] the old triremes [so that they might be sound
when they] *handed them over*, and it should build new ones *ea*|*ch*
[year, in addition to the ones at hand,] (to the number of) *ten*.[8] 'With-
in three days they came to the assistance | [of the Euboeans' - - -][9]

---

1 The question mark is Wilcken's. He felt the restorations were so tentative ('I
   insist yet again that [they] are intended to fill in the meaning, not the actual
   words,' p. 414) that he printed his restorations as footnotes to the text.
2 Or Mnesikles.
3 Euthydemos is the name attested for the archon of 431/30, Euthynos that of
   the archon of 450/49. But the ancients seem to have confused these names and
   so it is tenable that Euthydemos is a mistake in this document for Euthynos.
4 A correction of 'People' or 'government.'
5 The word stands in line 8.
6 This word stands in line 3.
7 The meaning of the word *polis*, used here, depends on whether the commentator
   is quoting from a fifth-century decree (as the editors of this version suppose), in

which case it means 'Akropolis'; the alternative (see Wilcken's text) is simply 'city.'
8 Compare the earlier restoration in *ATL* 1.572 (T9, lines 7-11): '...Aristei-|[des' assessment. "Triremes had to be available] to the city."' (This, of course, is a lemma, or rather, a semi-quotation of the words in Demosthenes, which the scholiast will proceed to explain. 'After this, [on the occurrence, once again, of alliance, it was resolved] that the Boule | *render* [account in the Assembly] of the old triremes, and build new ones *on ea|ch occasion*, [(namely) triremes or quadriremes] (to the number of) *ten.*'
9 This phrase is the next lemma. See the final words of Demosthenes quoted above.

95 The Peace of Kallias. 449 B.C. (?)

A: Isocrates 4.118-20; B: Isocrates 7.80; C: Demosthenes 19.273; D: Theon, *Progymnasmata* 2.67, 22 Spengel (Theopompus, *FGrHist* 115 F 153); E: Harpocration s.v. 'Attic letters' (Theopompus, *FGrHist* 115 F 154); F: Lycurgus, *Leokrates* 73; G: Diodorus 12.4.4-6; H: Plutarch, *Kimon* 13.4-5 (Callisthenes, *FGrHist* 124 F 16; Craterus, *FGrHist* 342 F 13); I: Livy 33.20.1-2; J: Aristodemus, *FGrHist* 104 F 13; K: Plato, *Menexenos* 242a; L: *Suda* s.v. 'Kallias'; M: The 'Missing' Tribute quota List of 449/8 B.C. (*IG* I^2 196, 198, 199 (I^3 263ff.)); N: Athens honors Herakleides (*IG* II^2 8), no. 138; O: Andocides 3.29. Cf. Herodotus 4.42.2, 7.151; Thucydides 8.5.5, 8.56.4; Isocrates 12.59; Pausanias 1.8.2; Aelius Aristeides, *Panathenaicus* 153.

Wade-Gery, *Essays* 201-32, S. K. Eddy, *CP* 65 (1970) 8-14, 68 (1973) 241-58 (for authenticity); D. Stockton, *Historia* 8 (1957) 61-73, C. L. Murison, *Phoenix* 25 (1971) 12-31 (against). Discussion and additional bibliography in Meiggs, *Empire* 129-51, 487-95, on this much debated issue ('Statistically an article on the Peace of Callias can be expected every two years' (ibid. 598)); Bury–Meiggs 222; Sealey, *History* 278-82.

A. Isocrates 4.118-20[1]

(We so chastised the barbarians) (118) that they not only ceased from making expeditions against us but even tolerated their own territory being ravaged. We brought them, who had been sailing the sea with twelve hundred ships, so low that they did not launch a ship of war this side of Phaselis but remained quiet and awaited a favorable opportunity and did not trust in their existing strength .... (120) One can best comprehend the magnitude of the change (in our fortunes between then and now) if one compares the treaty which was made in our time (of leadership) with that which is now written up.[2] For it will appear that at that time we shall be seen to have set boundaries to the empire of the King, assessed some of his subjects for tribute and prevented him from using the sea.

B. Isocrates 7.80

The barbarians were so far from interfering in Hellenic affairs that they did not sail this side of Phaselis in their ships of war or advance west of the Halys river with their forces, but were very peaceful.

C. Demosthenes 19.273

Now they (our ancestors) – and I well know that all of you have heard this story – almost put Kallias son of Hipponikos to death and fined him fifty talents at his euthynai because he appeared to have taken bribes as ambassador when he negotiated that peace which everyone now keeps talking about, to the effect that the King was not to advance toward the sea by land within a day's ride by horse and was not to sail with a ship of war beyond the Chelidoniai and Kyaneai.[3]

D. Theon, *Progymnasmata* 2.67, 22

From Theopompus' twenty-fifth book of the *Philippika*: [The] Hellenic oath is a fabrication, which the Athenians say the Hellenes swore before the battle of Plataea against the barbarians,[4] and so is the Athenian treaty with King Dareios in regard to the Greeks.[5] Furthermore, the battle of Marathon was not as everyone hymns it to have been; 'nor all those other things,' he says, 'in which the city of Athens makes her boasts and deceives the Hellenes.'

E. Harpocration s.v. 'Attic letters'

... Theopompus in Book 25 of the *Philippika* says that the treaty with the barbarian was a fabrication, and that it was not inscribed on the stele with Attic letters[6] but with the letters of the Ionians.

F. Lycurgus, *Leokrates* 73

And as the crown of their victory (i.e. at the Eurymedon) they were not content to have set up the trophy at Salamis, but they fixed the boundaries for the barbarians (which were required) for the liberty of Hellas and they prevented them from overstepping them. They made a treaty that (the King) was not to sail in a ship of war beyond the Kyaneai and Phaselis, and that the Hellenes, not only those in Europe but also those dwelling in Asia, were to be autonomous.

G. Diodorus 12.4.4-6 (at 449/8 B.C.)

When King Artaxerxes learned of the defeats in Cyprus, and after he consulted with his friends about the war, he judged it advantageous to make peace with the the Hellenes .... (He enquired about Athenian terms (5) and his commanders sent envoys to Athens.) The Athenians gave them a hearing and sent fully empowered ambassadors of which the leader was Kallias son of Hipponikos. There resulted a treaty of peace with the Persians for the Athenians and their allies, of which the chief terms are the following: All Hellenic cities throughout Asia shall be autonomous; the satraps of the Persians shall not advance within a three-day journey of the sea; nor shall a warship sail beyond Phaselis and the Kyaneai. If this is fulfilled by the King and his generals, the Athenians shall not conduct military expeditions against the territory which the King {Artaxerxes}[7] rules. (6) When the treaty was concluded the Athenians withdrew their forces from Cyprus.

H. Plutarch, *Kimon* **13.4-5**

(The double victory of Kimon at the Eurymedon, followed by a further naval victory,) so humbled the pride of the King that he concluded that much talked-about peace (in which he promised) always to keep away from the Hellenic sea by the distance a horse will travel (in a day) and not to sail with a bronze-prowed warship within the Kyaneai and Chelidoniai. Yet Callisthenes says that the barbarian did not sign an agreement to this effect, but that he in fact acted in this way because of his fear arising from that defeat and stayed so far away from Hellas that Perikles with fifty vessels and Ephialtes with a mere thirty sailed beyond the Chelidoniai without a fleet of the barbarians approaching them. (5) But in the (book entitled) *Public Decrees* which Craterus collected, copies of the agreements are set down as having been made.

I. Livy 33.20.1-2

Although the Rhodians ventured to undertake many distinguished actions both on land and on sea in their good faith towards the Roman people and for the sake of the entire Hellenic nation, (2) nothing was more noble than their action in this period (197 B.C.). Undeterred by the colossal magnitude of the approaching war, they sent envoys to the King (Antiochos) to forbid him from sailing past Chelidoniae – a promontory of Cilicia which is celebrated because of the ancient treaty of the Athenians and the Persian Kings.

J. Aristodemus, *FGrHist* 104 F 13

Immediately (after the battle at Oenophyta) they campaigned against Cyprus with Kimon son of Miltiades as general. There they were afflicted by famine and Kimon became ill in the Cyprian city of Citium and died. The Persians perceived that the Athenians were in distress and in their contempt of them attacked with their ships. A struggle arose at sea in which the Athenians prevailed. (2) They elected as general Kallias – the one nicknamed Lakkoploutos ('pit-wealth') – because he became wealthy by discovering a treasury at Marathon and appropriating it.[8] This Kallias made a treaty with Artaxerxes and the rest of the Persians. The treaty was made on these conditions: the Persians were not to sail in warships beyond the Kyaneai, the River Nessos[9] and Phaselis, which is a Pamphylian city, and Chelidoniai. Nor were they to advance within a three-day journey of the sea as covered by a horse at speed.

K. Plato, *Menexenos* 242a[10]

(The war against Xerxes was brought to its ultimate completion by Athens after 479 in campaigns at the Eurymedon, Cyprus, Egypt and elsewhere.) But when peace was made and the city held a position of honor, first rivalry and then from it jealousy arose against the city – something that men tend to direct toward those who are successful. When war broke out after this, the Athenians joined battle at Tanagra (*ca.* 458), fighting the Lakedaimonians for the freedom of the Boeotians.

L. *Suda* s.v. 'Kallias'

Kallias, surnamed Lakkoploutos, confirmed the terms of the treaty (made) in Kimon's time (by going) as general to Artaxerxes. . . .

M. The 'Missing' tribute quota list of 449/8 B.C.

1. The prescript of *IG* I² 196 (I³ 264); *ATL* 2, List 7, p. 13 (449/8 *or* 448/7); 2. The prescript of *IG* I² 198 (I³ 265); *ATL* 2, List 8, p. 14; 3. *IG* I² 199 (I³ 266); the prescript of *ATL* 2, List 9, p. 15.

A. W. Gomme, *CR* 54 (1940) 65-7; S. Dow, *AJA* 45 (1941) 642; B. D. Meritt, *CP* 38 (1943) 223-39, *Hesperia* 41 (1972) 403-5; *ATL* 277f.; D. M. Lewis, *BSA* 49 (1954) 25-9; M. F. McGregor, *Phoenix* 16 (1962) 267-75; W. K. Pritchett, *Historia* 13 (1964) 129-34, *GRBS* 7 (1966) 123-9; Meiggs, *Empire* 154; R. Sealey, *Phoenix* 24 (1970) 13-15.

(1) THE PRESCRIPT OF *ATL* LIST 7 (LIST 6)
In the (year of the) [board] (of the Hellenotamiai) in which Menet[i-mo]s of Lamptrai was Secretary.

(2) THE PRESCRIPT OF *ATL* LIST 8 (LIST 7)
In the (year of the) [-6 or 7[11] board] | in which Diod [-2 or 4-[12] was Secretary,] | of Paionidai.

(3) THE PRESCRIPT OF *ATL* LIST 9 (LIST 8) (?)
(a) *ATL* McGregor
[In the (year of the)] *ninth* [board in which - - -]

(b) D. M. Lewis
- - Be]rg[aioi[13]- - -]

The *lapis primus*, or first stele, records the tribute quota paid to Athena from 454/3 to 440/39, a period of fifteen years. See no. 85 for the first date; the lower terminus is fixed because the series is continued on a 'second stele' covering the years 439/8–433/2. Six lists are engraved on the obverse face; the first two of these continue onto the right lateral face. A seventh list fills the rest of the right lateral face. Five *or* six lists (see below) are inscribed on the reverse, and two on the left lateral face.

The main problem raised by the stele concerns the number of lists it contained. Many believe that the stele has space for fourteen lists only, and not fifteen, and thus that there is a 'missing year.' In that case it is open to postulate that the Peace of Kallias not only occurred, but also entailed the cessation of tribute for the year 449/8. On that view, then, the first five lists on the obverse recorded the tribute quota from 454/3 to 450/49, while the last list on the obverse recorded the tribute quota for the year 448/7. If so, this quota will naturally also have been designated as that received by the *seventh* board of Hellenotamiai, not the sixth.

Unfortunately, though the first five lists have serial numbers for the board of Hellenotamiai in their prescripts, the sixth does not ((1) above). Hence the importance of the serial number of the fragmentary prescript of the next list in the sequence ((2) above), that inscribed on the right lateral face (just beneath the continuation of list number 2). If this list were the 'eighth' (i.e. that for the year 447/6), the hypothesis making 449/8 the 'missing year' would be confirmed (*ATL*), and the layout of the stone would have been as follows:

(A)		*Left*		*Right*
	Reverse	*lateral face*	*Obverse*	*lateral face*
			List 1 (454/3)	
			List 2 (453/2)	
	Lists 9–13	Lists 14–15	Lists 3–5	List 8
	(446/5–442/1)	(441/40–440/39)	(452/1–450/49)	(447/6)
			List 7 (448/7)	

On the other hand, if it were numbered the 'seventh' list (Dow, Gomme), and hence were of the year 448/7, then the one preceding it, the last list on the obverse, must be the 'sixth', dated to 449/8, and a missing year can be sought elsewhere (447/6). In that case the layout would have been as follows:

(B)	*Reverse*	*Left lateral face*	*Obverse*	*Right lateral face*
	List 9 (446/5)		List 1 (454/3)	
			List 2 (453/2)	
	Lists 10–13 (445/4–442/1)	Lists 14–15 (441/40–440/39)	Lists 3–6 (452/1–449/8)	List 7 (448/7)

Alternatively, it is possible to believe that there is space for fifteen lists on the stele. The crucial area of the stone is its reverse side where five lists are usually restored; but six might fit *if* what is usually read as a prescript on the stone ((3a) above) were in reality merely an item included in a list ((3b) above). In that case another list including that item could be located on the upper section of the reverse, as follows:

(C)	*Reverse*	*Left lateral face*	*Obverse*	*Right lateral face*
			List 1 (454/3)	
			List 2 (453/2)	
	Lists 8–13 (447/6–442/1)	Lists 14–15 (441/40–440/39)	Lists 3–6 (452/1–449/8)	List 7 (448/7)

N. See no. 138, Athens honors Herakleides

O. Andocides 3.29

First we made a treaty with the Great King[14] – (and I mention this because) we must consider the past in order to make a proper decision – and a compact of friendship for all time. Epilykos son of Teisandros, my maternal uncle, negotiated it for us. Then, persuaded by Amorges, the runaway slave of the King, we threw it off as if it were worthless and chose Amorges' friendship in the belief that it was more advantageous.[15]

1   This reference (about 380 B.C.) to the Peace of Kallias is the earliest known.
2   The 'King's Peace' of 387/6 B.C. was a compact made by Sparta with Persia yielding all states in Asia to Persia and guaranteeing the autonomy of all states in Greece (to Sparta's advantage). It marked the successful involvement of Persia in Greek affairs.
3   The Chelidoniai are a small group of islands just southeast of the Hieron Promontory on the southwest coast of Lycia; the Kyaneai are usually taken to be

two small islands at the mouth of the Euxine (though Wade-Gery, *Essays* 213 with note 2, suggests that they form the southernmost point of Lycia).

4 See no. 57.
5 Some emend this statement to read 'the treaty of the Athenians with the King.'
6 See the Glossary.
7 Deleted by Vogel (editor of the Teubner text of Diodorus).
8 See Plut. *Aristeides* 5.
9 The river is unidentified.
10 Socrates is speaking and allegedly repeating a funeral oration delivered by Aspasia. This dialogue contains several apparently irresponsible historical allusions and must be used with care as a historical source.
11 '[eighth]': *ATL*; '[seventh]': Pritchett.
12 'Dio[des]': *ATL*; 'Diod[oros]' or 'Diod[otos]' are the alternatives. Diodes is an extremely rare name.
13 The restorations in (a) and (b) are mutually incompatible. McGregor read EN (en[ates=ninth]); Lewis (together with W. G. Forrest) read PΓ (rg). The first could form part of the prescript, the second, part of the body of the text. (The Bergaioi inhabited the upper Chalcidice.)
14 Dareios the Bastard, son of Artaxerxes, who came to the throne in 424 B.C.
15 See Thuc. 8.5.5, 8.28, 8.54.3.

96 Aspasia. After 450 B.C.

A: Plutarch, *Perikles* 24.2–11 (Aeschines Socraticus F 45, 46 Krauss; Cratinus F 241 Kock; Eupolis F 98 Kock); B: Athenaeus 13.56, p. 589de. Cf. Aristophanes, *Acharnians* 526–9 (quoted in no. 122B); Scholiast to Plato, *Menexenos* 235e.

U. von Wilamowitz-Moellendorff, *Aristoteles und Athen* (Berlin 1893) 2.99; E. Meyer, *Forschungen zur alten Geschichte* (Halle 1899) 2.55f.; A. R. Burn, *Pericles and Athens* (London 1948) 128–30; Bury–Meiggs 258; E. F. Bloedow, *Wiener Studien* 88 (1975) 32–48.

A. Plutarch, *Perikles* 24.2–11

Since Perikles appears to have taken these actions against the Samians[1] to please Aspasia, this may be the most proper time to raise questions about the woman, the art or power she possessed to such a degree as to overwhelm the first rank of statesmen and provide philosophers with subject matter about herself that was neither paltry nor limited. (3) It is agreed that she was Milesian by birth, the daughter of Axiochos. They say that she emulated a certain Thargelia, an Ionian woman of earlier times and went after men of the greatest power. (4) For Thargelia too was beautiful and possessed both charm and cleverness. She lived with a great number of Hellenes and brought over to the King's interest all who made love with her; and so she sowed the beginnings of medism in the cities through them inasmuch as they were powerful and great men.

(5) Aspasia, some say, was courted by Perikles since she was a very wise and statesmanlike woman. For even Socrates would visit her on occasion with his well-known friends, and her own intimates brought their wives to listen to her even though she managed a business that was neither seemly nor respectable: she raised young girls as courtesans.

(6) Aeschines says that Lysikles[2] the sheep dealer, though of ignoble and base nature, became first among the Athenians by living with her after Perikles' death. (7) Plato's *Menexenos* (235e), even if the first part has been written in jest, has at least this much of historical truth in it: the woman had the reputation of studying public speaking with many Athenians. All the same, Perikles' love of Aspasia appears to have been rather more sexual (than philosophical).

(8) Perikles had a wife who was related to him but who earlier had been married to Hipponikos, to whom she had borne Kallias 'the rich.'[3] She then bore Xanthippos and Paralos[4] to Perikles. After that, since their marriage was not satisfactory, with her approval he gave her up to another man, while he himself took Aspasia and loved her with extraordinary affection. (9) For they say that when he left the house or returned from the agora he even embraced her with a kiss.

In the Comedies she was called 'New Omphale,' 'Deianeira,' and, again, 'Hera.' Cratinus calls her a concubine[5] outright in these lines: 'And the goddess of pederasty bears, as his Hera, Aspasia, / (the) dog-eyed concubine.' (10) It seems that he also had his illegitimate son by her.[6] Eupolis in his *Demes* has (Perikles) asking (Myronides),[7] 'Is my bastard alive?' and Myronides answering, 'He would have been a man long ago if he were not a little afraid of the disgrace of (being the son of) the whore.' (11) They say that Aspasia became so famous and celebrated that even Kyros – he who waged war against the King for the rule over the Persians[8] – named his best-loved concubine, theretofore called Milto, Aspasia.

B. Athenaeus 13.56, p. 589de

See no. 116C.

1 I.e. the war of 440 B.C.; see nos. 113, 115.
2 This demagogue had a high standing in Athens after Perikles' death, holding the 'second place' after Eukrates (Aristophanes, *Knights* 132 with scholia). He died as general in Caria in 428/7 (Thucydides 3.19).
3 See no. 95.
4 See no. 117 lines 13f. They died of the plague (Plutarch, *Perikles* 36.6–8).
5 After the passage of Perikles' citizenship law in 451 B.C. (no. 86), which limited citizenship to those having Athenian parents on both sides, marriage to a foreigner became legally invalid; cf. J. H. Lipsius, *Das attische Recht* (Leipzig 1905–15) 417f.

6 Named Perikles, he was specially granted Athenian citizenship (cf. Aristotle, *Ath. Pol.* 26.4, Plut. *Per.* 36.5–6). See also nos. 154, note 5 and 161, note 2.
7 The famous general, victor at Oenophyta; see Thucydides 1.105.4, 1.108.3, Diodorus 11.83.1.
8 Kyros the younger, who met his death at Cunaxa in 401 B.C. Xenophon accompanied his army and the *Anabasis* is his account of the adventure.

97 Athenian Decree Enforcing the Use of Athenian Coins, Weights, and Measures. 450–446 *or* 425/4 B.C. *or* before 414 B.C.

The text is a composite based on fragments of the decree found at Syme, Cos, Aphytis, Siphnos, Odessa, and the copy of a fragment, now lost, from Smyrna. As section 10 makes clear, the decree was published throughout the Empire. The fragments are in Ionic letters, except for the one found in Doric Cos, which has Attic lettering and 3-bar sigma. The clauses are numbered for convenience, since lines cannot be indicated.

ATL 2.D14, pp. 61–8, with photos on Plates 5–7; *GHI*, no. 45, pp. 111–17; *IG* I³ 1453. Cf. Aristophanes, *Birds* 1040f. (415/14).

M. N. Tod, *JHS* 69 (1949) 104f.; H. B. Mattingly, *Historia* 10 (1961) 148–69, *CQ* 16 (1966) 187–90, *BSA* 65 (1970) 141f. (425/4); B. D. Meritt and H. T. Wade-Gery, *JHS* 82 (1962) 67–74 (449/8); Meiggs, *Empire* 167–72, 406f., 599–601 (before 445 with qualifications); Bury–Meiggs 226; Sealey, *History* 306.

[(1) - - -] *governors*[1] [in the] cities or[2] [-*c*. 30- (2) The] Hellenotamiai [-*c*. 24-] are to make a record[3] [- - -][4] of any of the cities, [the man who wishes shall immediately] *bring* [before] the law court (Heliaia) of the [Thesmothetai those who have acted against the law.] *The* Thesmothetai shall [institute proceedings for the] *denouncers* of each (malefactor) [within] *five* [days.] (3) If [someone other] than the *governors* [in] the cities does not act *according to what has been decreed*, whether *citizen* or alien, [he shall] *lose his citizen rights* [and his] *property shall be* confiscated, the goddess (Athena) receiving *the* [tithe. (4) If] there are *no* Athenian governors, the chief magistrates[5] [of each city shall perform all that is in the] decree. If they do not act in compliance with [what has been decreed, let there be directed against] these magistrates [prosecution at Athens] involving [loss of citizen-rights. (5) In the] mint, [after receiving] the *money*, [they shall mint no] *less* than half and [-*c*. 31-][6] the cities. *The fee exacted* [by the superintendents (of the mint) shall invariably be three] drachmas out of each *mna*. [-*c*. 23-] they shall *convert* (the money) or [be] liable [-*c*. 12-[7] (6) Whatever] is *left over* of the money [that has been exacted shall be minted and handed over] either to the *generals* [or to the -*c*. 15-][8] (7) *When* it has been handed over, [-*c*. 31-] and to Hephais[tos -*c*. 14-][9] (8) If] *anyone* proposes [or] puts to a vote regarding [these matters that it be permissible for foreign currency] to be used or *loaned*, [an accusation shall immediately be lodged against him with][10] the Eleven. The [Eleven are to punish him with] *death*. [If] he disputes the charge, [let them bring him to court.] (9) Heralds shall be elected by the [People -*c*. 37-][11] one to the *Islands*, [one to Ionia, one to Hellespo]nt, and *one to* [the] Thracian [region. -*c*. 49- they are to] dispatch [-*c*. 19-][12] they are to be *subject* (to a fine of) *ten thousand* [drachmas. (10) This] decree shall be [set up by the] *governors* in the cities, [after they have inscribed it on a] *stele* of marble, in the marketplace of [each] *city*, and (the same shall be done) by the *superintendents* [in front] of the mint. This [the Athenians shall do] *if* (the peoples) themselves are not willing.[13] (11) The herald making the journey shall require of them (that they accomplish) all that the Athenians *command*. (12) An addition shall be made to the oath of the Boule by the Secretary of the [Boule, in future, as] *follows*: 'If someone coins *money* of silver in the *cities and* does not use [Athen]ian *coins* or weights or *measures* [but (uses instead) foreign coins] and measures and weights, [I shall exact punishment and penalize him according to the former] decree which Klearch[os moved.' (13) Anyone shall be allowed to turn in] the foreign money [which he possesses and to convert it in the same fashion] whenever he chooses. The *city* [shall give him in place of it our own coin.] *Each* individual (?) [shall bring] his money [to Athens and deposit it at the] *mint*. (14) *The* superintendents, having *recorded* [everything yielded up by each, are to] *set up* [a marble stele[14] in front of the] *mint* for scrutiny by *whoever wishes*. [They are to make a record of the total of the coin which is] foreign, *keeping separate* [the silver and the gold, and the total of our] *money* [-----]

1 Greek *archons*: here Athenian magistrates sent out to supervise local governments; cf. no. 92, line 47, and the Glossary. But the word can also be used of local magistrates, as may be the case in section 10 of the present decree, where I again translate 'governors.'
2 '(or) *governors* [from Athens': *ATL*, which requires that the same word (*archons*), in the preceding phrase, be understood to refer to local (non-Athenian) magistrates.
3 'The] Hellenotamiai are to make a record [of the mints in the cities]': *ATL*.
4 '*If* [someone incorrectly records the (minting)]': *ATL*.
5 See note 1.
6 '[they shall so return it that sufficient coin will be available to]': *ATL*.
7 This sentence, as restored in *ATL*: 'They shall *convert* [the other half within five months] or [be] liable [according to the law.'
8 'Apodektai immediately': *ATL*.
9 '[a vote shall be held about Athena's and Hephais[tos' debts]': *ATL*.
10 'used or borrowed, [he shall be haled before]': Lewis, *Phoros* 84.

11 'and they shall be sent to the cities according to what has been decreed]':
   ATL; 'to announce what has been decreed]': Tod.
12 The preceding, as restored in *ATL*: '[their individual itinerary having been
   drawn up by the generals, let (the generals)] dispatch (them). [If they do not,
   one by one]'.
13 The text and meaning of this section are uncertain.
14 Tod; 'set (it) up [by the side of the stele': *ATL*.

98 Decree on the Payment of Tribute, Passed on the motion of Kleinias. 448/7 *or* 430s *or* 426/5 B.C.

Marble stele, Attic writing, stoichedon, Athens.

IG I^2 66 (I^3 34); *ATL* 2.D7, pp. 50-1, with photos on Plate 2; *GHI, no. 46, 117-21.

H. B. Mattingly, *Historia* 10 (1961) 150-69, *BSA* 65 (1970) 129-33 (426/5); B. D. Meritt and H. T. Wade-Gery, *JHS* 82 (1962) 67-74 (448/7); R. Meiggs, *JHS* 86 (1966) 97 (448/7 or 430s), *Empire* 212f.; de Ste Croix, *Origins* 310-14; Sealey, *History* 285.

Gods. | Resolved by the Boule [and the] Peo|ple, Oineis held the pry-
5 tany, [Sp]ou|dias was Secretary, [-6-]on || presided, Kleini[as[1] made
   the motion.] The B|oule, the governors[2] [in] th|e cities and the *epis-
   kopoi*[3] shall s|ee to it *that* the tribute payments | be collected each ||
10 year and *be brought* to Athe|ns. Identification seals *shall be made* f|or
   the cities, *so that* it will be imposs|ible that fraud be committed by
   those *bringing* the t|ribute payments. *And* after [the] city has inscribed
15 in || an account book whatever *tribute payment* it is sending, and has s|et
   its *seal* to it, the book shall be sent to Athens. Let those b|ringing it give
   up the account book in the Boule, to be re|ad *at the same time as* they
   are paying in the tribute money. And let the Pr|ytaneis, after the Dio-
20 nysia, summon an Assembly for th||e Hellenotamiai to make known to
   the Athenians which of the cit|ies paid *the tribute money* in full and
   which fe|ll short; these separately, as many [-9-].[4] Let the Athenians
   sele|ct men, *four* [in number, and send them to] the cities to give a
25 r|eceipt for *the* [tribute payment made] *and* to de||mand what was not
   [remitted -14-],[5] t|wo of them to sail *to* [the cities of the Islands and
   of Ionia on a] s|wift trireme, [the other two to sail to those of the Hel-
   lespont] an|d of Thrace. [The Prytaneis] *shall bring up* [this matter in
   the] | Boule and in the [Assembly at once after the Dionysia, and they]
30 shall c||onsider it [without interruption until] *a decision has been
   tak*|*en.* And if any Ath[enian or ally is guilty of wrongdoing in respect
   to] th|e tribute which it is required [-28-]|[..][6] for those *carrying it*
   [-16-[7] (the culprit) may be] in|dicted before [the Prytaneis by] any-
35 one who wishes, [Athen]||ian or *ally.* [The] *Prytaneis shall bring* |

before the Boule [whatever indictment] may have been drawn up, [or]
they shall *be | called to account* for bribery and (be liable to a fine of)
[-8-⁸ drachmas] each. [As to the man | charged by *the* [Boule, sen-
tence on] *him* shall [not] be in its hands, [but] he shall | be brought
before *the* [Heliaia immediately]. If and when he shall be found
40 [guil‖ty], judgment shall be *passed by* [the] Prytaneis⁹ as to what
seems proper for | *him* as a punishment or [as a fine.¹⁰ And] as to the
bring|ing of the cow or [the panoply],¹¹ if anyone commits a wrong, a
similar indictment *shall | lie* against him [and the penalty shall be] the
same. The [Hellen|otamiai, after registering it on a] notice-board
45 *whitened ‖ over*, [shall publish both the assessment] of the tribute and
[-8-] | [-21-¹² and] *write down* [-7-]

(Approximately ten lines lost)

[-24-] Boule *entering of|fice* [-25-]. All those who *have brought |*
(payment) [to Athens and who on the notice-board] are listed as ow‖-
60 ing [-18-] publish to the Peop|le [-20- If] any of the cities | [raises
any dispute about the tribute] *payment*, claiming to have | *paid it* [-16-]
65 the government (?) of the | [city -20-] the cities and ‖ [-20-] not be
permitted | [-25-] let the liability be the | [accuser's -17-]. The indict-
ment shall be | [lodged with the Polemarch in the month of Game]lion.
70 If anyone | [disputes -17-] prosecutions, the Boule, *hav‖ing considered*
[-17-]. Let the | [Eisagogeis] bring [into the Heliaia those whose] tri-
bute to the [Athe]nians | [is owing, in the order of the] *list* of denun-
ciations. | [-21- of the current year's] tribute and of the previous |
75 year's [-12- the Boule,] framing a preliminary decree, shall ‖ [refer
-18-] is concerned at the next | [day's meeting -22-] of the election to
tra|nsact (?)

(The rest of line 77 is lost, but there is a vacant
space at the end of the line)

1 The mover has been identified by proponents of the earlier date with that
   Kleinias who was the father of Alkibiades and who died at the battle of Koron-
   eia in 447 or 446 B.C.
2 'archons': here meaning governors of tributary cities; cf. no. 97, note 1.
3 Inspectors: see the Glossary.
4 '[as many as there may be]': *ATL.*
5 '[according as it fell short]': *GHI.*
6 '[that the cities, having written (their sums) on a tabl|et]': *GHI.*
7 '[to send to Athens]': *GHI.*
8 '[one thousand': *GHI;* '[ten thousand]': *ATL.*
9 I.e. it would at this stage be the duty of the prytanis to bring the matter of
   punishment before the Boule for deliberation.
10 This standard expression, 'punishment or fine,' distinguishes between penalties

that would affect the accused's person and those that affected his property. Those that would affect his person (my 'punishment') were death, imprisonment, exile, and the loss of citizen-rights. A fine could be anything from a nominal sum to the confiscation of the entire estate of the man convicted. See Harrison 2.168ff.

11 For the 'cow and panoply' (full suit of armor), see no. 136, line 57 and, for this demand upon an Athenian colony, see no. 100, lines 11-12. See also the Glossary.

12 '[those cities | which have paid the complete sum]': *GHI*.

99 An Athenian Treaty with Colophon. 447/6 *or* 427/6 B.C.

Four fragments of marble, two of them joining. Attic writing with strong admixture of Ionic, 3-bar sigma, nonstoichedon, Athens.

IG I² 14, 15 (I³ 37); *ATL* 2.D15, pp. 68f., and Plate 8; *GHI, no. 47, pp. 121-5. Cf. Thucydides 3.34.

ATL 3.282-4; B. D. Meritt and H. T. Wade-Gery, *JHS* 83 (1963) 102f. (447/6); H. B. Mattingly, *Historia* 12 (1963) 266f., *Ehrenberg studies* 210-12 (427/6); Meiggs, *Empire* 162; A. G. Woodhead, *Akten des 6. Internationalen Kongresses für griechische und lateinische Epigraphik, München 1972* (Vestigia 17, Munich 1973) 351f.; cf. 354; Sealey, *History* 289.

(B)¹

10 [--] of² [--] | [-8-] *decree* becomes [--] | [-13-] the time [--] | | [-9-] of
15 the [Co]lophonians and *the* [--] | [-10-] Athens' Protectress³ [--] | | | [-11-]
of his (?) to the [--] | [-10-] of the Colophonians [--] | [-11-] comes
about [--] | | [-5-Athen]ians, unless someone [--] | [-8-] the *five* men
20 elected [--] | | | [--] *that* which has been voted [--] | [-8-] they shall so
that⁴ [--] | [-10-] with the *People* [--] | [-7-] *their* holy places [--] | [-7-]
25 each for [each] *day*⁵ [--] | | | [-5- The] money [must be] *paid* [--] | [-6-]⁶
and the Diosiritai [--] | [-6-] of the Colophonians [--] | [-10-] *whatever*
30 may [--] | [-10-] of each [--] | | | [-6-] when [--] | [...the] *names* [--] |
[---] | | [---]

(C)

35 [---] | | | [---] | | [---] | | [This] decree [and the oath shall be inscribed by the]
Sec | *retary* of the *Boule* [on a marble stele on the Akropolis at the ex-
40 pens | e] of the Colophonians. [At Colophon⁷ this and the oa | | th] shall be
inscribed [on a marble stele by the - 10-]⁸ | oikists (colonists) [--] | [--]⁹
I shall s | *peak* and counsel [as fittingly and as well as I can] *reg* | *arding*
45 the People [of the Athenians -21-] | | [..]¹⁰ and I [shall] not *rebel*
[against the People of the Athenians, either] | in word or deed, [neither
I myself nor shall I let another persuade me,] | and I shall cherish the

[People of the Athenians and] I shall [not defe|ct] and [--]¹¹ | I *myself*
50 nor [shall I let] *another* [persuade me--] || [....] city [--] | [..] *these*
things (as) true [--by | Z]eus and Apo[llo and Demeter. And if] | I
transgress [this (oath), may I be utterly destroyed, both myself and]
55 my *fa|mily* [for all time, but if I keep my oath may there be] || an
abundance of [good] things for me.

1 The first fragment, (A) (lines 1–10), is very badly preserved and is omitted
   here. Bradeen and McGregor, *Studies* 94–9, provide the most recent epigraphical commentary on it. Their most important observation is that 'C]olophon'
   should be read in line 1. Mattingly had stressed the absence of the name as one of
   his arguments for a later date for the inscription.
2 'of Triopion': *ATL*; it is situated in the Cnidian Chersonese.
3 See no. 55, line 5, for another use of this epithet of Athena.
4 (From line 19) '[as oikists (colonists) of Co|llophon] *shall declare that* which
   has been voted [to the cities, an|d] they shall [take care] so that': *ATL*.
5 (From line 23) '[Of those elected, let there be pa|id to] each for [each] *day*
   [as traveling money a dr||achma': *ATL*.
6 '[--by the Colophon|ians] and the Diosiritai': Hiller (*IG* I² 14/15); '[by the
   Colophonians and the L|ebedians] and the Diosiritai': *ATL*.
7 *ATL*; '[in Notion': Mattingly.
8 'Colophonian]': *ATL*; 'elected]': Mattingly.
9 '--The Colophonians shall] *swear* [as follows: I shall act and]': *ATL*. Cf. the
   oath for the Erythraeans, no. 72, lines 20ff.
10 '[and their alli|les]': *ATL*.
11 '[I shall not destroy the] *democracy* [at Colophon either]': *ATL* (from line
   48); Mattingly restores 'in Notion' in the place of 'Colophon.'

100   The Foundation of an Athenian Colony at Brea. 447/6 *or* about 445 *or* 439/8 *or* 426/5 B.C.

Two fragments of a marble stele, developed Attic letters, stoichedon,
Athens.

IG I² 45 (I³ 46); B. D. Meritt, *Hesperia* 10 (1941) 317–19; **GHI*, no. 49, pp. 128–
33 (*c.* 445). Cf. Plutarch, *Perikles* 11.5; Stephanus of Byzantium s.v. 'Brea.'

ATL 3.287f. (447/6); A. G. Woodhead, *CQ* n.s. 2 (1952) 57–62 (439/8); H. B.
Mattingly, *CQ* n.s. 16 (1966) 172–86 (426/5); Meiggs, *Empire* 158f.; Bury–Meiggs
533.

(A)

[-19-] to which [he] *denounces* [or | indicts (a man),] let him *prose-*
cute. If he prosecutes, [--] | [-7-]¹ by the informant or the prosecutor
5 [-7-] | [-7-]² are to be provided for them by the *apoikist* ||s³ *to obtain*
good omens for the colony, [however many | they] decide. Geonomoi⁴

shall be elected, [ten | in number,] one from (each) tribe. These *are to*
distribute [the | land. Dem]okleides shall establish the [colon|y] *at his*
10 *discretion* as [best] he can. [T||he sacred] *precincts* which have been
reserved (for the gods) shall be left as [they ar|e, and] others shall not
be consecrated.[5] A cow and [panopl|y][6] shall be *brought* to the Great
Panathenaia [and to the D|ionysi]a a phallos. If anyone *wages* a cam-
paign [agai|nst the territory] of the settlers, aid shall be dispatched by
15 *the* [cities a|ls swiftly] as possible, as prescribed by the agreements
[which, when . .]||[-6-] tos was Secretary (of the Boule), were contrac-
ted [for t|he cities] in the Thrace-ward region. (They shall) inscribe
[this | on a stele] and set it up on the Akropolis. [Provis|ion shall be
20 made for] the stele by the settlers [at] their *own* [ex||pense]. If any-
one proposes a decree contrary to the [stel|e or if a] *public speaker* ad-
vises or [attempts] to induce (anyone) | to *rescind* or cancel any part
of what has been voted, | let him and [his] children [lose their citizen-
rights | and his] property be confiscated (and let) the [goddess receive
25 the t||ithe,] except if the settlers themselves [....]||[.... make the
request (?)]. All those who are enrolled [to go as col|onists[7] who are]
soldiers, after they have returned [to Athen|s] are to be in Brea within
thirty days [as colon|ists]. (The settlers) shall lead out the colony
30 within *thirty* [d||ays. A]ischines shall accompany them and *provid|e*
[(them) with the] *money vv.*

(B)

[Ph]antokles made the motion. Concerning | the Brean colo|ny, (let all
35 the rest be) just as Demokl||eides moved. But Phantokle|s shall be
introduced by E|rechtheis, the tribe in prytan|y, to the Boule in it|s
40 first session. As to || Brea, thetes and ze|ugitai[8] shall go there as the
colon|ists.

---

1 '[let] *pledges* [be tak|en from him]': *IG* I[2].
2 '[Resources fo|r sacrificing]': Meritt.
3 Apparently subordinates of the *oikistes*, the founder and hero of a colony.
4 Those who distribute the allotments of the colony to the colonists.
5 Whether this refers to the preservation of the cult sites of the earlier inhabitants
  (cf. Thucydides 4.98.2) or to those already chosen for the gods of this very
  colony is uncertain.
6 For the 'panoply', a suit of armor, cf. no. 98, line 43, and the Glossary, Cow and
  panoply.
7 The soldiers are called *epoikoi*, 'colonists,' or 'additional settlers,' in contrast with
  the *apoikoi*, 'settlers,' already mentioned. Cf. no. 129.
8 The two lowest property classes in Athens; cf. Aristotle, *Athenaion Politeia* 7.

101   Memorial for Pythion of Megara. 446/5 B.C.
Marble stele, Ionic lettering, nonstoichedon, Athens. Hexameters.

IG I^2 1085; **GHI*, no. 51, pp. 137f. Cf. Thucydides 1.114-115.1; Diodorus 12.7; Plutarch, *Perikles* 22

Gomme, etc., *HCT* 1.340f.; Meiggs, *Empire* 177f.; Bury-Meiggs 223.

[This] memorial [is] set over the grave of the bravest of men. / Pythion | of Megara slew seven men / and broke seven s|pears in their bodies. / He chose the path of bravery, bri|nging honor to his father among his
5   people. // This man, who rescued thr|lee Athenian tribes / by leading them from Pegai through Boeotia to Athens, / brought | honor to Andokides[1] with his two thousand prisoners.[2] / No | mortal man suffered improper injury at his hands / and he went down to Hades most bl|essed in the eyes of all. The tribes are these: Pandionis, Kekr|opis, Antiochis.[3]

1 See no. 105.
2 Or 'slaves.'
3 The last sentence is added in prose.

102   Athenian Regulations for Eretria (?). 446/5 *or* 424/3 B.C.
Marble stele, Ionic lettering, nonstoichedon, Athens.

IG I^2 17+ (I^3 39); **ATL* 2.D16, pp. 69f., with a photo on Plate 9 (446/5).

Gomme, etc., *HCT* 1.343f.; H. B. Mattingly, *JHS* 81 (1961) 124-32 (424/3); J. R. Green and R. K. Sinclair, *Historia* 19 (1970) 519-27; Bury-Meiggs 223. Cf. Thucydides 1.114.3; Aristophanes, *Clouds* 211-13 (424/3), with scholia; Diodorus 12.7; Plutarch, *Perikles* 23.3-4. The evidence for the lower date is Philochorus, *FGrHist* 328 F 119, quoted in no. 86, above.

[- - this I shall guarantee the Ere|trians if they obey the People of the Athenian|s.] Oaths shall be administered [by the embassy coming from Ere|tria,] together with the [oath-commissioners, to the Athenians, and
5   a record shall be m|lade] of those who have sworn it. *That* [the oath be taken by everyo|ne] shall be the responsibility of the *generals.* [In these terms | shall they] take the oath: 'I [shall] not [rebel from the Peo|ple] of the Athenians either *by artifice* [or by device] *of an|y kind* either by
10 word or [by deed, nor will anyone in rebel|llion] persuade me; and [if anyone rebels I shall denounce him] | *to the* [Ath]e[n]ians. [I shall pay] the *tribute* [to the Athen|ians which] I shall persuade [the Athenians - -]

103   Athenian Regulations for Chalcis. 446/5 *or* 424/3 B.C.

Marble stele, Attic letters (with one Ionism), stoichedon, Athens.

IG I² 39 (I³ 40); *ATL* 2.D17, pp. 70–2, with a photo on Plate 10; **GHI*, no. 52, pp. 138–44 (446/5). For ancient testimonia see no. 102.

Gomme, etc., *HCT* 1.242, 293f., 342f. (446/5); *ATL* 3.297 (446/5); H. B. Mattingly, *JHS* 81 (1961) 124–32, *Ehrenberg studies* 201f. (424/3); J. R. Green and R. K. Sinclair, *Historia* 19 (1970) 520 (446/5); A. G. Woodhead, *Akten des 6. Internationalen Kongresses für griechische und lateinische Epigraphik, München 1972* (Vestigia 17, Munich 1973) 349–51 (mid-440s); Bury–Meiggs 223f. (446/5); Sealey, *History* 292–4 (446/5); C. W. Fornara, *CSCA* 10 (1977) 39–55 (446/5); A. Henry, *ZPE* 35 (1979) 287–91 (446/5).

Resolved by the Boule and the People, Antiochis held the *prytany*, Drak[on]tides presided, Diognetos made the motion:[1] The oath shall be taken as follows by the Athenian | Boule and the dikasts:[2] 'I shall
5   not deport Cha|lcidians from Chalcis or devastate the city | or deprive any individual of his ri|ghts or punish him with exile or impris|on him or kill him or take property f|rom anyone unheard in trial without (the
10   concurrence of) the People of the Ath|lenians. I shall not have a vote taken, without summons to attend trial, against | either the government or any private individual wha|tever. When an embassy has arrived, I shall introduce it | to the Boule and People within ten days when | I
15   hold the prytany, to the best of my power. This I shall gua|lrantee the Chalcidians if they obey the Pe|ople of the Athenians.' The oath shall be administered by an embass|y which is to come from Chalcis, together with the oath-commissioner|s, as regards the Athenians, and they shall inscribe the names of those who took the o|ath. That everyone takes
20   the oath shall be the respon|lsibility of the generals. *vv* | The Chalcidians shall take the following oath: 'I shall not rebe|l against the People of the Athenians either by artifi|ce or by device of any kind either by
25   word or | by deed. Nor shall I follow anyone in rebellion a|lnd if anyone does rebel, I shall denounce him to the Athenians. | I shall pay the tribute to the Athenians which | I persuade them (to assess), and as an ally I shall be | the best and truest possible. | And I shall assist the
30   People of the Athenians || and defend them if anyone does injury to the People | of the Athenians, and I shall obey the People of the Athle-nians.' This oath shall be taken by the Chalcidian adu|lts, all without exception. Whoever does not take the oath is to be deprived of his
35   citizen-rights | and his property shall be confiscated, and || Olympian Zeus[3] shall receive the tithe consecrate|d from his property. The oath shall be administered by an embas|sy of the Athenians which shall go to Chalcis, together with th|e oath-commissioners in Chalcis, and they shall inscri|be the names of the Chalcidians who swear it. *vv* ||

(A vacant space)

Antikles made the motion: With good fortune for Athe\|ns shall the oath be exchanged by the Athenians and Chal\|cidians just as it was voted for the Eretrians | by the People of the Athenians. That it be most speedil\|y accomplished shall be the responsibility of the generals. \|| As oath-commissioners who will go t\|o Chalcis, the People shall elect five me\|n immediately. As to the hostages, re\|ply shall be made to the Chalcidians that as of now the Athe\|nians are resolved to leave the matter as voted.[4] W\||hen it seems best, after consideration, they will make a\|n agreement[5] such as seems suitabl\|e for the Athenians and Chalcidians. As to the a\|liens in Chalcis who are resident there | and who are not subject to Athenian taxes, or who have been granted b\||y the People of the Athenians immunity from public burdens (ateleia), they | shall pay (taxes) to Chalcis like the othe\|r Chalcidians.[6] This decree and the | oath shall be inscribed at Athens by the Sec\|retary of the Boule on a marble stele and sh\||all be set up on the Akropolis at the expense of the Chalcidi\|ans; in Chalcis, in the temple of Zeus | Olympios, let the Boule of the Chalcidians inscrib\|e and set it up. This is decreed for the Chalc\|idians. *vv* The sacrifices required by the ora\||cles on account of Euboea shall be performed as quickly as possible by | Hierokles and three men chosen by th\|e Boule from among its members. That it be done most speedily | shall be the joint responsibility of the generals and | they shall supply the money required for it. *vv* \|| Archestratos made the motion: Let all the rest be as A\|ntikles (proposed), but the legal processes of punishment[7] shall be in the hands of the Chalcidians, as regards t\|heir own citizens in Chalcis, just as they are in Ath\|ens for the Athenians, except (when the penalty involved is) exile, deat\|h or loss of citizen-rights. In regard to these, appeal shall li\||e in Athens, in the law court (heliaia) of the Thesmoth\|etes, in accordance with the decree of the People.[8] As to the pro\|tection of Euboea, the generals shall have the responsibi\||lity, to their best ability, that it b\|e as excellent as possible for the Athenians. \|| (The) Oath.[9] | *vacat*

---

1 The name of the secretary of the Boule, normally mentioned, is omitted from the prescript. Since another stone had been affixed on the left of this one, with a third over the two of them, his name may have been inscribed at the top of the monument. The monument apparently contained more than one decree (see lines 49, 76).
2 The full panel of the 6,000 Athenian jurors: Aristotle, *Athenaion Politeia* 24.3.
3 In Chalcis: cf. lines 61f.
4 Hesychius states, s.v. 'Eretrian Catalogue,' that a decree was passed in 442/1 'to make a list of the sons of the richest men from Eretria as hostages.'
5 An alternative view holds that this word means not 'agreement' but 'exchange' or 'replacement' of one group of hostages by another.

6 The sentence is difficult to understand since it would seem to go without saying that resident aliens would pay their taxes to Chalcis: residents of any state, whether citizens or aliens, naturally paid taxes to the state in which they lived. The sentence is therefore probably intended to indicate a limitation of that general rule: certain resident aliens were *excused* from paying taxes to Chalcis. The aliens in question have been supposed to be (a) Athenian klerouchs (*ATL* 3.296f., P. A. Brunt, *Ehrenberg studies* 88); (b) non-Athenian resident aliens who pay taxes to Athens or who have received grants of immunity from Athens (Henry; *GHI*); or (c) simply Athenians resident at Chalcis (Fornara).

7 Or, 'the public examination of the conduct of magistrates.' See Glossary, 'Euthynai.'

8 By this means, Athens could ensure that her friends in Chalcis would not be oppressed by anti-Athenian elements in that state and, at the same time, that her enemies would not be unjustly acquitted of serious offenses.

9 In large letters filling the line. The oath is not inscribed, probably because it has already been incorporated into the body of the decree.

104   The Bribery of Pleistoanax and Kleandridas of Sparta. 446/5 B.C.

Scholiast to Aristophanes, *Clouds* 859 (424/3) (Ephorus, *FGrHist* 70 F 193). Cf. Thucydides 1.114.2, 2.21.1; Plutarch, *Perikles* 22.2-4; Diodorus 13.106.10.

Gomme, etc., *HCT* 1.341; de Ste Croix, *Origins* 196-200; Bury–Meiggs 223.

Aristoph. *Clouds* 858-9: (Pheidippides) What have you done with your shoes, you idiot? / (Strepsiades) Like Perikles, I lost them 'for what was necessary.'

Scholion: Of the abundant money on the Akropolis, Perikles spent most for the war. They say that when he was rendering accounts he stated simply that he had spent twenty talents 'for what was necessary.' Ephorus says that the Lacedaemonians later learned of this and confiscated the property of Kleandridas and fined Pleistoanax 15 talents. They supposed that (these men) had been bribed by the agents of Perikles because of their having spared the rest of the Athenian territory and that Perikles had not wished to state baldly: 'I gave the missing amount to the Kings of the Lacedaemonians.'

105   Andocides the Orator and His Forebears. 446/5-416/15 B.C.

A: *Suda* s.v. 'Andokides' (Hellanicus, *FGrHist* 323a F 24c); B: [Plutarch] *Lives of the Ten Orators* 55 (*Moralia* 834bc (Hellanicus, *FGrHist* 323a F 24a). Cf. Thucydides 6.60.4; Plutarch, *Alkibiades* 21. Cf. no. 147.

D. M. Macdowell, *Andokides on the Mysteries* (Oxford 1962) 1-6; Bury–Meiggs 223.

A. *Suda* **s.v. 'Andokides'**

Andocides. An Athenian, one of the ten famous orators, the son of Leogoras, a descendant of Telemachos son of Odysseus, and of Nausikaa, as Hellanicus says.

B. [Plutarch] *Lives of the Ten Orators* **55 (***Moralia* **834bc)**

Andocides was the son of Leogoras whose own father, ⟨Andokides,⟩[1] once made peace with the Lacedaemonians for the Athenians (446/5). He had as his deme either Kydathenaion or Thorai and was of a Eupatrid family.[2] According to Hellanicus he was also (descended) from Hermes. For he was related to the family of the Kerykes.[3] Thus[4] he[5] was appointed at one time to go with Glaukon and twenty ships to the aid of the Corcyraeans when they were at war with the Corinthians. After that he[6] was accused of impiety as having mutilated the Herms and having sinned against the Mysteries of Demeter (416/15). Condemned for this he was freed on condition that he inform against the guilty.

1 This name is Ruhnken's addition to the text (cited in the *apparatus criticus* of *FGrHist* 323a F 24a), which, in the original Greek, would otherwise wrongly make Leogoras a signatory of the peace. An ostrakon exists which reads '[Ando]-kides son of [Leog]oras' (*GHI*, p. 41).
2 For the Eupatrids see Hignett, *Constitution* 65ff.; R. Sealey, *Essays in Greek politics* (New York n.d.) 9–41.
3 Pseudo-Plutarch is our only authority for this family connection, and it must be rejected. See Jacoby, *FGrHist* IIIb Suppl. 1.53, and J. K. Davies, *Athenian propertied families* (Oxford 1971) 27.
4 I.e. because he was allegedly a herald; 'kerykes' means 'heralds.'
5 Another error: either the grandfather or the father of Andocides is meant; but it is uncertain that an Andokides was general in 433/2 as Thuc. 1.51.4 alleged; see Fornara, *Generals* 51, and no. 126 below.
6 The orator himself: see, in general, his own apology, *On the Mysteries*.

106   The Establishment of a Board of Eleusinian Superintendents. After 450 *or* before 445 *or* about 432/1 B.C.

Marble stele, Attic writing, 3-bar sigma, stoichedon, Eleusis.

SEG X 24 = *Hill, B 41, pp. 296f. (after 450) (*IG* I[3] 32); B. D. Meritt and H. T. Wade-Gery, *JHS* 83 (1963) 111–14 (before 445). Cf. no. 75.

H. B. Mattingly, *Historia* 10 (1961) 171–3 (about 432/1); R. Meiggs, *JHS* 86 (1966) 96 (no. 26) (mid-440s).

[-32-]|*Hieropoioi* and [-19-]| *and* spend [-19-]|[..] of the same. *The*

5 Prytaneis are to bring ‖ before the Boule the [-10-] when they re|quest
   (it). Thespieus [made the motion: Let all the] rest be a|s (resolved) *by
   the Boule*. But [men shall be elected] from the Athenian|s, five in num-
   ber, and *they* [shall draw the pay of] *four* obol|s each from the Kola-
10 kretai, and one ‖ of them *shall be Secretary* [according to] *vote*. Thes|e
   men shall take charge of the money of the two g|oddesses[1] just as those
   (administering) the Akropolis wo|rks were in charge of the temple and
   the statue.[2] | Refusal of the office shall not be allowed. [Those] who
15 are electe|ld shall approach the Boule, if anything is ow|ed the two god-
   desses, and they shall declare it and exa|ct it. They shall hold office for
   a year, after taking the oath be|tween the two altars at Eleusis, and in
20 the futu|re, elections shall be held in the same way every year for t|lhe
   men. They shall also administer the yearly reven|ues which accrue to
   the two goddesses, and if | they discover that anything has been lost,
   they *shall recover it*. The | Logistai shall calculate in Eleusis the money
25 | expended in Eleusis, and in the city the money ‖ expended in the
   city, summoning the archite|ct Koroibos and Lysanias to the Ele|usin-
   ion[3] (for this purpose); and at Phaleron (they shall calculate) in the
   temple that (which was) | spent for Phaleron. They shall spend for
30 whatever is mo|st necessary, consulting[4] with the priests and the Boul‖e
   henceforth. They shall summon back (prior boards), | *beginning* with
   the *board* [-12-]|[-6-][5] the money. A record shall be set up of this *dec-
   re|e* on a stele in Eleusis *and* [in the city and in Ph]|al[e]ron in the
35 Eleusinion. [-8-[6] made the motio‖n:] Let all the rest be *as* [Thespieus
   (moved). But the co|unting] shall be done [of the monies which the]|
   treasurers gave over [-17-]|[....][7] the *architect* [-14-]

1 Demeter and Kore (Persephone).
2 Either the temple of Athena Polias and the statue of Athena Promachos (said by
   Pausanias 1.28.2 to be an offering from Persian booty taken at Marathon but not
   erected until the mid-fifties) or the Parthenon and the gold-and-ivory statue of
   Athena Parthenos, which were completed in 439/8; cf. no. 120.
3 In Athens.
4 This word is in the next line.
5 '[by which Ktesias was g|iven]': Meritt and Wade-Gery.
6 Lysanias' name is generally restored (because he is an interested party (line 26)
   and has the right number of letters in his name).
7 '[by the elected fiv|e (men) and]': Meritt and Wade-Gery.

**107 Extracts from Pseudo-Xenophon ('The Old Oligarch'). 445–441
B.C. *or* before 432 *or* not before 431 *or* 420–415 B.C.**

H. Frisch, *The constitution of the Athenians* (Copenhagen 1942) 11–37 (before
432); *G. W. Bowersock, *HSCP* 71 (1967) 33–5 (445–441).

A. W. Gomme, *HSCP* Suppl. 1 (1940) 211–45 (420–415); de Ste Croix, *Origins* 307–10 (not before 431); R. Sealey, *CSCA* 6 (1973) 253–63; Bury–Meiggs 267f.

1.1–3

(1.1) As to the Athenian form of government, I do not approve of the fact that they adopted this type of government because in adopting it they chose to favor the rabble instead of the better people. For this reason, therefore, I do not approve of this. But since this was their decision, I will demonstrate that they are good at keeping their form of government secure and at managing everything else which the Hellenes suppose they do wrongly.

(1.2) First of all I say that the poor and the people[1] rightly have[2] the better of the nobles and the rich there because the people are the ones who row the ships and who bring the city its power far more than the hoplites, the nobles, and the better people. Since this is the case, it seems to be just for everybody to share in the offices, both by lot and by election, and for anyone who wishes to be able to speak (in the Assembly). (1.3) Secondly, of all those offices which bring security when properly performed and, when not properly performed, bring danger to the entire people, of none of these do the people want a share. They do not think it right for themselves to share in the generalship or the hipparchy by way of the lot.[3] For the people know that they get more benefit from not holding these offices themselves but by allowing the most influential men to hold them. But as to all those offices which exist for the sake of wages and domestic gain, these the people are anxious to hold.

1.10

The slaves and metics enjoy at Athens the greatest degree of license. There it is neither possible to strike them nor will they get out of your way. I will state the reason for this local peculiarity. If it were the law that a slave - or a metic or a freedman - might be hit by the free man, he (the free man) would frequently strike an Athenian on the assumption he was a slave. For the people there dress no better than the slaves and the metics, and they are in no way better in appearance.

1.14–18

(1.14) As to the allies - that they (the Athenians) sail out and make denunciations, as they are thought to do, and hate the better people, knowing that it is inevitable that the ruler be hated by the ruled, and that if the rich and the better people have power in the cities the empire of the people of Athens will be of the briefest duration – for this reason, then, they dishonor the better people and take away their property and drive them out and kill them while they strengthen the rabble. But the better Athenians preserve the better sort in the allied cities, since they know that it is a good thing for them always to preserve the best elements in the cities. (1.15) Someone might say that it is precisely the strength of the Athenians to have their allies capable of contributing money. But the populace thinks it a greater good for each single Athenian to possess the money of the allies and for their allies to have a bare subsistence and, by working for a living, to be incapable of fomenting plots.

(1.16) The Athenian people are thought to act ill-advisedly in this matter also, namely, in forcing the allies to sail to Athens for litigation. But their response is to calculate all the advantages from this which accrue to the Athenian people. First, they receive their pay through the year from the court fees.[4] Next, sitting at home and without sailing out on ships, they control the allied cities and save the men of the people, and ruin their opponents, in the courts. If each of the allies brought their law suits at home, out of their detestation of the Athenians they would ruin those of their number who were most the friends of the Athenian people. (1.17) In addition, the Athenian people profit as follows because the law suits of the allies are brought at Athens. First of all, the one percent tax in the Piraeus[5] is the larger for the city. Secondly, whoever has lodgings can do better (in renting), and anybody who has a carriage or a slave to rent out. Further, the heralds do better on account of the allies' visits. (1.18) In addition, if the allies did not go (there) for law suits, they would pay honor only to those Athenians who sail out – the generals, trierarchs and envoys. As it is, each and every man of the allies is compelled to fawn on the Athenian people, knowing that when he comes to Athens he must bring suits and submit to them under (the jurisdiction of) no one else but the people, as is the law at Athens. He is compelled to be a suppliant in the courts and to grasp by the hand anybody who enters. Therefore, on account of this, the allies are made even more the slaves of the Athenian people.

2.1–6

(2.1) Their hoplite force, which is thought to be in very poor condition at Athens, has been so constituted, and they believe that though they are both inferior to the enemy and less in number, yet they are even by land far more powerful than the allies who bring in the tribute; and they consider that the hoplite force is adequate if they are more powerful than the allies. (2.2) In addition, it is their fortune to be in this kind of situation: though it is possible for men who are ruled by land to combine from small into large cities and fight united, those ruled by sea – all who are islanders – cannot combine their cities. For the sea is in their midst, and their rulers are masters of the sea. Even if it is possible for the islanders to escape notice in concentrating together on one island, they will die of starvation. (2.3) As to all the cities on the mainland ruled by the Athenians, the large ones are ruled through fear, and the small completely by need. For no city exists which does not need to import something or export it. This will consequently be impossible for it (to do) unless it obeys the rulers of the sea. (2.4) Furthermore, it is possible for the rulers of the sea to do what sometimes land powers (do) – devastate the land of more powerful states. For it is possible for them to sail along to a place where there is no enemy or where there are few, and if the enemy advances, to embark and sail off. By doing this they will have less difficulty than the man who brings assistance on foot. (2.5) Furthermore, it is possible for those who rule by sea to sail away from their own land on as far a voyage as you please, but those who rule by land cannot depart from their own land on a march of many days. For marches are slow, and it is impossible to have food for a long period when going on foot. And the man going on foot must go through friendly country or win his way by fighting while it is possible for the man on shipboard to disembark where he is in superior strength 〈. . .〉[6] this territory but to sail by it until he reaches friendly country or inferior powers. (2.6) Further, though the power by land is seriously affected by crop diseases, which stem from Zeus, the sea power (bears them) easily. For every land is not simultaneously struck by disease, so that (produce) reaches the rulers of the sea from the place that is thriving.

2.9-10

(2.9) As to sacrifices and offerings and festivals and temple-precincts, the people, knowing that it was not possible for each poor man to make sacrifice and to hold feasts, to set up temples and live in a lovely and great city, have devised the means of bringing it about. This is why the city makes public sacrifice of many victims, but it is the people who are feasted and who obtain an allotment of the victims. (2.10) Gymnasiums and baths and dressing rooms are privately possessed by some of the rich, but the people themselves build for their own personal use many wrestling schools, dressing rooms and baths, and the masses enjoy more of these than the few and the wealthy.

2.14-16

(2.14) One thing do they lack. If the Athenians inhabited an island and controlled the sea, they could inflict damage, if they wished, but suffer none so long as they ruled the sea, and not have their own country devastated or await the enemy. But as it is, the farmers and the rich Athenians come more heavily under enemy attack while the people, inasmuch as they well know that they (the enemy) will not set fire to any of their property or ravage it, live carefree and do not fawn on them. (2.15) In addition to this, they would be free from another fear if they lived on an island – the city would never be betrayed by a few men or the gates be opened or the enemy pour in. For how could this happen if they lived on an island? Nor, again, (would they fear) that anyone would foment revolution against the people if they lived on an island. But should they (dissidents) attempt revolution now, they would do so with their hope on the enemy whom they would intend to bring on by land. But if they lived on an island, they would not need to fear this either. (2.16) Therefore, since from the first they happen not to have been living on an island, they now act as follows. They store their property on the islands, trusting in their empire of the sea, and they allow the land of Attica to be devastated. They know that if they have pity on it they will be deprived of other goods still greater.

3.1-5

(3.1) . . . I see some people blaming the Athenians for this too – that sometimes it is impossible there for a man to transact business with the Boule or the people[7] even if he waits for a year. This happens at Athens for no other reason than that because of the multitude of their concerns they cannot transact the business of everyone and then send them away. (3.2) For how can a people be able (to do so) who first must celebrate such a number of festivals as no other Hellenic city – during which it is the less possible for anyone to transact the business of the city – and then to adjudicate civil cases, public cases, and euthynai in a number which not even all (the rest of) mankind together adjudicate, while the Boule considers many things relating to the war, many things relating to the provision of revenue, many things relating to lawmaking, many things relating to the daily business of the city, many things relating to the allies, to the receipt of tribute, and to the care of the shipyards and the shrines. Is it, then, very amazing that with all these matters before them they are not able to transact every man's business? (3.3) But some people say that if a man has money and approaches the Boule or the people he will get his business done. I would agree with them that much is accomplished at Athens with money and that even more would be accomplished if still more people offered money. Even so I well know that the city is incapable of acting on everyone's needs even if someone were to offer them unlimited gold and silver. (3.4) They must also hold enquiry as to whether someone is not repairing his ship[8] or is building something on public land. In addition to this (they must) judge (disputes) among choregoi for the Dionysia, Thargelia, Panathenaia, Promethia, and Hephaistia year by year. Four hundred trierarchs are appointed each year, and year by year they must judge (disputes) among those of them who ask for it.[9] In addition to this, they must make scrutiny of officials (dokimasia) and judge (disputes) among them, verify orphanhood,[10] and appoint keepers of the prisons. These matters, then, year by year (they oversee). (3.5) On occasion they must make judgment about desertion and any other sudden crime that occurs, and as to whether people perpetrate some unusual outrage or act impiously. I omit a very great deal, but the greatest part has been mentioned – except for the assessments of the tribute. This generally occurs every four years.

3.10-13

(3.10) I think that the Athenians are ill-advised in their resolve to take the part of the vulgar in cities torn by faction. But they do this purposely. For if they took the part of the better people they would be preferring men whose opinions run counter to their own. For in no city is the best element favorably disposed to the people; rather is the worst element in each city well disposed to the people. Kindred spirits feel mutual attraction. Because of this, then, the Athenians take the part of their own type. (3.11) Every time they attempted to favor the best element it was disadvantageous for them. Within a short period of time the people (i.e. the democrats) in Boeotia were enslaved.[11] And when they took the part of the best element in Miletus, within a short period of time it rebelled and massacred the people.[12] And when they took the part of the Lacedaemonians instead of the Messenians, within a short period of time the Lacedaemonians subjugated the Messenians and made war against the Athenians.[13] (3.12) Someone might argue that nobody has been unjustly deprived of his citizen-rights at Athens. I affirm that there are some who have been deprived of them unjustly, but they are few. But more than a few are necessary to attack the democracy at Athens. Since that is the case, one must take thought not as to whether some men have lost their citizen-rights justly but whether some (have lost them) unjustly. (3.13) How, then, can one suppose that the majority[14] has lost its citizens-rights at Athens unjustly, where the people are the holders of the offices? It is as a result of their having been corrupt in office and unjust in speech and action that people are without citizen-rights in Athens. Taking this into consideration, it is right to believe that no danger will be posed by the disenfranchised at Athens.

1 The word 'people' (=*demos*) is ambiguous, since it can denote 'commoners' or the 'democratic element' or the government itself. Context determines the shade of meaning intended by the author, but the ambiguity is sometimes deliberate.
2 Reading MS M.
3 Both magistracies were elective offices.
4 *Prytaneia*: see the Glossary, 'Court fees.'
5 Probably duty collected from those disembarking at the Piraeus en route to Athens.
6 Kirchhoff inferred a lacuna here. The likely sense, found in one manuscript but probably a mere conjecture, is '⟨and where he is not, to refrain from disembarking on⟩'.
7 I.e. people in the official sense, as constituting law courts.
8 Cf. no. 166 lines 27-32; see the Glossary, 'Trierarch.'
9 A process existed, called *diadikasia* (referred to here), which provided for the resolution of conflicting claims. According to the *Lexica Segueriana* 5 (Bekker, *Anecdota Graeca* 1.236): 'Every suit is not called a *diadikasia* as a general term, but those in which there is a dispute about something, as to whom it more properly belongs.' This instance provides an example of the negative aspect of *diadikasia*: determination was to be made of which trierarch-appointee need *not* serve.
10 Aristotle, *Athenaion Politeia* 24.3, speaks of the maintenance of orphans. This is therefore probably a reference to the means adopted by the state to ensure the legitimacy of orphans' claims.
11 Sometime between 457 and 446. Cf. Arist. *Politics* 5.2.1302b.
12 The date is uncertain; see no. 92.
13 See Thucydides 1.102 and no. 104.
14 Of all those deprived of citizen-rights. The thought seems to be that those who deservedly were punished are, unlike the few unjustly deprived of their rights, nevertheless democrats and hardly the kind of people to make an attack against democracy itself.

108   The Foundation of Thurii. 444/3 B.C.

A: Photius, *Lexicon* s.v. 'Thouriomanteis'; B: Scholiast to Aristophanes, *Clouds* 332 (424/3); C: *Anonymous Life of Thucydides* 7. Cf. Diodorus 10.3-7; Plutarch, *Nikias* 5.3.

Wade-Gery, *Essays* 255-8; Kagan, *Outbreak* 156-69; Fornara, *Generals* 48; de Ste Croix, *Origins* 381; Bury–Meiggs 225; Sealey, *History* 309.

A. Photius, *Lexicon* s.v. 'Thouriomanteis'

Thouriomanteis. Those with Lampon.[1] For some ascribe the colony at Sybaris[2] to Lampon, others to Dionysios the Bronze-Man,[3] others to

Xenokritos, others to Katharios (Klearidas: Wade-Gery) the Laconian, others to Plexippos the Athenian.

B. Scholiast to Aristophanes, *Clouds* 332

Aristoph. *Clouds* 331–2: Because you don't know, by Zeus, that these (clouds) foster the greatest number of sophists: / Thurian-seers (Thouriomanteis) . . . (there follows a list of other 'sophists').

   Scholion: . . . Thouriomanteis are not seers from Thurii but those who were sent to Thurii to found it. Ten men were sent among whom was also Lampon the seer, whom they called exegete. He also was much active in politics. He appeared to be introducing oracles continuously about the colony of Thurii.

C. *Anonymous Life of Thucydides* 7

When he became arrogant in public affairs, inasmuch as he loved money, he[4] was not permitted to be leader (*prostates*) of the People for a longer time. For first, after he had gone to Sybaris, when he returned to Athens he was charged by Xenokritos and convicted of court-violation (?).[5] Later he was ostracized for ten years.

1 Cf. Plut. *Perikles* 6.2–3; Aristotle, *Rhetorica* 2.18, p. 1419a.
2 Thurii was built at the site of Sybaris.
3 Wade-Gery's emendation of 'the Chalcidian Dionysius.'
4 Thoukydides son of Melesias (see no. 109), whom the author of this brief life of Thucydides the historian has confused with the latter (Wade-Gery, *Essays* 239ff.).
5 It is not clear what these words signify. Wade-Gery (261 n. 4) suggested some kind of 'failure to substantiate'; the root meaning of the verb ('confuse,' 'confound') suggests something more violent, e.g. 'disturbance of the court,' but cf. no. 109A.

109   The Ostracism of Thoukydides Son of Melesias. 444/3 B.C.

A: Scholiast to Aristophanes, *Wasps* 947 (423/2) (Philochorus, *FGrHist* 338 F 120; Ammonius, *FGrHist* 350 F 1; Theopompus, *FGrHist* 115 F 91; Androtion, *FGrHist* 324 F 37); B: Marcellinus, *Life of Thucydides* 28 (Polemon F 5 Preller; Androtion, *FGrHist* 324 F 57). Cf. Aristotle, *Athenaion Politeia* 28.2; Plutarch, *Perikles* 14.3, 16.3.

Jacoby, *FGrHist* IIIb Suppl. 1.149, 482–4; Wade-Gery, *Essays* 238–69; Meiggs, *Empire* 186; Bury–Meiggs 224–6; Sealey, *History* 303; A. Andrewes, *JHS* 98 (1978) 1–8.

A. Scholiast to Aristophanes, *Wasps* 947

Aristoph. *Wasps* 946-8: No, but he seems to me to have experienced what once Thoukydides experienced when on trial. / His jaws were suddenly paralysed.

Scholion: He is speaking of Thoukydides son of Melesias of Alopeke. The Athenians ostracized him for the (statutory) ten years according to the law....[1] Another explanation: Thoukydides son of Melesias who had been Perikles' political opponent. There are four Athenians named Thoukydides: the historian, the one from Gargettos, the Thessalian, and this one, who was in fact a fine orator but who, when under indictment, was unable to speak for himself in the trial but held his tongue as if it were being constrained, and thus he was convicted and then ostracized. Another explanation: Applied to the history (of Thucydides?). Perhaps the man who was Perikles' political opponent. This Philochorus relates ⟨--⟩[2] (Thucydides, the historian) who did not become very famous, not even in comedy, because he was condemned to exile after being entrusted for a short time with the expedition with Kleon in Thrace. Some say, among them Ammonius, that (he was the son) of Stephanos.[3] But one may doubt this, as has been said. The ostracism which took place indicates that the son of Melesias was indeed the man ostracized. However, the historian Theopompus says that the son of Pantain⟨et⟩os was Perikles' opponent. Not Androtion, however, but he too (like Philochorus?) claims that it was the son of Melesias.

B. Marcellinus, *Life of Thucydides* 28

Let us not fail to recognize that there were many men named Thoukydides: this one (Thucydides, the historian), the son of Oloros, and, second, the demagogue,[4] the son of Melesias, who indeed was the political opponent of Perikles. Third is a Pharsalian[5] in nationality whom Polemon mentions in his *About the Akropolis*, saying that his father was Menon. Another (and) fourth Thoukydides was the poet of the deme Acherdous, whom Androtion mentioned in his *Atthis*, saying that he was the son of Ariston.

1 A discussion follows of the difference between banishment and ostracism, for which see no. 41C (2).
2 Something has dropped out of the text.
3 *Prosopographia Attica* 12884 (Stephanos son of Thoukydides of Alopeke).
4 Without a derogatory context, this means no more than 'leader of the People.'
5 The Thessalian of (A); cf. Thuc. 8.92.8.

110   The Board of Athenian Generals at Samos. 441/40 B.C.

Scholiast to Aristeides 46.136, p. 225 Dindorf (Androtion, *FGrHist* 324 F 38). Cf. Thucydides 1.115–17; Diodorus 12.27–8; Plutarch, *Perikles* 24, 1–2, 25–8. See also nos. 113, 115.

Jacoby, *FGrHist* IIIb Suppl. 1.148f.; Hignett, *Constitution* 354f.; Fornara, *Generals* 49; H. Avery, *Historia* (1973) 509–14 (Sophocles' political career); Hammond, *Studies* 376f.; Sealey, *History* 309–11.

Aristeides 46.136, p. 225: At Samos (Perikles) himself general with nine others effaced all the other generals....

Scholion: (The following are) the names of the ten generals in Samos according to Androtion: Sokrates of Anagyrous; Sophokles of Kolonos, the poet;[1] Andokides of Kydathenaion;[2] Kreon of Skambonidai; Perikles of Cholargos; Glaukon of Kerameis; Kallistratos of Acharnai; Xenophon of Melite; Lampides of Piraeus;[3] Glauketes the Athenian;[4] Kleitophon of Thorai.

1 See Athenaeus 13.81, pp. 603–4. According to the scholiast to Aristophanes, *Peace* 697 (422/1), 'it is said that he extorted money in Samos from his position as general.'
2 See no. 105 and note 1.
3 Lampides is a regular Greek name but is unattested for Athens.
4 If the name is genuine, this word must be a mistake for a deme, perhaps 'of Azenia': Wilamowitz (cited Jacoby, p. 149); 'of Aphidna': Lenz (cited Jacoby, p. 149). See Jacoby for various attempts to explain the presence of eleven names. Fornara would expunge Glauketes as a doublet of Glaukon; Hammond accepts all eleven generals.

111   Athenian Restrictions against Comedy. 440/39 B.C.

Scholiast to Aristophanes, *Acharnians* 67 (426/5). Cf. [Xenophon,] *Athenaion Politeia* 2.18; Aristophanes, *Acharnians* 377f., 502f. (harassment by Kleon in 427/6).

G. Busolt, *Griechische Geschichte* (Gotha 1897) 3.1.560f.; Bury–Meiggs 241.

Aristoph. *Acharnians* 65–7: You sent us to the Great King / with two drachmas daily as our pay / in the archonship of Euthymenes.

Scholion: This is the Archon in whose term of office the decree about prohibiting ridicule was repealed, which had been passed in the archonship of Morychides (440/39). It was in effect for that year and the next two, in the archonships of Glaukinos (439/8) and Theodoros (438/7), after which it was repealed in Euthymenes' archonship (437/6).

112 Victory of Tarentum over Thurii. After 440 B.C.

On three faces of a bronze spear-butt, Laconian–Tarentine writing, Olympia.

Jeffery, *LSAG*, no. 10, p. 282 and Plate 53; *GHI*, no. 57, p. 154. Cf. Strabo 6.1.4, p. 264.

E. A. Freeman, *The history of Sicily* (Oxford 1891) 2.14; F. E. Adcock, *CAH* 5.169.

Spoils from the Thurians the Taran|tines dedicated to Zeus Oly|mpios as a tithe.

113 Expenses of the Samian War. 441–439 *or* 440–439 B.C.

Marble stele, developed Attic writing, stoichedon,[1] Athens.

IG I² 293+ (I³ 363); B. D. Meritt, *AJP* 55 (1934) 365f.; *GHI*, no. 55, pp. 149–51. Cf. Plutarch, *Perikles* 28.1; Nepos, *Timotheus* 1.2; Diodorus 12.28, where '⟨one thousand⟩ two hundred talents' should probably be read.

Gomme, etc., *HCT* 2.30f.; Meiggs, *Empire* 192; Bury–Meiggs 240f.; C. W. Fornara, *JHS* 99 (1979) 7–18 (441–439).

5   [---]|[---]|[---]|[...] of (the deme) Phrearrhioi [---]|| 128 T. [---]|
Athenians [spent---][2] | against the Samia[ns the following --]| of
Athena P[olias? --]|[.] for whom Phyro[machos was Secretary,---]
10 *Secre*||*tary*.[3] The Treasurers [---Eu]bou[lides] o|f Oion. Naus[---]|
368 T. [---]| from the Treasurers [---[4] Epichar]|inos of Pira[eus---]||
15 [....].[5] These [were the Treasurers---]| of Aphidna [---]| 908 T.[6]
[---]| The total's [sum---]| 1,400 T.[7] [---]

1   The length of line is very uncertain (editors now holding that each line contained about sixty-five letters) and most restorations are no less so.
2   'when Timokles and Morychides were Archons for the Athenians (441/40 and 440/39) for the (war)]': *GHI*.
3   'in the (year of the) Boule in which -*c.* 12- was the first] *Secre*||*tary*: *GHI*.
4   '[of the Akropolis, for whom Demostratos was Secretary, in the (year of the) Boule in which': *GHI*.
5   'was the first Secretary (440/39), to the generals sent against Samos, expenditure the] *se*||*cond*.': *GHI*.
6   There is a misprint here in the first printing of *GHI*.
7   Figures less than 100 may have followed. The figures in lines 5, 12 and 17 (none of them necessarily complete) must have added up to the total in line 19.

114 Accounts of Pheidias' Gold-and-Ivory Statue of Athena. A: 440/39 B.C.; B: 438 B.C.[1]
Marble stelai, all stoichedon except A (1), developed Attic writing, Athens.

A: *IG* I^2 355, 355a+ (I^3 458, 459); **GHI*, no 54A, pp. 146f.

R. P. Austin, *Stoichedon style* (Oxford 1938) 62f., with a photo on Plate 8; Bury-Meiggs 229f.; S. K. Eddy, *AJA* 81 (1977) 107–11.

(1)

Gods. Athena. Fortune. | Kichesippos was Secretary of the statue's
5 Com|missioners, of (the deme of) Myrrhinous. || Receipt from *vv* |
vacat[2]

(2)

Kichesippos was Se|cretary of the stat|ue's Commissioner|s, of Myr-
5 rhinous. R||eceipt from the Treasurer|s[3] for whom Demostra|tos was
10 Secretar|y, of Xypete: 100 T.[4] The Trea|surers: Ktesion, St[r]||osias,
Antiphat[e]|s, Menandros, Th[ym]|ochares, Smokor[d]|os, Pheide-
15 leid[es]. *vacat* | Gold was bough||t; in weight: 6 T. 1,618 dr. 1 ob.[5] |
The cost of this: 87 T. 4,652 dr. | 5 ob.[6] *vv* | *vacat* | Ivory was bought: |
20 2 T. 74||3 dr.

B: *IG* I^2 354+ (I^3 460); W. B. Dinsmoor, *Arch. Eph.* 1937, 507–11; **GHI*, no. 54B, pp. 148f.

Commissioners [---]| *received* the following [---] *sil|ver. vv*| 700 T.
5 [---] || 520 dr. [---] | *Of* gold [---]|[...] 200 dr. [---]| Kalla[ischros--]
10 *dedi|cated* [---]|| *Expenditures* [---] |[.] 100 T. [---]| 70 dr. [---] |
15 *Execution* [---]⁷| 770 dr. [---]|| *Armature*[8] [---]| 30 T. [---]| 300 dr.
[---]| Golden [---] *for the st|atue* [---][9]

---

1 The statue was begun in 447/6 B.C. For a general account see G. Richter, *The sculpture and sculptors of the Greeks* (New Haven 1950) 217–20; cf. Thucydides 2.13.5; Philochorus, *FGrHist* 328 F 121, no. 116A, below; Diodorus 12.39; Plutarch, *Perikles* 13.
2 This version was cut unskillfully and nonstoichedon; perhaps this is why the work was redone (Austin). Meritt (*Athenian financial documents of the fifth century* (Ann Arbor 1932) 30–41) believes that it was redone because the first block of marble lacked room for its figure column.
3 Of Athena.
4 The sum is carved on line 6, to the left of the main text.

5 The sum is on the right side of the text, lines 15f.
6 The sum is to the left and below the text, lines 14–17. The following figure, on the left, extends from 18–20.
7 '[of the pedestal]': Donnay (cited *GHI*, p. 146).
8 I.e. the inner framework of the statue. This difficult word has also been understood to mean the fringe of Athena's mantle (Cavaignac (*Etudes sur l'histoire financière d'Athènes au Ve siècle* (Paris 1908) XLIX)) or a curtain assumed to have been hanging behind the statue (Dinsmoor). 'Armature' is Donnay's interpretation.
9 Dinsmoor restores 847 T. 520[+]dr. in lines 4f.; in lines 11f., 850 T. 4,270 dr.

115 Athenian Treaty with Samos. 440/39 *or* 439/8 B.C.

Four fragments of a marble stele, developed Attic letters, stoichedon, Athens.

IG I² 50+ (I³ 48); H. T. Wade-Gery, *CP* 26 (1931) 309–13; *ATL* 2.D18, pp. 72–4, and Plate 11; *GHI*, no. 56, pp. 151–4 (439/8); Bradeen and McGregor, *Studies* 120f. Cf. Thucydides 1.117.3; Diodorus 12.28.3–4; Plutarch, *Perikles* 28.1–3.

Gomme, etc., *HCT* 1.353ff.; Meiggs, *Empire* 190–3; C. W. Fornara, *JHS* 99 (1979) 7–18 (440/39).

5 [---]|[---]|[---]|[--]Lemno[s¹--]||[--] *just as* [--]|[---]|[--Pelo]pon-
nese [--]|

(Lines 8–14 are almost completely illegible)

(Lacuna)

15 [-- 'I shall a|ct and speak and deliberate in the interests of the People of the Athen|ians, to my uttermost ability, rightly] *and fittingly,* [and I shall not r|ebel against the People of the A]thenians either [by] *w|ord*
20 [or by deed nor (shall I rebel) from the] allies of the A||[thenians, and I shall be loyal] to the People of the Athl[enians.' The (Samian) Boule² shall swear:] 'I shall *act* and speak and | [deliberate rightly towards the People of the] Samians in whatever way | [I can and -12-³ Sa]mians
25 according [...]|[-25-] Athenians [..]||[-35-]|[-35-]⁴

(Lacuna)

Generals [took the oath: -8- of Ere]|chtheis,⁵ Dem[-26- of Pa]|n-
30 dionis,⁶ Ch[-20- Perikl]||es, Glaukon, (of) A[kamantis? -16-]|[-26-]⁷ Tlemp[olemos]|[-25-] Boule in office [....]|[-22-] was Secretary, Rha|[--]⁸ *vacat.*

1 Samian hostages had initially been deposited there (Thuc. 1.115.3).
2 Fornara; 'the Athenians': *GHI*. The possibility should be noted that the fragment containing lines 15–27 has been restored with too few letters to the line. Fornara

would expand lines 20 ('I shall be a loyal ally]'), 21 ('shall swear as follows]'), 22 ('rightly and fittingly'). It is impossible to lengthen similarly the fragment containing the list of generals.

3 'I shall take responsibility for the' is usually restored.

4 (From line 23) 'according to what [w|as agreed by the generals of the] Athenians [an|l]d the ruling magistrates of the Samians. Kalli]krate[s made a motio|n': *ATL*.

5 Sokrates' name is usually restored. The tribes of the generals, not their demes, are given. Fornara doubts that this fragment is a part of the treaty.

6 'Dem[okleides of Aigeis, Phormion of Pa]|ndionis': Wade-Gery.

7 'Kall]i[sstratos of Oi|neis, Xe[nophon of Kekropis]' is generally supplied.

8 'was *first* Secretary, of Rha|[mnous' is generally supplied.

116 Attacks against Pheidias, Anaxagoras, and Aspasia. 438/7 *or* about 433 B.C.

A: Scholiast to Aristophanes, *Peace* 605 (422/1) (Philochorus, *FGrHist* 328 F 121); B: Diogenes Laertius 2.12 (Satyrus, *Fragmenta Historicorum Graecorum* 3.163); C: Athenaeus 13.56, p. 589de (Clearchus F 30 Wehrli; Stesimbrotus, *FGrHist* 107 F 10a; Antisthenes). Cf. Plutarch, *Perikles* 31.2-5, 32.1-2, 5-6; Diodorus 12.39.1-2. See no. 123.

Jacoby, *FGrHist* IIIb Suppl. 1.484-96 (438/7); Wade-Gery, *Essays* 258-60 (about 433); F. Frost, *Historia* 13 (1964) 385-99; Kagan, *Outbreak* 193-202; de Ste Croix, *Origins* 236f.; Bury–Meiggs 257; J. Mansfeld, *Mnemosyne* s.4, 32 (1979) 39-69; 33 (1980) 17-95.

A. Scholiast to Aristophanes, *Peace* 605

Aristoph. *Peace* 605-9: First of all Pheidias started it by faring badly. / Then Perikles, afraid of sharing his fate, / ... / . fired the city / by casting into it the tiny spark of the Megarian decree.

Scholion: Philochorus says this (occurred) in the archonship of ⟨The⟩odoros[1] (438/7): 'And the golden statue of Athena was set up in the great temple, having the weight of 44 talents[2] of gold. Perikles was the superintendent in charge, Pheidias was the sculptor. Pheidias, after he had made it, was judged to have cheated in his accounting of the ivory used in the scales (of the serpent) and was condemned. Having fled to Elis he is said to have been hired to execute the statue of Zeus in Olympia and, when he had completed it, to have been put to death by the Eleians.' In the archonship of ⟨P⟩ythodoros[3] (432/1), who is the seventh (Archon) after the aforementioned,[4] (Philochorus) says regarding the Megarians that they also complained against the Athenians to the Lacedaemonians, claiming that they were unjustly excluded from the marketplace (agora) and harbors of the Athenians. For the Athenians decreed this on the motion of Perikles, having accused them of working the land that was sacred to the goddesses.[5] Some say that when Pheidias the sculptor had been judged to be cheating the city and had been banished, Perikles, fearful because of his superintendence of the making of the statue and his complicity in the theft, wrote the bill against Megara and precipitated the war so that he would not render account to the Athenians since they were totally concerned with the war. His charge against the Megarians was that they had worked the sacred land of the two goddesses.

B. Diogenes Laertius 2.12

Satyrus says in his *Lives* that the prosecution (of Anaxagoras) was brought by Thoukydides (son of Melesias) in political opposition to Perikles (and that he was charged) not only with impiety but also with medism. He was condemned to death in absentia.

C. Athenaeus 13.56, p. 589de

Did not Perikles the Olympian, as Clearchus says in the first book of the *Erotica*, throw all of Hellas into confusion for the sake of Aspasia – not the 'younger' but the one who held converse with the learned Sokrates[6] – in spite of his possession of great reputation for intelligence and political ability? This man was extremely prone to sexual pleasure. He even had intercourse with his son's wife, as Stesimbrotus of Thasus relates, a man who lived in his time and set eyes on him. (This) in his work entitled *On Themistokles, Thoukydides, and Perikles*. Antisthenes the Socratic says he (Perikles) was in love with Aspasia and embraced the woman twice a day when he entered (the house) and when he left her. Once when she was a defendant on the charge of impiety, he spoke on her behalf and shed more tears than when his life and his property were in danger.[7]

1 An emendation of Pythodoros (archon in 432/1).
2 Cf. Thucydides 2.13.5 (40 talents); Diod. 12.40.3 (50 talents).
3 An emendation of Skythodoros, not an archon name.
4 Both termini were normally counted – hence 'seventh.'
5 The two goddesses of Eleusis (see no. 140 below). Cf. Thuc. 1.139.2. For the Megarian Decree, see no. 123.
6 See no. 96.
7 In 430/29. See Thuc. 2.65.3.

117 Work on the Athenian Water Supply. 437/6 *or* 435/4 *or* about 432/1 B.C.
Marble stele, developed Attic writing, stoichedon, Athens.

IG I² 54 (I³ 49); *ATL* 2.D19, p. 74 (text for the first five lines); A. Wilhelm, *JHS* 68 (1948) 128; H. B. Mattingly, *Historia* 10 (1961) 164f., *BCH* 92 (1968) 469 (about 432/1); *B. D. Meritt and H. T. Wade-Gery, *JHS* 83 (1963) 105f. (437/6); A. G. Woodhead, *Archeologia classica* 25-6 (1973-4) 751-61 (435/4).

W. E. Thompson, *Athenaeum* 49 (1971) 328-35.

5   [--Hipp]|oniko[s--]| each [--] d|rachma[1] [--] || [.] of the aqueduct [--Nikomachos made the motion: L|et] *all the* rest be *as* [(resolved) by the Boule, but let care be taken of the fountains in the ci|ty] so that the flow [of all of them will be as excellent and pure as possible. But in order that the] m|inimum sum [may be expended for the task, those Prytaneis who by the lo|t]'become the first to hold the prytany [shall
10   introduce the architect into the first of the] || regular assemblies, *immediately* [after the report on sacred matters.[2] They shall do what seems] *be*|st to the People of the Athe[nians. They shall ensure that delay (?) of] *n*|*o kind* arises and that it shall be managed for the Athe-[nians in the best possible fashion.[3]-7-] *made the m*|*otion.* Let all the rest be as Nikoma[chos (proposed), but let praise be given to Perikles and Par]|alos and Xanthippos and the *sons*[4] [--They shall spend (on the
15   work) the money] || which [is] paid into the tribute of the Athenians [after the goddess has from it] *rece*|*ived* her accustomed share. *vv*

1   Lines 3-5 as restored in *ATL*: '[--They shall receive pay of a] d|rachma for [each day, and they shall have the care of the spring an||d] of the conduit [for the water.'
2   In a regular assembly – one not specially summoned, as, for example, by the generals (see the Glossary) – the agenda was prescribed, and cult had first place on it.
3   Lines 6-12 are modified by Meritt and Wade-Gery without substantial change of sense.
4   'and (their) *sons*': *ATL*; 'and the *sons* [of Kleinias': Mattingly.

118   The Cost and Construction of the Propylaia. 437/6-433/2 B.C.

A: Harpocration, *Lexicon* s.v. 'Those Propylaia' (Philochorus, *FGrHist* 328 F 36; Heliodorus, *FGrHist* 374 F 1); B: Building accounts of the Propylaia. *IG* I[2] 366 (I[3] 465); *GHI*, no. 60, pp. 165f.

ATL 3.124 and n. 15; J. J. Keaney, *Historia* 17 (1968) 507-9; Bury-Meiggs 233. Cf. Plutarch, *Perikles* 13.12; and no. 94 above.

A. Harpocration, *Lexicon* s.v. 'Those Propylaia'

As to the Propylaia of the Akropolis, that the Athenians began to build them in the archonship of Euthymenes (437/6), and that the architect was Mnesikles,[1] has been related by Philochorus, among others, in his fourth book. Heliodorus, in Book I of his *On the Athenian Akropolis*, in addition to other things, says this: 'It was completely finished[2] in five years and 2,012 talents were spent (on it). They made five gateways through which they enter the Akropolis.'

B. Building accounts of the Propylaia

IG I[2] 366 (I[3] 465); **GHI*, no. 60, pp. 165f. 434/3 B.C. Marble stele (not properly finished), developed Attic letters, irregular stoichedon, Athens.

[Gods. A]thena. [Fortune. I In (the year of) the] *fourth* board,[3] in which Dioge[nes] *was Secretary*, I [-9-] during the Boule in which Meta[genes was] *first* [Secre I tary,] *Commissioners*: Ari[styl]los of
5   M[elite], M[-9-] II [-9-], Diktys of Ko[i]le, Tim[ostratos] of Ke[-7-]I [-8-of Th]orai. Their [receipts] *for the year* [are these:]I[4]

[---]319 dr.   From the *preceding Commissioners* [for whom]
             Epikles *was Secretary*, of Thorikos.
10 [---]   From the Treasurers *in charge* [of the] Goddess's TreasuryII
             for whom Krates *was Secretary*, of Lamptrai.
    [---]   From the Hellenotamiai for whom Proton[ikos]
             was *Secretary*, of Ker[ame]is, out of the *all-*
             ies' [tribute], one *mna* from each *talent*.[5]
    [---]   [From the Treasurers] of the Hepha[is]tikon[6] in
15   L[au]r[eion]II
             [-14-] *of the* five *parts*.[7]
             [From the Hellenotamiai],[8] *from* the campaign [-4-]
    [---]   [---]sippos of Agryle,
             [----] *from* Timosthenes.[9]

1 See R. Carpenter, *The architects of the Parthenon* (London 1970) 136, for spe-
   culation about the choice of this architect.
2 They were in fact not completed.
3 Since each board held office for a year, and since this particular year is fixed by
   the mention of Krates and Metagenes, Philochorus' testimony in (A) is corro-
   borated; it may independently be inferred that work on the Propylaia com-
   menced in 437/6.
4 The remainder of my text follows the stone line by line.
5 This was the quota (one sixtieth) paid to Athena out of the tribute. See nos. 85
   and 95L.
6 A silver mine; they were frequently named after divinities.
7 Probably, five-sixths of the revenue of the mine.
8 Restored on the basis of the parallel with *IG* I[2] 365 (I[3] 464) (the building account
   of 435/4), line 14: '[from the Hellenot]amiai from the *campaign*.'
9 'From the expedition of a given general (--sippos of Agryle, line 17) by means
   of the Hellenotamias Timosthenes (line 18)': *ATL* 3.329-32. The money is
   possibly surplus funds left unspent by the generals (*ATL*) or perhaps a tithe of
   the booty taken by them (W. E. Thompson, *CQ* 20 (1970) 39f.).

119   Financial Decrees Moved by Kallias. 434/3 *or* 425/4 *or* 422/1 *or* 418/17 B.C.
Marble stele carved on the front (A) and the back (B), by the same hand (?), developed Attic letters, stoichedon, Athens.

IG I² 91, 92 (I³ 52); *ATL* 2.D1, 2, pp. 46f.; W. K. Pritchett, *CSCA* 4 (1971) 219–25; **GHI*, no. 58, pp. 154–61. Cf. Thucydides 1.144.2, 2.13, 16; Andocides, *On the Peace* 8.

H. T. Wade-Gery, *JHS* 51 (1931) 57–85 (422/1); *ATL* 3.326–8 (434/3); H. B. Mattingly, *BCH* 92 (1968) 450–85, *BSA* 65 (1970) 147–9; *Phoros* 94–7, *GRBS* 16 (1975) 15–22 (422/1); C. W. Fornara, *GRBS* 11 (1970) 185–96 (418/17); D. W. Bradeen, *GRBS* 12 (1971) 469–83; Meiggs, *Empire* 519–23, 601 (434/3); D. M. Lewis, *Phoros* 82–4; Bury–Meiggs 535; Tullia Linders, *The Treasurers of the Other Gods in Athens and their functions*, Beiträge zur Klassischen Philologie 62 (Meisenheim am Glan 1975); Sealey, *History* 323.

(A)

Resolved by the Boule and the People, Kekropis held the prytany, Mnesitheos w|as Secretary, Eupeithes presided, Kallias made the motion. Repayment shall be made to the gods | of the money that is owed them, since Athena's three thousand talent|s, which were voted, have been brought up to the Akropolis, in our own coinage. It shall be
5   pa|lid back from the monies which were allocated for repayment to the gods by vo|te, (namely,) both that which is now in the hands of the Hellenotamiai and the rest which is part of this | money, and also the money from the ten percent tax, when it is farmed out.[1] Calculation shall be made by t|he thirty Logistai now in office of that which is owed to the gods preci|sely, and the Boule shall be solely competent (*autokrator*) to determine when the Logistai are to meet together. The
10   repayment || of the money shall be made by the Prytaneis together with the Boule, and they shall cancel records (of debts) a|s they pay them back, after searching the registers and ledgers and wherever | else claims are recorded. These records shall be produced by the pries|ts and by the Hieropoioi and by anyone else who knows of them. Treasurers shall be selected by lo|t for these funds, whenever the other magistracies
15   (are filled), just as are the (Treasurers) of the sa||cred monies of Athena. Those selected are to serve as treasurers on the Akropolis in the Opis-th|[odo]mos (administering) the funds of the gods capably and piously, and they are to share the openi|ng and closing and sealing of the entran-ces of the Opisthodomos | with the Treasurers of Athena. (As they receive the treasures) from the present treasurers and the super|inten-
20   dents and the Hieropoioi in the temples, who now have charg||e of them,

they shall count them and weigh them in front of the Boule | on the Akropolis, and (then) the Treasurers selected by the lot shall take them over from the current | officials and shall record on one stele the whole of the treasure, both according to | the individual gods, how much belongs to each of them, and the entire su|m, with silver and gold (lis-

25 ted) separately. In future, records shall be inscribed by || successive Treasurers on a stele. They shall draw up accounts (showing) the balance of the monies (they receive), | and the revenue of the gods and whatever is spent throughout the y|ear, (and shall submit them) to the Logistai, and (the Treasurers) shall submit to scrutiny (at the expiration of their term of office). From Panathenai|a to Panathenaia they shall draw up their accounts, in the same way as Athena's T|reasurers. The

30 stelai on which they shall inscribe the treasures of the god||s shall be set up on the Akropolis by the Treasurers. When repayment has been made to the gods | of the *money*, (the Athenians) shall apply what remains of the mon|ey to the dockyard and the walls [---]

(B)

[Resolved by the Boule and the People, Kekropis held the prytany, Mnesithe|os was Secretary, E]up[e]i[th]e[s presided, Kalli]as [made the motion:[2] (The Athenians) shall complete the] | [-5-][3] *of marble* and the *golden Nikai*[4] and the Pro[pylaia....] | [-13-][5] completely,

5 [-10-] shall be utilized [-13-] || [-9-][6] according to what was *voted*, and the Akropolis [-10-] | [-15-][7] and they shall *make it ready*[8] [by spending] ten talents | every [year] until (it) is [-6-][9] and prepared [-6-] | [-5-][10] Let there be [joint] supervision [of the task] by *the* Treasurers and [the Superintendent|s. The] *plans* are to be [made][11]

10 by the architect *just as* (was done) for the Pro[pylaia. H||e is to] *see to it* together with the *Superintendents* that the *best* [-9-] | [-10-] shall be[12] the Akr[opolis] and that restoration *shall be made* [of what is requ|ired. The] rest of the money of Athena *which* [now i|s on the Akropolis] *and* whatever *in future* is taken up (to the Akropolis) shall not be used [nor shall there be exp|enditures made][13] *from* it *for* any

15 purpose *other* [than] this, above (the sum of) *ten thousand* [drachma||s, except for] *restoration*, if any is needed. But [for] no [other] purpose shall use be made [of the moni|es unless] the People [pass a] vote of immunity[14] just as [when they pass a vot|e about] *property taxes*. If anyone [proposes or] puts to a vote, without [a decree grantin|g immunity having been passed,] that *the funds* of Athe[na] be utilized, [he shall be lia|ble to the] same (penalty) as one proposing to have a *pro-*

20 *perty tax* or *putting this to the vote*. [..] || [-10-][15] shall deposit be made *through the* year of what *each* [is ow|ed, (the deposit to be made)

with] *the* Treasurers [of Ath]ena by the *Hellenotamiai.* [Wh|en from the] two hundred[16] *talents* which [were] *voted* for repayment [by t|he People] *to the* Other Gods [payment has been made] of that which is owed, [the administration o|f Ath]ena's treasure shall be located [in the] area on the right-hand side of the Opis]thodomos, and that || of the Other] Gods in the area on the *left. vv* | [(As to) all the sacred] treasures which are unweighed or *uncounted,* [t|he Treasurers] now in office, together with the [four] boards[17] which *rendered* [accou|nts from Pa]nathenaia to Pan[athena]ia (shall take) all the *gold* | [and silver] and *gilded silver* (and) *weigh it,* [while the] *rest* [- - -][18]

25

1 Taxes were not collected by the government but by private corporations, which made bids for the tax, paid the state their bid and then collected their tax money. The difference was their profit or loss. Cf. Andoc. *On the Mysteries* 133ff.
2 This more conservative reading of the names Eupeithes and Kallias is based on the new examination of the stone by Pritchett.
3 '(Parthenon) pediments]': Preuner (reported in Tod I, p. 110); 'sculptures]': *ATL*; 'bases (of the statues of Nike)]': Tod I (pp. 105, 110), Mattingly.
4 Winged Victories. Cf. no. 164B and note 4.
5 'So that they may be] *finished*': Wilhelm (cited Tod I, p. 104); 'While it is being] *finished*': *ATL*.
6 (From line 4) '[inspection] shall be made [as they spen||d for what is required]': Wilhelm; '[expenditure shall be made] *from* [the monie||s of Athena]': *ATL*; '[whatever is required]' (Gomme (*Historia* 2 (1953) 16)) 'shall be applied *from* [the (treasury) of Athen||a without fear of prosecution]': Mattingly.
7 '[shall be barred where it is no|t sufficiently] *closed off*': Wilhelm.
8 Or, 'repair it'.
9 '[barred]': Wilhelm.
10 '[most splen|didly.]': *GHI*.
11 *ATL* (from line 8); 'by *the* Treasurers and [they are to order that a model] be [made] by the architect': Wilhelm.
12 The root of this verb is missing; '[and chea|pest (means) of closing off] the Akr[opolis] shall be (found)': Wilhelm.
13 '[nor shall borrowings be made]': Lewis.
14 *adeia*: license to bring forward proposals which otherwise are debarred by law. See the Glossary, 'Immunity.'
15 '[for the go|ds, all of them]': editors generally.
16 'twelve hundred talents' is a possible restoration.
17 I.e. the four annual boards of the Treasurers of Athena which held office in the preceding four-year Panathenaic period.
18 '[shall be counted - -]': generally restored.

120 Building Accounts of the Parthenon. 434/3 B.C.

Marble stele, developed Attic letters, irregular stoichedon, Athens.

IG I[2] 352 (I[3] 449); W. B. Dinsmoor, *AJA* 17 (1913) 53–80, *AJA* 25 (1921) 233–45; **GHI*, no. 59, pp. 162–5. Cf. Plutarch, *Moralia* 351a, *Perikles* 13.7; Strabo

9.1.12, p. 395, 1.16, p. 396; no. 93, above. A. Burford, *Greece and Rome*, Suppl.
to vol. 10 (1960) 23–35; Bury–Meiggs 229.

For the Commissioners, for whom | Antikles was Secretary, | in the
5 (year of the) fourte|enth Boule,[1] in which Meta|lgenes was first Secre-
t|ary, in Krates' arch|onship over the Athenians (434/3), | the receipts
for this year | (are) as follows: ||

10 1,470 (dr.)	Balance from the previous year.
7[4] 15 27 and 1/6	Gold staters[2] [of Lamps]acus [Gold] staters of C[yzic]us
25,000 (dr.) (i.e. 4 T. 1,000 dr.) 20	*From the Treasurers* [of the] Goddess'[3] *Treasury* for whom Krates was sec- retary, of Lamptrai:
1,372 (dr.)	From gold sold *off*; in weight, 9[8 dr.]: payment for it:
1,305 (dr.) 4 (ob.) 25	From ivory *sold off*, in weight, [3] T. 60 dr.: payment [for it]:

Expenditures

[...] 200 [--] 2 (dr.) 1 (ob.)[4]	for purchases
30 1,[9]26 (dr.) 2 (ob.)	For contracting for the workmen [at Pentelicu s who also have the marble load- ed on to the wagons]:[5]
16,392 (dr.) (i.e., 2 T. 4,392 dr.)	*For sculptors of the pediment-sculptures: the pay:*

[1,]800

35

For monthly wages.

[..] 11 (dr.) 2 (ob.)

[--]   *Balance* (at the end)
[--]   *of this* [year]:
[74]   [Gold staters]
                    [of Lampsacus]

40 [27]   [Gold staters]
     [1/6]   [of Cyzicus][6]

1 I.e. the commission which was formed to supervise the construction of the Parthenon is in its fourteenth year of operation, the years being counted by years of
office of the Boule. The first Parthenon account (*IG* I² 339=I³ 436) dates to
447/6; the last was 433/2 (*IG* I²353=I³ 450).
2 In fact electrum (gold alloyed with silver); see W. E. Thompson, *AC* 40 (1971)
574-88, on their value.
3 Athena.
4 This figure is spread over two lines. Of the part standing in the first line the last
two symbols (each 100) survive. That part of the figure must therefore have
totaled at least 900 dr., since only a symbol equal in value to or greater than
what follows the lacuna can have occupied that position (i.e. at least one 500
and two 100s) and must precede the two surviving 100s. See the Introduction.
In the second line, symbols for 100, 50, 10, 5 or single drachmas may have
stood in the lacuna, continuing from the two 100s at the end of the preceding
line.
5 The restoration is secured from the repetition of the formula in other accounts.
6 Lines 38-41 are so restored because these coins had been carried unspent in the
balance from the time they had been given over to the first year's board. Con-
tractors and workmen apparently found them undesirable.

**121 Accounts of the Delian Temples when Delos Was under Athenian
Control. 434-432 B.C.**
Marble stele (now lost), nonstoichedon, except lines 1-6, Ionic letters
with the numerals written slightly larger, Athens.

IG I² 377+ (I³ 402); B. D. Meritt, *Hesperia* 5 (1936) 378-80; *GHI*, no. 62, pp.
169-71.

Meiggs, *Empire* 291f.

5 [--] | [*vv*] Dioph[-*vv*] | *vv* Xanthes *vv*| *vv* Bolakles *vv*|| *vv* Demothales
vv| *vv* Anaxidemos[1] *vv* | [--] *from* the Delians *owe*[--]|[--] *came to* (?)
and that from [--] | [-*c*.4- the sum of money] in all: 55,410[2] [(dr.)--]
10 || [-*c*.21-] they made the boundaries of the bath [--]||[-*c*. 8-] *was built
by them*, they delimited Rheneia[3] [--] | [-*c*. 11-] they made loans of 9
T. 20 dr. *at ten percent interest* [for five years so that the re|payment

by the] borrowers (would come to) 13 T. 3,0[30 dr. as both principal and interest of what] | they *borrowed*. The period begins with the month of Metageitnion in Athens, [in the archonship of Apseudes
15 (433/2); ‖ in] Delos in the month of Bouphonion, in the archonship of Eupteres. [The Delian territory which is] | sacred was leased by them, and the orchards, houses and [-*c*. 4- for ten years. The period be|gins] in the month of Posideion at Athens, in the archonship of Krates (434/3); *in* [Delos in the month of - -⁴] | in the archonship of Eupteres; so that payment of the rent [for all this by those] wh|o *lease* it is as the
20 contract stipulated. The rent's *sum* [for the first year:] ‖ 716 dr.; for the other years: 800⁵ [(dr.) -*c*. 7- The land in Rhenei]|a which is sacred they leased for ten years. The period [begins - -] | month, in the archonship of Apseudes, in Delos in Hieros [month, in the archonship of - -] |[. .] so that payment will be made by the *lessee*, [for each year, of the]
25 r|ent of one T. 1,110 dr. The sea⁶ which [- -]‖[-*c*. 4-] in Rheneia they leased for ten [years - -]

1 The list of names, probably Delian, represents a board of officials.
2 Further symbols for 10 or smaller amounts may have followed.
3 The island is about one-half mile west of Delos; unlike Delos, it paid tribute to Athens.
4 *GHI*: 'Lenaion.'
5 Further symbols for 100 or smaller amounts may have followed.
6 Probably a pond or lagoon rather than the open sea (*GHI*, p. 171).

122 The Murder of Anthemokritos and the Decree of Charinos. About 433 *or* 431 *or* about 350 B.C.

A: The Megarian Decree; B: Philip's Letter = [Demosthenes] 12.4; C: Pausanias 1.36.3; D: Scholiast to Aristophanes, *Peace* 246 (422/1); E: Harpocration, *Lexicon* s.v. 'Anthemokritos' (Isaeus F 21 Thalheim). Cf. Thucydides 1.139.2; Plutarch, *Perikles* 30; Demosthenes 13.32.

W. R. Connor, *AJP* 83 (1962) 225–46, *REG* 83 (1970) 305–8 (about 350); K. J. Dover, *AJP* 87 (1966) 203–9 (431); de Ste Croix, *Origins* 246–51 (about 433), 392–3; C. W. Fornara, *YCS* 24 (1975) 213–28 (about 433).

A. The Megarian Decree

See no. 123.

B. Philip's Letter = [Demosthenes] 12.4

And yet the commission of criminal acts against a herald and envoys is considered impious not only by all others but especially by you (Athnians). Thus when the Megarians murdered Anthemokritos the People

were affected to such an extent that they barred them from (partic-
pating in) the Mysteries and set up a statue in front of the gates as a
reminder of this injustice.[1]

C. Pausanias 1.36.3

As one goes to Eleusis from Athens on the road the Athenians call the
Sacred Way, (there) the memorial of Anthemokritos has been erected.
A most impious action was committed against him by the Megarians.
They killed Anthemokritos when he came as a herald to stop them
from working the territory in the future. Blood-guilt remains with them
even to this day for doing it.

D. Scholiast to Aristophanes, *Peace* 246 (422/1)

Peace 246f.: O Megara, Megara, how quickly you have been ground to
bits, / made into one whole mincemeat.
  Scholion: . . . The Megarians were allies of the Lacedaemonians. And
because the whole reason for the war appears to have come about because of them, Charinos[2] wrote up the notice board[3] directed against
them as a favor to Perikles, to the effect that the Megarians were not to
venture on the land or the harbors of the Athenians. . . .

E. Harpocration, *Lexicon* s.v. 'Anthemokritos'

Anthemokritos. Isaeus in the *In Reply to Kalydon*: 'the bath next to
the statue of Anthemokritos.' This is at the Thriasian Gates. He was an
Athenian herald and was murdered by the Megarians when he forbade
them to work the sacred tract of land of the two goddesses.

1 This letter of complaint by Philip is doubtless inauthentic.
2 This name results from the emendation of the text. Compare Plut. *Perikles* 30.
3 I.e. the tablet on which the alleged decree was written.

123   The Megarian Decree or Decrees.[1] Before 433 *or* 433–432 B.C.

A: Scholiast to Aristophanes, *Peace* 605 (422/1 B.C.); B: Scholiast to Aristophanes,
Acharnians 532 (426/5 B.C.); C: Harpocration, *Lexicon* s.v. 'Anthemokritos.' Cf.
Thucydides 1.67.4, 139.1–2, 144.2; Diodorus 12.39.4; Plutarch, *Perikles* 29–31.

P. A. Brunt, *AJP* 72 (1951) 269–82 (before 433); Kagan, *Outbreak* 251–72 (433–
432); Meiggs, *Empire* 430f.; de Ste Croix, *Origins* 225–89, 392–3; C. W. Fornara,
YCS 24 (1975) 213–28 (about 433); Bury-Meiggs 246; R. Sealey, *CP* 70 (1975)
103–5; Sealey, *History* 317f.; T. E. Wick, *AC* 46 (1977) 74–99.

A. Scholiast to Aristophanes, *Peace* 605

See no. 116A.

B. Scholiast to Aristophanes, *Acharnians* 532

515   Aristoph. *Acharnians* 515-38: Some of us - and I do not say the city: / remember that I do not say the city! - but rascally little men, base coin, / dishonored men and counterfeits and half-foreigners, / kept on

520   denouncing Megarian jackets as contraband, // and if they saw a cucumber or a little rabbit somewhere, / or a piglet or a clove of garlic or a lump of salt, / these were Megarian and (confiscated and) sold off forthwith. / These were small matters and the custom of the country. / But

525   when some drunken youths went for the whore Simaitha // and stole her away, / then the Megarians, garlicked with the pain, / stole in return two whores of Aspasia. / Then the start of the war burst out / for all

530   Hellenes because of three strumpets. // Then Perikles the Olympian in his wrath / thundered, lightened, threw Hellas into confusion, / passed laws that were written like drinking songs / (decreeing) that the Megarians shall not be on our land, in our market, / on the sea or on the con-

535   tinent.[2] // Then the Megarians, since they were starving little by little, / begged the Lacedaemonians (to see) that the decree / arising from the three strumpets was withdrawn. / But we were unwilling, though they asked us many times. / Then came the clash of the shields.

   Scholion: 'Passed laws.' He imitated the writer of drinking songs. Timocreon of Rhodes ... (wrote one on which this parody of Perikles' law is modeled). Perikles, when he wrote the decree, moved that 'Megara shall not be admitted in the marketplace, on the sea, or on the mainland.' ... Perikles charged the Megarians with farming the sacred tract of land.

C. Harpocration s.v. 'Anthemokritos'

See no. 122E.

1   Some have inferred (see Gomme, etc., *HCT* 1.447; cf. de Ste Croix, *Origins* 226) on the basis of Aristophanes, *Acharnians* 515-22, that, by a decree earlier than that of 433, the Athenians excluded Megarian products from Athens' harbor.
2   'in heaven': Bentley.

124   Athenian Alliance with Rhegium. 433/2 B.C.
Marble stele, Attic letters, stoichedon, Athens.

IG I^2 51 (I^3 53); **GHI*, no. 63, pp. 171-5. Cf. Thucydides 1.36.2, 3.86.3 and no. 125 (alliance with Leontini).

ATL 3.277; Gomme, etc., *HCT* 1.198, 2.387; H. B. Mattingly, *Historia* 12 (1963) 272; Meiggs, *Empire* 138; J. D. Smart, *JHS* 92 (1972) 144-6; Bury–Meiggs 254; D. M. Lewis, *ZPE* 22 (1976) 223-5; Sealey, *History* 308.

[Gods. The envoys from Rhegium] *by whom* the alliance | [was concluded, and who took the oath:] Kleandros son of Xen|[-19-(son of)-]tinos, Silenos son of Phokos, | [-15-in Ap]seudes' archonship
5   (433/2) a||nd [in the Boule for which Kritia]des was first *Secre|tary.*
     [*vv*[1] Resolved by the] *Boule* and the People, A|[kamantis held the prytany, Ch]arias was Secretar|y, [Timoxenos[2] presided,] Kalli-[3] *vv* (10 spaces) | [--as made the motion: Alliance shall be made] between the
10   Athenians and || [the Rhegians. The oath] shall be sworn by the Athen|[ians so that everything will be] trustworthy and guileless and s|[traightforward on the Athenians' part,] *forever*, in relation to the Rhegians. |[They shall swear the following:[4]] '*As allies* we shall be
15   *trustw|orthy* [and just and] *steadfast* and reliable || [forever to the Rhegians and] we shall provide them with aid *if* [.] | [---]

1 A gap of two empty spaces must be assumed because the formula is invariable.
2 The name is restored because it appears in the related decree, no. 125.
3 This entire prescript (lines 1-8) was carved after the erasure of the original one; an extra letter was added to each line and an extra line was inserted; cf. no. 125. The reason for the erasure is not known.
4 '*an|d* [(their) allies': Hiller (*IG* I[2], cit.).

125   Athenian Alliance with Leontini. 433/2 B.C.
Marble stele, Attic letters, stoichedon, Athens.

IG I[2] 52 (I[3] 54); *GHI*, no. 64, pp. 175f.

See no. 124.

     Gods. The envoys from Leont|ini by whom the allian|ce was concluded
5   and who took the o|ath; Timenor son of Agathok|lles, Sosis son of Glaukias, Ge|llon son of Exekestos, the Secre|tary being Theotimos son of Tauris|kos. In Apseudes' archonsh|ip (433/2) and in the Boule for
10   which Kr||itiades was Secretary. | Resolved by the Boule and | the People, Akamantis h|eld the prytany, Charias was Se|cretary, Timoxe-
15   nos || presided, Kallias ma-[1] *vv* |de the motion: Alliance | shall be made between the Athenians and | Leontinians and the oa|th shall be given
20   and tak||en. [The oath shall be sworn] by the Atheni|[ans as follows:] '*As allies we shall b|e* [to the Leont]in[ians] *foreve|r* [guileless] *and*
25   *reliable.*' | [The Leontinians likewise shall] *swe||ar:* ['As allies we shall | forever be to the Athenians] *gui|leless* [and reliable.] *As to*[2] | [---]

1 As with no. 124, the alliance with Rhegium, this prescript (lines 1-15) was inscribed over an erasure and is longer than the original one.
2 An additional five lines follow in which no more than three letters at the right-hand margin are preserved.

126 Expenses of the Athenian Squadrons Sent to Corcyra. 433 B.C.
Marble stele, developed Attic letters, stoichedon (though syllabic division is observed), Athens.

IG I² 295+ (I³ 364); *GHI*, no. 61, pp. 167f. Cf. Thucydides 1.45, 1.51.4.

Gomme, etc., *HCT* 1.196f.; Meiggs, *Empire* 201, 259; Bury–Meiggs 246; Sealey, *History* 314f.

[The Athenians] *spent* for Corcyra [the following. When A|pseudes] was Archon (433/2), and in the (year of the) Boule for which Kr[i|tiades son of Phaeinos] of Teithras was first *Secre|tary*, [the Treasurers] of
5   the sacred monies of Athena, ‖ [-6- of Ker]ameis and his colleagues, for whom | [Krates son of Nau]pon of Lamptrai was Secretary, | [gave over] to the generals (sent) to Corcyra, the | [first (group)] to sail there, Lakedaimonios of Lakia|[dai,[1] Proteas] of Aixone, Diotimos of Euony-
10 mon, ‖ [in Aian]tis' prytany, the first *pry|tany* (of the year, of which) thirteen days had *elap|sed*: [2]6 T.[2] *vv* | [In Apseudes'] archonship and in the Boule | [for which Kritiades] son of Phaeinos of Teithras was first
15 S‖*ecretary, the Treasurers* of the sacred monies of A|[thena, Pronap]es of Erchia and his colleagu|es,[3] [for whom Euthias son of Ai]schron of Anaphlystos | [was Secretary,] gave *over* to the generals (sent) to Cor-|
20 [cyra, the second (group)] to sail there, Glaukon ‖ [of Kerameis, Meta-g]enes of Koile, Drakonti|[des -7-[4] in] Aiantis' prytany, | [the first prytany (of the year),] on the *final* [d|ay of the prytany: 50 T.[5]] *vv*

1 Kimon's son; see his dedication as a Knight, no. 83.
2 The other formal possibility is [6]6 T. The name of the tribe and the number of the prytany are supplied from the second entry.
3 The treasurers took up and laid down their office at the time of the Panathenaia (cf. no. 119A lines 27-8); the explanation for the double board here is that the time of the Panathenaia must have fallen between these two payments.
4 'of Thorai' is usually restored. These names differ, except for Glaukon's, from those given by Thuc. 1.51.4. For possible explanations see *GHI*, p. 168; Fornara, *Generals* 51.
5 One space is available for the figure and 50 is the most reasonable conjecture.

127 The Invasion of Attica. 432/1 B.C.

A: Scholiast to Sophocles, *Oidipous at Kolonos* 698 (Philochorus, *FGrHist* 328 F 125; Androtion, *FGrHist* 324 F 39); B: Scholiast to Sophocles, *Oidipous at Kolonos*

701 (Istrus, *FGrHist* 334 F 30). Cf. Herodotus 9.73; Thucydides 2.10.2, 2.19.2; Diodorus 12.42.3; Plutarch, *Perikles* 33.5.

F. E. Adcock, *CAH* 5.196f.; Jacoby, *FGrHist* IIIb Suppl. 1.150; Gomme, etc., *HCT* 2.13; Bury–Meiggs 254f.

A. Scholiast to Sophocles, *Oidipous at Kolonos* 698

Soph. *Oidipous at Kolonos* 694–700 (Pearson): There is something which // I have not heard tell of on Asian land / and which is never born in the great Dorian island / of Pelops, a growth / indestructible and self-renewing, / making a blaze of terror to the spears of the enemy, / which greatly flourishes in this land, // the leaf of the gray child-nourishing olive.

Scholion: That the Lacedaemonians did no injury to the sacred olive trees is stated by Philochorus as well as by others. . . . For the Lacedaemonians, when they invaded Attica with –[1] tens of thousands of Peloponnesians and Boeotians under the leadership of Archidamos son of Zeuxidamos, king of the Lacedaemonians, kept away from the so-called 'sacred olives' out of fear of Athena, as Androtion says.

B. Scholiast to Sophocles, *Oidipous at Kolonos* 701[2]

. . . . Istrus has also disclosed their number by writing as follows:[3] They say that the shoot[4] of the olive tree in the Academy was grown from the one on the Akropolis.[5] They laid invaders under a curse if anyone, friend or enemy, were to cut them down.[6] On account of this the Lacedaemonians, though they devastated the rest of the land, refrained from harming the Tetrapolis (Oinoe, Marathon, Probalinthos, Trikorythos) on account of the Herakleidai and (from harming) the sacred olives because of the curses.

1 The text is corrupt; a wrong word stands here. Plutarch gives 60,000 as the number. See Jacoby's discussion.
2 = verse 700 in passage A above.
3 The text is corrupt and a sentence seems to have dropped out.
4 Papageorgius' correction (*Scholia in Sophoclis tragoedias vetera* (Leipzig 1888) 435).
5 According to Photius and the *Suda*, 'moriai' (sacred olives), the trees originally were twelve in number, 'which were transplanted from the Akropolis to the Academy.' But the term was not restricted to the trees of the Academy.
6 See note 4.

128   Athenian Relations with Methone and Macedon. 430 *or* late winter 429/8 *or* 427/6 B.C. and later.
Marble stele, Attic letters (with two instances of Ionic), stoichedon, Athens.

IG I² 57 (I³ 61); *ATL* 2.D3–6, pp. 48f., and Plate 1; *GHI*, no. 65, pp. 176–80. Cf. Thucydides 2.29.6, 2.80.7 and *IG* I² 71 + (I³ 89) (relations with Perdikkas).

ATL 3.133–7 (first decree 430); H. B. Mattingly, *CQ* 11 (1961) 154–65 (first decree 427/6); Meiggs, *Empire* 534–6 (first decree 430); Bury–Meiggs 278f.; N. G. L. Hammond and G. T. Griffith, *A history of Macedonia* 2 (Oxford 1979) 124–7 (429/8).

The Methonaians from Pier[ia. | Ph]ainippos son of Phrynichos was Secretary.[1] | Resolved by the Boule and the People, Erechtheis *held the*
5 *prytan|y*, Skopas was Secretary, Timonides presided, D[iop‖ei]thes made the motion: The People shall vote their preference immediately [regardi|ng the M]ethonaians as to whether it seems best for the People to assess tribute [stra|ight]away or whether it shall be sufficient for them to pay what the *goddess* | had coming [from] the tribute[2] which in the previous *Panathenai|a* they had been assessed to pay and to be
10 exempt from the rest. [As to the] *d‖ebts* which the Methonaians are recorded as owing to the public treasury [of the Athe|ni]ans, if they are *cooperative* with the A|thenians as they are now, and even more so, [concession shall be granted in the matter of a] *specia‖l assessment* by the Athenians regarding the collection of the arrears. If a [genera‖l]
15 decree about the debts on the [recor‖|d tablets] is passed, it shall not affect the Methonaians [unles|s a] separate decree is passed concerning the Methonaians. [Envoy|s,] three in number, more than fifty years *of age*, shall be dispatched | [to] Perdikkas, and they shall declare to Perdikkas that it seems [ju|st] to allow the Methonaians to ply the sea
20 [and that it shall n‖ot] be permitted that (they be) circumscribed;[3] that he shall allow them *to* enter his territory and trade[4] [jus|t as] formerly; that he shall neither do them injury nor [receive inju|ry from them]; nor shall [he lead] an army through the territory of Methone | if the Methonaians object. If there is agreement [betwe|en the two parties,] the envoys shall arrange for the signing of a treaty. If not, [an
25 em‖|bassy] shall be sent by *each of* the parties to (arrive at) the Dionysia, with full powers to settle | what is in dispute, to meet with the Boule and [the] | *People*. (Our envoys) shall *tell* Perdikkas that if the *soldiers* | [who] are in Potidaea speak well of him, a favorable opinion [will be held | toward] him by the Athenians. The People voted that
30 the [Methon‖aian]s pay *as much* to the goddess as was coming to her from the tribute [which] | in the previous Panathenaia they had been assessed to [pay, the] | rest to be remitted.[5] *v* Resolved by the Boule and [the Peop‖le, H]ippotho[ntis] held the prytany, Megakleides [was Secre|tary,] Ni[k]o[-5-] presided, Kleonymos made the motion.[6] The
35 M[ethonaia‖|ns] *shall be permitted to import* grain from Byzantium up to the amount of [....] | *thousand* medimnoi each year. The [Helles-| p]ontine guards shall not themselves prevent them from exporting it

o|r allow *anyone else* to prevent them, or (if they do,) they are to be liable to a fine of ten thousand *drach|mas* each. After giving notice to
40   the Hellespon||tine guards they shall export up to the permitted amount. Exemption *shall also apply* | *to* the ship carrying it. Whatever general *decre|e* is voted concerning the allies by the Athenians, *relating to* (military) a|ssistance or enjoining some other action upon the cities, whether concernin|g (the Athenians) themselves or concerning the
45   cities, any that specifically name *the* [c||ity] of Methone, which they may vote, [shall] apply | [to it,] but no others. Instead, if they guard *their ow|n* [land,] they shall be doing what is required of them. As to what they say of Perd[ikk|as' mistreatment of them,] the Athenians shall consider whatever [se|ems best] regarding the Methonaians at *the*
50   *meet||ling before* the People of the envoys (returning) from Perdikkas – [both thos|e] who went with [Pl]eistias and those who went with Leo-go[ras. As regards th|e other] cities, their business shall be attended to on the *entrance into office* [of the] | *second prytany*, which, after the dockyard [session,] | shall *immediately* arrange for an assembly to be
55   held. They shall continuously hold [the || session there] until the matter *is concluded*, and nothing else [shall] take precedence | over this unless the generals require it. *v* [Reso||lved by the] Boule and the People, Kekropis *held the prytany*, [.]|[-6-]es was Secretary, H[i]erokleides
60   [presided...]|[-6-] made the motion:[7] Since [-25-]||[---]

(Lacuna)[8]

1   This stele contained at least four decrees, Phainippos having been secretary of the Boule when the last was passed, probably in 423 B.C. (Thuc. 4.118.11).
2   I.e. the *aparche* of one-sixtieth.
3   A minor modification of the text in *GHI*; cf. Alan Henry, *JHS* 97 (1977) 155f.
4   Apparently in the interior.
5   This sentence records the decision mandated in lines 5–9 of the decree.
6   For the date, 426/5, see no. 134, line 5.
7   This decree belongs in 426/5 or 425/4.
8   At least one other decree followed (see note 1).

129   Resettlement of Potidaea. 429 B.C.

Marble base, developed Attic writing, nonstoichedon, Athens.

IG I² 397; *DAA*, no. 306, pp. 328f.; *GHI*, no. 66, p. 181. Cf. Thucydides 2.70.4, 4.120.3; Diodorus 12.46.7 (1,000 colonists).

ATL 3.285; V. Ehrenberg, *CP* 47 (1952) 143f.; Meiggs, *Empire* 535; Bury-Meiggs 257.

(Dedicated by the) Epoikoi[1] | to Potidaea

1   'Immigrants' or 'additional settlers'; cf. no. 100, note 7.

130   The Fining and Reinstatement of the Athenian General Phormion. 428/7 B.C.

Scholiast to Aristophanes, *Peace* 347 (422/1) (Androtion, *FGrHist* 324 F 8). Cf. Thucydides 3.7.1; Pausanias 1.23.10.

Jacoby, *FGrHist* IIIb Suppl. 1.125–37; Fornara, *Generals* 56; Bury–Meiggs 263.

Aristoph. *Peace* 347: 'I endured the many troubles and straw mattresses which were the lot of Phormion.'

Scholion: This Phormion was an Athenian by birth, the son of Asopios. He became a pauper after being incorruptible as a general. After losing his citizen-rights, because he was unable to pay the 100 mnai (he had been fined at) his euthynai, he stayed idle in the countryside until the Acarnanians demanded him as general. He did not consent, but said that it was not permitted to men without citizen-rights. The People, wanting to free him from the ban, farmed out by contract to him for 100 mnai, †of the Dionysion,[1] as Androtion says in the third book of his *History of Athens*.

1   The passage is corrupt. Boeckh added the word 'festival' and changed the noun to 'Dionysos'; 'festival of Zeus': Mueller–Struebing. The general sense is clear. In order to free Phormion from the ban, the Athenians vastly overpaid him. They appointed Phormion to perform an act of cult for which they allotted him enough money to pay the fine.

131   Kleon and the Knights. 428–427 B.C. (?)

A: Scholiast to Aristophanes, *Knights* 226 (425/4) (Theopompus, *FGrHist* 115 F 93); B: Scholiast to Aristophanes, *Acharnians* 6 (426/5) (Theopompus, *FGrHist* 115 F 94).

Gomme, etc., *HCT* 2.289f.; W. R. Connor, *Theopompus and fifth-century Athens* (Washington, D.C. 1968) 50f.; C. W. Fornara, *CQ* 23 (1973) 24.

A. Scholiast to Aristophanes, *Knights* 226 (425/4)

Aristoph. *Knights* 225f.: But there are the Knights, a thousand brave men / who hate him and who will come to your aid.

Scholion: Theopompus says in the tenth book of the *Philippica* that the Knights hated him (Kleon). For having been insulted by them, and worked up into a rage, he made an attack against the constitution[1] and continuously devised evil against them. For he charged them with desertion (on the field of battle).

B. Scholiast to Aristophanes, *Acharnians* 6 (426/5)

Aristoph. *Acharnians* 6: (Dikaiopolis' heart was warmed) by the five talents which Kleon vomited up.

Scholion: ... For Kleon was fined five talents because he insulted the Knights. Kleon received five talents from the islanders to persuade the Athenians to lighten the burden of the eisphora. The Knights, perceiving this, spoke against him and demanded it from him. Theopompus mentions it.

1 'against the payment of their equipment-money': Fornara, suggesting that, since the word for cavalry equipment-money (*katastasis*) also means 'constitution', the scholiast understood the word in the latter sense and replaced it with its synonym *politeia*.

132 Contributions to the Spartan War Fund. 427 *or* about 405 *or* 396/5 B.C.

Marble stele,[1] Doric Greek, nonstoichedon, near Sparta.

IG V (1) 1; Jeffery, *LSAG*, no. 55, p. 197; *GHI*, no. 67, pp. 181–4 (?427; Lewis suggests 396/5).

E. Meyer, *Theopomps Hellenika* (Halle 1909) 266 (about 405); F. E. Adcock, *Mélanges Glotz* (Paris 1932) 1.1–6 (427); Meiggs, *Empire* 314, 352, 359.

[- - to the Lac]edaemonian[s -6 -] | [- -] hundred darics. [-11 -] | [- - to the L]acedaemonians, for the | [war,] *nine* mnai and ten staters. ‖
5 [There was given to the Lac]edaemonians by Lykeidas' son | [- -]os of Ole[n]os[2] *gave* [to the Lace|daemonians,] for the war, trireme [-6 -] | [-[3] in silver,] thirty-two mnai. [....] | [- -] from friends among the
10 Chians who[4] [- -] ‖ [- -] Aeginetan staters. [- -] | [- - to the] Lacedaemonians for the [wa|r, -][5] *four thousand*, and another | [- -] *four thousand* and, of raisins, | [- -] talents. ‖ [- - (someone's)] son *gave to* [the Lace-
15 daemo|nians - -] in abundance, and 800[6] darics | [- - in] *silver*, three talents. | [- -] *gave*, for the war, | [a silver] *talent*, thirty mnai [and] ‖
20 [- -] three thousand medimnoi (of wheat) and [further | medimnoi (?) (totaling) - -]ty[7] and, in *silver, sixty* | [mnai. There was given by] the Ephesians to the Lacedaem[o|nians, for the] war, *one thousand darics*.

(On the side of the stele)

5 Given by the Me|lians to the | Lacedae|monians ‖ in silver, | twenty |
10 mnai. | Given by Mo|lokros[8] to the ‖ Lacedaemo|nians, tale|nts[9] of
15 silver. | Given by the Melians ‖ to the Lacedae|monians | [- - -][10]

1 'We are dependent on Fourmont's copy except for ll. 1–10, and even they have suffered since he read them … we can see nothing of ll. 11–23 on our squeezes and are puzzled about the original layout of the inscription' (*GHI*, p. 183).
2 In Achaea. 'Oleros' (in Crete) is another possibility. Line 6 has very little space for both the gift of Lykeidas' son and the name of the contributor from Ole-[n]os, but the latter is presumably the donor of the gift named in lines 7f.
3 'trireme]s' p|ay': Dittenberger (*SIG* I, p. 108).
4 'From friends of the Chians *who are* [Lacedaemonian]' was Fourmont's reading, subsequently emended to '*for the* [war.'
5 'medimnoi (numbering)]': *GHI*.
6 Additional figures under 100 presumably followed in line 17.
7 The ending of a multiple of 10 between 30 and 90 survives here.
8 Perhaps the name of a Spartan; possibly Molobros (cf. Thucydides 4.8.9); or, with Wilamowitz (cited *GHI*, p. 183), 'Mo⟨lon⟩ | the Locrian.'
9 The line seems to be corrupt.
10 For a possible fragment, which adds as benefactors 'the Apell[--]', see *LSAG* 197, reprinted in *GHI*, p. 183.

133   Appointment of Tribute Collectors. 426 B.C.

Fragments of a marble stele, crowned by a relief (most of it lost), representing jars and sacks for tribute. Attic letters, stoichedon, Athens.

IG I² 65 (I³ 68); *ATL* 2.D8, pp. 52f.; B. D. Meritt, *AJP* 88 (1967) 29–32; **GHI*, no. 68, pp. 184–8. Cf. Antiphon F 52 Thalheim (tribute collectors were wealthy foreign nationals).

Gomme, etc., *HCT* 2.18; H. B. Mattingly, *BSA* 65 (1970) 129–33; Sealey, *History* 336.

[---] | Tribute. | Resolved by the Boule and *the* [People,] Kekropis
5 held the p|rytany, Polemarchos *was Secretary*, Onasos p‖resided,
[K]leonym[os made the motion: All] cities tri|butary [to the Ath]e-
nian[s shall elect] in each | city [tribute collectors (eklogeis) so that]
from all part|s the [entire tribute will be collected for the Athe]n[ians
or the] *lia|bility* [will be the collectors'--]¹ ‖

(Lacuna)

10 [---]|[---] *whi|ch holds the prytany* [-10- after the] Dionys|[ia. They]
shall read out [before the People those] *cities wh|ich have paid the* [tri-
15 bute, those which] have not p‖aid [and] *those which* (have paid) [in
part]. *To* those in *arr|ears there shall be sent five* [men to] exac|t [the]
tribute. A list is to be made [by the] *Hellenota|miai* on a display board,
containing the [cities] *in default* of tri|bute and [-9-]² of those who
20 bring (the tribute). It shall be placed ‖ on each occasion in front of
[-9-].³ For the Sa|mians and Therans⁴ shall [-19-] *t|he* monies which
[-13-] the selection | of the men and *any other* city which was assessed
| to bring money [to] Athens. This decree (shall be inscribed) on a

25 s‖tele (and) the *prytany* of Kekropis is to set it up on the Akropolis.
P|[...]kritos[5] made a motion: *Let all the rest be* as Kleonym|[os
(moved)]‚ but so that the Athenians may *best and most easily* carry on
| the war, [this matter] shall be brought [before] the People | [and an]
30 *assembly* [shall be held] tomorrow. Resolved by the ‖ [Boule and the
People, Kekr]opis held the prytany, Pol|[lemarchos was Secretary,
H]ygiainon presided, | [-9[6] made the motion: (Let) all the rest] (be)
as in the earlier | [decree - - -] |

(Lacuna)

35 [- - -] ‖ [- - -] | [- - -] | [- -] *Commissi|oners* shall be elected *for* the [other (?)]
40 suits relating to] the A|thenian monies [-15-][7] decre‖e and [one]
general [shall be ordered] to be *in attendanc|e* when any of the [cities
has a suit to be judge|d]. If anyone *schemes to* [render voi|d] the
tribute-decree [or to prevent the bringi|ng] of the tribute to Athens
45 (from a city), *a charge* [of treason shall be lodged against] h‖im by
any man from that *city* [who wishes (and it shall be brought)] b|*efore*
the Commissioners. *The* [Commissioners shall ta|ke] (the case) to the
[court] within a month [of the] S|ummoners' return. *Twice as many*
[Summoners shall there be] | as there are men whom anyone [wishes]
50 to indict. [If anyone] is co‖*ndemned*, the *court shall assess* [the proper]
p|*unishment* or fine. The heralds, [in whatever number th|ey] may be,
whom the Prytaneis *together* [with the Boule shall have e|lected,] shall
be sent to the cities *in* [Kekropi|s'] prytany *to secure the election* [of
55 the men w‖ho] will collect the tribute *and* [(their names) shall be writ-
ten down in|] *the* Bouleuterion. As to the stele, [the Poletai] shall *l|et
60 the contract. vv* | Tribute *collection vv* | *from* the *cities. vv* ‖ *vacat*

1   Restorations, the rationale for which is comparison with the Decree of Kleinias
    (no. 98), are very precarious. A number of them, supported by minimal evidence
    on the stele, are ignored here.
2   '[the names]': Wilhelm (cited *GHI*, p. 186).
3   '[the Metroon]': Meritt; '[the podium]' or '[the (statues of the) Heroes]': *ATL*.
4   Samos and Thera are not recorded as having made tribute payments. Samos was
    perhaps still paying her war indemnity (cf. Thucydides 1.117.3), and the same
    has been inferred for Thera.
5   Pythokritos or Polykritos.
6   '[Kleonymos]': Meritt.
7   '[according to the presently existing]': *ATL*.

134 Loans to the Athenian State from the Treasury of Athena Polias. 426/5–424/3 B.C.[1]

Fragments of a marble stele, developed Attic writing, stoichedon,
Athens.

IG I² 324+, 306 (I³ 369); B. D. Meritt, *Athenian financial documents of the fifth century* (Ann Arbor 1932) 136ff.; W. K. Pritchett and O. Neugebauer, *The calendars of Athens* (Cambridge, Mass. 1947) 102ff.; W. K. Pritchett, *Ancient Athenian calendars on stone*, Univ. of Calif. Publ.: Class. Archaeology 4.4 (Berkeley and Los Angeles 1963) 290-312; M. Lang and B. D. Meritt, *CQ* 18 (1968) 84-94; *GHI*, no. 72, pp. 205-17. Cf. Thucydides 2.13; Andocides, *On the Peace* 8.

Gomme, etc., *HCT* 2.432-36; B. D. Meritt, *The Athenian year* (Berkeley and Los Angeles 1961) 60-71; H. B. Mattingly, *BSA* 65 (1970) 137f.; W. K. Pritchett, *The Choiseul Marble*, Univ. of Calif. Publ.: Class. Studies 5 (Berkeley and Los Angeles 1970) 98-103.

[The following was calculated] by the Logistai [in the] *four* years from Panathenaia to [Panathenaia as outs│tanding. The following was paid out *by the* Treasurers [Andro]kles of Phlya and his colleagues to the Hell[enotamiai . . . .]│[-10-]es and his colleagues for the *generals* Hippokrates of Cholargos and his *colleagues* [in the]│ prytany of [Kekropis],
5   the second prytany, (of which) four days had *passed*, [in th││e Boule for which] Megakleides was first *Secretary*, in Euthynos' archonship (426/5), 20 T. Interest [on this came to │ 5,69]6 dr. *v* Second payment in Kekropis, the second prytany, [there were] *remaining* [seven d│ays] to the prytany, 50 T. Interest [for this *v*] : 2 T. 1,970 dr. *v* Third payment in Pan[dionis' pryta│ny], the fourth prytany, five days *had passed* of the prytany, [28 T. 5,6--dr.² I│nterest] for this: *v* 1 T.1,719 dr.³ 2 ob.
10   *v Fourth* payment in Akamantis' prytany, [the eighth prytan││y], five days *had* passed *of the* prytany, 44 T. 3,000 dr. Interest for this: [*v* 1 T. 4,7-dr. (?-ob.)]. │ *Fifth* payment in Akamantis' prytany, the eighth prytany, there had *passed* [ten da│ys of] the prytany, 100 T. Interest [for this *v*]: 3 T. 5,940 dr. *v* Sixth payment in Ere[chtheis' prytan│y], the tenth prytany, seven days of the prytany *had passed*, 1[8 T. 3,000 dr. Interest for th│is] came to 4,172[-dr.]⁴ *Total* of the principal spent
15   in Andr[okles' magistracy an││d (that)] of his *colleagues*: 261 T. 5,6[--dr. ?ob.] Total interest for the money which was spent [in Androk│les'] magistracy and (that) of his colleagues: [11 T. 1]99 dr. 1 ob. *vv* The following was given over by the *Treasurers* [Phokiades o│f Oi]on and his colleagues, in S[tra]tokles' archonship (425/4) and in the Boule for which Pl[eistias was first *v*] │ *Secretary*, to the generals *around* [Pe]loponnesus, De[m]osthenes son of Alkisthenes of Aphid[na, in . . .]│ │ [-5-]⁵ prytany, the fourth *prytany*, on the third *day* of the prytany in
20   [progress, from ││ (the) Opisth]odomos:⁶ 30 T. Interest for *this came to* 5,910 dr. *v* Another payment to the generals [Nikias son of Nikerat│os of Kyda]ntidai and his *colleagues* [in] Pandionis' prytany, the ninth *prytany*, [on the -5-]│[-5-]teenth⁷ day of the *prytany* in progress, 100 T. Interest for this *came to* [2 T. 3,---dr.]⁸ │ *Total* of the principal *spent* in Phokiades' magistracy and (that) of his colleagues: 1[30 T.

The interest-tot|al for the] money which was *spent* in Phokiades' magis-
25 tracy and (that) of his colleagues: [3 T. 3, - - - dr.[9] || The following] *was
given over* by the Treasurers Th[ouky]dides of Acherdous and his col-
leagues, in Is[archos' archonship (424/3) an|d in the Boule for which
Epi]l[y]kos was *first* Secretary, to the Hellenotamiai of the previous
year, D[-14-]|[-6- and his colleagues, and to the new ones,] Charopides
of Ska[mb]onidai and his colleagues, [in Hippothon|tis' prytany, the
first] *prytany*, on the twenty-sixth day of the prytany, [-12-]|[..[10]:
32 T. 5, - - - dr.[11] Interest for] this came to 4,665 dr. 5 ob. Second *pay-*
30 *ment* [in the -5-]||[-21-] prytany,[12] on the twelfth day of the prytany,
23[+ T.[13]-15-]|[-21-[14] Third] *payment* in Erechtheis' prytany, [-18]|
[-28-][15] Interest for this came to 632 dr. 1½ ob. *v Fourth* [payment in |
Akamantis' prytany, the eighth] prytany, on the thirtieth day of the
prytany, [100 T. Interest -7-]|[-17-[16] Total] of the principal spent in
35 Thoukydides' [magistracy and (that) of his colleag||ues: -6-. Total of
interest for the] money which was spent in Thoukyd[ides' magistracy
and (that) of his collea|gues: -15-][17]

(Lines 112–23. Totals for eleven years, 433/2–423/2)

[The principal of Athena Nike (which) they owe in] eleven years: ⟨2⟩8
T. 3,548 dr. 2 ob. *vv* | [Interest for Athena Nike came to 5 T. . . . .] 31
dr. 2½ ob.[18] *vv* | [Of Athena Polias in eleven years] the principal they
115 owe: 4,748 T. 5,[775 dr. || Interest for Athena Polias came to, in]
eleven *years*, 1,243 T. 3,803 dr. *vv* | [In eleven years (the principal) of
Athena Nike and] (Athena) Polias: [4]777 T. 3,[323 dr. 2 ob.[19] | In
eleven years (the) total of (Athena) Polia]s' and Nik[e's interest]:
1,248 T. [--] | [*vv*] *vv* | [For the Other Gods, the expenditure of the]
120 *principal* in eleven [years in total: 821 T. 1,087 dr. || For the Other
Gods, the entire interest] *in* eleven *years* [in total: - - -] | [- - *vv*] *vv* |
[The entire principal in eleven years (owed)] *to all* the *gods*: [5,594 T.
4,900+ dr. - -] | [The entire interest (owed) to all the gods in] eleven
years [in total: - - -]|[--] *vv*

1   This document is as difficult as it is important. The stoichedon pattern is irre-
    gular. The method used by the Athenians to compute interest, perhaps with
    the abacus, is not yet recovered; and a further complicating factor is the
    assumption by some scholars (Lang, Meritt) that the stele had a blemish in
    certain portions of the right-hand margin (which is missing totally), with the
    result that some lines (it is supposed) may have not run on to the end.
2   '[5,610 dr. 3½ ob.': *A(thenian) F(inancial) D(ocuments)* 136. *(The) Cal(endars
    of Athens)* 103; L(ang)–M(eritt, *CQ*) 8: '[5,665 dr.'
3   *IG* I[2] reports no reading in the two spaces after the talent sign.
4   4,172 dr. [4 ob.: *AFD* 138, *Cal.* 103; 4,17[3 dr. 4 ob.: L–M 89 (more than the
    space allows).
5   The possible prytanies are Aigeis and Oineis.

6   The room in which the treasures were stored; cf. no. 119, lines 15–16, and the Glossary.

7   'fif]teenth': *AFD*, L–M; 'eigh]teenth': *Cal.* 102, *(Ancient Athenian Calendars on)Stone* 295.

8   '[3,760 dr.': *AFD*; '[3,740 dr.': *Cal.*; '[3,800 dr.': L–M.

9   '3,670 dr.': *AFD*; '3,650 dr.': *Cal.*; '3,710 dr.': L–M.

10 '[from the Opisthodo|mos': *Cal.* 99, L–M.

11 '33 T. 550 dr.': *AFD*; '32 T. 5,983 dr.': *Cal.*; '32 T. 5,983 dr. 2 ob.': L–M; '32 T. 5,986 dr. 4 ob.': *Stone* 304.

12 '[third]': *AFD, Cal.*; '[fourth]': L–M.

13 '23 T. [4,250 dr.]': *AFD*; '[4,817 dr.]': *Cal.*; '2[4 T. 1,216 dr. 4 ob.]': L–M; '23 T. [4,718 dr.': *Stone*.

14 This interest payment was computed at 3,057 dr. 5 ob.: *AFD* 139; 3,077 dr. 5 ob.: *Cal., Stone*; 2,957 dr. 4 ob.: L–M.

15 'the s[eventh prytan|y, on the second day of the prytany, 6 T. 1,2]00 dr.' *AFD*. 's[eventh prytan *vv*|y, on the first day of the prytany, 6 T. 1,2]00 dr.': *Cal.*; 's[ixth prytany, | on the sixth day of the prytany, 5 T. 4,8]00 dr.': L–M; 's[eventh prytan|y, on the third day of the prytany, 6 T. 13]00 dr. 2 ob.': *Stone* (with a misprint). The last two figures are only partially preserved (*Stone* 271ff.).

16 '1 T. 2,900 dr.': *AFD*; '2,960 dr.': L–M.

17 The inscription continues through 423/2 B.C. and goes on to record loans from the Other Gods.

18 I follow *GHI* and do not provide the most speculative restorations. Incomplete figures will therefore be slightly larger. Eleven years of interest for the Other Gods (line 120) cannot be computed.

19 Ten talents of this sum are added as a correction.

135   Thank-Offering of the Messenians and Naupactians. 425 *or* about 421 B.C.

Near the foot of the triangular marble basis which supported the Nike of Paionios at Olympia. Lines 1–2 generally Ionic alphabet, 4-bar sigma, Doric Greek; lines 3–4 Ionic, smaller. Olympia.

Tod I, no. 65, pp. 146–8 (425); *GHI*, no. 74, pp. 223 f. (about 421). Cf. Thucydides 4.9.1, 4.36.1, 4.41.2; Diodorus 12.63; Pausanias 5.26.1 in the edition of J. G. Frazer, *Pausanias' description of Greece*[2] (London 1913) 3.643 ff.; F. W. Mitchel, *Phoros* 107–9.

The Messenians and Naupactians[1] dedicated (this) to Zeus | Olympios as tithe from the enemy. |

Paionios of Mende made it, | and in making the akroteria[2] on the temple he won the victory.[3]

1   See no. 47 above.

2   Statues or ornaments placed on the angles of a pediment. Here the bronze-gilt Nike (Victory) atop the temple pediment and the cauldrons at its extremities (Paus. 5.10.4).

3   I.e. in competition for the design of the akroteria.

136 Reassessment of the Tribute of the Athenian Empire. 425/4 B.C.[1]
Fragments of a marble stele, developed Attic letters, stoichedon,
Athens.

IG I² 63 (I³ 71); *ATL* 1.A9, pp. 154–7; 2.A9, pp. 40–3; *GHI*, no. 69, pp. 188–201.
Cf. Plutarch, *Aristeides* 24.3.

ATL 3.70–80; Gomme, etc., *HCT* 3.500–4; H. B. Mattingly, *BSA* 65 (1970) 140f.;
Meiggs, *Empire* 324–32; Rhodes, *Boule* 90; Bury–Meiggs 274; Sealey, *History* 336.

Gods. | *Assessment of tribute.* | Resolved by the [Boule and the People,
-7-]² *held the prytany*, [....] on *was Secretary*, [-7-] *pre|sided*, Thou-
di[ppos made the motion. Heralds shall be sent] from the [-8-³ who]
5   *shall be elected* [by the Boule, to th|le] cities, two [to Ionia and
Caria], two *to* [Thrace, two] to the I[slands, two to the Hellesp]|ont.
These [are to announce to the] public authority [of each city that en-
voys are to be present in Mai]|makterion [month -11-] Eisagogeis⁴ [-8-
These] shall elect both a *Secre|tary* and a co[-Secretary -11-]⁵ The
Boule [-25- ten] m|en.⁶ These [shall enroll the cities within five(?)]
10   *days* from that on which [-34-⁷ or] f|lor *each* day *each* [shall make
payment of one thousand (?) drachmas. Let the taktai (assessors) be
put on oath by] *t|he* oath-commissioners [on the very day on which
they] *happen* [to be elected or each (of the oath-commissioners) shall
be liable to th|e] same *penalty.* [-55- it is]⁸ *vo|ted* by the [People. The
Eisagogeus who is] *selected by lot*⁹ and the Polemarch [are to make
(preliminary) examination of the suits in] *t|he* Heliaia [just as in the]
15   *other* [suits (judged)] by the Heliasts. [If -20-¹⁰ the] || cities in accor-
dance with [the diadikasiai (adjudications)], let [each of them] be
liable *to pay at his euthyna* ten thousand *drachmas* [according to the
law]. | The [-4-]thetai¹¹ are to establish a new [court of one thousand
dikasts(?). As to the tribute, sinc|e] *it has become* too little, the [pre-
sent assessments] *are to be made by* (the jurors) *together* with the
Boule [just as (was done) in the la|st] term of office, with [all (assess-
ments)] *proportionate*, in the month of *Posideion.* [They shall also
deliberate daily] | *from the first of the month* [using the same proce-
dure in order that assessment may be made] of the tribute in the [month
20   of] *Posideion.* [The Boule, in full sessio|ln(?)] *is to* deliberate *quite*
[continuously so that assessments] may be made unless [the People
votes otherwise. T|he] tribute is not [to be assessed] for any [city for
less] than [the amount it previously happened to pa|y] unless *there
appears to be* [impoverishment so that] its area is unable [to pay more.
This] | *resolution* [and this decree and the] *tribute* which *is* assessed
[on each city shall be inscrib|ed] by the *Secretary* [of the Boule on

two] *stelai* of marble, [and he is to set one of them up in the] *Bouleu-*
25 *te*|*rion and the other* [on the Akropolis. The contract shall be let] by
the Poletai [and the money shall be supplied] by the Ko|lakretai. [In
future, announcement shall be made to the] *cities* about the [tribute
before the] *Great* [Panathenaia. | The prytany which] *happens to be in
office* [shall introduce (the business of) the assessments during the]
Panathe|*naia*. [If the Prytaneis do not at that time introduce] to the
People *and* [to the Boule and to the] *court*[12] | (the business) of *the*
[tribute, or if they do not immediately deal with it] *in their own term
of office, there shall be due* [(a fine of) one hundred drachmas,] *sacred*
30 *to* || Athena, [from each of the Prytaneis,] *and* to the public treasury
[one hundred (drachmas from each), and at their euthynai (a fine of)]
one thousand | *drachmas* [from each of the Prytaneis.] If anyone else
proposes [a motion that the cities] shall *not* be a|ssessed [during] the
[Great Panathenaia] in the prytany [which] *first holds office*, his
citiz|en-rights *shall be* forfeit [and] his *property* shall be *confiscated*,
the goddess [receiving the tithe]. These (proposals) are to be *brought* |
before [the] People *in the prytany* [of -6-],[13] compulsorily, *after* [the]
35 *expedition*[14] [has returned], on the second d|lay, *immediately after the
religious business* (has been transacted). *If* (the matter) *is not finished*
on *that day*, they shall [deliberate] *about it* first of a|ll on the *succeed-
ing day*, (and they shall deliberate) *without interruption until it is
finished* in *the* prytany [-9-].[15] If they do *n*|*ot* bring the matter before
[the People] or do [not] finish it in their *own* term of office, *at their
euthynai* let a fine of ten thousand *drachm*|*as* (be imposed) on *each* of
the [Prytaneis on the ground of] preventing additional (?) *tribute from
being given* [for the] *armies*. Those *summoned* [to] tr|ial[16] *are to be
brought by* [the] Public Klete[res] *(Summoners)* [in order that] *the*
40 *Boule* [may judge immediately] *whetl*|*her* they do not appear [to be
performing their duties] *correctly*. *The routes* the heralds [are to travel
shall be prescribed, according to] t|*he* oath, *by the assessors*, [(who will
indicate) how far] *they shall proceed*, so that not [-33-] | the *assess-
ments* to the [cities -15-] *wherever* it seems best [-22-[17] What], rela|t-
ing to the assessments and [this decree], is to be *said* [to the cities, this
the People] *shall de*|*cree*, and likewise [anything else the Prytaneis may
introduce], *dealing with* [what is necessary. That the tribute] shall be
45 pa|lid by the cities [shall be the responsibility of the generals] *as soon
as* [the Boule has made] *the assessmen*|*t* [of the] *tribute*, so that there
may be [sufficient money for the People for the] *war*. [The generals]
shall take | [the] tribute *under careful consideration* [every year, inves-
tigating by land] *and* sea, (as their) *fi*|*rst* (business), [how much] must
[be spent] either *on* [the expeditions or on anything else. At the] *first*
[session of] *the* Boule | [they are to introduce suits regularly about this

50   without (consulting) the Heliaia and] *the* other courts unles‖s [the]
     People [decrees that they introduce them after the jurors have] *first*
     [made a decision]. The heralds who are going | [are to] *receive* [their
     pay from the Kolakretai. -9- made the motion]. Let all the rest be as
     the Boule (advises). [But (as to)] the | [assessments] which [-24-¹⁸
     the] Prytaneis who happen then *to be in o*|*ffice*, (together with) *the*
     Secretary [of the Boule shall bring them before] *the* court when the
     assess|*ments* [are at issue] *so that* [the jurors may give their concur-
55   rence]. *v* Resolved by the Boule and the People, A‖[igeis] held the
     prytany, [Phil]ip[pos was Secretary, -7-]oros *presided*. Thoudippos
     made the motion. *All th*|*ose cities* for which tribute [was assessed in
     (the year of)] *the* [Boule in which Pleisti]as was first *Secretary*, in
     Stratokl|[les'] archonship (425/4), [shall bring a] *cow* [and a panoply
     of armor¹⁹ to the] *Great Panathenaia* without exception. They are to
     take part | [in] the procession [just as colonists (?) (do)]. *vv* [The
     following is the ass]essment of the trib[ute] *for the* cities by the Boule |
     in which [Pl]eistias *was first Secretary* [-11-],²⁰ *in* Stratokl[es'] archon-
60   ship, in the term of office *of the* Eis‖lagogeis for whom Ka[-*c*. 18- was
     Secretary].

*(An uninscribed portion follows after which are inscribed
the lists of the cities, according to districts, in four columns)*

*(Extract from column I)*²¹

	Island Tribute			1 T.	Athenitians
	30 T.	Parians	80	1 T.	Syrians (from Syros)
	15 T.	Naxians		2,000 dr.	Grynchians
	15 T.	Andrians		1,000 dr.	Rhenaians
65	15 T.	Melians		2,000 dr.	Diakreis from
	9 T.	Siphnians			(the Chalcidians²²)
	15 T.	Eretrians	85	1,000 dr.	Anaphaians
	5 T.	Therans		*(Vacant)*	Keria 10 dr. 3 ob.
	10 T.	Ceians		2,000 dr.	Pholegandros
70	5 T.	Carystians		300 dr.	Belbina
	10 T.	Chalcidians		1,000 dr.	Kimolos
	6 T.	Cythnians	90	1,000 dr.	Sikinetians
	10 T.	Tenians		100 dr.	Posideion in
	2 T.	Styrians			Euboea
75	[2 T.]	Mykonians		1 T. 2,000 dr.	Diakrians
	[2 T.]	Seriphians			in Euboea
	[1 T.]	Ietians	95	*(Vacant)*	[H]eph[ais]ți[ans],
	[1 T.]	Dionians		4 T.	*Those* [in Lemnos]

(Vacant)   [Myrrhinians]   100   [Total]
[1 T.]   [Imbrians]   [163T. 410 dr. 3 ob.][23]
[Of Island Tribute]

1 Some twenty of this decree's surviving forty-three fragments have been reconstructed with plaster, but more than half of it is missing, including much of the right-hand margin. Restoration of detail is therefore very uncertain, even though the main provisions can be grasped. The decree is remarkable for its strong language as well as because it was not passed in a Great Panathenaic year, as was customary, and provides for an extraordinary increase in the tribute demanded, and unrealistically lists all possible tribute-paying states.

2 'Leontis]': *ATL*; the alternative is Aiantis.

3 There is no satisfactory restoration of the group from which the heralds were to be selected.

4 Magistrates who brought cases into court; see the Glossary. *ATL* 1 restores: 'The Boule shall also have] Eisagogeis [elected by lot.'

5 'from among themselves]': Béquignon and Will; 'from the entire citizen body': *ATL*.

6 '[shall elect, as assessors of the tribute, ten] m|en': *ATL* 2.

7 This sentence, as restored in *ATL* 1: 'These [shall enroll the cities within five days] from the time [they happen to have been elected.]'

8 '[The Eisagogeis are to take charge of the adjudications (diadikasiai) about the tribute when it is]': *ATL*.

9 *GHI*, following *ATL* 4.ix; '[They and the] *Archon*': *ATL* 2.

10 '[If the assessors do not assess]': *ATL* 2.

11 '[Nomo]theta[i': *ATL*; '?[Thesmo]theta[i': *GHI*, assuming an omitted letter, since Nomothetai are not known at this time and, when they later do appear, have quite different functions. See Hignett, *Constitution* 299–305.

12 *ATL* 1; 'and [if they do not vote a] *court*': *ATL* 2.

13 'Oineis]': *ATL*; '[Leontis]': *GHI*, tentatively, assuming an irregularity in the orthography of the preceding word.

14 Perhaps Kleon's, from Sphakteria, or Nikias', from Corinth.

15 '[already named]': *ATL* (i.e. Oineis); '[of Leontis]': *GHI*.

16 *ATL* 1; 'The her|alds who are summoned': *ATL* 2.

17 (From line 41:) '[they may] not [journey uninstructed. The heralds | are to be compelled to announce] *the assessments* to the [cities] *wherever* it seems best [to the (local) rulers': *ATL* 2, or, '[to the People who proclaim it': *ATL* 1.

18 '[shall be subject to adjudication for individual cities': *ATL* 2.

19 See no. 98 above, line 43; no. 100, lines 11–12.

20 Pleistias' demotic filled this lacuna.

21 Where the name can be regarded as certain, restoration has not been indicated. The names completely restored are supplied from other lists.

22 The central part of Euboea was called the Diakria; hence the Diakreis and the Diakrians (line 93). The former were counted as Chalcidian.

23 Other partially preserved tribute totals: Hellespontine: 250 T. [--], Col. III, line 123; Thracian: 310 T. [--], Col. IV, line 125; the grand total: [1],460 T. [--], at the very bottom of the inscription.

137 An Agreement Between Andros and Delphi. Second half of the fifth century B.C.[1]

Two fragments of a limestone stele, Dorian and Ionian dialects in mixture, stoichedon with irregularity, Delphi.

G. Daux, *Hesperia* 18 (1949) 58–72, with a photo on Plate 1; *F. Sokolowski, *Lois sacrées des cités grecques*, Suppl. (Paris 1962) no. 38, pp. 76–80.

(A)

5   [---]|[---]|[---]|[-5-] the *three* houses[2] [.||-10-] to the c|*hiefs* of the
    sacred embassy. The following | shall *not* provide *food* or [....]|[..][3]:
10 three chiefs of the sacred embassy, a s|eer, commander,[4] herald, ||flutist,
    steersman, bo|atswain, the officer commanding at the bow. A *hi|de*[5]
    shall be provided to herald, flut|list, boatswain, and each | of the state-
15 priests. Fo||od shall be provided (by the Delphians) on the fi|rst (day):
    barley-cake, meat, wine – a|s *much as* they desire – and whatever *el|se*
20 is appropriate. For the (next) two da|ys, *in addition to the food*, p||ay-
    ment shall be made by each person, both boy a|nd man, of an Aegine-
    tan obol | for each day. The | chiefs of the sacred embassy shall make
25 sa|crifice with one (victim costing(?)) more than half.[6]|| The reserved
    portions[7] shall be rendered up: the *pe||anos* – four (obols); the metax-
    en|ia[8] – two (obols); for the priest – six (obols), out of | each *hecatomb*.
30 A *pri|vate individual*[9] shall obtain the third part[10] of the hide||s *from*
    what he sacrifices | except for victims sacrificed for the sake of consul-
    tation (of the oracle) and for *p|urification*, and (except for) all those
35 who together with [..]|[-8-][11] go to consult the oracle. | [---]||[---]

(The stele breaks off)

(Aa)

This portion of the inscription, containing seven lines, is too poorly preserved to be restored. The mention, however, in lines 6f. of the 'Andria|[ns' permits the identification of the people involved in this compact with Delphi.

(B)

  [---]|[-5-] Archiadas, | *just* like his ances|tors. The Boule, out of those
5 || sailing to Del|phi, shall select fiv|e men and bind them b|y oath.
10 Food shall not | be provided by (these men themselves) be||cause of
    this official duty. They | shall be empowered to f|ine a disord|erly per-
15 son up to fi|ve drachmas ea||ch day. Whomever | they fine they shall
    present a re|cord of to the Boule.

1 About 425: Daux.
2 Apparently the lodgings in which members of the Andrian community would stay while visiting Delphi. The multitude of pilgrims flocking to Delphi made it desirable, if not mandatory, that various states would have houses available in which to lodge their nationals.
3 'roast me|at': Daux, who interprets this document differently. He supposes that what is in question here is a sacrificial *offering* which the group is not obliged to make.
4 I.e. of the vessel bringing the Andrians to Delphi. Daux takes the word (*archon*) to refer to the archon eponymous of Andros.
5 The hides from sacrificial victims were customarily apportioned out. See no. 93, line 10.
6 This is a very difficult passage, and its interpretation is in doubt.
7 The equivalent in money of portions normally reserved for obligatory dedications now transmuted into a tax.
8 The *pelanos*, a cake made from the meal of barley and wheat, which normally was offered as a preliminary to sacrifice, is valued at four obols. The *metaxenia* (26f.) was perhaps a payment made to certain individuals, such as *proxenoi*, who possessed the right to attend the banquet.
9 From Andros.
10 These three words appear in lines 30f.
11 'th|e [King]': Daux; Sokolowski tentatively suggests 'th|e (man) [in charge].'

138 Athens Honors Herakleides for Help in Concluding a Treaty with the King of Persia. 424/3 *or* 415 *or* 389 B.C.[1]
Marble stele, Ionic lettering, stoichedon, Athens.

IG II² 8 (*IG* I³ 227); **GHI*, no. 70, 201-3. Cf. Plato, *Ion* 541d; Andocides 3.29; Demosthenes 20.60; Aristotle, *Athenaion Politeia* 41.

Wade-Gery, *Essays* 207-11 (Herakleides of Klazomenai: 424/3); D. Stockton, *Historia* 8 (1959) 74-9 (Herakleides of Byzantium: 389); A. Raubitschek, *GRBS* 5 (1964) 156 (415). Meiggs, *Empire* 135, 138, 493; J. Pečírka, *The formula for the grant of enktesis in Attic inscriptions* (Prague 1966) 22ff.

3 Resolved by the Boule [and the People, -6-]|[..]s held the prytany,
5 S[....was Secretary, || (?) N]eokleides *presided*, [-12-]| *made the motion.* Herakleides [-14-]² *shall be re|corded* by the *Secretary* [of the Boule as a prox|enos] and benefactor [in accordance with what the Peopl|e] decide and (the Secretary) shall set up (the inscription) on [the Acro-
10 polis, since (Herakleides) was of be||nefit] to the Athenian [embassies and in a|ll things] is a *good man* [toward the People] | of the *Athenians.* Thoukydide[s made the motion. Let all the rest be] | *as* (resolved) by the Boule. [But] *since* [the envoys | who] *have returned* from the King³
15 [announce that He||rak]leides *cooperated* [with them zealous|ly] both as to the treaty [with the King and a|s to] any other thing they *enjoined,* [there shall be granted to Herakle|ides] the right to possess land and [a dwelling at Athen|s and] *immunity* from public burdens just *as*

20 [for the other pr‖oxenoi.] If [he should die] anywhere by a *violent*
[death, punishment shall be (exacted)] *for* him [jus‖t as - - -]

1 This inscription is the second of (at least) two, and parts of the last two lines of
the preceding one remain preserved stating that it should be engraved and set up
on the Acropolis. The lettering of the inscription here translated 'suggests the
early fourth century' (*GHI*).
2 '[of Klazomenai]': Wade-Gery and others; '[of Byzantium]': Stockton. Stockton's restoration of this ethnic presupposes a departure from the usual formula
and irregularity in the mason's spelling.
3 The 'King' (used without article in Greek) is invariably the King of Persia; yet
Stockton here suggests a Thracian king, Seuthes or Medokos.

139 Payment to the Priestess of Athena Nike. 424/3 B.C.
Marble stele (the reverse side of no. 93), stoichedon, Attic and Ionic
lettering, Athens.

IG I² 25 (I³ 36); **GHI*, no. 71, pp. 204f.

H. B. Mattingly, *Historia* 10 (1961) 169–71; B. D. Meritt and H. T. Wade-Gery,
JHS 83 (1963) 110f.; Meiggs, *Empire* 135f., 138, 493; and see no. 93.

Resolved by the Boule and the Pe‖ople, Aigeis held the prytany, Neo-
k‖leides was Secretary, Hagnode‖mos presided, Kallias made the motion.
5 To t‖he Priestess of Athena Ni‖ke [[*v*]].[1] The fifty drachmas ‖ which
have been written down on the stele ‖ shall be paid (annually) by the
10 *Kolakretai* ‖ who hold office in *Thargel‖lion*[2] to the *Priestess* of A‖thena
Nike [-8-]

1 Lines 1–6 are written in Attic, the rest, from the erasure, in Ionic. What has been
erased was the sign for 50 drachmas. The two references in lines 6 and 11 to the
priestess of Athena Nike are as puzzling as the change in lettering.
2 Or, by changing punctuation (see Tod I, 178f.), 'shall be paid by the Kolakretai,
whoever hold the office, in Thargelion.'

140 Athenian Decree Regulating the Offering of First-Fruits at Eleusis.
425/4 *or* about 422 *or* 416/15 B.C.
Marble stele, developed Attic writing, stoichedon (with irregularity),
Eleusis. A small fragment exists of another copy at Athens.

IG I² 76+ (I³ 78); **GHI*, no. 73, pp. 217–23.

B. D. Meritt, *Athenian financial documents of the fifth century* (Ann Arbor 1932)
172 n. 3, *CW* 56 (1962) 39–41 (416/15); H. B. Mattingly, *PACA* 7 (1964) 53–5
423/2); Gomme, etc., *HCT* 4.270; Meiggs, *Empire* 303f.; H. B. Mattingly, *Phoros*
90–7 (425/4).

[Timo]tel[e]s of Acharnai was Secretary.[1] | *Resolved* by the Boule and
the People, Kekropis held the prytany, Timotel[les] was Secretary,
Kykneas presided. The following the Commissioners (syngrapheis) dralf-
ted: First-fruits shall be offered to the two goddesses, in accordance
5 with ancestral custom and thlle oracular response from Delphi, by the
Athenians (as follows): from each one hundred medimnoi of blarley
not less than one-sixth (of one medimnos); of wheat, from each hundred medimnoi, nlot less than one-twelfth. If anyone produces more
grain than [this amounlt] or less, he shall offer first-fruits in the same
proportion. Collection shall be made by [the] Demlarchs deme by
10 deme and they shall deliver it to the Hieropoioi || from Eleusis[2] at
Eleusis. (The Athenians) shall construct three (storage) pits at Eleusils
in accordance with the ancestral custom, at whatever place seems to
the Hieropoioi and the architlect to be suitable, out of the funds of the
two goddesses. *The* grlain shall be put in there which they receive from
the Demarchs. | The allies as well shall offer first-fruits according to
15 the same procedure. The cities shall have *collellctors* chosen for the
grain by whatever means seems best to them for grailn collection. When
it has been collected, they shall send it to Athens, | and those who have
brought it shall deliver it to the Hieropoioi from Eleusils at Eleusis. If
(the latter) do not take delivery of it within five days *vv* | after it has
been reported to them, although it was offered by (the envoys) of
20 whatever city [was the sourclle] of the *grain*, the Hieropoioi at their
euthynai shall be fined one thousand *v* drachmas [elach]. They shall
also receive it from the Demarchs in accordance with the same procedure. [Herlalds] shall be chosen by the Boule, which shall send them to
the cities announcing [the | present] decree of the People, in the pre-
sent instance as quickly as possible and in the fluture, whenever it (the
Boule) thinks best. Let an exhortation be pronounced both by the
25 Hierophant[3] and by [the] || Daidouchos[4] for the Hellenes to make
offerings of the first-fruits at the Mysteries in accordance | with the
ancestral custom and the oracular response from Delphi. After writing
on | a notice board the weight of the grain (received) from the Demarchs
according to *dleme* and of that (received) from the cities according to
city, | (the Hieropoioi) shall set up (copies of) it in the Eleusinion in
30 Eleusis and in the Bouleutellrion.[5] The Boule shall also send a proclamation to the other cities, [the] Helllenic cities in their entirety, where-
ever it seems to the Boule to be feasible, tellling them the principles on
which the Athenians and their allies are offering first-fruits, and | not
ordering them but urging them to offer first-fruits, if they so desire, | in
accordance with the ancestral custom and the oracular response from
35 Delphi. The acceptance || of any (grain) that anyone may bring from
these cities as well shall be the duty of the Hieropoioi accorlding to the

same procedure. They shall perform sacrifice with the pelanos[6] in accordance with what the Eumolpidai[7] [dic|tate]; and (they shall sacrifice) the triple sacrifice, first, a bull with gilt horns to each of the two goddesses *separate|ly, out* of (proceeds from) the barley and the wheat; and to Triptolemos and to the [go|d] and the goddess and Euboulos[8] a

40 full-grown victim each; and || to Athena a bull[9] with gilt horns. The rest of the barley and wheat shall be s|old by the Hieropoioi together with the Boule and they shall have votive offerings dedicat|ed to the two goddesses, having made whatever seems best to the People of the Athenians, | and they shall inscribe on the votive offerings that it was out of the first-fruits of the grain | that they were dedicated, and (the name) of every Hellene who made the offering of first-fruits. [For those] who

45 do this || there shall be many benefits in abundance of good harvests if *they are men who | do not* injure the Athenians or the city of the Athenians or the two goddesses. *v* | Lampon[10] made the motion: Let all the rest be as (advised) in the draft-decree (of the Commissioners) for the first-fruits of the | grain for the goddesses. But their draft-decree and this decree shall be ins|cribed by the Secretary of the Boule on two

50 stelai of marbl|le and set up, the one in the sanctuary in Eleusis, the other o|n the Akropolis. The Poletai are to let out the contract for the two stelai. The *Kol|lakretai* are to supply the money. These things concerning the first-fruits of the grain to t|he two goddesses shall be inscribed on the two stelai. There shall be intercalation[11] of the month Hekatomb|laion by the new Archon. The King (Archon) shall delimit the

55 sanctuaries in t|lhe Pelargikon,[12] and in the future altars shall not be erected in the Pela|rgikon without the consent of the Boule and the People, nor shall (anyone) cut stones out of the P|elargikon, or remove soil or stones. If anyone transgresses *v* | a[13]ny of these regulations, he shall be fined five hundred drachmas and impeached[14] by t|he King (Archon) before the Boule. As to the first-fruits of olive oil, a draft-

60 dec||ree shall be produced by Lampon before the Boule in the ninth prytany | and the Boule shall be obliged to bring it before the People.

1 This line is a heading and is outside the stoichedon pattern.
2 See no. 106.
3 The initiating priest at Eleusis, an office held by the Eumolpid family.
4 'Torch-bearer,' another ancestral office, in this case belonging to the family of the Kerykes.
5 In Athens.
6 Cake made from choice wheat and barley; cf. Aristophanes, *Ploutos* 661, and no. 137.25f. (with n. 8).
7 For this family see F. Jacoby, *Atthis* (Oxford 1949), 26f.
8 Probably Pluto, Persephone, and a god of the underworld respectively.
9 Or 'cow.'
10 For this man see no. 108; he must be one of the syngrapheis.

11 See Introduction; B. D. Meritt, *The Athenian year* (Berkeley and Los Angeles 1961) 3–5; W. K. Pritchett, *The Choiseul Marble*, Univ. of Calif. Publ.: Classical Studies 5 (Berkeley and Los Angeles 1970) 62–4. The general practice was to duplicate the month Gamelion in an intercalary year. Hekatombaion (the first Attic month) probably was chosen in this instance in order to give longer notice to those willing to offer first-fruits at Eleusis, the date for which ritual probably fell in the month Boedromion (the third Attic month) during the Eleusinia.

12 For this site, below the Akropolis, see Gomme, etc., *HCT* 2.63–5. Reference in this inscription to the Pelargikon may not be arbitrary or merely a response to Apollo's injunction (cf. Thucydides 2.17.1) as is commonly thought. For there was a mythical figure named Pelarge, daughter of Potneus, the eponymous hero of Potniai (near Thebes), who is closely connected with Demeter and the Mysteries. With her husband she was believed to have reintroduced the Mysteries of the Kabeiroi (original inhabitants of the area after whose departure the rites had lapsed), which they themselves had received from Demeter (Pausanias 9.25.7f.). Pelarge herself received sacrifice; and there was also a shrine of Demeter and Persephone at Potniai. See J. Krischan, *RE* s.v. 'Pelarge', coll. 250f.

13 A punctuation mark, apparently covering an erasure, divides this word.

14 See the Glossary under 'Eisangelia.'

141 Inventory of the Treasures in the Parthenon. 422/1 B.C.

Marble slab (now lost), developed Attic writing, Athens.

IG I² 280+ (I³ 351); W. S. Ferguson, *The treasurers of Athena* (Cambridge, Mass. 1932) 110 ff.; *Tod I, no. 69, pp. 168–71; W. E. Thompson, *Hesperia* 34 (1965) 25–8. Cf. Thucydides 2.13.4.

Gods. [Ath]e[na. Fortune.] | The following was paid over by the four boards, which rendered *their* [account from (Great) Panathenaia] *to* (Great) P[anathenaia, to the] T|reasurers for whom Presbias son of Semi[os of the Phe]⟨g⟩aia was Secretary. [The Treasurers, for whom Pres]bias son of Se[mios of Phegaia | was Secretary, paid over to the Treasurers for whom Nikeas son of Eu[thykles of Halimous] *was*
5   *Secretary*, [to Euphemos] ‖ of Kollytos and (his) colleagues, in the Parthenon:¹ Crown *of gold*, [weight] *of this*, 60 dr. Saucers [of gold, 5], *we*|ight of these, 782 dr. Uncoined gold, weight of this, [1 dr. 4 ob. Drinking cup] of gold, its *bottom gilt silv*|er, consecrated to Herakles of *Elaious*, weight *of this*, 138 dr. Pair of nails, underneath silver, gi|lt, weight of these, 1[8]4 dr. Mask with silver underneath, *gilt, weight* of this, 116 dr. *Saucers of si*|lver, 138 dr. Silver drinking horn. Weight of these: 2 T. 3,30[7 dr. By number], the following: Short (Persian)
10 swords *set in gold*, [6]. ‖ Standing crop set in gold, ears of corn. 1[2]. Breadbaskets, wooden underneath, gilt, [2. Censer], wooden underneath, *gilt*, | 1. Maiden on a stele, gilt, [1]. Bed, wooden underneath, gilt, [1]. *Gorgon* mask, with skull gilt. [Hor|se], griffin, front part of a griffin, griffin, lion's head, *necklace of flowers*, [snake]: these gilt.

[Helmet] gi|lt. Shields gilt with wood underneath, 15. [Chian-made beds, 8]. Milesian-made [beds], 10. *Saber|s*, 9. Swords, 5. Breastplates, 1[6]. Shields with devices, 6. Shields [covered with bronze, 3]1. *Chairs,*
15 6. Stools, [4]. *Camp||stools*, 9. Lyre, gilt, 1. Lyres of ivory, 4. Lyres, 4. [Table] inlaid with ivory. Helmets [of bronze, 3]. B|edposts covered with silver, [13]. (Small leather) *shield.* Saucers of silver, 4. [Small cup covered with silver, 2].² Horse of *silver.* [Weigh|t] of these, 900 dr. Shields, gilt, with wood underneath, [2]. Short (Persian) sword, *gilt, unweighed.* Saucers [of silver, 8]. *We|ight* of these, 807 dr. Chalcidian drinking cups of silver, 4, weight [of these], 124 dr. *Flute case* [from Methy]|mna of ivory, gilt. Shield from Lesbos with device. Helmet
20 from [L]esbos, of Illyrian [bronze.³ Saucer||s] of silver, 2. Drinking cups of silver, [2]. Weight of these, 580 dr. L[e]s[b]ian [cups] *of silver,* 3, *weight* [of these, 3]|70 dr. Crown of gold, weight of this, 18 dr. 3 ob. Crown of gold, *weight* of this, 2[9 dr. Athena N] |ike's golden crown, weight of this, 29 dr. Crown of *gold, weight* of this, 3[3 dr. Athena N]|ike's crown of gold, weight of this, 33 dr. Tetradrachm [of gold], weight of this, 7 dr. [2½ ob. Onyx stone]| on a golden ring, *unweighed.*⁴

1 See no. 119A, lines 27–9.
2 Thompson: *'winecups*, [13], *of silver'*: Tod.
3 Meritt, *Hesperia* 30 (1961) 240.
4 This is one of a series of records extending from 434/3 to 407/6. Portions of most of these are preserved, and thus an interlocking series of restorations of objects and their weights is possible.

142 Athenian Tribute Quota List. 418 B.C.
Five fragments of a marble stele, developed Attic letters, stoichedon, Athens.

H. B. Mattingly, *PACA* 7 (1964) 47; B. D. Meritt and M. F. McGregor, *Phoenix* 21 (1967) 85f. (abandoning the date 422/1 suggested by Meritt earlier); *GHI,* no. 75, pp. 225–7; *B. D. Meritt, *Hesperia* 41 (1972) 419 (a new fragment) (*IG* I³ 287).

[In the year of the Boule for which -6 *or* 7- of A]phidna [was] *first* [Secretary, the Archon | at Athens was Antiphon of Sk]ambonidai, in *the* [seven-and-thirt|ieth board the Hellenotamiai] were, for whom
5 Ant[-16-¹] | [-16- of Perg]ase, Mnesitheo[s of Araphen -6-] || [-16- of Eupy]ridai, Aischines of P[erithoidai -7-] | [of Thymait]ada[i, Ergokles of Bes]a. *vv* | These [cities paid the] *quota* to the goddess, a mna *from* each talent [*v*]

	I		II
	Of the Islands		Of the Hellespont
	[---]	Anaphaians[2]	100 dr.	Sigeians
10	[---]	Therans	2,000 dr.	Cyzicenes
	[---]	Seriphians	6[6 dr. 4 ob.]	[Arta]kenians
	[---]	Ietians	[---]	Kianians
	[---]	Tenians	[---]	Bysbikenes
	[---]	Siphnians	[---]	Prokonnesians
15	[---]	Andrians	[--]1 dr. 4 ob.	Parianians
	[--]2 ob.	Sikinetians	[---]	Chalchedonians
	[---]	Cythnians	[---]	Sely[mbrians]
		(Lacuna)	[---]	Seri[oteichitians]
			[---]	Didy[moteichitians]
20			[---]	Dauni[oteichitians]
			[--]1 dr. 4 ob.	Sombia
			[--]18 dr. 2 ob.	Perinthians
			[--]1 dr. 4 ob.	Brylleianians
			[---]	Lampsacenes
25			[---]	[Aby]denes
				(Lacuna)
			[---]	[.]e[---]
			[--]2 ob.	Che[rronesites]
				from [Agora]
			[---]	K[allipolitans]

1 After Ant-'s name would come the statement that he was secretary (to the Hellenotamiai).

2 Where the names are certain, restoration has not been indicated.

143 Inventory of Treasures in the Hekatompedon. 418/17 B.C.
Marble stele, developed Attic writing, stoichedon, Athens.

IG I[2] 268+ (I[3] 329); W. B. Dinsmoor, *AJA* 51 (1947) 123ff.; *GHI*, no. 76, pp. 227-9. Cf. Thucydides 2.13.4 and no. 141.

The following was paid over by the four boards, *which* [rendered their account from (Great) Panathenaia to] (Great) *Panathenaia*, to the Treasurers Pythodoros of Halai [and (his) colleagues, for whom Phormion son of Aristion of] Kydathenai|on was Secretary. The Treasurers, for whom Pho[rmio]n son of A[ristion of Kydathenaion was] *Secretary*, pa|id over to the Treasurers Anaxikrates of La[mp]tra[i and

5 (his) colleagues ⟨for whom⟩ Euxenos son of Euphanes] of Pros‖palta was Secretary, in the sanctuary, the H[ekatomped[on:[1] saucers of gold,

3, weight] *of these*, 2,5|44 dr. Maiden of gold on a stele, unweighed. [Silver vessel for sprinkling holy water, unweighed. Pair of] *crowns* of go|ld, [2], weight of the pair, 80 dr. Crown *of gold which* [the Nike has,[2] weight of this, 60 dr.] *Saucers* of silver, 8, weight of these, [8]00 dr. Drinking cup [of silver, weight of this, 200 dr. Drinking cup] *of silver* of Ze|us Polieus, weight of this, 200 dr. Crown [of gold, weight
10 of this,...3 dr. 2 ob.] Pair of *crowns of gold*, wei|lght of the pair, 63 dr. Crowns of gold, [4], *weight* [of these, 135 dr. 2 ob. Crown] *of gold*, weight o|f this, 18 dr. 3 ob. Pair of golden vessels, 2, weight of the pair, [293 dr. 3 ob. Golden vessel, weight] of this, 138 dr. [2] ob. | Golden vessel, weight of this, 119 dr. *Crown* [of gold, weight of this, 26 dr. 3 ob.] Silver vessel, weight | of this, 192 dr. Censer *of silver*, [weight of this, 1,000 dr. In the year there were added]: *crown* of go|ld, weight of this, 1,250 dr. Crown *of gold*, [weight of this,..1 dr.
15 Crown] of gold, weight o|lf this, 35 dr.[3]

1 The Pronaos, Hekatompedon, and Parthenon were, respectively, the porch, east cella and west cella of the building we call the Parthenon.
2 This is the winged figure of the goddess Nike, resting on the right hand of Pheidias' gold-and-ivory statue of Athena.
3 For the restorations, see no. 141, note 4.

144 Payments from Athena's Treasury for Public Purposes. 418/17–417/16 B.C.
Fragments of a marble stele, developed Attic writing, stoichedon (with irregularity), Athens.

IG I[2] 302 (I[3] 370); B. D. Meritt, *Athenian financial documents of the fifth century* (Ann Arbor 1932) 160–74; **GHI*, no. 77, pp. 229–36.

Gomme, etc., *HCT* 4.129, 153f.

Gods.[1] | [The Athenians spent in Antiphon's archonship (418/17) and in the year of the Boule for which -7- was first Secretary], the Treasurers of the s|*acred* [monies of Athena, Pythodoros of Halai and (his) colleagues, for whom Phormion son of Aristion] of Kydathenai|on [was Secretary, transferred to the Hellenotamiai, Ergokles son of Aris-
5 teides of Besa and (his)] *colleagues*, and to the Paredroi H|lierokles son of Archestratos of Athmonon and (his) colleagues in -10-, the first] *prytany* and on the day (which was) *sec*|*ond*[2] [-62-][3] to those with Demosthenes [.]||[-65-][4] the Hellenotamiai 'and [t|he Paredroi to the Treasurers of the] goddess, Pyth[odoros of Halai and (his) colleagues and that the] *Treasurers* of the goddess *shall* in turn transfer i|t [to the Hellenotamiai] and to the *Paredroi*, [and they shall give it to the

10 generals in Th]race, Euthydemos son of Eudemos [.] ‖ [-21 (or fewer)-].[5]
    vv | [In -10-] *prytany*, the second [prytany, to the Hellenotamiai
    Er]gokles son of Aristeides of Besa [.] | [-17- of Ai]xone and (his) col-
    leagues [and to the Paredroi Hierokles son of Arche]stratos of Ath-
    monon and (his) *colleag|ues* [on the -19-] (day) of the prytany, [we
    transferred -14- golden] Cyzicene staters: 4, [..] | [-21-]. The silver

15 money for this [came to -20-] 2 ob.[6] This money we transferre‖d [to
    the trierarchs (?) at A]rgos who were with Dem[osthenes, the People
    having voted the] immunity.[7] *vv* | [In -16-] prytany, on the *eight*-[and-
    twentieth day of the] *prytany*, to the generals *we* trans|ferred [-21-],[8]
    Autokles of Anaphl[ystos -20 (or fewer)-]. *vv* | [In Pandionis', the]
    ninth prytany, on the *thirteenth* [day of the] prytany, we transferred
    from the [payment from S|amos (?)] coming in [for the year] to the
    Hellenotamiai [Ergokles son of Aristeides of Bes]a and (his) colleagues

20 and to the *Par‖edros of the Hellenotamiai*, [Hi]erokles son of Arches-
    tratos [of Athmonon -19- to the] generals[9] Nikias son of Nikerat|[os
    of Kydant]idai, Kal[listr]atos son of Empedos of Oia, K[-26 (or
    fewer-]. *vv* |
    Sum of expenditures during the | term of office: 56 T. 1,8[-8-]2 ob.[10]
    The Athenians spent in [Euphemos'] archonship (417/16) and [in the
    year of the Boule for which -9-] was *first* Secretary, the Treasurers of

25 the sac‖red monies of A[thena, Anaxikrates of Lamptrai and (his)
    colleagues, for whom] Euxenos son of Euphanes of Prospalt|a was
    Secretary, [transferred -28- to the generals in] the Thracian region and
    to Rhinon son of Ch|arikles of Paiania [in -8-, the -6-[11] prytany, the]
    twenty-*second* day of the pryta|ny, the vote [of immunity] having
    been taken [by the People -32 (or fewer)-]. *vv* | In Aiantis', [the -6[12]
    prytany, we transferred to the generals at Melos, Teisi]as son of Teisi-

30 machos of Kephale, ‖ Kleomedes son of Lyko[medes of Phlya[13] on the
    -18- of the prytany, the vote] of immunity [having been taken] by the
    People, 10 T. *vv* | In Antiochi[s', the -6 (or) 7-[14] prytany, we trans-
    ferred to the Hellenotamiai -9 (or) 10-] of Auridai, to Timarchos of
    Pal‖lene and *to the generals* [at Melos, Teisias son of Teisimachos of
    Kephale, Kleomedes son of Lykomed]es of Phlya, on the thirte|enth
    day [of the prytany, the People having voted immunity -22 (or
    fewer)-]. *vv*

(The record of payments continues through the year 415/14 B.C.)

---

1 This word, of which only the last letter survives, was spaced out over the line
   as a heading.
2 '*second* [and twentieth of the prytany' or '[and thirtieth of the prytany'. A
   sum of money followed.
3 '[in order to give it to the trierarchs at Arg]os': Dittenberger (*SIG*, p. 123);

same with 'at Eion]': West–McCarthy (cited *GHI*, p. 230). Demosthenes' activities are not alluded to by Thucydides until after the battle of Mantinea, when he was ordered to withdraw the Athenian force stationed at Epidaurus (5.80.3).

4 '[R|esolved by the People in accordance with the decree of -8- that the money which was transferred shall be paid over by]': *GHI* (a slight variation on prior restorations). Whatever the restoration, it is clear from the language that survives that the treasurers quoted a portion of the decree authorizing this transferral of funds.

5 These proceedings are obscure. Thucydides says nothing of the expedition to Thrace, and it is not known what may have induced the Athenians to cancel their payment to Demosthenes (whether he was intended to advance to Thrace or was at Argos; see note 3).

6 I.e. the value of the (electrum) staters when converted into Athenian money. The rate of exchange is not precisely known but was probably very close in value to 25 Attic drachmas for one Cyzicene stater. Bogaert, *AC* 32 (1963) 107f., restores the lacunae to yield 4,[287 4/6 staters = (line 14) 18 T. 3,737 dr.] 2 ob. (minimum), 4,[9|97 5/6 staters = 23 T. 1,939 dr.] 2 ob. (maximum), which is a little high in both cases, assuming roughly 25 dr. per stater. See W. E. Thompson, *AC* 40 (1971) 574–88; Meiggs, *Empire* 442f.

7 See no. 119B, line 16.

8 '[to Alkibiades of Skamboni]dai': Meritt.

9 The usual restorations, which leave five spaces unaccounted for, presuppose an error for 'these gave to the] generals'. Thucydides 5.83.4 mentions an abortive expedition to have been mounted against Perdikkas in Thrace. Probably it was for this that the money was paid over to Nikias and his colleagues, and later it was canceled.

10 1,946 dr. 2 ob. maximum; 1,829 dr. 4 ob. minimum; see the Introduction.

11 First or third.

12 Eighth or ninth.

13 Cf. Thuc. 5.84.3. These were the generals who invested Melos at the time of the 'Melian Dialogue' of Thucydides.

14 Ninth or tenth.

145 Ostracism and Death of Hyperbolos. 418/17–411 B.C.

A: Scholiast to Lucian, *Timon* 30 (Androtion, *FGrHist* 324 F 42); B: Scholiast to Aristophanes, *Wasps* 1007 (423/2) (Theopompus, *FGrHist* 115 F 96b). Cf. Aristophanes, *Peace* 680f.; Thucydides 8.73; Plutarch, *Nikias* 11.7.10, *Alkibiades* 13. See also no. 41.

Hignett, *Constitution* 395f.; Jacoby, *FGrHist* IIIb Suppl. 1.151; Bury–Meiggs 288f.; Sealey, *History* 353.

A. Scholiast to Lucian, *Timon* 30

Lucian, *Timon* 30: You do well to lead me, Hermes, for if you left me, I would quickly run into Hyperbolos or Kleon as I wandered (in Athens).

Scholion: This Hyperbolos, as Androtion says, was the son of Antiphanes of (the deme) Perithoidai, and was ostracized because of his worthlessness.

B. Scholiast to Aristophanes, *Wasps* 1007

Aristoph. *Wasps* 1007: Hyperbolos will not grin as he cheats you.

Scholion: Theopompus says that his corpse was thrown into the sea, writing that 'they ostracized Hyperbolos for six years. After sailing down to Samos and making his home there he died.[1] They put his corpse into a wine bag and sank it in the sea.'

1 He was murdered (Thuc. 8.73.3).

146 Decrees Relating to the Sicilian Expedition. 415 B.C.

Eight fragments from two or more marble stelai, developed Attic writing, stoichedon, Athens.

IG I^2 98, 99+ (I^3 93); Tod I,[1] no. 77, pp. 192–5; *GHI*, no. 78, pp. 236–40; *Gomme, etc., HCT* 4.224–7. Cf. Aristophanes, *Lysistrata* (412/11) 387ff.; Thucydides 6.8–26; Plutarch, *Nikias* 12, *Alkibiades* 17f.; Meiggs, *Empire* 346–8; Bury–Meiggs 292–305; Sealey, *History* 354.

Fragment b

[---]|[-the choice shall be made by the People] immediately as to whether it seems best for one *gener*|*al* [or ---] to be elected with good fortune at this time who [.]|[---] the enemy to the extent that they
5 are able [....]|||[--] also of the allies *al*|*l* [who---] *cities* to the Boule of the Athenians | [---] of sixty ships at whatever time [...]|[---] if [they] wish [-9-]|[----]|[---]

(The fragment is broken off)

Fragment c

[...] Boule as best [---] *i*|*f* from the rateable property it seems best [---if]| (it seems best that) the city shall spend as much as [--- th|e]
5 sixty ships if [---]|||[.....] it has been [--] to tax property whenever it is *necessary* (?)[---] *ass*|*embly* is to be summoned by them [within] ten days [---] *a*|*bout* nothing else before [---]|[.] the *Prytaneis* shall sum-
10 mon an Assembly [---]|[..] to the generals of the ships [---]|||[...] As to the departure of the ships [---] *b*|e corrected by the People[2] [---]

a|ssembly is to be summoned by them whenever [---]|[..] and of the
15   rest of the crew [---]| and of money for auspicious sacrifice [---]|||[.]
one thousand six hundred [---]|[---]

(The fragment is broken off)

Fragments d+g

[---]|[---]|[--] or they guard *the* [city or] *the* land [.]|[--] whoever
5   does not *patrol* [or] *serve for hir*|*e*[3] (in the armed forces?) [--] except
for all those who [-7-] *the* Boule and | [--] shall be subject to penalty
[-8-] nor the [...]|[--] *Prytaneis*. Repeal shall be made [-9-] the *dec-
r|ee* [--] of *the* departure of the *sixty ships* until [...]|[--] *on* no other
10   task *nor* [on another] campaign ||[--] three thousand. *If* [anyone
should move] or *put to the* | *vote* [---]|[---]|[---]

(The fragment is broken off)[4]

1   Tod's text, like earlier ones, is adventurous in view of our ignorance of the
length of the lines of this document. Restorations which amount to extrapola-
tions from Thucydides' text are here ignored.
2   I.e. in assembly, as the Greek makes clear.
3   Though this meaning is given to the verb by Liddell–Scott–Jones, an Athenian in
the army or navy cannot be said to 'serve as a mercenary'; perhaps the other
meaning, 'to receive pay for public service,' is better here.
4   Of the other fragments it is notable that Fragment f mentions 100 triremes.

147   Confiscation of the Property of Athenians Convicted of Sacrilege.
414 B.C.

A: Pollux, *Onomasticon* 10.97; B: Scholiast to Aristophanes, *Lysistrata* 1094
(412/11) (Philochorus, *FGrHist* 128 F 133); C: Scholiast to Aristophanes, *Birds*
766 (415/14) (Cratinus F 66, 174 Kock; Philochorus, *FGrHist* 328 F 134); D:
Extracts from the 'Attic Stelai,' *GHI*, no. 79, pp. 240–7. Cf. Thucydides 6.27–9,
6.60–1; Andocides, *On the Mysteries, passim*, and especially 12–18 for the names
of those denounced; Plutarch, *Alkibiades* 19–20. See no. 105.

Jacoby, *FGrHist* IIIb Suppl. 1.504–7; D. M. Macdowell, *Andokides on the Mysteries* (Oxford 1962) 167 ff.; Gomme, etc., *HCT* 4.264–88; Bury–Meiggs 294f.;
C. A. Powell, *Historia* 28 (1979) 15–31; C. W. Fornara, *Panhellenica. Essays in
honor of T. S. Brown* (Lawrence, Kansas 1980) 43–55.

A. Pollux, *Onomasticon* 10.97

On the Attic Stelai, which are set up in Eleusis, there is inscribed the
property of those who committed sacrilege against the two goddesses
which was publicly sold.

B. Scholiast to Aristophanes, *Lysistrata* 1094

Aristoph. *Lysistrata* 1093–4: If you are wise you will hold on to your clothes for fear that / one of the Hermokopidai will see you.

Scholion: ... In so far as the Hermokopidai mutilated the Herms when (the Athenians) were about to sail to Sicily, four years before the production of this play. Some attributed the blame for this to Alkibiades and his associates, as Thucydides (says); some to the Corinthians, as Philochorus (says). He writes that only the Herm of Andocides was ⟨not⟩ mutilated.

C. Scholiast to Aristophanes, *Birds* 766

Aristoph. *Birds* 766: But if (Meles) the son of Peisias wants to betray the gates (of the city) to those without citizen-rights....

Scholion: We have no certain information about who the son of Peisias was or about the betrayal. That he was one of the very worthless people is indicated by Cratinus in his *Chirones, Meeting of the Amphictyons*, and *The Hours*. The son of Peisias may have been associated with the Hermokopidai who, as Philochorus says, were condemned to death in the archonship of Chabrias (= Charias, 415/14) and their names were inscribed on stelai and ⟨their property⟩ was confiscated and proclamation was made of a talent reward per man for anyone who killed one of them. (See Plato, *Gorg.* 502 for Meles son of Peisias.)

D. Extracts from the 'Attic Stelai'

Fragments from marble stelai, developed Attic writing, partly stoichedon, Athens.

W. K. Pritchett, *Hesperia* 22 (1953) 240–9, 268–79; 25 (1956) 276–81; 30 (1961) 23–5, 28; *GHI*, no. 79, pp. 240–7 (*IG* I³ 421, 426).

Pritchett, *Hesperia* 25 (1956) 178–317; D. M. Lewis, *Ehrenberg studies* 177–91. The name 'Attic Stelae' is due to Pollux (A above).

(A) (STELE I, COL. I)

```
 7¹  [--]²      [---]      [-7-]
     [--]       [---]      [-6-]
     [--]       [---]      [Slave boy, P]eisistratos of Caria
10                         [Total] from Hephaistodoros:
                           [-8-]2 dr. 4½ ob.
                           [Of Alkibiades]³ son of Kleinias
                           [of Skambonid]ai, the following house-gear was sold:
```

	[--]	[---]	[-7-]
15	[--]	[---]	*Pot* of bronze
	[--]	[---]	*Pot* of bronze
	[--]	[---]	*Pot* of bronze
	[--]	[---]	[-6-] of bronze

(The fragment breaks off)[4]

	[--]	[.]10[-]	[---]
20	[3] ob.	18 dr.	Crops at Thria
	[3] ob.	20 dr.	Crops at Athmonon
			Total with tax:
25			4,723 dr. 5 ob.
			Of Polystratos son of Dio[doros] of Ankyle
	2 dr. 1 ob.	202 dr.	Pistos[5]
	[1] dr.[6]	42 dr.	Crops at An-
30			kyle
			Total with tax:
			247 dr. 1 ob.
			Of Kephisodoros[7] the metic in Pira[eus]
	2 dr.	165 dr.	Thracian slave-girl (or woman)
35	1 dr. 3 ob.	135 dr.	Thracian slave-girl (or woman)
	[2] dr.	170 dr.	Thracian slave
	2 dr. 3 ob.	240 dr.	Syrian slave
	[1] dr. 3 ob.	105 dr.	Carian slave
	2 dr.	161 dr.	Illyrian slave
40	2 dr. 3 ob.	220 dr.	Thracian slave-girl (or woman)
	1 dr. 3 ob.	115 dr.	Thracian slave
	1 dr. 3 ob.	144 dr.	Scythian slave
	1 dr. 3 ob.	121 dr.	Illyrian slave
	2 dr.	153 dr.	Colchian slave
45	2 dr.	174 dr.	Carian slave-boy
	1 dr.	72 dr.	Carian child
	[3] dr. 1 ob.	301 dr.	Syrian slave
	[2] dr.	151 dr.	Meletenian slave[8]
	1 dr.	85[..]1 ob.[9]	Lydian slave-girl (or woman)

(End of Column I)

(B) (STELE VI)

50   [--]   [---]   [....] and [their young] [10]

(Two lines are uninscribed)

[Of Adeimantos] [11] son of Le[uk]olophides of Ska[m-
             bonidai]
     [--]   [..]   The man [Ar]istomachos
55   Country-farm [in] Thasos in I[--]
                               and private residence
     [--]   [...]250 dr. Included are *jars* (?): *nine*; [amphorae (?)]
                               unbroken: 20[..] *unsound* [--]
                               [with] lids
                               Amphoreis of wine [---] :
60   [--]   [..]180 dr.
                               590, three choes [12]

(This line is uninscribed)

Of [P]anaitios
                               Amphoreis of wine, Attic
65   [--]   [.]20 dr.
                               unmixed: 104, *seven* choes
                               Beehives on the *country-farm*
     [3] dr.   [2]60 dr.
                               in Is[-6-] 15 dr. [--]
     [1 dr. 1 ob.] [100] dr.   *Two working* oxen in Ar[--]
     [1] dr.   [7]0 dr.   [Two] oxen
70   [--]   [--]   Four cows [13] and *calves* [--]
     [--]   [--]   Sheep: 84
                               and their young
     [7 dr. 3 ob.] [7]10 dr.   Goats, 67, and [their] young

(This line is uninscribed)

75   [Of Polystra]tos son of Diodoros of Ankyle
                               Private residence in Kydathenaion [in which
                                    the porch is]
                               two-columned, adjoining [the temple]
     [--]   [....]50 dr. of Artemis, from Athmonon,
                               Amarysia.
80   [--]   Land at Ankyle *south of*
                               the hill where the *temple* [--]

(Three lines are uninscribed)

85   Of Nikid[es son of] Phoiniki[des of M]elite
       1 dr. 52 dr. [--][14]

       (This line is uninscribed)

       Of Euphiletos son of T[imotheos of Kydathenaion]
       (Guilty) in respect of both.[15] *Private residence* [--]
90   15 dr. 1,500 dr. [--]

       (Two lines are uninscribed)

       Of Pherekles son of Phe[ren]ika[ios of Themakos]
       (Guilty) in respect of both.[15] *Private residence in* Bate
                    [and] land

95   *(This line is uninscribed)*

        Another (piece of) land [--]
        [--]
        Land beside the Pyth[ion[16]--]

       (This line is uninscribed)

100 12 dr.   1,200 dr. *House-site, swampy, without a crop,*
              beside [the P]ythion
              Another (piece of) land beside *the*
              Hera[kle]ion
              Half the *orgas*[17] [--][18]
105   Pythion *and* of the canal from [the temple,]
              [the other] half in Kykale
              This was sold all together as a parcel.

       (Two lines are uninscribed)

110   Payments were made of these rents
     of the men who committed impiety toward the two goddesses.[19]
     Of Phaidros[20] son of Pytho[kles] of Myrrhinous:
        60 dr.   Rent paid down for the *private residence*
              [For land in Myrrh]inous rent
115   350 dr.   [was paid down]
  [--]

    From the (property) of Adeim[antos son of L]eukolophides of
     Skambonidai
    1,632 dr. 4 ob. [---]

From (the property) of Axioch[os[21] son of Alkibiades of S]kam-
bonidai

120

1,633 dr. 2½ ob.　[---]
　　　　250 dr.　[---]
162 dr. 4 ob.　　[---]
From [----
------]

1　The first six lines are missing.
2　This column listed the tax on the sales. How it was computed is obscure, but it was close to a one percent tax, which increased in steps for sums over 100 dr.; see Pritchett, *Hesperia* 22 226-30. The column adjacent to it posted the value of the property; the third column gives the description of the items sold.
3　The famous Alkibiades; see the literature cited at the beginning of the entry.
4　Enough uninscribed space on the right-hand side indicates that the list contained short items (Pritchett).
5　A slave.
6　An overcharge of 3 obols (Pritchett)
7　Macdowell 211 identifies him with a comic poet mentioned by Lysias 21.4. If that is correct, he managed to rehabilitate himself, like Adeimantos (note 11) and Axiochos (note 21).
8　Probably Melitene in Cappadocia. The ending is missing and we cannot tell whether this slave is male or female.
9　A new reading in *GHI*. The two missing figures may be drachmas or obols.
10　I.e. livestock.
11　He became general in 407 and remained after the fall of Alkibiades to serve as general at the defeat at Aegospotami (405), when he was accused of treachery (Xenophon, *Hellenica* 1.4.21, 1.7.1, 2.1.30, 32; Lys. 14.38).
12　I.e. 590 amphoreis (a unit of measurement probably equivalent to 12 choes) + three choes = 7,083 choes. (Pritchett's figure, 6,963 choes (*Hesperia* 25 200) seems to be an error.)
13　Or, 'oxen.'
14　'[crops] *from Chalcis*': Lewis; '*bronze objects*': Tod. The letters legible on the stone are EKCHAL.
15　I.e. implication in both crimes, the desecration of the Mysteries and the mutilation of the Herms.
16　The temple of Pythian Apollo at Athens.
17　Apparently, a 'woody, mountainous tract,' perhaps originally sacred land (Pritchett); cf. no. 122E.
18　'hard by': Meritt; 'within': *GHI*. In the first case, half the canal is assumed to have been sold along with half the *orgas*; in the second, the boundaries of the *orgas* would be the temple and the canal.
19　I.e. rents now received by the state from tenants of the violators of the Mysteries.
20　Phaidros was the friend of Sokrates whose name appears as the title of one of Plato's dialogues. Lys. 19.15 speaks of his poverty; the explanation is his involvement in this episode.
21　The uncle of Alkibiades, he survived to move the second decree of no. 156. A Socratic dialogue bears his name.

148   The Athenian Commissioners of 411 B.C.

Harpocration, *Lexicon* s.v. Syngrapheis (Androtion, *FGrHist* 324 F 43; Philochorus, *FGrHist* 328 F 136). Cf. Thucydides 8.67; Aristotle, *Athenaion Politeia* 29.

W. S. Ferguson, *CAH* 5.321ff.; Jacoby, *FGrHist* IIIb Suppl. 1.151f.; Hignett, *Constitution* 356-64; P. J. Rhodes, *JHS* 92 (1972) 115-27; Bury-Meiggs 306; Sealey, *History* 358ff.

Syngrapheis: Isocrates in the *Areopagiticus* (58). It was customary among the Athenians, whenever necessary, to elect a certain number of men who announced their resolutions to the People on a stipulated day.[1] This happened also before the establishment of the Four Hundred, as Thucydides says in Book VIII (67.1): 'At that moment the colleagues of Peisandros arrived and immediately set to work on what remained. First they assembled the People and introduced a motion to elect ten men as Commissioners with plenary powers; these men were to draft a resolution and introduce it before the People on a stipulated day, on how best to order the state.' But the total of Commissioners who were elected at that time, according to Androtion and Philochorus, each in his *History of Athens*, was thirty. Thucydides mentioned only the ten Probouloi.[2]

1 See, for example, no. 140, lines 59f., though there the time specified is not a day but a prytany.
2 I.e. the ten probouloi of Thuc. 8.1.3. According to Aristotle, *Ath. Pol.* 29, 2, this board (established in winter 413/12) became that of the Commissioners with the addition of twenty men in 411 B.C.

149   A Decree Passed by the Oligarchy in Athens. 411 B.C.
Fragment of a marble stele, Ionic script, stoichedon, Athens.

IG II² 12+; *IG* I², p. 297 (I³ 98); *GHI*, no. 80, pp. 247-50. Cf. Thucydides 8.67.3; Aristotle, *Athenaion Politeia* 30.

W. G. Ferguson, *CP* 21 (1926) 73f. (passed under the Five Thousand); G. E. M. de Ste Croix, *Historia* 5 (1956) 17-19 (passed under the Four Hundred); Bury-Meiggs 309f.; Rhodes, *Boule* 29.

[---]|[---]|[-6-]ates of Ika[ria was Secretary.]|[....]s presided[1] [-17-]
5 ||[...] *and* with him [-17-]|[.]² of Xypete, Diop[-16-]|[..] of Kephale,
Kal[-16-]|[.Hi]ppomenes made the motion: [-16-]|stian,³ since he
10 [is] *proxenos* [of the Athenian]|ls and benefactor, *and* [does whatever
good he ca|n] for the city of the Ath[enians -9-]|stians,⁴ the decree
which [was previously voted] for h|im shall be inscribed on a *stele* [of

15 marble by th|e] Secretary of the *Boule* [now] *in off|lice*, and shall be
set up by him [on the Akropolis. The]| property which is possessed
[by] Pythopha[nes at Athens] | or wherever else the Athenians [hold
sway, and,] | as to what he says about the ship and [about his] *pro-|
perty*,[5] no one shall injure (property and claims); *and* [inviolability is
20 g|liven] him and [his] property [both when he] *c|omes* and when he
goes. This [shall be] *de|creed* for all (territory) over which the Athe-
nians [hold sway for al|l] the family of Pythophanes in the *same way.*
25 [That] | this be effected, the *generals* [at any || given time] in office
shall take care (to ensure), [and (with them) t|he] Boule at any given
time in *office.* [There shall be further] *ins|cribed* this *decree* as well [on
the] *s|ame* stele by the *Secretary* [of the Boule]. | *vv* In Aristokrates'
30 archonship (399/8).[6] [*vv*] || [Resolved by the] *Boule*, Kekr[opis held
the pryta|ny, -7-] *was Secretary*, [-9-]|[-15-][7] *presided* [--]|[---]

1 '[Over the Boule there] presided': Wilhelm (cited *GHI*, p. 248); if so, the pre-
    script has no parallel. [Plutarch], *Lives of the Ten Orators* (*Moralia* 833d); re-
    cords (almost certainly inaccurately) the other known decree of the period; it
    begins: 'Resolved by the Boule, on the twenty-first day of the prytany, Demo-
    nikos of Alopeke was Secretary, Philostratos of Pallene presided, Andron made
    the motion.' See no. 151.
2 '[the Proedroi were]': Wilhelm; '[the Prytaneis were]': Kahrstedt (cited *GHI*,
    p. 248). (The initial letter, pi, is preserved.)
3 The surviving letters seem to be the dative ending of an adjective formed from
    a city name in -*stos*. '[To Pythophanes the Cary]|stian', though generally read,
    is too long by one letter.
4 '[and for (the city) of the Cary]|stians': Wilhelm (one letter too long); '[and
    for (the city) of the Phai]|stians': *GHI*.
5 '*merch|andise*': Wilhelm.
6 A new decree begins dated 399/8 B.C.
7 '[Aristokra|tes was Archon, -8-]': *GHI*.

150 Expenditures of the Treasurers of Athena under the Oligarchy. 411 B.C.
Marble stele, Ionic letters, nonstoichedon, Athens.

IG I[2] 298 (I[3] 373); B. D. Meritt, *Athenian financial documents of the fifth century*
(Ann Arbor 1932) 93 and Plate 1; **GHI*, no. 81, pp. 250f. Cf. Aristotle, *Athenaion
Politeia* 33.1.

W. S. Ferguson, *The treasurers of Athena* (Cambridge, Mass. 1932) 145f.

[The Atheni]ans *spent* [in | Mnasil]ochos'[1] *archonship.* | *vacat* | *The*
5   *Treasurers* of the sacred *moni|les of* Athena, [Aso|podo]ros of Kyda-
th[en|aion] and (his) *colleagu|les*, for whom Euandros son of Er|ithal-
10   ion of Euonym||on was Secretary, | transferred to the Helleno|tamiai,

15   Antisthen|es of Hermos and (his) col|leagues, it having been decre||ed
by the Boule,[2] in Hekat|ombaion, the ninth day | from its *end*, from
20   the | [monies] of Athena | [Polia]s, 27 T. 2,||[-4 *or* 5-]74 dr. 4 ob.;[3]
fr|om Athena [Nike,] from [-11-]640[4] | [---]

1   Mnasilochos was archon for two months at the beginning of 411/10, under the
Four Hundred; he later became one of the Thirty (Xenophon, *Hellenica* 2.3.2).
2   Note the alteration by the Four Hundred of the usual formula, 'after a decree of
the People' (cf. no. 154, line 3).
3   The missing figures may include up to two additional thousands and must include
at least two hundreds.
4   These are drachmas; there may be up to nine more, plus obols.

151   The Trial of Antiphon. 411/10 B.C.

[Plutarch], *Lives of the Ten Orators* 55 (*Moralia* 833d–834b). Cf. Thucydides
8.68.1-2, 8.90. 1-2; Aristotle, *Athenaion Politeia* 32.2; Lysias 12.67.

Hignett, *Constitution* 375-8; Bury–Meiggs 311.

Caecilius has quoted the decree (passed) in the archonship of Theopompos (411/10), the year in which the Four Hundred were overthrown, according to which it was resolved that Antiphon stand trial:
'Resolved by the Boule on the twenty-first day of the prytany.[1] Demo-
nikos of Alopeke was Secretary, Philostratos of Pallene presided, Andron
made the motion: Concerning the men whom the generals denounce as
going on an embassy to Lacedaemon to the damage of the city of the
Athenians, as sailing from the military encampment on an enemy vessel,
and as going by land through Decelea, (that is to say) Archeptolemos,
Onomakles, and Antiphon, (it is resolved) that they be arrested and
handed over to the law court to stand trial. The generals, together with
those whom the generals decide to include from the Boule, to the number of ten, shall ensure their appearance so that the trial will take place
with them present. The Thesmothetai shall summon them tomorrow
and bring them into court when the summonses have reached the court,[2]
for the public advocates who are chosen, and the generals, and any
others who wish, to prosecute them for treason. Whomever the law
court condemns, it shall deal with according to the law which has been
established concerning traitors.' To this resolution is subjoined the sentence passed. 'Archeptolemos son of Hippodamos of Agryle, being present, and Antiphon son of Sophilos of Rhamnous, being present, were
convicted of treason. They were sentenced to be given over to the
Eleven,[3] their property to be confiscated, with the tithe consecrated to
the goddess, their homes to be leveled to the ground and markers placed
on the sites, inscribed "(the property) of Archeptolemos and Antiphon,

the traitors"; and the two demarchs (of their respective demes) to make an account of their property. It shall not be permissible to bury Archeptolemos and Antiphon at Athens or where the Athenians hold sway. Archeptolemos and Antiphon and their posterity, both bastards and legitimate, shall be without citizen-rights. If anyone adopts a descendant of Archeptolemos and Antiphon, he shall lose his citizen-rights. (The Athenians) shall inscribe this on a bronze stele and set it up where the decrees about Phyrnichos[4] are standing.'

1 The decree belongs to the rule of the 5,000. Note the absence of 'the People' in the prescript.
2 It was part of normal procedure that a trial begin with the arrival of summoners, who thus guaranteed that the defendant had received notification.
3 So as to be put to death.
4 For Phrynichos see no. 155.

152 Eretria Revolts from Athens. 411 B.C.
Marble stele, Ionic letters, Eretrian dialect, stoichedon, Eretria.

IG XII 9.187A+; *SIG*, no. 105, p. 136; **GHI*, no. 82, pp. 251f. Cf. Thucydides 8.95.

W. S. Ferguson, *CAH* 5.336; Bury–Meiggs 311.

Gods. | Resolved by the Boule.[1] Hegelochos | of Tarentum shall be
5 proxenos | and benefactor, both he himself || and his sons, and public maintenance shall b|e (granted) both to him and to his sons when t|hey are in the country, and ateleia (immunity from public burdens), and | seating privileges at the games, since he j|oined in the liberation of the
10 city || from the Athenians.[2]

1 This formula marks the decree as passed under an oligarchy.
2 Another decree of later date follows this one. Its prescript contains the democratic formula: 'Resolved by the Boule and the People.'

153 Two Laws Offering Rewards for Information Regarding Plots against the Government at Thasos. 411–409 B.C.(?)[1]
Marble block, Parian alphabet, nonstoichedon, Thasos.

Jeffery, *LSAG*, no. 76, p. 303; **GHI*, no. 83, pp. 252–5. Cf. Thucydides 8.64.

H. Pleket, *Historia* 12 (1963) 75–7; Meiggs, *Empire* 575.

(A)

Whoever informs against an insurrection planned against Thasos and proves the truth of his allegations, a thousand stater|s[2] from the city

shall be his. If a slave informs, he shall also become free. If more than one informs, | three hundred men[2] shall decide, after adjudging the claims. If one of the plotters informs, the money | shall be his and no sworn accusation shall be lodged against him, nor any suit either sacred
5 or secular, relative to it (i.e. his involvement in the plot), || nor shall he be included in the curse – except only if he be the one who was the instigator of the plot. This (law) takes effect on the twenty-first of Apatouri|on,[4] when Akryptes, Aleximachos, Dexiades were Archons. |

(B)

Whoever informs against an insurrection being planned in the colonies (of Thasos), or (reports) treason being planned against the city (of Thasos) by a Thasian | or a colonist, and proves the truth of his allegations, he shall have two hundred staters from the city. If the | property of the insurgent is worth more than two hundred staters, four hundred
10 staters from the city || shall be his. If a slave informs, he shall both get the money and be free. If more than one informs, three hundred men[5] | shall decide, after adjudging their claims. If one of the plotters informs, the money shall be his and no sworn accusation | shall be lodged against him, nor any suit, either sacred or secular, relative to it, nor shall he be included in the curse – except only if he be the one who | was the instigator of the plot. The law takes effect on the third of Galaxion,[6] when Phanodikos, Antiphanes, Ktesillos | were Archons.

1 The context of this law is uncertain. Use of an adapted Parian alphabet, when texts dating as early as 430–425 use Ionic, suggests conscious archaizing (a conservative penchant), and reference to 'three hundred' men (line 3 with n. 2), together with other indications (see *GHI*, p. 254), seems to indicate that the decree was passed under the oligarchy which was installed after the Athenian general Dieitrephes disbanded the democracy in early summer 411. The rule of the oligarchs ended in summer 407 (Xenophon, *Hellenica* 1.4.9; Diodorus 13.72), if not before, in winter 411/10 (Xen. *Hell.* 1.1.12).
2 Worth 1,600 Athenian drachmas.
3 Or 'the Three Hundred.' Reference to 'three hundred' in an early fifth-century inscription, as well as allusion to 'three hundred' in another contemporary with this one (*IG* XII 8.263), has been taken by some scholars to indicate that the oligarchic organ of government was a council of three hundred, and that it is being referred to here. Against the assumption is the lack of the definite article 'the'.
4 Apatourion was an autumn month, and Galaxion (line 14) fell in the spring. It is now believed likely that Apatourion was the first month of the Thasian civil year (*GHI*, p. 254). Therefore, because of the different boards of archons, the two laws were not only of different civil years but some seventeen months apart. If so, and if these measures are oligarchic, it follows (see note 1, above) that the oligarchy was not abolished in winter 411/10.
5 See note 3.
6 See note 4.

154   Expenditures of the Treasurers of Athena. 410/9 B.C.[1]
Marble stele, developed Attic writing, nonstoichedon, Athens.

IG I[2] 304A+ (I[3] 375); B. D. Meritt, *Athenian financial documents of the fifth century* (Ann Arbor 1932) 62, 94–8, with Plates 2–6; *GHI*, no. 84, pp. 255–60; *W. K. Pritchett, *The Choiseul Marble*, Univ. of Calif. Publ.: Class. Studies 5 (Berkeley and Los Angeles 1970) 18–21.

Pritchett, *The Choiseul Marble, passim*; Meiggs, *Empire* 234, 370, 468.

The Athenians spent in Glaukippos' archonship (410/9) and (in the year of) the Boule for which Kleigenes of Halai was first I Secretary: the Treasurers of the sacred monies of Athena, Kallistratos of Marathon and (his) colleagues paid over from the year's revenue, after decrees of the People:[2] in Aiantis', the first prytany: to the Hellenotamiai there was paid over, to Kallimachos of Hagnous, Phr[.]sitr[.]ides[3] of Ikaria
5   there was paid allowance for grain for horses,[4] from Athena Po[lialls]: 3 T. 3,237 dr. ½ ob.; from (Athena) Nike: 91 dr. 3¼ ob. In Aigeis', the second prytany, to the organizers of the contests (Athlothetai) was paid over, for the Great Panathenaia, to Philon of Kydathenaion and (his) *colleagues*, from Athena Polias: 5 T. 1,000 dr. To the Hieropoioi for the I year, Diyllos of Erchia and (his) colleagues, for the hekatomb: 5,114 dr. In Oineis', the third prytany, there was paid to the Hellenotamiai, Perikles of Cholargos[5] and (his) colleagues: allowance for grain for horses was paid: 2 T. 5,420 dr. I Another (payment) was made to the same Hellenotamiai as allowance for grain for horses: 2 T. 5,400 dr.
10   Another (payment) to the same Hellenotamiai II was made for Hermon, commander at Pylos: 6 T. Another to the same Hellenotamiai for the diobelia:[6] 2 T. In Aklamantis', the fourth prytany, there was paid over to the Hellenotamiai, Perikles of Cholargos and (his) colleagues: allowance for grain for (ho)rses was paid: 3 T. Another to the same Hellenotamiai was paid for the diobelia: 8 T. 1,355 dr. In I Kekropis', the fifth prytany, there was paid over to the Hellenotamiai, Perikles of Cholargos and (his) colleagues *for* I the diobelia: 4 T. 2,200 dr. In Leontis',
15   the sixth prytany, on the third day of the prytany, II there was paid over to the Hellenotamiai, Dionysios of Kydathenaion and (his) colleagues: 1,284 dr. On the ninth day of the prytany, to the Hellenotamiai Thrason of Boutadai and (his) colleagues: 3 T. 1,083 dr. 2 ob. On the eleventh day of the prytany to the Hellenotamiai there was paid over, to Proxenos of Aphidna and (his) colleagues for the general from Eretria, Eukleides, a record of paymelnt[7] of 3,740 dr. 1¼ ob. On the thirteenth day of the prytany, to the Hellenotamiai Perikles of Cholargos and his colleagues: [.]I4,906 dr. On the twenty-eighth day of the

prytany, tо́ the Hellenotamiai, Spoudias of Phlya and (his) colleagues:
20 2 T. 2, [.]‖ 100 dr.[8] On the thirtieth day of the prytany, the (payment?) from Samos[9] was recorded as paid to the Hellenotamias, Anaitios of Sphettos, and to the Paredros, Pʃolyaratos of Cholargos: 57
T. 1,000 dr. In Antiochis', the seventh prytany, on the fifth day of the
prytany, there was paʃid over to Dionysios of Kydathenaion and (his)
colleagues for the diobelia: 1 T. On the seventh day of the prytany, to
the Hellenotamiai Thraʃson of Boutadai and (his) colleagues for the diobelia: 1 T. 1,232 dr. 3¼ ob. On the same day, to the Hellenotamiai,
Phalanthos of Aʃlopeke and (his) colleagues, as allowance for grain for
horses: [.]3 T.[10] On the sixteenth day of the prytany, to the Helleno-
25 tamiai Pro[xe]ʃlnos of Aphidna and (his) colleagues: 1,534 dr. 3 ob.
On the twenty-fourth day of the prytany, to the Hellenotamiai Eupolis
of Aʃphidna and (his) colleagues: 5,400 dr. On the twenty-seventh day
of the prytany, to the Hellenotamiai Kallias of Euonymon aʃnd (his)
colleagues: 1 T. 2,565 dr. 4½ ob. In Hippothontis', the eighth prytany,
on the twelfth day of the prytany, to the Hellenoʃtamiai there was
paid, to Proxenos of Aphidna and (his) colleagues: 3 T. 634 dr. 4 ob.
On the twenty-fourth day of the prytaʃny, there was paid to the Hellenotamiai Dionysios of Kydathenaion and (his) colleagues: 3 T. 4,318 dr.
30 1½ ob. On the thirty-sixth day ‖ of the prytany, there was paid to the
Hellenotamiai Thrason of Boutadai and (his) colleagues: 1 T. 3,329 dr.
3 ob. In Erechtheis', ʃ the ninth prytany, on the twelfth day of the
prytany, there was paid to the Hellenotamiai, Proxenos of Aphidna and
(his) colleagues: [.][11] ʃ 2,188 dr. 1 ob. On the twenty-third day of the
prytany there was paid to the Hellenotamiai Dionysios of Kydathenaion
and (his) colleaguesʃ[.] 3 T. 793 dr. 3 ob.[12] On the thirty-sixth day of
the prytany there was paid to the Hellenotamiai Thrason of Boutadai
and (his) colʃleagues: 2 T. 3,850 dr. 2½ ob. On the thirty-sixth day of
the prytany, the (payment?) from Samos was recorded as paid [by the]
35 *allies* ‖ *to the* generals at Samos:[13] to Dexikrates of Aigilia: 21 T.
1,000 dr.; to Pasiphon of Phrearrhioi: 6 T.; to Aristokra[tes -9-]: 5 T.;
to E[...]ʃ [....][14] of Euonymon: 5 T. 3,896 dr.; to Nikeratos of
Kydantidai, trierarch: 3,000 dr.; to Aristophanes of An[-9-],[15] *trierarch*: ʃ [-6-]. In Pandionis', the tenth prytany, on the eleventh day of
the prytany, to the *Hellenotamiai* [there was paid], to Pro[xʃenos of
Aphidna] and (his) colleagues: 5 T. 442 dr. 5 ob. On the twenty-third
day of the prytany, to the *Hellenotamiai* [there was paid....]ʃ[-(about)
14- and (his) colleagues]: 2 T. 5,090 dr. 3 ob. On the thirty-sixth day
40 of the prytany, to the *Hellenotamiai* [there was paid...]‖[-(about) 19-
and] (his) *colleagues*: 5 T. 4,656 dr. 4 ob. The total of the money in its
entirety which K[allistratos of Marathon][16] ʃ and (his) colleagues paid
over: -(about) 5-] *vv*

1   The Choiseul Marble (this inscription and that on the reverse of the stele, *IG*
    I² 304B, no. 158 below) is fundamental for the study of the Athenian calen-
    dar, providing abundant if controversial evidence for the progression of days,
    intervals in days between fixed points in the prytany calendar, and of the
    relationship between the archon year and the conciliar or prytany year.
2   See no. 144, line 15, above.
3   A new reading by Pritchett which, if correct, rules out the traditionally accep-
    ted 'Phrasitelides.'
4   For the cavalry, cf. no. 131, note 1.
5   The son of Perikles and Aspasia (no. 96, note 6). He became general in 406/5
    and was put to death after the battle of Arginusae (Plutarch, *Perikles* 37;
    Xenophon, *Hellenica* 1.5.16, 1.7.2).
6   The nature of the diobelia ('two-obol payment') remains obscure. It was instituted
    by Kleophon (Aristotle, *Athenaion Politeia* 28.3) and apparently was increased
    thereafter (Arist. *Politics* 2.7.1267b). The diobelia has been variously identified
    with the Theoric Fund (which provided fourth-century Athenians with admis-
    sion money for the theatre), jury pay, assembly pay and relief payments for
    those rendered destitute by the Peloponnesian War. There are difficulties in all
    these explanations.
7   Literally 'a promise to pay,' it was a book transaction. The money collected at
    Eretria passed directly into Eukleides' hands, but since the money was the pro-
    perty of the goddess, the Treasurers entered the sum, indicating that they did
    not receive or disburse it.
8   The missing figure must be either 1,000 or 500 or 100 dr.
9   'The Samian payment' is perplexing. Some hold that it marks the continued re-
    payment of Samos' debt (see no. 133 n. 4), others refer it to the centrality of
    Samos as a base of operations, where money was aggregated. Cf. line 34.
10 4 T. is probable. (The first numeral could not be read by Pritchett, but is
    probably 1 T., as traditionally given.)
11 The last letter space in line 31 is so reported by Pritchett.
12 Either a numeral (Meritt, in his most recent text (cited *GHI*, p. 257)) or a
    punctuation mark (Meritt, earlier: *Athenian financial documents of the fifth
    century* (Ann Arbor 1932) 96; Pritchett) began this line.
13 That is, these funds were paid by the allies to the generals instead of to the
    Treasurers, but were recorded by the Treasurers; this makes the procedure
    above (see note 9) clear.
14 'E[u|machos]' has been proposed by Bradeen (*Hesperia* 33 (1964) 49 n. 65).
15 'of An[agyrous]' or 'of An[aphlystos].'
16 The demotic may have been omitted, since more than about five spaces is re-
    quired for the total at the end of the line (*GHI*).

155 Phrynichos' Assassins Honored. 409 B.C.

Marble stele, developed Attic writing, stoichedon, except for the first
two lines, Athens.

IG I² 110 + (I³ 102); W. S. Ferguson, *CAH* 5.336f.; *GHI*, no. 85, pp. 260-3. Cf.
Thucydides 8.92; Lysias 13.71; Plutarch, *Alkibiades* 25.14.

[In Glauki]ppos' *archonship* (410/9). | [Lobon of] Kedoi was Secre-
tary. | [Resolved by the] Boule and the People, Hippothonti|s *held the*
5 *prytany,* Lobon was Secretary, Philistide||s [presided], Glaukippos was
Archon. Erasinides made the motio|n: Thrasyboulos[1] [shall be com-
mended] since he is a good man | [toward the] *People* of the Athen-
ians and zealous [t|o do whatever] good [he can]. In return for the
10 good he has d|one [to both the city[2]] and the *People* of the Athenian||s,
[he shall be crowned with a golden] *crown,* [and] they *shall* mak|e [the
crown (at a cost of) one thousand] *drachmas.* The [H|ellenotamiai are
to provide the money. Proclamat|ion shall be made by the herald, at
the Dionysia(?) during the] festival, of the *rea|sons* [why the People
15 gave him a crown]. Diokles moved: || [Let all the rest be as the Boule
(proposed)], but Thrasy|[boulos] shall be [an Athenian (citizen); and
in whatever tribe] *and* phratry[3] | [he prefers, he shall be enrolled], and
the other things which [h|ave been voted by the People] *shall be* [valid]
for Thrasyboulo|s. [It shall be permissible for him to acquire] *from* the
20 Athenians || [in addition any other thing which seems good to them][4]
on account of his *good d|eeds* [toward the People of the Athenians].
And a record shall be set | up [by the Secretary of what has been de-
creed]. There shall be elected | [five men from among the Boule][5]
immediately, wh|o [are to] *determine* [what Thrasyboulos'] *portion*
25 shall b||e. The [others who at that time] *benefited* the Peo|ple of the
Athe[nians -10-]is and Agorato|s and Komon [and -13-] and Simon
an|d Philinos *and* [-9-], they shall as benefactors be record|ed on the
30 Akropolis [on a stele of] *marble* by the Secretar||y of the Boule. [The
(same) right of owning land] shall be theirs which | Athenians (pos-
sess), [both plots of land] and houses, and a residen|ce in Athens, and
they shall be *entrusted to the care* of the Boule | at any given time *in*
office, and to the Prytaneis, so that they ma|y not *suffer harm.* [The]
35 stele shall be let out for contrac||t [by the Poletai in the] *Boule.* The
Hellenotam|iai [shall provide the money]. If it is decided that they are
also | [to receive other (benefits), the] Boule, after having formulated a
preliminary decree, | [shall bring it before the People]. Eudikos made
the motion: Let all the rest | [be as Diokles (moved), but as to] those
40 who brib||ed [for the sake of the decree] which was voted for Apol-
l|[odoros,[6] the Boule shall deliberate] in its first *sess|ion* [in the Bouleu-
terion], and it shall exact punishment, with those who were *brib|ed*
being condemned and [handed over][7] to a cou|rt in accordance with
45 what seems best to it. T||he [Bouleutai who] are present shall reveal
what|ever [they know (about the affair) and (so shall)] anyone (else)
who knows anything further about i|t [-12-][8] private person (to testify)
if anyone wishes.

1 Thrasyboulos was a Calydonian.
2 'Boule' is also possible.
3 *GHI*; 'tribe and deme] and phratry': *IG* I² (two letters too long).
4 *GHI*; '[any other good thing if he should be in need]': *IG* I².
5 *IG* I²; '[by the People three men]': Michel (cited *GHI*, p. 262).
6 Lys. 13.72, in a speech against Agoratos (named on lines 26–7), refuting his claim to have killed Phrynichos and been made a citizen, speaks of a decree conferring citizenship on Thrasyboulos and Apollodoros; our decree certainly suggests that this earlier decree was rescinded. Perhaps the enquiry to be held by the Boule vindicated Apollodoros' claim [*GHI*] (not incompatible with Lys. 13.71, where Apollodoros is said not to have struck a blow). Thucydides offers a different version.
7 This verb is in the next line.
8 '[It shall be permissible also] for a': *IG* I².

156 Athens Honors Neapolis in Thrace. 410/9–408/7 B.C.

Fragments of a marble stele, Attic writing, with lines 1–46 showing Ionic influence, stoichedon from line 48, Athens.

IG I² 108 (I³ 101); B. D. Meritt and A. Andrewes, *BSA* 96 (1951) 200–9; *GHI, no. 89, pp. 271–5. Cf. no. 154.

Meiggs, *Empire* 365, 575; de Ste Croix, *Origins* 42; Bury–Meiggs 313.

Gods. | Neapolitans | near Thas[os].¹ | Resolved by the *Boule* and the
5 People, Leontis *held the* prytany,² ‖ Sibyrtiad[es] was Secretary,
Chairimenes *presided*, [Gl]|aukippos was *Archon* (410/9), [....]theos
made the motion: *Commendation* shall be given to the Neap[olitans]|
near Thasos, [first, because though colonists of the Thasians and under
s̲i̲]ege b̲y̲ t̲h̲e̲m̲³ and the Pelo[ponn]esians [first,

*(The underlined was erased and reinscribed as follows)*⁴

|because they] carried on the war together with the Athenians [and]|

|under si|lege | by [the Thasians]| and the Peloponnesians they were not
willing t|o rebel [against the Athenians, and (because)] *they showed*
10 *themselves* good *men* [both to th|le army and to the] *People* [of the
Athenians] *and the* [all|ies - - -]

(Lacuna of 9 lines)

[--] *Athenians* [--]|[--] property [--]|[--] of the Athenians [--]|[--]
25 shall be (for the?) Neapo[litans --]‖[--] and lend 4 T. 2,[--dr.-]|[--]
they requested so that *they* might *have* (it) [for | the war. -(about) 8-]
shall make it to them from the *monies* | [-(about) 10- of Neap]olis
from the harbor. The [generals]⁵ at [Thasos | are each year to record]

30 (them) as having received from [themselves (what they received) ‖
    until it is completely] repaid.[6] They shall do this *as long as* [th|ey are at
    war with] the Thasians. That which is being given *now* [by the Neapo-
    lit|ans -(about) 12-] both willingly and spontaneously [was given by
    them to the] | *Hellenotamiai*: 5 T. 4,800 dr.; and they are zealous [to
    do all poss|ible] *good*, having made profession of this themselves both
35 in *word* [and in deed to t‖he] *city* of the Athenians, and in return for
    [this] *benefaction* [these shall no|w] and in future time (have) from
    the Athenians [-(about) 12-] *for th|em* on the grounds that they are
    good men and [access shall be] *the|irs* to the Boule and the People
    [right after the sacred business, since] | they are benefactors of the
40 Athenians. *The* [envoys shall have the recor‖ds] of that money which
    the Neapolitans *gave* [handed over in their entirety to the] *Se|cretary*
    of the Boule, keeping apart [that which has now been given from the]
    re|st, and this decree shall be *inscribed* by [the Secretary of] | the
    Boule on a stele of marble and set up [on the Akropolis at the expense
    of th|e] Neapolitans. In Neapolis (the Neapolitans) themselves [shall
45 inscribe it and set it ‖ up] in the temple of the Virgin Goddess on a
    stele [of marble. An invitation shall also be issued] | to the embassy for
    hospitality at the *Prytaneion* [tomorrow. *vv*] | To Oinobios of Decelea,
    general, 3 T. 6[34 dr. 4 ob. (?)][7] | Axiochos made the motion:[8] Com-
    mendation shall be given to the Neapolitans from [Thrace since they
    are good men] | both to the army and to the city of the Athenians and
50 because [they went on campaign against Thasos], *laying* ‖ *siege* (to it)
    with the Athenians, and because, together with (the Athenians), they
    fought a battle by sea [and conquered], and [joined in the land fight-
    ing during the] *who|le* time, and because in all other respects they
    keep benefiting the Athenians. [In return for] this [-16- from the]
    A|thenians shall be for them just as was voted *by the People.* And in
    order that [they] shall *not* [suffer any harm eithe|r] from a·private
    person or from a city's government, the *generals* who on each occasion
    [have command shall all] take c|are of them in regard to whatever they
    may require. And the Athenian governors[9] who *on each occasion* [-9-]‖
55 [..] the city guarding the Neapolitans and being zealous to do whatever
    may [-15-]|[..] And now they shall themselves acquire from the
    People of the Athenians whatever seems *good* [-9-[10] As to]| the first-
    fruits to the Virgin Goddess *which* even earlier were given to the god-
    dess,[11] [(the matter) shall be discussed] in (the Assembly of) the People
    [with] *th|em.* In the *previous* decree the Secretary of the Boule shall
    make correction [and write on it] | in place of (their being) a *colony*
    [of the Thasi]ans[12] that they carried on the war *together with* [the
60 Athenians....]‖[-36-]. They shall be commended inasmuch as they
    now say *and* [do go|od to the People of the Athenians and because]

they are zealous to do whatever they can to *benefit* [the ar|my and the city in the future] *precisely as* in the past. They shall also be invited for *hospitality* [tomorrow]. | [-7- made the motion: Let all the rest be as (resolved) by the] Boule. For the Virgin Goddess *they shall set apart* [the first-fruits ju|st as formerly -15- the] People[13] pray for.

1 These lines are spaced out to form a heading.
2 The sixth prytany: see no. 154, line 14.
3 Thasos had rebelled in 412/11 (cf. no. 153).
4 The correction was required by the second decree, lines 58f.
5 The word is on line 29.
6 This sentence (as restored) is unusually compressed and lacks its main verb as well. The Neapolitans are presumably receiving installment payments on the loan from the Athenian generals, and the generals are to record the payments.
7 This line was inscribed by a different hand. The payment is usually identified with that of no. 154, line 28, and is restored accordingly.
8 This decree is by a third hand, stoichedon. Axiochos is probably the uncle of Alkibiades; see no. 147, line 118.
9 The Greek is 'archontes'; see the Glossary.
10 'to the Boule': Meritt and Andrewes.
11 Taken by Tod to be the Athena of Athens, by Meritt and Andrewes to be the Athena of the Neapolitans.
12 See note 4.
13 'which the Neapolitan] People': Meritt and Andrewes.

157   A Contract for the Ransoming of Prisoners of War. 408/7 B.C.

Scholiast to Aristotle, *Nicomachean Ethics* 5.10.1134b (Androtion, *FGrHist* 324 F 44).

Jacoby, *FGrHist* IIIb Suppl. 1.152f.

Arist. *Nicomachean Ethics* 5.10.1134b: Conventional justice (as against natural justice), which does not matter originally whether it is one way or another, does matter after it is enacted, as, for example, redeeming (men) for a mna.

Scholion: Redeem for a mna. This the Athenians and the Lacedaemonians contracted in their war against each other – to ransom prisoners for a mna each. Androtion mentions this contract: 'Euktemon of Kydathenaion. In his archonship (408/7) there came from Lacedaemonia to Athens, as ambassadors, Megillos, Endios, and Philocharidas.'[1] And he adds, 'As to the surplus, they returned them at the price of one mna for each man.'[2] For he had previously said that this had been agreed by them with regard to the captured men.

1 These names are corrections of the corrupt 'Metellos, Eudikos, and Philochoros.' Megillos is probably the man mentioned by Xenophon, *Hellenica* 3.4.6; for

Endios see Thucydides 8.6.3, Diodorus 13.52.2; for Philocharidas see Thuc.
4.119.2, 5.19.2, 5.24.1.
2 I.e. after an exchange of man for man, those left over were returned for a mna
   each.

158   Expenditures of the Treasurers of Athena. 408/7–407/6 *or* 407/6 B.C.

Marble stele (reverse side of no. 154), developed Attic writing, stoichedon with irregularity (except lines 12–27, which are nonstoichedon),
Athens.

IG I² 304B–C (I³ 377); B. D. Meritt, *Athenian financial documents of the fifth
century (*Ann Arbor 1932) 116–27; W. K. Pritchett, *BCH* 88 (1964) 455–87; Meritt,
TAPA 95 (1964) 204–12 (407/6). *W. K. Pritchett, *The Choiseul Marble*, Univ.
of Calif. Publ.: Class. Studies 5 (Berkeley and Los Angeles 1970) 7–10 and *passim*[1]
(408/7–407/6); see no. 154.

[....] to the Logistai, K[-22-] of monies and from [-23-]|[..... (to)]
(son of?) Noumenios[2] of Marathon, A[rch]edemos of [P]aion[id]ai,
D[-34]|[-6-], Phainippos of Paionidai on the *three-*[and]-twentieth
day [of the] prytany, the third of Mounichion *from its* | *beginning*: [.]
5   1 T. 2,814 dr. [.] ob.[3] To the Hellenotamiai and *Paredroi* [-31-]||[-5-]
on the six-and-twentieth day of the prytany, the sixth of *Mounichion
from its beginning*, 2 T. 520[-6-]. *In* | Aigeis' (prytany), to the Helleno-
tamiai and Paredroi, [L]ysitheo[s of Thymaita]dai and (his) *colleagues
on the second day* | *of the* prytany, the seventeenth of Mounichion,
[..]110[-6-]. To the *Hellenotamiai and* Paredroi, A|[the]nodoros of
Melite and (his) colleagues, on the fourth day [of the] *prytany*, the
eighth[4] of *Mounichion, for* [the] *di*|*obelia:*[5] *v* 2 T. 50 dr. to the Logis-
tai [Ar]chedemos of [M]arath[on and] (his) *colleagues* and [to the]
10 *Hellenotamiai* [....] || [.....] of *Kopros*, on the seventh day of the
prytany, the *sixth* of Mounichion from its end, [for the] obol[6] (?)
[.....]|100 dr. To the Logistai [Ar]chedemos of [M]a[r]athon and
(his) *colleagues* [and to the Hellenotamiai Athenod]oros of M[elite]|,
on the fifteenth day *of the prytany*, the second of *Thargelion* from its
beginning, [for] the [---]|[....] the Logistai [for?] the obol (?): 1,250
dr. [To] the Logistai [---]| of the prytany, the *eleventh* of Thargelion,
15 [--[7] In the prytany of] Antiochis [-- to the Logistai Archede]||mos of
Paionidai and (his) colleagues and to the Hellenotamiai [Protar]chos of
Pro[ba]li[nth]os [and] (his) *colleagues* [on the twelfth day of the pry-
tany], *the fif*|*th* of Skirophorion from its beginning [for those (in
charge?)] of the obols: 1,100 dr. *To the Logistai* [Arche]d[e]mos of
Paionidai [and (his) colleagues and to the Hellenotamiai --]|[...] of
Phaleron and (his) colleagues on the twelfth day *of the* prytany, the

fifth of Skirophorion from its beginning: 100 dr. [To the Logistai - - - and] the *Hellenota|miai* and Pared⟨roi⟩, Lysitheos of Thymai⟨tadai⟩ and (his) colleagues, on the *seventeenth* day of the prytany, [- - of Skirophorion, 620 dr.]. To the *Hellenota|miai* and Paredroi, [P]rotarchos of Prob[al]inthos and (his) colleagues, on the *seven-*[and-twentieth day of

20 the] *prytany*, the *seventh of* ‖ Skirophorion from its end, *for* Thorikos:[8] 1 T. To the Logistai [Arch]edemos of [M]a[rathon and (his) colleagues and to the Hellenotamiai and Paredroi --]|[..] of Kopros and (his) colleagues, on the three-and-twentieth day of the *prytany*,[9] the *sixteenth* of *Skirophorion*: 100 dr. [--]|[...] of Euaiteles and of Amphikedes (?) [-20-] 640 [-dr.-]. *To the Hellenotamiai and Paredroi*, Ly[sitheos of Thy]mait⟨adai⟩ | and (his) colleagues, on the three-and-thirtieth day [of the] *prytany, the last day* | of *Skirophorion*: 160[- dr. - In the prytany] of *Antiochis*, [the first] *prytany* (of the year), to the Hellenotamiai and Paredroi, Lysith[eos] of [Thym]ai[tadai] and (his)

25 *colleagues*, on the *twentieth* day of the prytany, [the twentieth] ‖ of the month Hekatombaion, [for the] diobelia: 630 dr. [-6-] with everything (?) [-14 OR 15-twentieth day] *of the prytan|y*, the twentieth of the month Hekatombaion: 17 T. 1,620 [.] dr. [To the Logistai] and Paredroi, A[-5-]mos [--]. *I|n* Erechtheis' (prytany), on the first day of the *prytany*, the eighth of the month, 1 T. [..] *vv* |

(An uninscribed space follows, equivalent to three lines)

In Erechtheis', the second [-10- to the] *Hellenotamiai* [and] Paredroi, [Lysi]theos of Thymaita*v|*dai and (his) colleagues, on the *thirteenth*

30 *day* of the prytany, the *twentieth* of Metageitnion, *v* ‖ for the diobelia for Athena Nike (?): 215 dr. 4 ob. To the Hellenotamiai and Paredroi, Thr[asyl]ochos of Thorik*v|*os and (his) colleagues, on the seventeenth day of the prytany, the sixth of Metageitnion from its end, *v* | for the diobelia: 113 dr. To the Hellenotamiai and Paredroi, [Lysi]theos of Thym[ait]adai and (his) colleagues, | on the seventeenth day of the prytany on the sixth of Metageitnion from its end, *for* the diobelia for A*v|*thena Nike (?): 9[8]6 dr. 1 ob. To the Hellenotamiai and Paredroi,

35 [P]ro[ta]rch[o]s of Probalinthos and (his) *cv*‖olleagues, on the eighteenth day *of the* prytany, the fifth of Metageitnion from its end, for th*vv|*e diobelia: [1]2 dr. To the Hellenotamiai and Paredroi, P[rota]rchos of Proba[linth]os and (his) colleagues, on the nin*v|*eteenth day of the prytany, the fourth of Metageitnion from its end, for the diobelia: 25[.] dr. | To the Hellenotamiai and Paredroi, Lysitheos of Thymaitadai and (his) *colleagues*, on the two-and-twentieth day | of the prytany, the last day of Metageitnion, for the diobelia: 17 dr. 4 ob. To the Helleno-

40 tamiai [and] ‖ Paredroi, Thrasylochos of Thorikos and (his) colleagues, on the three-and-twentieth day of the prytany, the *firv|st* day of

Boedromion, for the diobelia: 16[2] dr. 2 ob. To the Hellenotamiai and Paredroi, Lysitheos of Thymai|tadai and (his) colleagues, on the four-and-twentieth day of the prytany, the second of Boedromion, for [the] | diobelia: 6 dr. 3½ ob. To the Hellenotamiai and Paredroi, Lysitheos òf Thymaitadai and (his) colleagues, on the *six-v*|and-twentieth day of the prytany, the fourth of Boedromion from its beginning, for the diobelia:
45   85[0+ dr.]. To the Hel|llenotamiai and Paredroi, Lysitheos of Thymaitadai and (his) colleagues, on the thirtieth day of the prytan|y, the eighth of Boedromion from its beginning, for the diobelia for Athena Nike (?): 506[+ dr.]. To the Hellenotamiai *an*|d Paredroi, Lysitheos of Thymaitadai and (his) colleagues, on the thirtieth day of the prytany, the eighth of | Boedromion from its beginning, for the diobelia: 82 dr. To the Hellenotamiai and Paredroi, Protarchos [[Protar|chos]] of Probalinthos and (his) colleagues, on the six-and-thirtieth day of the pry-
50   tany, the fourteenth of Boe|ldromion, [for the] *diobelia*: 28 dr. 1¼ ob. To the Hellenotamiai and Paredroi, Lysitheos of Thymaitadai | *and* (his) colleagues, on the [six-and-]*thirtieth* day of the prytany, the *fourteenth* of Boedromion, [for the | diobelia - - - -]

1   Pritchett's text supersedes all previous ones. I ignore earlier restorations which are incompatible with his new readings.
2   The genitive case of the name Noumenios (which would be a patronymic) is probably the mason's error; a dative must have been intended.
3   The first and last parts of the figure are not certain.
4   There is an omission here by the mason, for the figure should read 'eighteenth.'
5   See no. 154, note 6.
6   This new reading apparently reveals the existence of a purse unattested elsewhere in Attic inscriptions; its nature is therefore even more obscure than that of the diobelia (see no. 154, note 6). It is possible (see Pritchett 117) to identify it with the fund for jurors' pay (cf. Aristophanes, *Clouds* 863), or with the obol added to the diobelia by Kallikrates (Aristotle, *Athenaion Politeia* 28.3).
7   A sum of money is lost here.
8   Payments for Thorikos are probably to be connected with the expense incurred by its fortification against the incursions of Agis and his troops stationed at Decelea. See Xenophon, *Hellenica* 1.2.1.
9   Note that this entry is dated four days earlier than the preceding one, according to the prytany date, and seven days earlier (Skirophorion 16–23) according to the month date. Pritchett has shown (see especially pp. 24–33) that the archon freely intercalated or suppressed days in the calendar under his control.

159   The Date of Alkibiades' Return to Athens. 408/7 B.C.

Scholiast to Aristophanes, *Frogs* 1422 (406/5) (Androtion, *FGrHist* 324 F 45). Cf. Xenophon, *Hellenica* 1.4.8–21; Diodorus 13.68.2–69.3; Plutarch, *Alkibiades* 33.

W. S. Ferguson, *CAH* 5.483–5; Jacoby, *FGrHist* IIIb Suppl. 1.153f.; Bury–Meiggs 314; Sealey, *History* 373f.

Aristoph. *Frogs* 1422-3: First of all, as to Alkibiades, what / advice do each of you have? For the city (still) suffers from its labor pangs.

Scholion: He is speaking about his second withdrawal, into voluntary exile.[1] He had returned in the archonship of Antigenes (407/6), one year before the production of *The Frogs*, (and he fled) because he had entrusted the fleet to Antiochos his steersman and, being defeated by Lysandros,[2] he became hated by the Athenians. Androtion[3] differed from Xenophon about (the date of) the return.[4]

1   The first withdrawal was from the Sicilian Expedition in 415 B.C. (Thucydides 6.53).
2   At the battle of Notion, March 406 (Antigenes' year). A fragmentary, but detailed, description of this battle is provided by the Oxyrhynchus Historian, fr. 4 (Bartoletti, in the Teubner text).
3   A correction of 'Andron.'
4   I.e. Androtion dated Alkibiades' return correctly to 408/7, where Diodorus sets it. Xenophon, whom the scholiast followed, put it in the context of Antigenes' archonship (*Hell.* 1.3.1). It is worth noting that Xenophon also sets the battle of Notion into the archon year of Antigenes (407/6). Alkibiades returned to Athens in May, when the Plynteria was celebrated, and the battle was fought the next spring, in March. Since the new Attic year began in summer, both events cannot be placed in the same archon year, and therefore Xenophon may safely be supposed to have been mistaken.

160   Athens Honors Oiniades. 408/7 B.C.

Marble stele, Ionic letters, stoichedon, Athens.

IG I^2 118 (I^3 110); *GHI*, no. 90, 275-7.

Meiggs, *Empire* 214, 217.

Gods. | Resolved by the Boule and the Peop|le, Antiochis held the pry-
5   tany, Euk|leides was Secretary, Hierokl|les presided, Euktemon was
Archon (408/7). | Dieitrephes made the motion: Since | he is a good
man, Oiniades of Pal|aiskiathos, to the city | of the Athenians, and
10   zealous to d|o whatever good he can, and is of b|enefit to (any) Athe-
nian who comes | to Skiathos, commendation shall be given | him and
15   he shall be recorded | as proxenos and benefactor of the Athe|lnians,
and his descendants (as well); a|nd that he be not harmed shall be the |
responsibility both of the Boule, whichever i|s in office, and of the gen-
20   er|als and the (Athenian) governor in Ski|lathos, whoever he may be on
each occasion. This d|ecree shall be inscribed by the S|ecretary of the
Boule on a stel|le of marble and shall be set up on the A|kropolis. He
25   shall also be invited fo|lr hospitality to the Prytaneion for t|omorrow.

Antichares made the motion: Let all the | rest (be) as (resolved) by the
Boule, but | there shall be an alteration made in the resolution in plac|e
30   of 'of Skiathos', so that there be *wri*||*tten* 'Oiniades of Palais|[kia-
thos'].[1]

1   Cf. no. 156, lines 58f. Oiniades was perhaps 'touchy' about his proper designa-
tion (*GHI*, p. 277). Note that the correct form was actually engraved (lines 7-8),
but the amendment was still included.

161   Athens Orders the Building and Manning of Ships and Honors Archelaos (?) of Macedon.[1] 407/6 B.C.?

Marble stele, Attic letters, stoichedon, Athens.

IG I² 105 (I³ 117); Tod I, no. 91, pp. 222–4; B. D. Meritt, *Athenian financial documents of the fifth century* (Ann Arbor 1932) 107–15, *Classical studies presented to
Edward Capps* (Princeton 1936) 246–50: **GHI*, no. 91, pp. 277–80. Cf. Diodorus
13.49; and, for the importance of timber, Thucydides 4.108.1, Xenophon, *Hellenica*
6.1.11; and see Andoc. 2.11.

[Resolved by the Boule and] *the* People, Aka[ma|ntis held the prytany,
Phel]leus *was Secretar*|*ly*, [-13-² Sib]yrtio[s] *presided*, | [-10- made the
5   motion: For] *the construction* of the [sh||ips, a loan shall be made by
the] *generals* with P[e|rikles³ (taking) money] *from* the present A|[po-
dektai (and paying it) to the (?)shipwrights]. Whatever they *le*|*nd* [shall
be paid back to] *them* by the *tri*|*eropoioi*.⁴ [Those] *assigned* to sail
10   to || [man the vessels] shall as quickly as possible | [be dispatched by
the generals]. If (they are) not, [.....]||[-13- into] court.⁵ *The* | [-17-]
15   *not* willing to *de*|*part*, [-9-⁶ The] conveyance of the *sh*||*ips* [which the
(?)shipwrights send] *from* Macedonia | shall be *supervised* [by the
Boule] so that | [they may be sent as quickly as possible] ·to Athens
and [may b|e manned and· the army] shall be brought [to Ioni]a (?) |
20   [to keep] guard as effectively as possib||le. [If anyone does not act] in
accordance with this, he shall be *liab*|*le to pay* [-6-⁷ drachmas] dedicated
to Athl|[ena. The first man] *to arrive* and *to br*|*ing* [a ship shall receive
a gift] *in accordance* [with what has | been decreed by the People. And
25   since Archelaos (?) is || now and in former] *times has been* | [a good
man toward the Athenians], for the | [(?)shipwrights] *who sailed out*
he *has received* and to the [..]||[-18-] has sent (them?) off, *and* |
30   [-19-] encampment, *a*||*nd* [he has given them timber] and oar-spars
and | [all other things they required of] him, of excellent quality,
comm|*endation shall be given* [to Archelaos (?) on the grounds that] *he
is* a good man | [and zealous to do] *whatever* he can of *ben*|*efit*, [and
35   in return for his benefactions] to the city ||[and the People of the
Athenians], an inscription shall *be set* | *up* (recording) both himself and

his sons as proxenoi] and [bene|factors, on the Akropolis on a stele of marble, and ...]|[---]

1 The honorand of this decree is designated (36f.) as proxenos and benefactor, and he is thanked for spars for oars. Since Macedon is mentioned in the decree (15) and the name Archelas fits the spaces of line 32, the conjecture has been made that the benefactor is Archelaos of Macedon.
2 '[Antigenes was Archon' (407/6): Meritt, *GHI*.
3 This is the son of the great Perikles and Aspasia; see no. 96, note 6.
4 Men responsible for the construction of triremes; see Aristotle, *Ath. Pol.* 46.1.
5 '*let them* (i.e. the generals) *be brou|ght* [by the Eleven into] court': Mattingly; '*they are to be pros|ecuted* [for treason in the] court': Meritt.
6 (From the beginning of line 13:) '[Heliasts in the case of any man] *not* willing to de|part* [shall try him': Tod; '[generals – (THE SAME) – [shall bring him into court': *GHI*.
7 One thousand *or* ten thousand.

162 Athens Ratifies a Treaty with Selymbria. 407 B.C.
Marble stele, mixed lettering, inaccurate stoichedon, Athens.

IG I^2 116 (I^3 118); *GHI*, no. 87, 267–9. Cf. Xenophon, *Hellenica* 1.1.21, 1.3.10; Diodorus 13.66.4; Plutarch, *Alkibiades* 30.

W. S. Ferguson, *The treasurers of Athena* (Cambridge, Mass. 1932) 45 note 1; Gomme, etc., *HCT* 1.240; A. Andrewes, *JHS* 73 (1953) 8; Bury–Meiggs 313.

(No complete words are preserved on the first six lines)

7 [--] list [.....]|[--] hostages who *are* he|ld [by the Athenians shall be
10 returned, and in] future (hostages) shall not be *tak|len*, [and the
Selym]brians [shall establish] their *cons|titution* [autonomously in]
whatever [fashion they] may *kn|ow* [(to be best)-17-] *is owed*[1] by the
government of the Sel[lymbrians or by a private citizen] of the Selym-
15 brians [...]|[-18-] if anyone's property *had been confisc|lated* [or if
anyone] was in debt [to the government] or if anyone *was* deprived of
his citizenship [-20-][2] exiles of the Selymbrians | [-17-] *same* people
enemies and friends | [-14-][3] As to what was lost in the war, | of [the
20 property of Athenians] or of their allies, or if there was anything *ow|led*
[or] a *deposit* of anyone's which was exacte|d [-10-][4], there shall be no
recovery except for land and *hou|se*. [All] *other* contracts which were
formerly concluded between [p|rivate person] and private person or
private person and [g|overnment or] *government* and private person *v*
25 or any other which may *ar|lise* shall be *discharged*. As to whatever they
may *dis|pute*, [litigation] shall be based on contractual agreements. The
settleme|nt [shall be inscribed] on a stele and be set up in the shrin|e
[of -7-]. Those who took the oath were, of the Athenians, the generals
30 | [and the trierarchs] and the hoplites and an|ly [other Athenian] who
was present, and the Selymbrians *i|n their* entirety, [*v* Al]kib[iades]

made the motion: What was agreed by the Sel[lym]bria[n]s *with the* Athenians, that shall be done, | and the agreement shall be engraved and set up on the *Akropolis* by the ge|*nerals* together with the Secre-
35 tary of t|l*he* Boule [[-18-]]⁵ on a stele of mar|ble at their expense⁶ together with this decree. | [Apo]llodoros son of Empedos shall be com-mended and he shall be rem|oved from the status of being a hostage; furthermore, the deletion of the nam|es of the Selymbrian *hostages* and
40 their sure||ties⁷ shall be carried out tomorrow by the Secretary of the Boule, *wherever* | (their names) [are] *written down*, in the presence of the Prytan|eis. [....]om[a]chos of Selymbria shall be *inscri|bed on the same* stele as *proxenos* of the Athenians. | [There shall also be given]
45 the status of proxenos to Apollodoros ju||*st as* (it was) *to his* father. The *envoys* [and] Apol|[lodoros] shall be invited to the Prytaneion *for hospitality for* | [tomorrow]. *vv*

1 'There shall be suits as to what] *is owed*': Wilhelm (cited *GHI*, p. 268).
2 '[There shall be a return of the]': Wilhelm.
3 (From 17:) 'if they consider the] --- [as those in the city]': Wilhelm.
4 '[by the rulers (archons)]': Wilhelm.
5 An erasure.
6 This may mean the generals', but it is much more likely to be the Selymbrians'.
7 I.e. other men who guaranteed the good faith of the hostage and who would be liable if the hostage absconded.

163 Athenian Treaty with the Clazomenians at Daphnus. 407 B.C.
Marble stele, Ionic writing, stoichedon, Athens.

IG I² 117 (I³ 119); *GHI*, no. 88, pp. 270ff. Cf. Thucydides 8.14.3, 8.23.6, 8.31.2–3; Xenophon, *Hellenica* 1.1.10–11; Diodorus 13.71.1.

Resolved by the *Boule* [and the] *People*. [-8-]¹ h|eld the prytany, Krates was *Secretary*, [Epigen]|es presided. Alkibiades made the motion: [The settlemen|t] which the generals made [with those who
5 dwell i||n] Daphnus shall be (ratified) for them as [it was agre|ed], since they have shown themselves *good* (men); [and] *an ins|cription shall be set up* by the *Secretary* [of the Boule on a stele]| of marble on [the Akropolis, containing both the settlement and this de|cree ---]

1 Erechtheis, Kekropis, or Antiochis is possible.

164 The Athenian Military and Financial Emergency of 407/6 B.C.

A: Scholiast to Aristophanes, *Frogs* 694 (406/5 B.C.) (Hellanicus, *FGrHist* 323a F 25); B: Scholiast to Aristophanes, *Frogs* 720 (Hellanicus, *FGrHist* 323a F 26; Philochorus, *FGrHist* 328 F 144). Cf. Xenophon, *Hellenica* 1.6.24; Diodorus 13.97.1.

W. S. Ferguson, *CAH* 5.355f.; Jacoby, *FGrHist* IIIb Suppl. 1.54f., 511; E. S. G. Robinson, *American Numismatic Society, Museum Notes* 9 (1960) 8-12; Bury-Meiggs, 314f.

A. Scholiast to Aristophanes, *Frogs* 694

Aristoph. *Frogs* 693-4: For it is disgraceful for men who have fought one battle by sea / to become Plataeans straightway and masters instead of slaves.

Scholion: Hellanicus says that the slaves who joined in the sea battle (of Arginusae) were given their freedom and were enrolled as joint-citizens with the (Athenians) on the same terms as the Plataeans.[1] (He said this) when narrating the events in the archonship of Antigenes (407/6), who was Archon in the year ⟨before⟩ Kallias.[2]

B. Scholiast to Aristophanes, *Frogs* 720

Aristoph. *Frogs* 718-20: It has often seemed to us that the city has experienced / the same thing in the case of its citizens of the best sort / and (in the case of) its (good) old silver coin and its new gold coin.[3]

Scholion: In the year before, in the archonship of Antigenes (407/6), Hellanicus says they minted gold coin. Philochorus likewise speaks of the (coin) minted from the Golden Nikai.[4]

1 See Thucydides 3.55.3, with Gomme, etc., *HCT* 2.339f.
2 The battle of Arginusae was fought in Kallias' year, 406/5, not long after Antigenes left office. This measure, like (B), can be assumed to have been implemented in advance of the battle and in Antigenes' year. The Athenians resorted to the desperate measure of enfranchisement of foreigners, metics, and slaves in order to meet the threat posed by Kallikratidas, who heavily outnumbered them on the sea, having captured thirty of Konon's seventy ships in June 406. In order to pay for the fleet thus raised, they took the unusual step of coining gold.
3 Subsequent verses make clear that Aristophanes views the new coins disparagingly (though they apparently were not debased). Athenians were accustomed to silver coins, the famous 'owls.'
4 On these see E. Schweigert, *Hesperia* 9 (1940) 309ff.; H. Thompson, *HSCP* Suppl. 1 (1940) 183-210; W. E. Thompson, *Numismatic Chronicle* 10 (1970) 1-6.

165   Athens and Carthage. 406 B.C. (?)

Two fragments of a marble stele, developed Attic writing, stoichedon, Athens.

IG I² 47+ (I³ 123); B. D. Meritt, *HSCP* Suppl. 1 (1940) 247-53, with a photo on p. 248; *GHI*, no. 92, pp. 280f. Cf. Thucydides 6.88.6; Diodorus 13.80.2, 13.86.3.

The restoration of this inscription is almost purely hypothetical.

[Resolved by the] *Boule and* [the People, - (about) 6 - held the pry-|
tany, - (about) 6-]s of Aphid[na was Secretary, . . .]|[-12-]s *presided,*
5 [- - made the motion: - - -]|[- - -]||[- - -]|[-11-]. *A record shall be set up*
[of the Carthaginians as ben|efactors of the Athen]ians by the [Secre-
tary of the Boule o|n the Akropolis on a] *stele of marble.* [-16-]|[-11-]
10 to Sicil[y shall be sent to the gen||erals Hanniba]l[1] son of Geskon [and
Himilkon son of Hannon]|[-10-] themselves [-20]|[- - -]|

(The fragment breaks off)

15 [t|o the generals Hannibal son of Geskon and Him]ilko||[n son of
Hannon. Commendation shall also be given the heralds] who | [came
to Athens because they are] *good* [men | toward the People of the
Athenians. They shall be invited] also *f|or* [hospitality to the Pry-
20 taneion for tomorrow. *vv*] *vv* | [- - - Hann]ibal || [- - - | - - -]

1 This name, strictly transliterated, is Annibas; Carthage = Karchedon. The full
names of the two generals are known from Diodorus 13.80.

166 Athens Honors the Samians. 405 B.C.
Marble stele, Ionic writing, stoichedon (sometimes observing syllabic
division of words), Athens. (Inscribed 403/2 B.C.) A relief above the
inscription depicts Athena and Samian Hera clasping hands.

IG II[2] 1 (I[3] 127); *GHI, no. 94, pp. 283–7. Cf. Thucydides 8.21.

W. S. Ferguson, *CAH* 5.363; A. L. Boegehold, *AJA* 76 (1972) 23–9; Bury–Meiggs 317.

Kephisophon of Paiania | was Secretary. | For all the Samians who
5 stood with the People of the Atheni|ans.[1] || Resolved by the Boule and
the People, Kekropis held the prytany, Polymnis of Euonymon | was
Secretary, Alexias was Archon (405/4), Nikophon of Athmonon pre-
sided. Resolution of Kleisophos | and his fellow Prytaneis. Commenda-
tion shall be given to the Samian envoys, both those who former|ly
arrived and those now (here), and to the Boule and the generals and the
other | Samians, because they are good men and zealous to do whatever
10 good they can, || and for their action, because they see fit to act rightly
for the Athenians and the Sami|ans. And in return for the benefits they
have conferred on the Athenians and (because) they now highly esteem
them and | propose benefits for them, it has been resolved by the Boule
and the People that the Samians shall be Athenians, | governing them-
selves in the manner they themselves prefer. And in order that this shall
be most advan|tageous for both parties, just as they (the envoys) them-
15 selves say, when peace comes, at that time || there shall be deliberation
in common about the rest. They shall use their own laws | and be auto-

nomous, and they shall act in all other respects in accordance with the oaths and the treaties just as I agreed by Athenians and Samians. As to disputes which may arise I toward each other, they shall grant and shall submit to legal proceedings according to the existing agreements. I If any emergency arises because of the war even earlier as regards the

20 conǁstitution, just as the envoys say themselves, they shall deliberate in the light of present conditions and act I in whatever manner it seems to them to be best. As to the peace, if it comes, the same terms shall apply I for the Athenians and also for those who now inhabit Samos.[2] If it is necessary to wage war, preparations shall I be made by them as best they can, acting (in concert) with the generals. I *If* the Athenians send an embassy anywhere, those present from Samos shall jointly with

25 them send ǁ any envoy they wish, and they shall offer whatever good advice they possess. The triremes I [which] are at Samos[3] shall be given to them to use when they have had them repaired in accordance with what *thǀey* think best. The names of the trierarchs whose ships these were shall be listed I [by the] *envoys* for the Secretary of the Boule and the generals, and if against them I [there is any debt] written down anywhere in state records from when they took over the triremes, ǁ

30 [(the debts) are all to be expunged] by the dockyard superintendents from all records, but the equipment is to be collected into public [posǀsession as quickly as possible] and the (dockyard superintendents) are to compel those in possession of any of it to return it I [in good condition. Resolution of Kleisophos and] his fellow Prytaneis: Let all the rest (be) as (proposed) by the Boule, I [but the privilege shall be conferred upon the Samians] *who have come*, just as they themselves request, and (the Athenians) shall distribute I [them immediately into the

35 demes and] *the* tribes in ten parts.[4] Traveling expenses shall be *pro* ǁ *vided* [for the envoys by the generals] *as* quickly as possible. And Eumachos and the I [other Samians, all who have come with Eumachos], shall be commended since they are I [good men toward the Athenians. Invitation shall be issued to Eum]achos *for* dinner[5] at the Prytaneion I [for tomorrow. What has been decreed shall be inscribed by] *the Secretary* [of the] *Boule* together with the I [generals on a stele of marble and they] shall *set it up* on the Akropolis, [and the Hellen]o-

40 tamiai ǁ [shall supply the money. They (the Samians) shall inscribe it at Sa]mos in the same way *at their own expense*.

1 The first four lines form a heading.
2 The expression is used to ensure that the anti-Athenian exiles shall be excluded.
3 Presumably these are the triremes left there before Aegospotami (see Diodorus 13.104.2).
4 'and they shall be distributed [immediately by the Archons into] the tribes': Wilhelm (cited *SIG*, p. 160).

5 The usual word *hospitality* (*xenia*), would apply to foreign guests, whereas Eumachos is now an Athenian citizen and is honored by an invitation to 'dinner.'

167 The Influx of Gold and Silver into Sparta. 405 B.C. and later.

Athenaeus 6.24, p. 233e-234a (Posidonius, *FGrHist* 87 F 48c); cf. Xenophon, *Constitution of the Lacedaemonians* 7.6; Diodorus 13.106; Plutarch, *Lysander* 16f.

M. Cary, *CAH* 6.29; Michell, *Sparta* 298ff.

The Lacedaemonians, forbidden by their customs from introducing (wealth) into Sparta, as the same Posidonius relates, and from acquiring gold and silver, acquired it nonetheless, but deposited it with the neighboring Arcadians. At a later time the latter became their enemies instead of their friends[1] in order that because of the hostility, (the government's) suspicions should not be tested. They relate that the gold and silver which had earlier been in Lacedaemonia had been entrusted to Apollo in Delphi; and that when Lysandros brought it into the city as public property he became the cause of many evils. For the report is that Gylippos, the man who liberated the Syracusans,[2] starved himself to death after he had been found guilty by the Ephors of filching from the money of Lysandros. Apparently, it was difficult for a mortal man to be indifferent to what had been dedicated to a god and bestowed upon him as an adornment and possession.

1 From 370 B.C., with the organization of the Arcadian League.
2 See Thucydides 6.93.2, 6.104.1-2, 7.1ff.

168 Lysandros' Treatment of Conquered Cities. After 404 B.C.

Polyaenus, *Stratagems* 1.45.4. Cf. Isocrates 4.110; Nepos, *Lysander* 2; Plutarch, *Lysander* 13f.

A. Andrewes, *Phoenix* 25 (1971) 206ff.; Bury-Meiggs 324.

Lysandros conquered the Thasians, and among them were many partisans of Athens who were hiding in fear of the Laconian. He assembled the Thasians in the temple of Herakles and spoke kindly words – 'that pardon should be given to those who were in hiding because of the reversal of things, and that they ought to take heart since they would suffer no evil, as he was speaking in a temple,[1] and, at that, the temple of ancestral {to the city} Herakles.' Those of the Thasians who were concealed had trust in the kindliness of his words and came forth. But Lysandros, after waiting a few days to make them less fearful, commanded that they be rounded up and killed.

1 I.e. and so telling the truth.

169   Laws Regulating the Wine Trade at Thasos. Late fifth century B.C.

(A) nonstoichedon; (B) stoichedon. Thasos.

IG XII, Suppl. 347, I and II; *H. W. Pleket, *Epigraphica* I (Leiden 1964), no. 2, I and II, pp. 8f. Both laws are engraved on the same stele, with part of the second having been effaced in the second century A.D., when another law was inscribed in its place.

H. W. Pleket, *Historia* 12 (1963) 73 n. 18a; de Ste Croix, *Origins* 43 n. 80.

(A)

Neither sweet wine nor (ordinary) wine from the crop on the *vines* shall be *bo|ught* before the first of Plynterion. Whoever [transgresses] | and buys it shall have to pay a fine of stater for stater,[1] [half] | to the city, half to the one who has prosecuted (him). The form of suit shall be *the*
5   *same* ‖ as in cases of violence.[2] But if someone buys wine in wine jars, the pur|chase shall be valid if (the seller) has stamped a seal on the jars. *vacat.*

(B)

[- - - the] | penalties and deposits shall be the same. If no one makes the *depo|sit*,[3] the Commissioners for the Mainland are to bring suit. When-ever | they win the suit, the whole of the penalty shall belong to the
5   city. If the Comm‖issioners do not bring suit, though they have the in-formation, they themselves shall have to pay[4] a penalty of dou|ble (the amount). Whoever wishes may bring suit (against them) in the same way, | and he shall keep half of the penalty, and the suit shall be gran-ted[5] by the Demiourgo|i against the Commissioners in the same way. No boat | of Thasos shall import foreign wine within (the points of)
10   Athos and Pacheia.[6] If it does, ‖ (the owner) shall have to pay the same penalty as a waterer of wine | and the pilot shall owe the same penalty. The sui|ts and the deposits shall be the same. Neither out of amphorae n|or out of a cask nor out of a 'false-jar'[7] shall anyone sell by the kotyle[8] (rather than wholesale). Whoev|er does sell (it thus), suits and sureties
15   and punishments shall be applied in the same way a‖s for the adultera-tion (of wine) with water. *vacat*

1   I.e. the guilty party will pay the same amount as a penalty that he paid for the illegal wine.
2   According to Harpocration s.v. 'Violence' (*biaion*), in Athenian cases of this sort 'the man convicted pays the same sum to the public treasury as to the pro-secutor (and victim).'

3 With the result that no legal action is brought by a private individual. A private citizen had to pay a deposit before starting an action.
4 The verb stands in line 6.
5 The verb stands in line 8.
6 Territory which Thasos appears now to have regained (cf. Thucydides 1.100f.).
7 I.e. of a different capacity from the standard size.
8 A liquid measure of nearly one-half pint.

170 The Rule of the Ten in Athens. 404/3 B.C.

A: Harpocration, *Lexicon* s.v. 'Ten and Holder of a place among the Ten' (*deka kai dekadouchos*) (Isocrates 18.5; Androtion, *FGrHist* 324 F 10; Lysias F 79 Sauppe); B: Harpocration, *Lexicon* s.v. 'Molpis' (Androtion, *FGrHist* 324 F 11). Cf. Aristotle, *Ath. Pol.* 35.1, 38.3-4, 39.6.

Jacoby, *FGrHist* IIIb Suppl. 1.137f.; Hignett, *Constitution* 292f.; Bury–Meiggs 321; W. J. McCoy, *YCS* 24 (1975) 131-45; Sealey, *History* 379ff.

When the Thirty Tyrants were overthrown, the Ten were installed in their place. Aristotle speaks of a second board of ten which succeeded this one, 'zealous' for reconciliation with the People, which 'received its charge in the oligarchy and rendered account of itself in the democracy' (*Ath. Pol.* 39.4). Neither Xenophon nor Lysias mentions it. The Ten are also to be distinguished from the board referred to in extract (B).

A. Harpocration, *Lexicon* s.v. 'Ten and Holder of a place among the Ten'

Isocrates in the *Special Plea against Kallimachos*: 'For the 10 were in control, those established after the 30.' Of the 10 men elected at Athens after the dissolution of the 30, and of subsequent events, Androtion has given an account in (Book) 3. Each of these officials was called 'dekadouchos' ('Holder of a Place among the Ten'), as Lysias makes clear in the (speech) *On Diogenes' Estate*.

B. Harpocration, *Lexicon* s.v. 'Molpis'

Lysias in the (speech) *On Diogenes' ⟨Estate⟩* says: 'Molpis, one of ⟨the 10⟩ in Piraeus.' For the ten men in the time of the 30, one of whom was Molpis, ruled in Piraeus, as Androtion says in *History of Athens* (Book) 3.

APPENDIX I

Athenian Archons 500–403 B.C.

See T. J. Cadoux, *JHS* 68 (1948) 70–123, for earlier archons and for full references to those listed here between 500 and 480. A complete list of the archons from 479/8 B.C. to 403/2 B.C. is preserved in Diodorus, Books 11–14; other documentation for the archons holding office in this latter period is supplied by R. Meiggs and A. Andrewes in Hill, *Sources*[2] 397–401. Only the year in which archons entered office is given here; it must be remembered that they held office from summer to summer, i.e. that the archon listed under 500 was in office from summer 500 to summer 499, etc.

500	Smyros	466	Lysanias
499	?	465	Lysitheos
498	?	464	Archedemides
497	Archias[1]	463	Tlepolemos
496	Hipparchos	462	Konon
495	Philippos	461	Euthippos
494	Pythokritos	460	Phrasikles
493	Themistokles	459	Philokles
492	Diognetos	458	Habron
491	Hybrilides	457	Mnesitheides
490	Phainippos	456	Kallias
489	Aristeides	455	Sosistratos
488	Anchises	454	Ariston
487	Telesinos	453	Lysikrates
486	?	452	Chairephanes
485	Philokrates	451	Antidotos
484	Leostratos	450	Euthynos
483	Nikodemos	449	Pedieus
482	?	448	Philiskos
481	Hypsichides	447	Timarchides
480	Kalliades	446	Kallimachos
479	Xanthippos	445	Lysimachides
478	Timosthenes	444	Praxiteles
477	Adeimantos	443	Lysanias
476	Pheidon	442	Diphilos
475	Dromokleides	441	Timokles
474	Akestorides	440	Morychides
473	Menon	439	Glaukinos
472	Chares	438	Theodoros
471	Praxiergos	437	Euthymenes
470	Demotion	436	Lysimachos
469	Apsephion	435	Antiochides
468	Theagenides	434	Krates
467	Lysistratos	433	Apseudes

432	Pythodoros	417	Euphemos
431	Euthydemos	416	Arimnestos
430	Apollodoros	415	Charias
429	Epameinon	414	Teisandros
428	Diotimos	413	Kleokritos
427	Eukles	412	Kallias of the deme Skambonidai
426	Euthynos	411	Mnasilochos (2 months)
425	Stratokles		Theopompos (10 months)
424	Isarchos	410	Glaukippos
423	Ameinias	409	Diokles
422	Alkaios	408	Euktemon
421	Aristion	407	Antigenes
420	Astyphilos	406	Kallias of the deme Ankyle
419	Archias	405	Alexias
418	Antiphon	404	Pythodoros[2]

1 For the evidence see D. M. Lewis, *CR* 12 (1962) 201.
2 Pythodoros did not count officially since he held office under the oligarchy. See Xenophon, *Hellenica* 2.3.1; Aristotle, *Ath. Pol.* 35.1, 41.1; Diodorus 14.3.1.

APPENDIX II

Athenian Demes

All demes mentioned in this volume, and indexed in the Index of Personal and Geographical Names, are identified here according to their location in the coastal, inland, and city (suburban) regions of Attica. Many identifications are uncertain; those that are the most tenuous are marked with an asterisk. The tribal affiliation of each deme is indicated by a Roman numeral following the official order of the ten tribes (for which see the Introduction, p. xxiii). For a good map see G. Westermann, *Grosser Atlas zur Weltgeschichte* (Brunswick 1972) 13; for a survey of the modern state of deme studies, see E. Kirsten in *Atti del terzo congresso internazionale di epigrafia greca e latina* (Rome 1959) 155–72 (written in German), with a useful chart of the demes on pp. 166–71, and J. S. Traill, *The political organization of Attica* (Princeton 1975). See also Glossary, 'Demes.'

Acharnai, inland, VI
Acherdous, *coast, VIII
Agryle, city, I
Aigilia, coast (SW), X
Aixone, coast (SW), VII
Alopeke, city, X
Anagyrous, coast (SW), I
Anaphlystos, coast (SW), X
Ankyle, city, II
Aphidna, inland (N), IX
Araphen, coast (E), II
Athmonon, inland, VII
Azenia, coast (NW), VIII

Besa, coast (SW), X
Boutadai, city, VI

Cholargos, city, V

Dekeleia, inland (N), VIII

Eleusis, coast, VIII
Erchia, inland, II
Euonymon, city, I
Eupyridai, inland, IV

Gargettos, inland, II

Hagnous, inland (S), V
Halai Aixonides, coast (SW), VII
Halai Araphenides, coast (E), II
Halimous, city, IV
Hermos, city, V

Ikarion, inland, II

Kedoi, *coast (SW), I
Kephale, coast (S), V
Kerameis, city, V
Koile, city, VIII
Kollytos, city, II
Kolonos, city, II
Kopros, *coast (NW), VIII
Kydantidai, *inland, II
Kydathenaion, city, III

Lakiadai, city, VI
Lamptrai, coast (SW), I

Marathon, coast (NE), IX
Melite, city, VII
Myrrhinous, coast (E), III

Oē, coast (NW), VI
Oinoe (1), coast (NW), VIII
Oinoe (2), coast (NE), IX
Oion, inland (N), VIII

Paionidai, inland (N), IV
Pallene, inland, X
Pergase, inland, I
Perithoidai, *city, VI
Phaleron, city, IX
Phegaia, * coast (NE), II
Philaidai (E), II
Phlya, inland, VII
Phrearrhioi, coast (S), IV
Piraeus, city, VIII
Prasiai, coast (SE), III
Probalinthos, coast (NE), III
Prospalta, inland (S), V

Rhamnous, coast (NE), IX

Skambonidai, city, IV
Sphettos, inland, V

Teithras, inland, II
Themakos, city, I
Thorai, coast (SW), X
Thorikos, coast (SE), V
Thria, coast (NW), VI
Thymaitadai, city, VIII
Trikorynthos, coast (NE), IX

Xypete, city, VII

APPENDIX III

Glossary

Apatouria. An Athenian festival basic to the phratry, which was so distinctively
Athenian that its celebration by Ionians established for Herodotus their ultimate
Athenian descent. It was celebrated for three days in the month of Pyanopsion
(Sept.–Oct.), and on the last day new members were enrolled in the phratries.
Herodotus 1.147.2; Hellanicus, *FGrHist* 323a F23; scholiast to Aristophanes,
Acharnians 146; Harpocration s.v.

Apodektai ('public receivers'). A board of ten men at Athens, elected by the lot,
who collected public revenues such as tribute, war taxes, tolls, and state debts,
and immediately dispensed them to the appropriate authorities. The board may
not have been instituted before the Peace of Nikias in 421, in spite of Androtion's assertion that it was established by Kleisthenes. Androtion, *FGrHist* 324
F 5; Aristotle, *Ath. Pol.* 47.5–48.1, 52.3; Pollux 8.97; Harp. s.v.; Bekker, *Anecdota Graeca* 198.1; see Jacoby, *FGrHist* IIIb Suppl. 1.118; Harrison 2.27.

Archon (eponymous). The powers of the archon waned as the state developed, but
the oath he took upon entering office to confirm people in the possession of
their property, however superfluous in historical times, gives an indication of his

earlier authority. It is possible that he presided over the Assembly until the reform of 487/6, when the archonship was in part thrown open to the lot, but in the fifth century his principal duties were to supervise family matters – the rights of parents and children, widows and orphans, and the maintenance of family lines. He conducted the major religious festivals and appointed choregoi for the Great Dionysia. He gave his name to the year (hence the later title 'Eponymous'), regulated the calendar of the lunar year, and he lived in the Prytaneion, the hearth of the state. Thucydides 6.54.6; Isaeus 7.30; Arist. *Ath. Pol.* 3.2-3, 56.2-7; *Lexicon Rhetoricum Cantabrigiense*, Hesychius, s.v.; Poll. 8.89; see Hignett, *Constitution* 41-5; Harrison 2.7f.

Archons (governors). The word *archon* is the term for *ruler* and so can designate anyone at the head of affairs. The Athenians used the term to refer to magistrates of their own resident in allied cities. Their powers were probably considerable, *de facto* if not legally, but they are not defined in the sources. Aristophanes, *Birds* 1049f.; see Meiggs, *Empire* 213f., 587.

Archons, the Nine. This group was not strictly a board or college, since archon, basileus, polemarch and the board of the six thesmothetai possessed different functions (as could be expected from their individual establishment at different times). The original requirement of high property qualifications, attributed to Solon, was dropped in 457/6 when zeugitai (possessors of an income of 200 medimnoi of wheat or its equivalent) were given access to the office. On the expiration of their term of office, they entered the Areopagus. In 487/6 the archons ceased to be directly elected and became chosen by lot from an initially elected body of (probably) 100 men. Thuc. 1.126.8; Arist. *Ath. Pol.* 3, 22.5, 26.2, 55; Poll. 8.85, 118; *Suda*, s.v.; see Hignett, *Constitution* 45-7, 321-6.

Areopagus ('[the Council of] the hill of Ares'). This Council (Boule), named from the hill on which it sat, was Athens' most ancient. According to one tradition Solon defined and regularized the Council, though another alleged that he established it. Little about it is certainly known since the Council did not become a subject of discussion and controversy until the fourth century, after its most important features had withered away, and it retained little more than its jurisdiction in some murder trials. After Solon (what came before is unknown) it consisted of ex-archons with lifelong tenure, and it is said to have exercised the dominant power in the state as overseer of the laws and the magistrates. Whatever its power during the time of Peisistratos and Kleisthenes (its role was ignored by Herodotus and Thucydides when treating these epochs), Aristotle (*Ath. Pol.* 23) credited the Council with major importance even after the period of the Persian Wars. Its influence, in any case, was sufficient to provoke in 462-461 the scarcely less obscure attack against it by Ephialtes, who transferred its more important powers to the Boule and the law courts and ended its career as a political agency. Isocrates, *Areopagiticus*, passim, but esp. 37, 43-6; Arist. *Politics* 1273b 35-1274a2, *Ath. Pol.* 3.6, 4.4, 8.2, 4, 25.2; Cicero, *De Officiis* 1.75; Plutarch, *Solon* 19; Poll. 8.117-18, 125; see Jacoby, *FGrHist* IIIb Suppl. 1.22-5, 112-17, 265-7; Hignett, *Constitution* 79-83, 89-92, 146-8, 198-213; R. Sealey, *CP* 59 (1964) 12-14; Rhodes, *Boule* 200-7.

Assembly (Ekklesia). After Kleisthenes' reforms, the Assembly was open (probably) to all Athenian citizens, thetes included, who had completed their eighteenth year. In the fourth century it sat regularly four times in every prytany, one of those meetings (kyria ekklesia = principal assembly) having a fixed agenda; special meetings also could be called. The Assembly was the sovereign body of the state (and thus is sometimes referred to simply as 'the People'): it passed on all major questions, elected major magistrates and could recall them from office; on occasion´tried important political cases and conducted ostracisms under the presidency of the nine archons and the Boule. Although no matter won final approval from the Assembly unless it had first been cleared by the Boule, it could, by means of amendments, modify propositions submitted to it, and it could instruct the Boule to initiate a desired proposal. Any Athenian could participate in debate or offer amendments; voting was by a show of hands. Thuc. 4.118.11, 4.122.6, 7.20.1, 8.9.2; Xenophon, *Hellenica* 1.7.7ff.; *Ath. Pol.* 42.1, 43.4–6, 45.4; Arist. *Pol.* 4.14.1298a3ff.; Poll. 8.95; Harp., Hesychius, s.v. 'kyria ekklesia'; see Hignett, *Constitution* 232–6; Rhodes, *Boule* 52–85.

Assessors (Taktai). This commission probably was elected at the time of the Panathenaia, when occasion for assessment arose, and it provisionally assessed the tribute payments of the allies, including those states which paid 'voluntarily.' In 425/4, the time of a major reassessment, they were elected to draw up a fresh (and optimistic) list of tributary cities, fix the sum of tribute required, and assign itineraries to the heralds charged with announcing these demands to the allies. Antiphon F 25–33, 49–56 Thalheim; Andocides 4.11; see Rhodes, *Boule* 90f.

Ateleia (immunity from public burdens). Freedom from certain public duties and liturgies (such as choregia or trierarchy) involving the expenditure of money. Some such immunitites were based on laws of general application to Athenian citizens – e.g. that which freed members of the Boule from the obligation of military service, or the archons from regular liturgies or from the trierarchy. But metics as well as citizens (in Athens and elsewhere) could specifically be decreed exemptions from regular burdens for services rendered. For metics the dispensation normally would apply to the special burdens imposed on them by the state (see Metics). Demosthenes 20.18, 107; Poll. 8.155.

Athlothetai (of the Panathenaia). Ten cult officials, probably elected in the fifth century, though picked by the lot in the fourth, who held office for the four-year cycle from Great Panathenaia to Great Panathenaia and had the responsibility of directing the Panathenaic contests and furnishing the prizes for the victors. In the final weeks before the festival was held they dined in the Prytaneion at state expense: Arist. *Ath. Pol.* 60.1, 62.2; Plut. *Perikles* 13.11; Poll. 8.87, 93.

Attic letters. The Athenians officially discontinued the use of their Attic alphabet in 403/2, when they adopted Ionic on the urging, purportedly, of the Samians, and on the motion of Archinos (see Arist. *Ath. Pol.* 34.3). Thus the kind of alphabet used in Athenian public inscriptions provides an indication of their relative date – though it is not invariably acceptable (note the alphabet used in no. 68). Photius, *Suda*, s.v. 'Samian demos.'

Axon. One of a series of rectangular wooden tablets, each revolving on an axis, which contained the laws of Drakon and Solon. The relationship between axon and kyrbis is uncertain, though most scholars assume their identity. Lysias 30.17 (kyrbis); Arist. *Ath. Pol.* 7.1 (kyrbis); Dem. 23.28, 31; Plut. *Sol.* 1.1, 25.1–2; Harp. s.v.; see Hignett, *Constitution* 13, 390; A. Andrewes, *Phoros* 21–8; R. S. Stroud, *The Axones and Kyrbeis of Drakon and Solon* (Berkeley 1979).

Basileus (king archon). Whatever the connection of the basileus (as he was simply called) with the kings of the ancient Athenian state, his duties in the fifth century were to supervise matters of ancestral cult – sacrifices, ceremonies, temple-precincts, the state religion, disputes about the succession of hereditary priesthoods. In his judicial capacity he presided over the homicide courts. Arist. *Ath.*

Pol. 3.1-4, 57; Harp. s.v. 'Epimeletes of the Mysteries'; Poll 8.90, 108; Bekker, *Anecd.* 219.16, 310.6; see Hignett, *Constitution* 39ff., 75f.; Harrison 2.8f.

Boule of 500. Kleisthenes formed the Boule of 500; it was open to all citizens over thirty years of age, and they were selected by lot from a larger group appointed by the demes, each of the ten tribes being represented by 50 men. It met daily (except for holidays), prepared the Assembly's agenda, fixed the time of its meetings, presided over it, and attended to the execution of its decisions. The Boule supervised the magistrates (e.g. the generals), introduced envoys to the Assembly, and oversaw the financial administration of the state. Thuc. 8.69.4; Arist. *Ath. Pol.* 24.3, 43.2-5, 45-9; see Hignett, *Constitution* 237-44; Jones, *Democracy* 99ff.; Rhodes, *Boule*, passim.

Bouleuterion. The primary meeting place of the Boule, built probably at the end of the sixth century and located on the west side of the agora. (It was replaced by the 'New Bouleuterion,' a building begun at the end of the fifth century.) It contained a raised platform from which men spoke, with special benches for the prytaneis. (See Prytaneis.) Aristoph. *Knights* 625ff.; Antiph. 6.40; Lys. 13.37f.; see Rhodes, *Boule* 30-5.

Cavalry at Athens (Hippeis). Though the name hippeis denoted the second of the Solonian census classes (having an annual income of between 500 and 300 medimnoi of wheat or its equivalent), it also refers to an aristocratic body of 1,000 cavalry organized about the middle of the fifth century. The 'knights' provided their own mounts and the state provided equipment-money (katastasis and 'grain for horses' [see the index]). The cavalry was divided according to tribe, each tribal unit headed by a phylarch and the whole corps headed by two hipparchs. Thuc. 2.13.8; Aristoph. *Knights* 225; Andoc. 3.5, 7; Hesych. s.v.

Choregoi. The richest citizens were required to undertake certain liturgies or public burdens (cf. trierarchs) of which the choregia was one. Like the others, it was a sort of progressive tax, working as an indirect source of revenue for the state. The choregos assembled a chorus, required at dramatic, comic, and musical competitions held at the festivals; he equipped and paid it, and hired a trainer for it. Lys. 21.1-4; Dem. 20.130; Arist. *Ath. Pol.* 56.3ff.; *Lex. Rhet. Cantab.* 670; see Jones, *Democracy* 101.

Collectors of tribute (eklogeis). In order to insure the collection of the full amount of tribute – or at least to fix securely the responsibility for its collection and have a means of redress in case the sum fell short – the Athenians in 426/5 appointed wealthy foreign nationals of the allied cities to the task. Antiph. F 52 Thalheim; Harp., *Suda*, s.v. See Meiggs, *Empire* 241.

Commissioners (syngrapheis). Usually members of an ad hoc committee, though one individual could serve alone, commissioners were elected to provide a draft (syngraphai) of a motion dealing with complicated matters, religious or political, which then was submitted for ratification by the Boule and Assembly. Andoc. 1.96; see Jones, *Democracy* 123.

Council of Elders (Gerousia). The establishment of the Spartan Council was ascribed to Lykourgos' famous rhetra bidding the Spartans 'to tribe the tribes and obe the obes, (and) establish a thirty-man council of elders including the two kings' (Plutarch, *Lykourgos* 6.1-2). The twenty-eight men, over sixty years of age, were chosen by the People's acclamation. Their function was to propose legislation which the People in assembly would ratify; except in cases where the Council was divided, submission of a proposal was tantamount to its acceptance. For though the Lykourgan rhetra made the voice of the people final and permitted it the right of criticism, the Gerousia was later enabled (by an addition to the rhetra) to dismiss the people if displeased with their voting. Hdt. 6.57.5; Plato, *Laws* 3.691; Arist. *Pol.* 1270b; Plut. *Lykourgos* 6, 26; see Michell, *Sparta* 135ff.; N. G. L. Hammond, *Studies* 47–103.

Court fees (Prytaneia). In private legal suits both parties were required to deposit a sum of money, the loser's going to the winner of the case (the winner's to the state); and the fee was also paid by the prosecutor of a public suit whenever he stood to realize a gain if victorious (i.e. a portion of the penalty). The fee was 3 dr. for suits valued at 100 to 1,000 dr.; 30 dr. for suits involving more. In some special cases, the court fee could amount to the sum the prosecutor hoped to win. Aristoph. *Clouds* 1136, 1179f., 1189–91; Dem. 43.71; Isae. 3.47; Poll. 8.38; Hesych. s.v. 'without prytaneia'; Harp. s.v.; see Harrison 1.116–18; 2.92–4.

Cow and panoply. Several inscriptions of the fourth century make it clear that some Greek states (e.g. Paros) brought a cow and a panoply (a complete suit of armor) to Athens at the Panathenaia in token of ancient kinship and friendship (*Inschriften von Priene* 5). How extended the practice was, when it arose, and when tributary allies of the Athenians were required to share in it are controversial questions depending on the preferred dates for no. 98 (see no. 98, line 42). Schol. to Aristoph. *Clouds* 386; see B. D. Meritt and H. T. Wade-Gery, *JHS* 82 (1962) 69–71.

Darics. The gold coinage of Persia, of excellent quality, and bearing the image of Dareios armed with bow and spear.

Demarch. This annual magistrate, (probably) elected by his demesmen (though in the fourth century the demarch of the Piraeus was selected by lot from all Athenians), was the chief officer of the deme. He kept a record of property ownership for the purposes of taxation, maintained the lexiarchic registers (see no. 55 n. 8), superintended the deme's financial affairs, religious sacrifices, and holy places. Dem. 54.37, 57.25; schol. to Aristoph. *Clouds* 37; Arist. *Ath. Pol.* 21.5, 54.8; Harp., *Suda*, Hesych. s.v.; see Hignett, *Constitution* 136.

Demes. Local communities in rural areas formed the basis for Kleisthenes' political organization of the deme, though the town of Athens was divided more artificially. Some 139 demes are known from the late fourth century. Kleisthenes divided them into thirty groups, ten containing demes from the coast, ten from the suburban–urban area, and ten from the interior. Each of these groups was called a trittys (probably 'a third'), and each of the ten newly formed tribes was composed of one trittys from each of the three localities. Thus the tribe became representative of all sections of Attica, for no tribe contained two trittyes from the same region – though it was possible to gerrymander in such a way that a given tribe could possess contiguous trittyes (e.g. coastland–urban). Membership in a deme was a requirement of citizenship, and it was inherited regardless of where one (later) happened to live. The practice of identifying oneself by deme name (demotic), instead of by patronymic or in addition to it, became standard in the fifth century, especially in official documents. Hdt. 5.69.2; Arist. *Ath. Pol.* 21.4–5; Strabo 9.1.16, p. 396; see Hignett, *Constitution* 132–7; D. M. Lewis, *Historia* 12 (1963) 22–40; J. S. Traill, The *political organization of Attica* (Princeton 1975).

Demiourgoi. Magistrates of high rank among the Dorians, chosen from leading families, with a fixed number and term of office. Virtually no detailed information about them exists. Hesych. *Lexicon*, s.v., who compares them with Athenian demarchs; see K. Murakawa, *Historia* 6 (1957) 385–415.

Dionysia. The City or 'Great' Dionysia was a feast celebrated in honour of Dionysos Eleuthereus, so named from the town of Eleutherai, from which it was introduced into Athens, probably by Peisistratos. It was celebrated in March and lasted for about five days. Foreigners and the envoys of tributary allies attended the celebration, which consisted of religious ceremonials, tragic, comic, and dithyrambic contests. (Tragedy, in fact, probably originated from this cult.) The archon eponymous, together with other functionaries, supervised the procession, in which phalli were carried. Isoc. 8.82; Aeschines 3.32ff.; Pausanias 1.29.2; 38.3; Poll. 8.89; cf. A. E. Haigh, *The Attic Theatre*[2] (Oxford 1948) 9ff.

Dokimasia. Magistrates and members of the Boule underwent an examination after their election or sortition and before their entrance into office. At this scrutiny various questions were directed to the individuals about their citizenship, participation in ancestral state cults, possession of a family burial site, treatment of parents, fulfillment of military duties, etc., in order to test their legal qualifications and personal worthiness. Charges could be brought by any citizen against a candidate, and if he failed the dokimasia he was barred from office. The bouleutai and archons were scrutinized before the Boule, others before the court of the thesmothetai. Lys. 16, 31; Arist. *Ath. Pol.* 45.3, 55.2, 59.4; Poll. 8.85f.; see Hignett, *Constitution* 205-8; Harrison 2.200-7.

Eisagogeis ('Introducers'). Officials who brought legal disputes concerning the tribute of the allies into court; they are to be distinguished from magistrates of the fourth century of the same name who dealt with court cases requiring treatment within thirty days (Arist. *Ath. Pol.* 52.2; Heysch. s.v.). The earlier board probably was instituted in the middle of the fifth century, when imperial business vastly increased traffic in the courts; see Hignett, *Constitution* 218; Harrison 2.21.

Eisangelia (impeachment). A procedure for dealing with subversion of the constitution, acts of treason, irreligion, and bribery. Its institution was attributed to Solon. Until Ephialtes' reforms (462/1), the Areopagus had jurisdiction over the defendant; after that, jurisdiction passed to the Boule and the Assembly. Final decision of guilt or innocence was made by the Assembly or the law courts. Aristoph. *Wasps* 590f.; Arist. *Ath. Pol.* 8.4, 43.4, 59.2; Philochorus, *FGrHist* 328 F 195; Plut. *Alkibiades* 22; schol. to Aeschin. 1.16; Poll. 8.53; Harp. s.v.; see Harrison 2.50-9; Rhodes, *Boule* 162-71, *JHS* 99 (1979) 103-14.

Eisphora (property tax). A special tax on capital (not income) which was levied on Athenian citizens and metics by decree of the Assembly after a vote of 'immunity' (adeia) was passed. In a disputed passage, Thucydides states *either* that an eisphora was levied in Attica for the first time in 428 B.C. *or* that in 428 it produced a revenue of 200 talents for the first time. Thuc. 3.19.1; Aristoph. *Knights* 923-6; Antiph. 2.12; Lys. 21.1-4; see Gomme, etc., *HCT* 2.278f.; J. G. Griffith, *AJAH* 2 (1977) 3-7.

Eleven (the). This board was elected by lot and charged with the conviction and punishment of ordinary malefactors (kakourgoi). They were empowered to put criminals to death when they were caught in the act of committing certain crimes. They also oversaw the prisons. Antiph. 5.17; Arist. *Ath. Pol.* 7.3, 52.1; Poll. 8.102; see Harrison 2.17f.

Ephetai (or 'the Fifty-One'). The fifty-one ephetai made up an ancient board of jurors set up beside the Areopagus and constituted to try cases of homicide (except when premeditated); it met under the presidency of the king archon. Details about this college are obscure and controversial. Andoc. 1.78; Dem. 23.37f., 43.57; Arist. *Ath. Pol.* 57.4; Plut. *Sol.* 19; Poll. 8.125; Harp. s.v.; see Jacoby, *FGrHist* IIIb Suppl. 2.108 n. 32; R. S. Stroud, *Drakon's law on homicide* (Berkeley and Los Angeles 1968) 47-9.

Ephors ('overseers'). The ephorate, which consisted of five men elected annually by the people at the beginning of winter, was considered the 'democratic element' of the Spartan government, and it became the preponderant political body in Sparta by the late sixth century. Debate about the origin of the college continues, and it is uncertain whether they were originally an ancient priesthood, or whether they were established by royal decree or by Chilon 'the wise,' or were the heads of the five phylai or komai which superseded the three main Dorian tribes. In any case, the college, presided over by the eponymous ephor, and following the principle of majority rule, was the administrative arm of the state. It presided over the Gerousia and Assembly, served both as prosecutors and as judges in criminal cases, controlled the education of young Spartans, mobilized the army after a declaration of war, and supervised the kings and generals on campaign. Hdt. 1.65, 5.39; Thuc. 5.36; Plato, *Epistulae* 8.354b; Arist. *Pol.* 4.9. 1294b19ff., 5.11.1313a25ff.; Diogenes Laertius 1.68-73; Plut. *Lyk.* 7, *Lysander* 30, *Agis* 16, *Cleomenes* 10; see Michell, *Sparta* 118-34.

Episkopoi ('inspectors'). Athenian officials selected by lot and sent out to watch over the political affairs of allied cities. Theophrastus (quoted by Harpocration) suggests that they were resident officials, but this has been doubted. The nature of their powers is not detailed in the ancient tradition. Aristoph. *Birds* 1022-61; Harp., *Suda*, s.v.; see Meiggs, *Empire* 585.

Euthynai ('corrections'). This term applied to examinations undergone by all magistrates at the expiration of their term of office. Charges of misconduct could be brought to the notice of the ten euthynoi, who referred complaints of a private character to the deme judges (Arist. *Ath. Pol.* 16.5, 26.3, 48.5, 43.1) and public infractions to the thesmothetai. Some ambiguity exists in the inscriptions as to whether an actual euthyna of a magistrate is contemplated or simply his punishment for wrongdoing (e.g. no. 103 line 71 with n. 7) because the verb from which the noun is derived means 'to correct' or 'chastise.' Antiph. 6.43; Andoc. 1.78; Lys. 30.5; Arist. *Ath. Pol.* 48.3-5; Harp. s.v. 'logistai and logisteria' and 'euthynoi'; see Hignett, *Constitution* 203-5.

Generals (Strategoi). Of great political as well as military importance, the ten Athenian generals were directly elected by the people, and they could be reelected continuously. Each general originally represented his own tribe, but by the middle of the fifth century instances occur of a tribe's double representation, either because the tribal restraint was allowed to lapse or because a given statesman was specially eminent and an exception was made. Apart from their command in the field and defense of home territory, the generals enrolled soldiers, appointed trierarchs, and made treaties (provisionally) with other states. Their duties and experience, and the political influence their election reflected, also made them shapers of public policy, and they duly received access to the Boule and were empowered to summon special assemblies. Strategoi are attested in other states besides Athens, e.g. Corinth, Argos, Syracuse. Thuc. 4.118.4, 6.8.2; 6.62.1; Arist. *Ath. Pol.* 22.2-3, 62.3, 66.1; Plut. *Aristeides* 5.1, *Per.* 16.3; Diodorus 13.97.6; see Hignett, *Constitution* 244-51; Fornara, *Generals*, passim.

Heliaia, heliasts. The People in its judicial capacity, the heliaia was a body of 6,000 jurors (heliasts, dikasts) chosen annually by the lot. Solon may have instituted the Heliaia in the sense that it became a function of the Assembly to sit as an appeals court in some instances, but properly speaking the Heliaia is no earlier than the time of Kleisthenes. When Perikles introduced jury payment, the Heliaia was in effect replaced by the separate law courts, one of which was called the Heliaia of the Thesmothetai. Aristoph. *Wasps* 662; Andoc. 1.17; Lys. 10.16;

Arist. *Ath. Pol.* 9.1, 27.4-5, 63.3; Poll. 8.122; Harp. s.v.; see Hignett, *Constitution* 97f., 216-18; Harrison 2.3, 44-9.

Hellenotamiai ('Treasurers of the Hellenes'). This Athenian board of imperial treasurers was instituted in 478/7, and until 411/10 (and excepting 424/3) when there were twenty, it consisted of ten men of the highest property qualification, elected yearly, and capable of reelection. More than one member of a tribe could be represented (cf. the generals). Whether they entered office at the beginning of the archon year (Hekatombaion 1) or on the day of the Panathenaic festival (Hek. 28) is disputed. The board moved from Delos to Athens in 454 and continued to receive the tribute of the allies. It kept accounts of the tribute, paying over to Athena one mna from every talent received (see no. 85), and dispensed funds as directed by the Assembly. After 411 they took over the functions of the kolakretai (see Kolakretai). Thuc. 1.96.2; Poll. 8.114; Hesych, *Suda*, s.v.; see Meiggs, *Empire* 234-8; W. K. Pritchett, *The Choiseul Marble*, Univ. of Calif. Publ.: Classical Studies 5 (Berkeley and Los Angeles 1970) 108-16, *Historia* 26 (1977) 295-306.

Hephaistia. A celebration held by the Athenians in October on the night after the festival of the Apatouria. Men held torches which had been lit from the sacred hearth (in the Prytaneion) in celebration of Hephaistos. Arist. *Ath. Pol.* 54.6; Harp., Hesych. s.v. 'lampas'; see Jacoby, *FGrHist* IIIb Suppl. 1.628.

Heralds (Kerykes). Anyone in private life could serve as a herald (e.g. in the marketplace), but they were regularly appointed and paid by the state to serve as subordinate officials for magistracies where proclamations were frequent (Boule and Assembly, law courts, the nine archons, poletai). When in foreign parts, they were believed to stand under divine protection and were thus inviolable, even in cases of war (except when the war was 'truceless'). A notable and special group at Athens was that of the Eleusinian heralds, who regularly proclaimed a sacred truce in foreign cities in order to ensure the peaceful participation of all Hellenes in the celebration of the Eleusinian Mysteries. One of the heralds was always a member of the clan of the Kerykes, a long-descended family, hereditarily entrusted (together with the Eumolpidai) with the conduct of the Mysteries. Hdt. 7.133f., 137; Andoc. 1.36; Aeschin. 1.20; Arist. *Pol.* 4.12.1299a19, *Ath. Pol.* 62.2, 64.3; Plut. *Per.* 30.3; Poll. 4.94, 103; Harp. s.v. 'Kerykeia'; Bekker, *Anecd.* 255.

Hieropoioi ('makers of sacrifice'). The great centers of cult originally possessed their own hieropoioi, whose name suggests their original function, but these were supplanted in the middle of the fifth century by state officials with wider duties. Some were elected ad hoc for specific sacrificial duties, others were annual officials who served as general superintendents of the temples. Hieropoioi oversaw the sacrifices at the Greater Panathenaia; in Eleusis they became the overseers of temple property; and at the temple of Nemesis they served as treasurers. Dem. 58.29; Arist. *Politics* 6.8.1322b18ff., *Ath. Pol.* 30.2, 54.6f.; see Rhodes, *Boule* 127-31.

Hipparchs. Leaders of the Athenian Cavalry, normally two in number, the hipparchs were elected to office and served as subordinates to the generals but as superiors of the phylarchs. They maintained the cavalry register and had disciplinary power over their men. Aristoph. *Birds* 799 with schol.; Lys. 15.11, 16.13, 26.20; Xen. *Hipparchicus* 1.7; Arist. *Ath. Pol.* 43.1, 61.4, 62.3; Harp., *Suda*, Phot. s.v.

Hyakinthia. A springtime Dorian festival of mourning for Hyakinthos, known from its description as celebrated by the Spartans. It lasted three days and feasting was austere to befit the occasion, except on the second day (probably), when a grand musical celebration was held with singing, dancing, horseback riding, maidens on highly adorned carriages in procession, and a sumptuous feast was provided, with many victims sacrificed. Hdt. 9.7.1, 11.1; Paus. 3.16.2, 19.3; Athenaeus 4.17, p. 139de; Hesych. s.v. 'Hekatombeus'; see Michell, *Sparta* 293f.

Immunity (Adeia). No proposal could be carried to restore an individual's citizen-rights or cancel his debt to the state (without recourse to stratagem; see no. 130) unless a majority of the Assembly, voting in secret with a quorum of six thousand citizens, first granted immunity from the law that barred such action. A vote of immunity also was required when a proposal would run counter to existing legislation, such as when Athena's funds were wanted for purposes other than what the People had decreed and when a property tax (eisphora) was to be levied. Thuc. 2.24.1, with 8.15.1; Andoc. 1.77; Dem. 24.45.

Karneia. A festival celebrated by the Dorians in August, which lasted nine days. Nine tents, each containing nine men, were set up in military fashion in which meals were taken, and youths also engaged in foot races. Hdt. 7.206.1; Thuc. 5.54.2; Ath. 4.19, p. 141ef. See Michell, *Sparta* 99.

Kings of Sparta. The double kingship of the Spartans was hereditary in the houses of the Agiadai and Eurypontidai, both of which claimed descent from Herakles. Originally the sovereign power of the state, they fell under the restraint of the Ephorate after the second Messenian War. By the fifth century the ephors could depose them from office, punish them, and recall them from duty. Each month the kings exchanged oaths with the ephors, swearing to uphold the constitution. From the late sixth century only one king could lead an expedition in the field. The kings were the guardians of Delphic oracles, exercised wardship over heiress-es, and had care of the public highways, as well as being the commanders of the Lacedaemonian army. The honors they were paid are fully described by Herodotus in Book VI. Hdt. 5.75.2, 6.56ff., 7.3; Xen. *Constitution of the Lacedaemonians* 15; Plato, *Epist.* 7.354b; Arist. *Pol.* 3.14.1285a; Plut. *Lyk.* 7.1f.; see Michell, *Sparta* 101-18.

Klerouchs ('allotment holders'). Athenian settlers of the poorest classes (though the more affluent, pentakosiomedimnoi and hippeis, may not always have been excluded specifically – however unlikely to participate, in any case) who were granted a piece of land (kleros) in a territory taken by conquest. The klerouchs maintained Athenian citizenship with all of its privileges and responsibilities and, because of their new status as landholders, could serve as hoplites when needed. Some suppose that they did not always reside on their allotments, but instead received income or rent from the resident population. Thuc. 3.50.2; Aristoph. *Clouds* 203; Xen. *Memorabilia* 2.8.1; Isoc. 4.107; Plut. *Per.* 11.6; see Jones, *Democracy* 168-74; Meiggs, *Empire* 260-2.

Kolakretai ('collectors of hams'). The domestic treasurers of Athens (cf. the Helle-notamiai). Holders of this pre-Kleisthenic magistracy probably served their term in the Conciliar year and dispensed state monies, providing pay to the jurors, general expenses such as the cost of publication of state documents on marble, banquets in the Prytaneion, and pay for such officials as the hieropoioi, heralds, and the priestess of Athena Nike. The office was abolished in 411 B.C. when the Hellenotamiai took over its functions. Schol. to Aristoph. *Birds* 1541; Arist. *Ath. Pol.* 7.3; Hesych., *Suda*, s.v.; see Hignett, *Constitution* 78 n. 1, 91; Jacoby, *FGrHist* IIIb Suppl. 1.117f.

Liturgy. Originally the performance of any public service by a citizen, 'liturgy' is
specially applied in fifth- and fourth-century Athens to a wide range of financial
contributions and personal services to civic life undertaken by the wealthy element of the state, whether citizens or metics. Some liturgies were regular and
shouldered by wealthy individuals in rotation; see, e.g., Choregos. Other liturgies
were extraordinary (ad hoc); see, e.g., Trierarch. Liturgies represented an alternative to taxation and, though they might be onerous, also conferred honor and
esteem on the man performing them. Pseudo-Xen. 3.4 (above, no. 107), Antiphon
5.77, Andoc. *On the Mysteries* 132; Arist. *Ath. Pol.* 27.3, 56.2-5. See J. K.
Davies, *Athenian propertied families 600-300 B.C.* (Oxford 1971) xx-xxxi and
(for legal questions) Harrison 2.232-8.

Logistai ('auditors'). Thirty state accountants chosen by lot from all Athenians;
they audited the books of magistrates handling public money when their books
were closed or when they underwent their euthyna. (Arist. *Ath. Pol.* 48.3, 54.2,
like the references in the lexica, refer to conditions in the fourth century.) Logistai are unattested until 454, when the first of the tribute quota lists mention
them (or rather their number, which permits their identification), and they may
have been established by Ephialtes (462/1) or on the occasion of the transfer of
the imperial treasury from Delos to Athens (454). Their tenure of office may
have run for four years from Great Panathenaia to Great Panathenaia (a pen-
teteris) rather than for merely one year. Andoc. 1.78; Bekker, *Anecd.* 276.17;
see Hignett, *Constitution* 303f.; Pritchett, *The Choiseul Marble* 118.

Metics. Resident aliens in Athens, who numbered 10,000 at one time in the fourth
century; their status and obligations were strictly defined in exchange for the
privilege of permanent domicile. They paid an annual tax (metoikion) and, it is
said, could be enslaved if they failed to pay it. They were prohibited from own-
ing landed property in Attica and in most legal disputes required the sponsorship
of a patron (prostates). Like Athenian citizens, they were liable to military service and subject to some liturgies. Pseudo-Xen. 1.12; Lys. 12.4; Xen. *De Vecti-
galibus* 2.6; Dem. 20.18, 20; Ath. 6.103, p. 272c; Poll. 8.144; Phot., Harp. s.v.
'metoikion'; Harp. s.v. 'prostates.' See D. Whitehead, *The ideology of the Athenian metic*, Cambridge Philological Society Proceedings, Supplement vol. 4
(Cambridge 1977).

Metroon ('The temple of the mother of the gods'). Probably the Old Bouleuterion,
since the temple proper does not appear to have been rebuilt after the destruction suffered by Athens during Xerxes' war. It housed decrees on stelai and probably became the state archive by the end of the fifth century. The name 'Metroon'
is not attested in fifth-century documents. See A. L. Boegehold, *AJA* 76 (1972)
23-30; Rhodes, *Boule* 31.

Oath-Commissioners (Horkotai). Envoys chosen ad hoc to administer oaths to a
community when a treaty dictated such mutual oath-taking. In the fourth century, at least, it was not necessary for (all of?) them to be magistrates (*IG* II^2
16.18-20). The oath-commissioners are to be distinguished from a group of the
same name, only slightly less obscure, which administered oaths to magistrates
upon their entrance into office and from envoys who swore oaths in foreign
parts on behalf of their community.

Opisthodomos. This building (probably not a back room of the Parthenon) served
as the bank of the Treasurers of Athena and the Treasurers of the Other Gods
(from the time of the passage of the Kallias Decrees (no. 119)). It housed coined
money, bullion, and dedications. Aristoph. *Ploutos* 1193 with schol.; Dem.

13.14; see W. S. Ferguson, *The Treasurers of Athena* (Cambridge, Mass. 1932) 131f.

Panathenaia. An Athenian festival celebrated every year in July/August. Every fourth year the celebration was on a grander scale and so was named the Great Panathenaia. Lasting six to nine days, it consisted of musical and athletic competitions, torch and boat races (the latter held at the Piraeus), and of a grand procession, pictured on the frieze of the Parthenon, when the robe of Athena was brought up to the Parthenon. It was also at this festival that tribute assessments were published. Plut. *Theseus* 24.3; Harp., Phot., *Suda*, s.v. 'Panathenaia'; Harp. s.v. 'peplos.'

Paredroi. Assistants to various magistrates, namely, the three major archons, the euthynoi (who had two each), and the Hellenotamiai (one each, and of the same tribe). The archons named their own paredroi, those of the euthynoi were selected by lot, and those of the Hellenotamiai were elected. All underwent dokimasia and euthynai. Andoc. 1.78; Arist. *Ath. Pol.* 48.4, 56.1; Poll. 8.92; Harp., *Suda*, s.v.

Phratry ('brotherhood'). A social unit antecedent to Cleisthenes' reform, which was absorbed by it. One proof of Athenian citizenship consisted in membership in a phratry, all members of which regarded themselves as relations (gennētai). Each phratry had its leader (phratriarchos), priest, and special place of assembly. The major festival for all phratries was the Apatouria, when votes were taken on the admission of new members. Arist. *Pol.* 6.4.1319b19ff., *Ath. Pol.* 21.6; Harp. s.v. 'Gamelia'; see Hignett, *Constitution* 55–60; Jacoby, *FGrHist* IIIb Suppl. 1.321–3.

Phrourarch ('Garrison commander'). An Athenian phrourarch is attested (in the fifth century) only at Erythrae. Perhaps such commanders later acquired a less invidious title, such as archon. See Meiggs, *Empire* 214.

Phylobasileis ('tribe-kings'). Whatever their earlier role as heads of the four archaic Athenian tribes, in historical times they exercised religious functions and, with the king archon, were in charge of the homicide court at the Prytaneion for cases in which the slayer was unknown or death the (accidental) result of contact with an inanimate object. Arist. *Ath. Pol.* 8.3, 57.4; Pol. 8.111, 120; see Hignett, *Constitution* 312f.

Plynteria. A festival at Athens which took place in spring (25 Thargelion) and in which the clothes of Athena were washed. On that day it was not considered propitious to conduct business of importance. Xen. *Hell.* 1.4.12; Plut. *Alk.* 34.1f.; Phot. s.v. 'Kallynteria and Plynteria.'

Polemarch. This Athenian archon commanded the Athenian military until his supersession by the ten generals either in 487/6, when the archonship ceased to be elective, or prior to the battle of Marathon in 490. He retained sacrificial duties and judicial competence over foreigners and resident aliens. Arist. *Ath. Pol.* 3.58; Poll. 8.91; Bekker, *Anecd.* 310.9; Harp. s.v.; see Hignett, *Constitution* 39f., 75, 169ff.; Fornara, *Generals* 6–12; Hammond, *Studies* 346ff.

Poletai ('sellers'). Ten officials, elected by lot from each tribe, who farmed out state contracts – for tax collection, mining-rights, rent, the purchase and erection of stelai, etc. – and sold off confiscated property. Arist. *Ath. Pol.* 7.3, 47.2; Harp., Phot., *Suda*, s.v.; see Rhodes, *Boule* 96f.

Proedroi. The revolution of 411 in Athens was effected when five proedroi (the leaders of the oligarchs; the term means 'presiding officers') coöpted 100 men including themselves, each of whom chose three more, in order to create the Council of Four Hundred, the governing body of the oligarchy in 411. These proedroi are to be distinguished from the fourth-century board of nine proedroi

(Arist. *Ath. Pol.* 44.2). Thuc. 8.67; *Ath. Pol.* 29–32; see Hignett, *Constitution* 356ff.

Promethia. This Athenian festival, like the Hephaistia, was celebrated in the Kerameikos, in connection with the Apatouria, and was based on thanksgiving for the gift of fire. Athens seems to have fostered the cult of Hephaistos, however, in preference to that of Prometheus. Schol. to Aristoph. *Frogs* 131; Hesych., Harp. s.v. 'lampas.'

Proxenia, proxenos. An individual from one *polis* with special ties to another often was publicly recognized by that city as its 'friend' or 'guest-friend.' As such he would naturally represent the interests of that community in his own. This status was also granted to metics by decrees of the People (in Athens and in some other cities) and, in Athens, entitled the recipient to access to the court of the polemarch without need for the normally obligatory introduction by an Athenian acting as patron (prostates) of metics. Frequently conferred together with proxenia were other privileges, such as freedom from liturgies, the right to possession of houses in Attica, and isoteleia, the condition of being subject to no more obligations to the state than were the citizens themselves. Thuc. 2.29.1, 2.85.5; Dem. 52.5; Aeschin. 3.42; Plut. *Alk.* 14.1; Poll. 3.59; see Meiggs, *Empire* 215–19.

Prytaneion. The town hall of a Greek city-state, originally the meeting place of the magistrates and the location of the sacred hearth of the polis. In Athens it was used to entertain dignitaries, certain magistrates, and even seers, and it was also the residence of the archon eponymous. A law court at Athens also was known as the 'court at the Prytaneion' (Andoc. 1.78). Hdt. 1.146.2; Thuc. 2.15.2; Aristoph. *Peace* 1084, *Birds* 521 with schol.; Paus. 1.18.3; and see 'Phylobasileis'.

Prytaneis ('presidents'). The Conciliar year, or year of the Boule, was (from at least the time of Ephialtes' reforms) divided into ten parts, so that the fifty men of each of the ten tribes served collectively as the prytaneis or presiding officers of the Boule for one tenth of the year. The presiding tribe was named 'the tribe in prytany.' During their prytany, the prytaneis lived and dined at state expense in the Tholos, a circular building next to the Bouleuterion. The order of the prytanies followed no set pattern but was determined by lot; nine separate sortitions were held in the course of the year so that the order in prytany of the tribes could not be known until the allotment of the ninth. The prytaneis convened the Boule and Assembly, presided over them, fixed the agenda of the Boule, and heard judicial complaints which fell in the Boule's purview. One member of the tribe in prytany was picked by lot to serve every twenty-four hours as epistates or presiding officer, and he chaired the Boule and Assembly. On duty continuously, he kept in his possession the keys to the state treasuries and the public seal. His name appears in the preamble of most decrees dating from the middle of the fifth century (e.g. no. 119A1f.: 'Mnesitheos w|as Secretary, Eupeithes presided'). Arist. *Ath. Pol.* 43.2; Harp. s.v.; Poll 8.95f.; see Rhodes, *Boule* 16–25.

Recorders of the Laws (Anagrapheis). When the democracy was restored in 410, the need felt for authoritative publication and revision of the laws led to the establishment of a commission of Recorders of the Laws, whose term of office was to be four months, and whose number is unknown. The complexity of the task led to the commission's continuation in office until 404 (and, on the fall of the Thirty, it recommenced). Its members, who were paid, were closely supervised by the Boule and Assembly. Lys. 30.2 (after the Thirty); schol. to

Aeschin. 1.39; Poll. 8.112; see R. S. Stroud, *Drakon's law on homicide* (Berkeley and Los Angeles 1968) 20-8.

Satrap. The title of the governors of the Persian satrapies or provinces; they possessed wide authority in their domains, even to the point of acting quasi-independently, though military and civil officials were appointed by the Great King to keep them in check. The subdivision of the empire into satrapies by Dareios the Great remained fundamental in subsequent times.

Secretary of the Boule. The most important of the public secretaries; his name appears on the prescript of Athenian decrees. A new secretary was elected in each prytany and, though he was always a member of the Boule, he was never a member of the tribe in prytany. The secretary was responsible for drafting and publishing decrees and maintaining an archive of related records. Arist. *Ath. Pol.* 54.3-5; Athen. 9.72, p. 407c; Harp., *Suda*, s.v.; Poll. 8.98; see Rhodes, *Boule* 134-7.

Summoner (Kleter). A witness (two in the fourth century) who accompanied a plaintiff when he summoned his antagonist to court. In cases of default, the witness testified to the issuance of the summons. In public cases, public summoners made formal announcement of the charge being brought and named the day when appearance before the magistrate was required. Aristoph. *Clouds* 1218, *Wasps* 408 with schol.; Dem. 21.87; Hesych., Harp., *Suda*, s.v.; Bekker, *Anecd.* 272.6; see Harrison 2.85f.

Thargelia. A Maytime festival (7 Thargelion) in honor of Apollo's birthday. Men and boys competed in choruses; the archon selected the choregoi and supervised the preparations for the performance. Antiph. 6.11-13; Lys. 21.1; Arist. *Ath. Pol.* 56.3; Harp. s.v.

Thesmothetai. The six junior archons, though the term sometimes applies to all nine. They were charged with the removal of discrepancies in existing laws; some believe that prior to Ephialtes' reforms (462/1), they could indict unconstitutional measures before the Areopagos. Unlike the other archons, they seem to have been concerned solely with the administration of justice, and this in spheres outside the competency of the others. Their other major duties were to fix trial dates and assign courts to the appropriate magistrates, preside over law courts in a variety of cases involving wrongdoing against the state (e.g. Eisangelia) and those in which defendants from allied cities were subject to penalties of death, exile, or loss of citizen-rights. Thuc. 1.126.8; Aeschin. 3.38f.; schol. to Aeschin. 1.16; Arist. *Ath. Pol.* 3.4-5, 59; Harp. s.v.; Poll. 8.87; Bekker, *Anecd.* 184.11; see Hignett, *Constitution* 76f., 211; Harrison 2.12-17.

Treasurers of Athena. The 'Treasurers of the sacred monies of Athena' (though their nomenclature varies) were magistrates/cult officials of great antiquity, ten in number (after Kleisthenes), of the highest census class (pentakosiomedimnoi: possessors of income totalling at least 500 medimnoi of grain or its equivalent), and elected by lot according to tribe. They were annual officials, whose tenure of office ran from Panathenaia to Panathenaia, though they rendered accounts to the logistai collectively in four boards at the time of the Great Panathenaia. They superintended the funds of the goddess, dedicatory offerings (see Opisthodomos) and the great statue of Athena. Athena's treasury became the major treasury of the state. Arist. *Ath. Pol.* 7.3, 8.1, 47.1; Poll. 8.97; Harp., *Suda*, s.v.; see Ferguson, *Treasurers of Athena* 96ff., 153ff.; Hignett, *Constitution* 323-6.

Tribes (Athenian). All Greek cities were organized into tribes, whether authentic social units or patently artificial constructions. Athens was originally divided into four 'Ionic' or 'Attic' tribes (Geleontes, Hopletes, Argideis, Aigikoreis), probably natural in origin, in which membership was hereditary. Kleisthenes reapportioned the Athenians into a new grouping of ten tribes (see Demes). These became the basic political units of the state, though vestiges of the older tribal arrangement lingered on (see Phylobasileis). Thus Athenians voted by tribe, and most collegiate boards consisted of ten men, each from his tribe; Athenians fought by tribe, at least initially, and developed and maintained religious tribal associations in spite of the artificial genesis of the Kleisthenic tribes. Hdt. 5.66; Arist. *Pol.* 3.2.1257b37, *Ath. Pol.* 21; Poll. 8.109f.; see Hignett, *Constitution* 51-5, 137-42; V. Ehrenberg, *The Greek State* (Oxford 1960) 9-16.

Trierarch. A wealthy man, selected by the generals, who maintained a warship in good order for a year as a compulsory public service or liturgy. (See Liturgy.) Late in the Peloponnesian War, because of relative impoverishment, two trierarchs were allotted to each vessel. This duty could be avoided only if the designee had already performed it within the past two years, possessed an exemption, or could demonstrate that someone else was better able to perform it (antidosis). The ship, normally its equipment, and the pay of the crew were provided by the state; the trierarch was required the keep the vessel in good repair during the year of his trierarchy. If he did not (barring unavoidable disasters), legal action was taken against him by his successor. The trierarch served as captain of his ship. Aristoph. *Knights* 911ff. with schol. at 912; Thuc 6.31; Lys. 21.2, 32.26f.; Arist. *Ath. Pol.* 61.8; Poll. 1.119; see Jones, *Democracy* 56f., 85-8; Harrison 2.233-6.

INDEXES

I. Personal and Geographical Names

All references are to item numbers and line numbers where appropriate. Except where patronymics, demotics, or other place-names are given in the translated texts or are obvious from context, I do not distinguish between men of the same name. Identity is not necessarily implied.

Abbateya, 45
Abydenes, 142 II.25
Academy, Athens, 30A; 127B
Acarnanians, 130
Achaea, 6B; 132 n. 2
Achaeans, 6A; 9A; 29
Achaimenides, 72
Acharna, 89B.36
Acharnai, 44A; 110; 140.1
Acharnaians, 89B.2f.
Acherdous, 109B; 134.25
Achilleus, 39A.1
Adeimantos son of Leukolophides of
    Skambonidai, 147D(B).53
Aegina, 1A at 895/3; 4DE; 43 n. 1; 74B; 78.3
Aeginetans, 55.17; 59.3
Aegospotami, 147 n. 11; 166 n. 3
Aetna, 2A
Aetolia, 67C
Aetolians, 3C
Agamestor son of Laios, 26A
Agariste, 26 n. 3
Agathoia, 89B.28
Agathokles, 125.4f.
Agenor son of Akestor, 26A
Agora, 142 II.24
Agorakritos, 90 n. 2
Agoratos, 155.26f., n. 6
Agryle, 65B.1; 118B.17; 151
Ahura, 34
Ahuramazda, 34
Aiakos son of Zeus, 26A
Aiantis, 58; 82 n. 1; 126.10, 21; 136 n. 2;
    144.29; 154.3
Aias, 21.2; 26A; 44A.14
Aigantians, 85.17
Aigeis, 115 n. 6; 134 n. 5; 136.54f.; 139.2;
    154.5; 158.6
Aigilia, 154.35
Aischines, 100.30; of Perithoidai, 142.5;
    tyrant of Sicyon, 39B.22
Aischron, 126.17
Aixone, 126.9; 144.12

Akamantis, 15B.3; 68.2; 115.30; 124.6f.;
    125.12; 134.9, 11, 33; 154.10f.; 161.1f.
Akestor son of Epilykos, 26A
Akr[- -, 85.20
Akropolis, Athens, 49 n. 1; 55.11f.; 68.26,
    75C.36, 38; 81.12; 94C.8; 99.38; 100.18;
    103.60; 104; 106.11; 113 n. 4; 118A;
    119A.4, 15, B.5–13 passim; 127B; 133.25;
    136.25; 138.9; 140.51; 149.15; 155.29;
    156.43; 160.23f.; 161.36; 162.33; 163.8;
    165.8; 166.39; Corinth, 53
Akryptes, 153.6
Akryptos, 78.130
Alexias, archon 405/4, 166.6
Aleximachos, 153.6; of Erechtheis, 78.70
Alkibiades, 147D(B).118; son of Kleinias,
    40B; 41B.2; 98 n. 1; 144 n. 8; 147B,
    D(A).12, nn. 3, 11, 21; 156 n. 8; 159;
    162.31; 163.3
Alkimos, 66.1
Alkisthenes, 134.18
Alkmeon, 65B.1
Alkmeonidai, 40; 41D.9; 65 n. 3
Alopeke, 41B.2; 109A; 149 n. 1; 151;
    154.23f.
Alpheios R., 27
Alyattes, 1A at 605/3
Amasis, 24A.4, n. 5
Ambracia, 39 n. 5
Ambraciots, 59.11
Amoibichos, 24A.5, D
Amorges, 95O
Amphictyony, 15B.28; 16B
Amphidamas, 7BC
Amphikedes, 78.60; 158.22
Amphiktyonians, 1A at 591/0; 16B; 57 n. 6;
    82.7f.
Amphipolis, 62
Amyklai, 88A.8
Anacreon, 2C; 32
Anactorians, 59.10
Anagyrous, 110; 154 n. 15
Anaitios of Sphettos, 154.20

217

I. Index of personal and geographical names

I. Index of personal and geographical names

I. Index of personal and geographical names

I. Index of personal and geographical names

I. Index of personal and geographical names

I. Index of personal and geographical names

I. Index of personal and geographical names

I. Index of personal and geographical names

Oenophyta, 42 n. 1; 95J
Oianthia, 87 passim
Oianthians, 14.2; 87 passim
Oineis, 98.3; 115 n. 7; 134 n. 4; 136 nn. 13, 15; 154.7
Oiniades, 160.7, 30
Oinobios of Decelea, 156.47
Oinoe, 127B
Oion, 113.11; 134.17
Olenos, 132.6
Oleros, 132 n. 2
Oloros, 26 n. 6; 109B; king of Thrace, 26 n. 6
Olympia, 116A
Omphaleon, 12A
Onasippos, 68 n. 1
Onasos, 133.4
Onetor, 92 n. 2
Onetorides, archon 527/6, 23C.1
Onomakles, 151
Opisthodomos, 119A.15ff., B.24; 134.20, n. 10
Opuntians, 47.11, 14
Opus, 47.33
Orchomenos, 12A
Oropus, 90A
Orthagoras, 10.15
Oulios son of Agenor, 26A
Oxylos, 3C

Pabis, 24F.1
Pacheia, 169B.9
Paiania, 144.27; 166.1
Paionidai, 95M(2).3; 158.2f., 15f.
Paionios of Mende, 135.3
Palaiskiathos, 160.7f., 30f.
Pallas, 42
Pallene, 144.31f.; 149 n. 1; 151
Pamphylia, 95J
Pamphyloi, 2 n. 1; 12C(1).8
Panaitios, 147D(B).63
Panamyes son of Kasbollis, 70.12, 30f.
Pandionis, 101.8; 115.28f., n. 6; 134.7, 21; 144.18; 154.37
Pankrates, 55 n. 11
Pantainetos, 109A
Pantaleon, 78.7
Panteleon of Pisa, 12A
Panyassis, 70.15f., n. 5
Paralos son of Perikles, 96A; 117.13f.
Parianians, 142 II.15
Parians, 136.62
Parium, 6 n. 1
Parnassus, 16D
Paros, 1A Heading, line 3
Partheniai, 9A
Parthenon, 79B; 94ABC.3; 106 n. 2; 119 n. 3; 120; 141.5; 143 n. 1

Parthia, 34.2
Pasikrateia, 91.5f.
Pasiphon of Phrearrhioi, 154.35
Pausanias son of Kleombrotos, 61 passim
Pedasians, 85.5
Pegai, 101.5
Peisandros, 148
Peisias, 147C
Peisistratidai, 1A at 511/10; 39A.1; 40A
Peisistratos of Caria, 147D(A).9; son of Hippias, 23C.6; 37.1; tyrant of Athens, 1A at 561/0, 511/10; 1B at 562/1; 23 n. 6; 26 n. 6; 30; 31; 39B.23f.; 40; 41A.1
Pelagon, 16A
Pelarge, 140 n. 12
Pelargikon, 140.55ff.
Pelasgian Wall, 1A at 511/10
Peleqos son of Eudamos, 24A.5
Pelion, 60.7
Pelleneans, 10.30f., 35
Peloponnesus, 12A; 39 n. 3; 52; 84; 134.18
Pelops, 12A; 127A.697
Pentelicus, 120.30f.
Perdikkas of Macedon, 1A at 420/19; 128.18, 27, 47f., 50; 144 n. 9
Pergase, 142. 4
Periander of Corinth, 39 n. 3
Perikleidas, 67A.1138
Perikles son of Perikles of Cholargos, 96 n. 6; 154.7, 11, 13, 18; 161.5f.; son of Xanthippos, 74; 79AB; 94ABC.5; 95H; 96; 104; 109AB; 110; 115.29f.; 116ABC; 117.13; 122D; 123B; 154 n. 5
Perinthians, 142 II.22
Perithoidai, 142.5; 145A
Perkothariai, 47.22, 27
Persephone, 75 n. 3; 91 n. 3; 106 n. 1; 140 n. 8; see also Kore
Persepolis, 45–6
Persia, 45; 65; 72; 138 n. 3
Persians, 1B at 472/1, 461/0; 21.3; 34; 35.28; 72; 95GIJ; 96A; 106 n. 2
Phaeinos, 126.3, 14
Phaidon, archon 476/5, 62
Phaidros son of Pythokles of Myrrhinous, 147D(B).112
Phainippides, 23 n. 7
Phainippos, archon 490/89, 23(D).1, n. 7; of Paionidai, 158.3; son of Phrynichos, 128.2, n. 1
Phaistians, 149 n. 4
Phalanthos of Alopeke, 154.23; of Sparta, 9A
Phaleron, 79AC; 106.27f., 33f.; 158.17
Phanodikos, 153.13; son of Hermokrates, 20.1
Phantokles, 100.32, 35
Phanyllos, 78.71
Pharsalus, 7D

I. Index of personal and geographical names

I. Index of personal and geographical names

II. Index of subjects and terms

II. Subjects and Terms[1]

All references are to item numbers.

1 For Athenian archons, see Appendix I; for Athenian demes, see Appendix II; for Athenian
 months, see p. xxii above; for Athenian tribes, see p. xxiii above.

II. Index of subjects and terms

punishment of leaders, 65
revolutionary governments, 148-51; 170
victory dedications, 43; 50; 83
walls, 79
wars: Aegina, 43 n. 1; Boeotia and Chalcis,
    42, 43 n. 1; Persia, *see* Persian Wars;
    Phocis (Sacred War), 16; Samos, 113;
    Sparta, *see* Peloponnesian Wars;
    Syracuse, 146
Athlothetai, 154.5. *See also* Glossary
Attic letters, 95E. *See also* Glossary
Attic stelai, 147ACD
Autokrator, 119A.9
Axon, 15B.10, n. 8; *see also* Glossary

Basileus (king): Aetna, 2A; Andros, 137 n. 11;
    Argos, 89B.43, n. 11; Athens, 1A
    Heading, line 3 and at 895/3; King
    Archon, 15.6,(?)12; 140.54, 59; *see
    also* Glossary, 'Basileus'; Chios, 19 n. 1;
    Cyrene, 18.27; Egypt, 24A, G; Lydia,
    1A at 605/3; 28; Macedonia, 1A at
    420/19; Miletus, 66 n. 3; Orchomenos,
    12A; Persia, 34; 35.1, 21; 61B.1;
    65B.2; 95 passim; 111; 138.14; Sparta,
    1B at 758/7; 2B; 9A; 12C.3; 39C; 104;
    127A; *see also* Glossary, 'Kings of
    Sparta'
Boule
    Andros, 137B.3, 17
    Argos, 89B.45
    Athens (of 400), 19 n. 2; (of 500), and
        addition to Bouleutic Oath, 97.12;
        cares for triremes, 94C.9; 161.14ff.; as
        date (?), 44B.12; determines particular
        matters, 92.81ff.; 146; elects heralds,
        133.52; 140.22, 30; hears envoys,
        103.12ff.; 128.26; and listing of
        responsibilities, 107.3.1-4; members
        elected for special tasks, 93.15ff.;
        103.66ff.; mobilizes forces, 55.37; oath
        to Chalcis of, 103.4ff.; performs ostra-
        cism (?), 41A.2; presides over ostracism,
        41B.1; protects benefactors, 155.30ff.;
        160.17f.; read to by Herodotus (!), 1B
        at 445/4; required by Assembly to hear
        certain matters, 100.39; requires that
        business be taken up, 106.5f.; role in
        tribute payment of, 98, 136 passim;
        supervises officials, 106.14f.; 119.9f.,
        20; 140.41f.; *see also* Glossary
    Chalcis, 103.62
    Cnossus, 89B.41
    Erythrae, 71 passim
    Samos, 166.8
    Tylissos, 89B.41

Bouleuterion, 41A.2; 133.56; 136.24f. *See
    also* Glossary

Calendric equations, 154; 158; intercalation
    of calendar, 140.53; 158 n. 8
Cavalry (hippeis): Athenian, 83.1; 107.1.3;
    131; 154 n. 3; *see also* Glossary; Persian,
    48; 60.12; Syracusan, 52; Thessalian,
    7 n. 1
Chariots, 7 n. 1
Choiseul Marble, 154; 158
Choregoi, 107.3.4. *See also* Glossary
Chronography, 1; 3A
Coinage, Athenian, 164; Athenian decree on,
    97; of Pheidon, 4CDE; in Sparta, 167
Collectors (eklogeis): of grain, 140.14f.; of
    tribute, 133.7, 9. *See also* Glossary
Colonies: Amphipolis (Ennea Hodoi), 62;
    Athenian, 136.58; Brea, 100; Colophon,
    99.41, n. 4; Croton, 6; Cyrene, 17-18;
    Megara (Sicilian), 5; Naupactus, 47;
    Naxos (Sicilian), 5; Neapolis, 156;
    Potidaea, 129; Tarentum, 9; Thasian,
    153.7f.; Thurii, 108
Commissioners (epimeletai), 92.40, nn. 3, 14,
    16, 19; 133.37f., 46
    for the Mainland (Thasos), 169(B).3, 4f., 8
    or superintendents (epistatai): of accounts
        (Cyrene), 18.21; of Athena's statue,
        114A(1).3f., (2).3, B1; of the mint,
        97.5, 10, 14; of the Parthenon,
        119B.8, 10; 120.1; of the Propylaia,
        118B.4, 7; of temples, 119A.18f.
    (syngrapheis), 71B.2; 92.3; 140.3; 148.
        See also Glossary
Council of Elders: Locris, 33(A).10; Sparta,
    12C.3. *See also* Glossary
Court fees (prytaneia), 92.32, n. 14; 107.1.16.
    See also Glossary
Cow and panoply, 98.42; 100.11f.; 136.57.
    See also Glossary
Curses, 18.42ff.; 33.12ff.; 57.40ff.; 63.30ff.;
    71A.15ff., B.16ff.; 99.52ff.; 153.5, 11

Daidouchos, 140.25
Dedications, 28; 30A; 33(E); 36-8; 42-3; 46;
    49-51; 53-4; 59; 64; 80; 83; 91; 112;
    129; 135
Dekadouchos, 170A
Demarch: Athens, 22AB; 90B.2f., 32f.;
    140.8f., 13, 21; 151; *see also* Glossary;
    Chios, 19 n. 1
Demes, 15 n. 1; 22AB; 55 n. 8; 140.9;
    155 n. 3; 166.34. *See also* Glossary and
    Appendix II
Demioi, 11.4

II. Index of subjects and terms

Demiourgoi: Argos, 36.1, 12; Chaleion, 87.16; Locris, 33(E).1; Thasos, 169.7f. *See also* Glossary

Diadikasia, 107.3.4, n. 9; 136.15, n. 7

Dikasts (jurors): Athens, 103.4, n. 2; 136.16; *see also* Heliaia; Halicarnassus, 70.20

Diobelia, 154.10–23 passim; 158.8–52 passim

Divorce regulations (Gortyn), 88A

Dockyard superintendents, 166.30f.

Dockyards, 84, 119A.32

Dokimasia, 107.3.4. *See also* Glossary

Eisagogeis, 98.71; 136.7, 13, 59f. *See also* Glossary

Eisangelia, 65B.1; 107.3.5; 140.58f. *See also* Glossary

Eisphora (property tax), 92.56, n. 23; 119B.17, 19; 131B; 146c.5. *See also* Glossary

Eleven (the), 97.8; 151; 161 n. 5. *See also* Glossary

Enomotarch, 57.26

Entry fees (Locris), 47.8

Envoys and embassies, 1A at 556/5; 52; 81.14; 18; 89B. 38–40; 95CGI; 102.3; 103.16f., 36f.; 107.1.18; 124.1; 125.1; 128.16f., 24f., 27, 50f.; 136.6; 137A.6, 8, 23; 138.10, 13; 140.19; 156.39, 46; 151; 157; 162.45; 166.7, 14, 20, 24f.

Ephetai or the Fifty-One, 15.13, 17, 19f., 35f. *See also* Glossary

Ephors, 1B at 758/7; 39B.17; 67C; 167. *See also* Glossary

Epimenioi (Miletus), 66 passim

Episkopoi (inspectors), 71A.12f., B.13f.; 98.7. *See also* Glossary

Epoptai, 75B.7

Eunomia, 12A

Euthynai, 44B.8; 95C; 103 n. 7; 107.3.2; 119A.27; 130; 136.15, 30, 37; 140.20. *See also* Glossary

Euthynos: Teos, 63B.3. *See also* Glossary, 'Euthynai'

Exile(s): Athens, 15.11; 65; 159; *see also* Ostracism; Chalcis, 103.7, 73; Erythrae, 71A.25, B.26; Halicarnassus, 70.37; Miletus, 66.2f.; Selymbria, 162.16

Exposure of children, 88A.8f.

Fines and punishments: Andros, 137B.10ff.; Argos, 36.11f.; Athens, 15 passim; 44B.5ff.; 68.15ff.; 97.3, 8, 12; 98.36–43; 100A.20ff.; 103.4ff.; 116AB; 119B.17ff.; 128.38f.; 130; 133.50f.; 136.9ff., 15f., 27ff., 31ff., 36ff.; 147; 151; 161.20f.; Chalcis,

103.33ff., 71ff.; Cyrene, 18.36–40; Dreros, 11; Eleusis, 75B.1–4, C.28–31; 140.20, 58f.; Elis–Heraia, 25.5ff.; Erythrae, 71AB passim; Halicarnassus, 70.32ff.; Locris, 33(A).7ff., (E); Locris (Eastern), 47.43ff.; Miletus, 66.6ff.; 92 passim; Oianthia–Chaleion, 87.4ff.; Teos, 63; Thasos, 153; 169A.2f., B

First-fruits, 75.32; 140; 156.37, 64; *see also* Tribute

Four Hundred (the), 148; 150–1

Generals (strategoi)
 allied Greek, 57.28f.
 Arcadian, 12A
 Athenian, appointment of trierarchs by, 55.19f.; attend suits arising from tribute, 133.40; bring charges of treason, 151; care for triremes, 161.10; 166.27f.; defense of territory by, 103.77; dispatch heralds (?), 97 n. 12 (cf. 136.40f.); elected, 107.1.3; election for Sicilian campaign of, 146 b, 2f.; fined at euthyna, 130; instructed by Assembly, 146C.9; management of funds by, 97.6; 113 n. 5; 118 n. 9; 126.7–9; 18–21; 134.3ff.; 18ff.; 144 passim; 154.17, 35; 156.28, 47; 161.5ff., mobilize forces, 55.38; named 61B(2).3f.; 78.5, 62; 95JK; 110; 115; precedence in Assembly of, 128.56; protection of state benefactors by, 149.24; 156.53f.; 160.18f.; provide money to envoys (?), 166.35; see to erection of stelai, 162.33, n. 6; 166.39; as step to tyranny, 41A.1; subject to prosecution, 161 n. 5; supervision of oaths by, 81.9; 103.20, 44; supervision of sacrifices by, 103.68; supervision of tribute payments by, 136.45ff.; taking of oaths by, 115.28ff.; 162.28; treatment by allies of 107.1.18; *see also* Glossary
 Carthaginian, 165.9f., 15
 Persian, 95G
 Pisatan, 12A
 Samian, 166.8
 Spartan, 12A; 39B.17f.

Geonomoi, 100.6

Grain for horses, 154 passim. *See also* katastasis

Hatarmabattiš, 45

Heiresses (Gortyn), 88C

Heliaia (heliasts), 92 n. 13; 98.39, 71; 136.14, 49; 161 n. 6; of the Thesmothetai, 97.1; 103.75f. *See also* Glossary

II. Index of subjects and terms

Hellenotamiai (treasurers of the Greeks): assume duties of kolakretai, 15.9; 155.10f., 35f.; 166.39; disburse funds from Athena's Treasurers, 118B.11; 134.2; 144 passim; 150.11f.; 154 passim; 158 passim; disburse funds from generals, 118B.16f., nn. 8, 9; disburse funds to other treasurers, 119B.21; funds of, 119A. 6; receive and record tribute, 85; 95M; 98.20, 43f.; 133.17f.; 142.3; receive money from Neapolis, 156.33; record mints of allied cities, 97.1. *See also* Glossary

Hellespontine guards, 128.36f., 39f.

Helots, 9AB; 12C.5; 13; 61C; 67

Hephaistia, 107.3.4. *See also* Glossary

Heralds: Andros, 137.9, 12; Athens, 81.17; 97.9, 11; 107.1.17; 122BCE; 133.51; 136.4, 40, 50; 140.21f.; 155.13; 165.15. *See also* Glossary

Herms, 105B; 147B

Hetaireia, 18.16

Hierophant, 140.24

Hieropoioi: Athens, 71A.4, B.5, 6; 154.6; Eleusis, 75C.37; 106.1; 140; Nemesis, 90B.33; the Other Gods, 119A.13, 19. *See also* Glossary

Hipparchs, 83.1; 107.1.3. *See also* Glossary

Homicide law, 15; 33.14

Honorary decrees, 138; 149; 152; 155–6; 160–2; 165–6

Hoplites, 7D; 67A.1143; 107.1.2, 2.1; 162.29

Hostages, 42A.1, B.3; 103.47f.; 115 n. 1; 162.9, 38f.

Hyakinthia, 89B.17. *See also* Glossary

Immunity (adeia), 119B.16, n. 14; 144.15, 28, 30, 33. *See also* Glossary

Inheritance: Gortyn, 88B; Locris, 33A.3ff.; Locris–Naupactus, 47.16ff., 29ff., 35ff.

Initiate in the Mysteries, 75 passim

Inventory of Athena's treasures, 141; 143; cf. 119A.19ff.

Isonomia, 39A

Karneia, 2C. *See also* Glossary

Katastasis, 131 n. 1; *see also* Grain for horses

Kings of Sparta. *See* Basileus

Klerouchs, 44; 62; 103 n. 6; 129. *See also* Glossary

Knights, *see* Cavalry

Kolakretai, 81.13; 106.9; 136.25f., 52; 139.8; 140.51f. *See also* Glossary

Kosmoi (Crete), 11.1–3; 89B.42

Lacedaemonian alliances and treaties, *see* Spartan alliances and treaties

Laws: Argos, 36; Athens: of Drakon, 1B at 624/3. 594/3, nn. 16, 20; 15; of Solon, 1B at 594/3; 22; of Kleisthenes, 22; 41A–C; 75; 86; 148; Chaleion, 87B; Chios, 19; Dreros, 11; Gortyn, 88; Halicarnassus, 70; Locrian, 33; 47; Miletus, 66; Samos, 166.15; Sparta, 12C.3, 27; Teos, 63; Thasos, 153; 169

Leagues: Arcadian, 167 n. 1; Amphictyonic, 1 n. 4; 16; Athenian, *see* Athenian alliances and treaties; Delian, 71; Hellenic, 59; Peloponnesian, 73; 80; Sybarite, 29.1f.

Lelantine War, 7

Lexiarchic registers, 55.29f. with n. 8

Logistai, 85; 106.23; 119A.8f., 27; 134; 158 passim. *See also* Glossary

Megarian Decree, 122; 123

Melian Dialogue, 144 n. 13

Memorials, tombs and cenotaphs, 14; 20; 21; 51; 60; 101

Mercenaries, 24; 146dg.4f. (?)

Messenian Wars, 1B at 746/5; 9; 12; 67; 73

Metaxenia, 137.26 and n. 8

Metics (aliens): Athens, 55.7, 13, 30; 86; 107.1.10; 147D(A).33; 164 n. 2; *see also* Glossary; Chalcis, 103.52f.

Mint and coinage, 97.5, 13f., n. 3

Myesis, 75 n. 1

Mysteries: dedication of first-fruits at, 140.25; Great, 75C.12; Lesser, 75B.33f., C.10; profanation of, 105B; 147

Naukrariai (naukraros), 22A–C

Nomothetai, 136 n. 11

Numerical system, Greek, *see* Introduction

Oath-Commissioners (horkotai), 81.10; 102.4; 103.17, 28, 45; 136.11. *See also* Glossary

Oaths, 18 passim; 47.10ff.; 57; 70.24–8; 71A.15ff., B.16ff.; 81.1ff.; 82.9; 87.17f.; 88A.1, 7ff.; 92.69ff.; 95D; 97.12; 99.40f.; 102.3ff.; 103.3–47; 106.17f.; 115.15ff.; 124.10ff.; 125.21ff.; 136.11, 40f.; 162.28ff.

Obol (? Athenian fund), 158.10 with n. 6, 13, 16

Obols (spits), 4E

Oikistes ('founder'), 100 n. 3

Olympic Games, 1B at 607/6; 2C; 3; 4AB

Olympic Truce, 3B

Oracles, 6A; 9A; 10.4; 12C.3; 16B; 17; 18.7–11; 58; 61D; 65B.2; 91(?); 103.64f.; 137A.31ff.; 140.5, 26, 34

Oratory, 74

II. Index of subjects and terms

Ostracism, 41; 55.45f.; 65; 76; 108C; 109; 145
Ostraka, 41D; 105 n. 1

Panathenaia, 26; 39A, 94C.6; 107.3.4; 119A.27f.; 126 n. 3; Great, 71A.2, B.3; 100.12; 119AB.28; 128.9f., 31; 136.26f., 32, 57; 143.1f.; 154.6. *See also* Glossary
Paredroi, 144 passim; 154.20; 158 passim. *See also* Glossary
Parian Marble, 1A
Peace of Kallias, 95
Pelanos, 137.25f. and n. 8; 140.36
Peloponnesian Wars: First, 41C.1; 73, 76, 78-80; 83-4; 95K; 101; 104; 105B; 107.3.11; Archidamian, 126; 127; 129-36; Decelean, 151-2; 154; 156-9; 161-2; 164; 166-8
Persian Wars, 1B at 461/0; 48-53; 55-61; 65A.2; 72.36; 73; 78; 94BC.4; 95
Phratry: Argos, 89B.45; Athens, 15.18, 23; 155.16; *see also* Glossary; Cyrene, 18.15
Phrourarch, 71A.13f., 39, B.14f., 38. *See also* Glossary
Phylobasileis (tribe-kings): Athens, 22A; *see also* Glossary; Chios, 15.12 with n. 4
Plynteria, 159 n. 4. *See also* Glossary
Polemarch: Athens, 22C; 30A; 49.3; 55.31; 68.10; 98.68; 136.13; *see also* Glossary; Sicyon, 10.54
Poletai, 15.8; 81.12f.; 93.7; 133.56; 136.25; 140.51; 155.40; *see also* Glossary; accounts of, 147D
Priestess of Athena, 93.139
Prisoners of war, 157
Proedroi, 149 n. 2. *See also* Glossary
Prosetairoi (Miletus), 92.7
Prostates, 47.34. *See also* Glossary, Metics
Proxenia (proxenos), 14.3; 41C.1; 67C; 76; 87.9, 11; 137 n. 8; 138.7f., 19f.; 149.9; 152.3; 160.14; 161.36; 162.43f.; *see also* Glossary; special meaning, 29.5
Prytaneis
Athens, 146dg.7; bring contested tribute assessments into court, 136.52ff.; as chairmen of Boule, 119A.10; 133.51ff.; 149 n. 2; 155.33; ensure the erection of stele, 133.25; receive indictments and bring them before Boule, 98.34ff.; resolution of, 166.7, 32; subject to penalties, 136.29ff.; submit special business for consideration, 98.28f.; 106.4; 117.8; 133.11f.; 136.27ff.; sum-

mon Assembly, 98.18f.; 128.52f.; 146c.8; supervise the Secretary, 162.41f.; *see also* Glossary
Halicarnassus, 70.5f.
Miletus, 92.65 with n. 24
Prytany, 134; 154; 158 passim; stipulated as date for the introduction of business, 41B.1; 100.37; 133.11; 140.60. *See also* Glossary, Prytaneis

Recorders (mnemones): Halicarnassus, 70 passim; Salmakis, 70.13f.; of the laws (anagrapheis ton nomon), 15.5f. *See also* Glossary
Rhetra: Elis, 25.1; Sparta, 12
Rylands Papyrus, 393

Sacred War, First, 16
Satrap, 34; 95G. *See also* Glossary
Sculptors, 116A; 120.33
Secretary (grammateus)
of Boule, amends Bouleutic Oath, 97.12; amends decrees, 156.58; brings contested tribute assessments to court with Prytaneis, 136.53; deletes names of hostages, 162.39ff.; provides for the inscription and erection of stelai, 15.6ff.; 68.23ff.; 81.12; 99.37f.; 103.58f.; 136.24; 138.7ff.; 140.49; 142.33ff.; 149.14, 28; 155.22, 29f.; 156.42, 58f.; 160.21f.; 162.34f.; 163.6f.; 165.7; 166.38; receives records from envoys, 156.40f.; *see also* Glossary
of commissioners for the Parthenon, 120.2
of commissioners for the Propylaia, 118B.8
of commissioners for the statue of Athena Parthenos, 114A(1).2-4, (2).1ff.
of the Eisagogeis, 136. 7f.
of Eleusinian superintendents, 106. 10
of hellenotamiai, 118B.12; 142.3
of Leontinian envoys, 125.6f.
of Treasurers of Athena, 113.9; 114A (2).6f.; 118B.10; 126.6, 18; 141.3; 143.2-4; 144.3f.; 150.8-10
Serpent Column, 59
Settlements, *see* Colonies
Sicilian Expedition, 146; 159 n. 1
Sitesis (public maintenance), 152.5
Slaves, 9A; 13; 70.39; 101 n. 2; 107.1.10, 17; 147D passim; 153.2, 10; 164A, n. 2; serfs, Gortyn, 88A.41, n. 5
Spartan (Lacedaemonian)
alliances and treaties: Athens (446/5), 105B; Elis, 4A; Megara, 116A; 122D; 123B.536; Peloponnesian League, 80; Tegea, 27; Thebes, 73

III. Index of translated passages

1 Collections of inscriptions are listed first and are followed by other publications in alphabetical order of authors. All items possessing a *GHI* or *IG* number are indexed accordingly; a different listing appears only when the text so listed has formed the basis of the translation and commentary or when the text is not contained in *GHI* or *IG*.

III. Index of translated passages

III. Index of translated passages

LITERARY TEXTS
Aelian
  Varia Historia
    12.10: 4 n. 5
    13.24: 41A.3
Aeschines
    2.31: 62
    2.75: 84
    3.107–9: 16B
Aeschines, scholia to
    2.31: 62
    2.75: 84
Aeschines Socraticus (Krauss)
    Ff. 45, 46: 96A
Alexis
  FGrHist 539
    F 2: 32
Ammonius
  FGrHist 350
    F 1: 109A
Andocides
    3.29: 95O
Androtion
  FGrHist 324
    F 2: 26B
    F 6: 41A.1
    F 8: 130
    F 10: 170A
    F 11: 170B
    F 37: 109A
    F 38: 110
    F 39: 127A
    F 42: 145A
    F 43: 148
    F 44: 157
    F 45: 159
    F 57: 109B
  Anecdota Graeca
    I 236 s.v. 'diadikasia': 107 n. 9
    I 283 s.v. 'naukraroi': 22C
Antiochus of Syracuse
  FGrHist 555
    F 10: 6A
    F 13: 9A
Antiphon
    F 37 Thalheim: 79C
Antisthenes
    ap. Athenaeus 13.55 p. 589e: 116C
Archilochus
    F 3 Diehl: 7 n. 2
Aristeides
    2.158: 41C.1
    2.287: 69
    46.14: 41C.1, 76
    46.136: 110
Aristodemus
  FGrHist 104

    F 6.1: 65A.1
    13: 95J
Aristophanes
  Acharnians
    6: 131B
    65–7: 111
    515–38: 123B
    980: 39A2
  Birds
    766: 147C
  Clouds
    331–2: 108B
    858–9: 104
  Frogs
    693–4: 164A
    718–20: 164B
    1422–3: 159
  Knights
    83–4: 65B 2
    225–6: 131A
    447–9: 30B
    855: 41B.2
  Lysistrata
    1093–4: 147B
    1137–44: 67A
  Peace
    246–7: 122D
    347: 130
    605–9: 116A, 123A
  Wasps
    715–18: 86
    946–7: 41C2
    946–8: 109A
    1007: 145B
    F 556 (Kock): 79C
Aristophanes, scholia to
  Acharnians
    67: 111
    532: 123B
    980: 39A2
  Clouds
    332: 108B
  Knights
    84: 65B.2
    449: 30B
    855: 41B.2
  Lysistrata
    1138, 1144: 67A
  Peace
    246: 122D
    605: 116A, 123A
    697: 110 n. 1
  Wasps
    947: 41C.2, 109A
Aristotle
  Athenaion Politeia
    8.3: 22A

III. Index of translated passages